D0962097

EZRA

·

NEHEMIAH

VOLUME 14

THE ANCHOR BIBLE is a fresh approach to the world's greatest classic. Its object is to make the Bible accessible to the modern reader; its method is to arrive at the meaning of biblical literature through exact translation and extended exposition, and to reconstruct the ancient setting of the biblical story, as well as the circumstances of its transcription and the characteristics of its transcribers.

THE ANCHOR BIBLE is a project of international and interfaith scope: Protestant, Catholic, and Jewish scholars from many countries contribute individual volumes. The project is not sponsored by any ecclesiastical organization and is not intended to reflect any particular theological doctrine. Prepared under our joint supervision, THE ANCHOR BIBLE is an effort to make available all the significant historical and linguistic knowledge which bears on the interpretation of the biblical record.

THE ANCHOR BIBLE is aimed at the general reader with no special formal training in biblical studies; yet, it is written with the most exacting standards of scholarship, reflecting the highest technical accomplishment.

This project marks the beginning of a new era of co-operation among scholars in biblical research, thus forming a common body of knowledge to be shared by all.

William Foxwell Albright
David Noel Freedman
GENERAL EDITORS

THE ANCHOR BIBLE

EZRA
·
NEHEMIAH

INTRODUCTION, TRANSLATION, AND NOTES
BY
JACOB M. MYERS

The Anchor Bible
Doubleday
NEW YORK   LONDON   TORONTO   SYDNEY   AUCKLAND

The Anchor Bible
Published by Doubleday, a division of
Bantam Doubleday Dell Publishing Group, Inc.,
666 Fifth Avenue, New York, New York 10103

The Anchor Bible Doubleday, and the portrayal of an anchor
with the letters AB are trademarks of Doubleday, a division of
Bantam Doubleday Dell Publishing Group, Inc.

ISBN: 0-385-04695-2
Library of Congress Catalog Card Number 65–23788

12   14   16   17   15   13   11

BG

Dedicated to
My Revered Teachers
and
My Colleagues on
The Faculty of
The Lutheran Theological Seminary
Gettysburg, Pennsylvania

PREFACE

The period and literary deposit of Ezra-Nehemiah pose for the student of the Old Testament some of the most difficult and tantalizing problems connected with biblical history and literature. Not only are those books enigmatic in arrangement; we possess, at present, relatively little detailed extra-biblical knowledge of the contemporary situation in Palestine. True, archaeology has shed a great deal of light on the activity of peoples and nations in the territory of the period involved. Seals, inscriptions, names and notes on potsherds, as well as other discoveries proliferate. Everything we know so far confirms the essential historicity of the biblical materials; at the same time it reflects the dynamic, vital faith of courageous and devoted leaders and their small group of loyal followers in postexilic times. It is doubtful if the general, over-all portrait will be substantially altered by further discoveries; the lines will become more distinct, the colors more pronounced, and the interrelationship of details clearer.

The present volume represents the literary fruit of many satisfying, though often perplexing, hours spent over the years studying treasures new and old garnered by earlier scholars and commentators. Every page bears clear evidence of the thought and work of others. Due credit has been given to those scholars whose work has been referred to explicitly. Grateful acknowledgment is hereby made to the many others not mentioned specifically, but whose studies have been invaluable. The writer, however, bears full responsibility for what is written here, though aware of its inadequacies and many shortcomings.

To the general editors of The Anchor Bible for their kind assistance and, more especially, to those members of the Doubleday staff who have so painstakingly and diligently labored for countless hours over a difficult and complex manuscript, I express my deepest gratitude.

J. M. Myers

Gettysburg, Pa.

CONTENTS

NEHEMIAH

APPENDIXES

PRINCIPAL ABBREVIATIONS

1. Publications

AASOR	Annual of the American Schools of Oriental Research
AfO	Archiv für Orientforschung
AGP	*Géographie de la Palestine*, by F. M. Abel
AJSL	American Journal of Semitic Languages and Literatures
ANET	*Ancient Near Eastern Texts*, ed. J. B. Pritchard
AP	*Aramaic Papyri of the Fifth Century B.C.*, ed. and tr. A. Cowley
APN	*Assyrian Personal Names*, by K. L. Tallquist
BA	The Biblical Archaeologist
BASOR	Bulletin of the American Schools of Oriental Research
BMAP	*The Brooklyn Museum Aramaic Papyri*, ed. E. G. H. Kraeling
BJRL	Bulletin of the John Rylands Library
BP	"The Biblical Period," by W. F. Albright
CBQ	Catholic Biblical Quarterly
CHI	*The Chronicler's History of Israel*, by C. C. Torrey
EAT	*Einleitung in das Alte Testament*, by O. Eissfeldt
EdS	*Esra der Schreiber*, by H. H. Schaeder
EJ	*Die Entstehung des Judenthums*, by Eduard Meyer
ES	*Ezra Studies*, by C. C. Torrey
GÄJZ	*Die politische Geschichte Ägyptens vom 7. bis zum 4. Jahrhundert vor den Zeitwende*, by F. K. Kienitz
GVI	*Geschichte des Volkes Israel*, by Rudolph Kittel
HPE	*The History of the Persian Empire*, by A. T. Olmstead
HUCA	Hebrew Union College Annual
IAT	*Les Institutions de l'Ancien Testament*, by R. de Vaux
IB	Interpreter's Bible
IDB	The Interpretor's Dictionary of the Bible
IEJ	Israel Exploration Journal
IPN	*Die israelitischen Personennamen im Rahmen der gemein-semitischen Namengebung*, by M. Noth
JAOS	Journal of the American Oriental Society

JBL   Journal of Biblical Literature and Exegesis
JNES   Journal of Near Eastern Studies
JPOS   Journal of Palestine Oriental Society
JSOR   Journal of the Society of Oriental Research
KS   *Kleine Schriften zur Geschichte des Volkes Israel*, by
             A. Alt
PEQ   Palestine Exploration Quarterly
PJB   Palästinajahrbuch des deutschen evangelischen Institutes
             für Altertumwissenschaft des heiligen Landes zu Je-
             rusalem
QAEN   *The Question of Authorship in the Ezra-Narrative*, by
             A. S. Kapelrud
RB   Revue biblique
SY   *Sepher Yerushalayim*, by M. Avi-Yonah
TLZ   Theologische Literaturzeitung
ÜS   *Überlieferungsgeschichtliche Studien*, by M. Noth
VT   Vetus Testamentum
VTS   Vetus Testamentum Supplements
VuH   *Verbannung und Heimkehr: Festschrift für Wilhelm
             Rudolph*, ed. A. Kuschke
ZA   Zeitschrift für Assyriologie und verwandte Gebiete
ZAW   Zeitschrift für die alttestamentliche Wissenschaft
ZDPV   Zeitschrift des deutschen Palästina-Vereins

2. VERSIONS

EVV   English versions generally
LXX   The Septuagint
  LXX^A Codex Alexandrinus
  LXX^L Codex Regius
  LXX^א Codex Sinaiticus
  LXX^B Codex Vaticanus
  LXX^V Codex Venetus
MT   Masoretic Text
1QIs   Qumran Isaiah
1QH   Qumran Hymn of Thanksgiving
1QM   Qumran War Scroll
1QS   Qumran Manual of Discipline
1QSa   Qumran Manual of Discipline a
3Q10   Qumran, Fragment 10 from Cave 3
4Q Dib Ham   Qumran, from Cave 4, *dbry hm 'rwt*, "the words of the
             lights"

4QT	Qumran Testimonies
Syr.	Syriac version, the Peshitta
Vrs.	Ancient versions generally
Vulg.	The Vulgate

3. OTHER ABBREVIATIONS

Akk.	Akkadian
Ar.	Arabic
Aram.	Aramaic
Heb.	Hebrew
MSS	Manuscripts
OT	Old Testament
Pers.	Persian

INTRODUCTION

HISTORY

The Chronicler's treatment of the Ezra-Nehemiah period can be understood only in light of a survey of as much of exilic and post-exilic history as can be gleaned from the available sources.

The events leading up to 587 B.C. and the fall of Jerusalem itself were in one sense of the word, tragic. But in another sense they marked a significant point of reference in the ongoing life of a great and resourceful people. Before the Exile had gone centuries of tri-umphs and defeats, successes and failures, times of exaltation and times of humiliation, a period of preparation for further challenges and of purposes for people and nation.

THE JEWS IN THE EXILIC PERIOD

Both Kings and Chronicles agree that there was a major deporta-tion from Jerusalem and Judah in the reign of Jehoiachin.[1] Only members of the upper classes and experts in certain crafts, together with the court, were taken to Babylon in 597.[2] The effects of the first deportation are clearly evident in the Book of Jeremiah, in the reports of affairs in Judah at the time. Stability was absent from po-litical and religious councils, and uncertainty prevalent everywhere. The catastrophe of 587 was a foregone conclusion. This time there was a thorough housecleaning at Jerusalem, though apparently fewer important persons were taken into captivity than in 597,[3] for

[1] Cf. II Kings xxiv 8–16; II Chron xxxvi 9–10. The latter presents no figures on the number of captives and does not characterize in any way those taken into exile. II Kings offers two sets of figures, neither of which agree with those given in Jer lii 28 (cf. fn. [3] below).

[2] For date see D. J. Wiseman, *Chronicles of Chaldaean Kings (626–556 B.C.) in the British Museum*, 1956, pp. 32 ff.

[3] The figures given in Jer lii 28–30 are, in terms of the regnal years of Nebuchadnezzar: 3023 in the seventh year; 832 in the eighteenth year; 745 in the twenty-third year. Those in II Kings xxiv 14–16 refer only to the captives of the seventh year of Nebuchadnezzar.

the simple reason that their ranks had already been radically deci-
mated. However, II Kings xxv 12 (cf. Jer xl 7) says that only vine
dressers and farmers were left in the land. After the debacle involving the murder of Gedaliah (II Kings xxv 22–26), another contingent probably found its way to Babylon (Jer lii 30).

Those remaining in the land

Conditions in Judah after the fall of Jerusalem and the withdrawal
of Johanan and his followers to Egypt are reasonably well described in Lamentations.[4] While there was desolation around Jerusalem and in many of the cities of Judah,[5] there is evidence that a
considerable portion of the populace remained in the land. The
power vacuum created by the removal of responsible elements
opened it to all sorts of dangers. Encroachments from north and
south made life insecure and uncertain.

Life did not, nevertheless, come to a complete standstill. There is
some indication that a temporary altar was set up, perhaps hastily
(cf. Jer xli 5), and that some kind of worship was carried on by the
faithful among those who were left in the land.[6] The returnees of
course would have nothing to do with it because to them such worship lacked proper cult appurtenances and officials. The terrible
stroke that had befallen people and land left all concerned dazed
and planless. Ensuing poverty, dislocation, and pressures from the
outside were not easily surmounted; indeed, things would never be
quite the same, not even in Maccabean and post-Maccabean times.
The difficulties experienced in the times of Haggai, Zechariah, Nehemiah, and Ezra show how adverse the lot of the Jews was after
587.

After the removal of Gedaliah, the governor of what was to be a
Babylonian province, the area of Judah around Jerusalem became,

[4] See H. J. Kraus, "Klagelieder," (Biblischer Kommentar Altes Testament,
XX, 1956), p. 12, who thinks it comes from around Jerusalem and dates from
the period following close upon the actual events. N. K. Gottwald (Studies in
the Book of Lamentations, 1954, p. 21) is not so specific, preferring a date
from the Exile, i.e., between 586 and 538 B.C. Cf. E. Janssen, Juda in der
Exilszeit, 1956, pp. 39–42.
[5] See W. F. Albright, The Archaeology of Palestine, 1960, pp. 140–42.
[6] Cf. Janssen, op. cit., pp. 101 ff.; J. Bright, A History of Israel, 1959, p. 325.
It is highly probable that occasional, perhaps regular, periods of fasting and
mourning took place among the ruins or at an improvised altar.

perhaps unofficially at first, a part of the province of Samaria. The southern area was apparently infiltrated by the Edomites, who were themselves under pressure from the expanding Arabian peoples.[7] For the people of Judah, the whole situation could hardly be considered hopeful.

Those taken to Babylon

It is no accident that subsequent leadership for the Jews centered in Babylon. The best of them, except for those who were slain (II Kings xxv 18–21), lived there in exile (II Kings xxiv 12–16), as, for example, Ezekiel and the author of Isaiah xl–lv. They were settled on the Kebar Canal, probably in the vicinity of Nippur. To judge from Ezekiel, the letter of Jeremiah (xxix 4 ff.), and archaeological discoveries,[8] these Jews fared exceedingly well in their new home. Naturally they must have felt somewhat dejected in their religion (Ps cxxxvii) but that was only a temporary condition. It is quite probable that the little community of Babylonian Jews was assisted in regaining its composure and developing a new perspective by hoping for restoration under Jehoiachin, who was still alive and well. Had Jehoiachin's family suffered the fate endured by that of Zedekiah things might have been very different.

Jozadak the son of Seraiah (I Chron vi 14), who was put to death by Nebuchadnezzar at Riblah (II Kings xxv 18–21; Jer lii 24–27), was the high priest, though he is nowhere spoken of as an active participant in the religious affairs of the exilic community. During the early part of the Exile, Ezekiel seems to have assumed a leading role. His house was the center of a kind of gathering (Ezek viii 1) where the fires of religion were kept burning. The exiles were addressed regularly as the house of Israel, which may have affected the development of the religious climate, (as reflected by the

---

[7] A. Alt has shown clearly how the provincial system developed in Palestine in the wake of the Assyrian conquests of the eighth century B.C. and how it continued under the Babylonians. Cf. Alt, "Die Rolle Samarias bei der Entstehung des Judentums" in KS, II, pp. 316–37, and "Judas Nachbarn zur Zeit Nehemias," *ibid.*, pp. 338–45. See also W. F. Albright, BP, p. 48.

[8] See the Weidner texts in *Mélanges Syriens offerts à Monsieur René Dussaud*, 1939, pp. 923–35, and W. F. Albright, BA 5 (1942), 49–55; and cf. the growth, later, of the great banking house of Murashu's sons at Nippur. On the Jews in Babylon, see E. Klamroth, *Die jüdischen Exulanten in Babylonien*, 1912.

Chronicler) and, indeed, in creating the temper of the postexilic religious community in Judah. But another important direction of advancing Jewish thought was supplied by the prophet of Isa xl–lv. His preachments had much to do with investing his hearers with a new sense of values, and though the effects of his teaching were not so immediately apparent, they clearly did manifest themselves in later conceptions and movements.

The Jews in Egypt

There is evidence of numerous Jewish colonies in Egypt, some of them attested in the Bible. The first substantial settlement of Jews in Egypt was that of the Sons of Jacob (Gen xlvii). A Canaanite colony was located at On (Heliopolis) in the Amarna period.[9] So far as we know, the second Jewish migration to Egypt took place after the murder of Gedaliah and involved Jeremiah (Jer xliii, xliv). This group settled at Tahpanhes (Daphnae) at the northeast corner of the Nile delta. We hear nothing more of them, though some may have drifted to other points in Egypt. Jeremiah prophesied their doom (Jer xliv 27 f.), which probably overtook most of them.

The origin of the military colony at Elephantine is uncertain.[10] There may have been an early settlement of Jews at Syene, since Isa xlix 12 refers to it as the place[11] from which exiles will return. However, Syene was regarded as the southernmost extremity of Egypt and so may be a poetic symbol here for that distant portion of the world from which the Jews will return from captivity. But it is more probable that "and these from Sinim" (1QIs "Sunim") actually refers to Jews living at Syene, even though the Isaiah passage itself is eschatological in character (eschatological literature is not completely devoid of history). If that is so, Jews were settled there before 540 B.C. Some scholars think the Elephantine colony goes back to the reign of Psammeticus I (663–609 B.C.), when the Egyptian king, faced with wholesale desertion at the vital southern point of entrance, could have settled there some of his mercenaries

---

[9] BJRL 44 (1961/62), 102.

[10] For a discussion of the views that have been put forth see *The Brooklyn Museum Aramaic Papyri* (abbr. BMAP), ed. E. G. H. Kraeling, 1953, pp. 41–48. Cf. further C. H. Gordon in JNES 14 (1955), 56–58, who believes it came from a Jewish enclave in Aram.

[11] See T. O. Lambdin's article in IDB, IV, p. 472.

from Asia; and the latter group may have included Jews.[12] Others think it dates from the time of Apries (Hophra), 588–569 B.C., who established a strong military garrison at Elephantine to hold in check the Ethiopians who plagued Egypt since the days of Pian-khi.[13] The earliest of the Elephantine documents dates from 495 B.C.[14] and has to do with property rights. Papyrus 30, line 13, reads: ". . . from the days of the king[s] of Egypt our fathers had erected this temple in the fortress of Yeb and when Cambyses came to Egypt he found this temple built"—an indication that the temple had been constructed before 525 B.C. A temple and property rights point to a settled community; how long it was settled is, of course, not known but it must surely have lasted for a number of years. It is, therefore, not impossible that the Elephantine colony was a permanent fixture for some time and that it was augmented from time to time. At any rate, as these documents show, the Jews of Elephantine must have been a rather vigorous group and they still regarded themselves as having claims upon their brethren in Palestine. Moreover, this was not the last of the Jewish communities in Egypt, as may be seen from the investigations of V. A. Tcherikover and A. Fuks.[15]

Elsewhere

At present there is no explicit record of enduring Jewish communities elsewhere during the Exile. The painful reverses suffered in connection with the first attempts at restoration seem to have discouraged enterprising groups and individuals, who, in consequence,

[12] So A. Vincent, *La religion des Judéo-Araméens d' Eléphantine*, Paris, 1937; F. K. Kienitz, GÄJZ, p. 39. Kienitz thinks Psammeticus I established a Jewish garrison at Elephantine. Aristeas speaks (pars. 12–14) of Jewish contingents in the army of Psammeticus II (592–588 B.C.) campaigning against the Ethiopians—though the reference is actually not clear as to whether Psammeticus I or II is meant. The garrison or settlement was augmented further by compromisers and those who feared Babylonian reprisals.

[13] This is the view of W. F. Albright, *Archaeology and the Religion of Israel*, 1942, p. 168, based on the investigations of W. Struve, whose work was not accessible to me.

[14] A. Cowley, AP, pp. 1–3.

[15] *Corpus Papyrorum Judaicarum*, I, 1957, especially pp. 1–47. On the possibility of an earlier Israelite community in middle Egypt see E. Drioton, "Une colonie israélite en Moyenne Égypt à la fin du viie siècle av. J. C." in *A la recontre de Dieu*, 1961, pp. 181–91. Cf. also the report of M. M. Kamil on Aramaic documents from Hermopolis-West from sixth century B.C. in *Actes du XXIe Congrès International des Orientalistes*, 1949, pp. 106 f.

turned elsewhere for opportunities.[16] Presumably some of the exiles of the Northern Kingdom lingered on in places to which they had been transported after the fall of Samaria in 722 B.C. Some Jews fled from the Babylonian invasion to neighboring countries (Jer xl 11); others doubtless sought refuge in the northern provinces of Samaria and Galilee.[17] In a very real sense it may be said that the Jewish diaspora began with the tragic events in Judah in the first quarter of the sixth century B.C. It initiated a long process of movements and migrations that continue to the present day.

THE EARLY RETURNS

The rise of a new star at last brought hope to the more zealous Jews looking for a deliverer, one who might restore them to their homeland where they could once more take up the songs of Zion and devote themselves to being Yahweh's people. Cyrus, the son of Cambyses I by the daughter of Astyages of Media, swept across the sixth-century world like a meteor. He became king of Anshan and established himself in the capital city of Parsagarda about 559 B.C. A man of restless spirit and boundless ambition, he soon drew to himself the allegiance of neighboring peoples and tribes and united them into a solid block of Persian power. Being of rugged mountain stock, Cyrus and his followers revolted against his father-in-law, Astyages of Media, and at about the same time, apparently, arranged a convenient treaty with Nabonidus of Babylon. When the crucial test came between Media and Cyrus, the outcome favored Cyrus. The armies of the Medes either deserted to him or mutinied. Soon he found himself in nominal control of the whole Median empire, including the territory once held by Assyria. That brought him into conflict with Babylon, which also claimed much of the same area. Cyrus did not attack Babylon directly. First he went to Asia

---

[16] See Albright, BP, p. 50.

[17] C. C. Torrey believed that Nabonidus' (555–538 B.C.) moving of the royal residence of Babylon to Teima was the signal for the establishment of Jewish trading colonies in the great centers of Arabian trade. These Jews, he thinks, came from Babylonia. See his review in JAOS 73 (1953), 224. This view receives support from the Harran Inscriptions of Nabonidus (*Anatolian Studies* 8 [1958], 63 f., 86–88) and from "The Prayer of Nabonidus" from Qumran Cave IV (J. T. Milik, RB 63 [1956], 407–15; D. N. Freedman, BASOR 145 [1957], 31–32).

Minor, where Croesus of Lydia as well as the Lycians submitted to
him. Then he turned to the north and overran the mountainous
region between the Caspian Sea and the northwest corner of India.
By 540/39 he was on the frontier of Babylon. Five years earlier the
Babylonian governor of Elam (Gutium) had defected to Cyrus: he
now joined his army. After several battles, the army of the great
king entered the Babylonian capital itself on October 13, 539 B.C.
Nabonidus was taken prisoner but was treated with clemency—even
respect—by Cyrus. Some sixteen days later (October 29) Cyrus entered the city.

The Jews in the time of Cyrus and Cambyses (540–522)

To judge from the biblical references, the Persians could have had
no more zealous supporters than the Jews. The Second Isaiah waxed
eloquent over Cyrus: "He is my shepherd and shall fulfill my purpose fully" (xliv 28a); "Thus says the Lord to his anointed, to
Cyrus, whose right hand I have grasped. . . ." (xlv 1). For the religious enthusiasts he was the anointed (messiah) of Yahweh sent as
deliverer for his people. The conquests of Cyrus were due to
Yahweh, though he did not know him (Isa xlv 4); his successes
were all part of Yahweh's plan, which was more than mere deliver-
ance. The people of Judah under Cyrus' command (guided by
Yahweh) were to rebuild Jerusalem with its temple (Isa xliv 28b;
II Chron xxxvi 23; Ezra i 2, 3). There is no overt adverse judgment against the Persians in the exilic or postexilic prophets or in
the work of the Chronicler.

According to documents preserved by the Chronicler (II Chron
xxxvi 22–23; Ezra i 1–4, vi 2–5), Cyrus in the first year of his
reign issued a decree permitting the reconstruction of the house of
God at Jerusalem and returning the temple vessels taken by Nebuchadnezzar. The decree, in its transmitted form, says nothing
about the rebuilding of the city. There can be no doubt as to the
authenticity of Cyrus' decree or of its basic provisions (see the discussion of Ezra i, vi below), because they were in harmony with
the policy of the great king.[18]

[18] See the barrel inscription in J. B. Pritchard, ANET, p. 316. Cyrus claims
to have returned the sacred images of the gods to cities in Mesopotamia and
Elam, restored their sanctuaries and gathered and sent home their former inhabitants.

Despite the difficulties, privations, and dangers involved, a goodly number of Jews did return between 538 B.C. and the accession of Darius (in 522). It is equally certain that many remained in Babylon and were not interested in returning, probably because they were prosperous. Those who remained are reminiscent of the great banking houses of Murashu and sons and of Egibi, the positions attained by others in the service of both Babylonians and Persians, and the difficulty experienced by Ezra later in persuading Levites to accompany him to Jerusalem (Ezra viii 15 ff.). Fired by the preaching of the Second Isaiah and no doubt possessed of the nationalistic and religious hopes that had been kept alive by enthusiasts inspired by the dreams and promises of Ezekiel, they were willing to undertake the task. The officials involved in carrying out the royal edict were Sheshbazzar (Sin-ab-usur), a scion of the royal family and a son of Jehoiachin, and Joshua, the high priest. Sheshbazzar was soon replaced by Zerubbabel, his nephew and a grandson of the king. Actual progress of the returned community is difficult to assess, though it cannot have been auspicious, as may be seen from conditions of land and people depicted in the prophecies of Haggai and Zechariah. Rehabilitation required more than a royal decree; it required even more than material support for the religious enterprises. The very first contingent must have met with serious opposition on the part of the Samaritans who had gradually taken over the territory around Jerusalem and claimed hegemony over it, though it had not been officially assigned to them by the Babylonian conquerors. Nor had outsiders been settled there, as was the case with Samaria after the Assyrian conquest. The Samaritans and other peoples of the land, including the poorer classes of Jews who had escaped deportation, had, to all intents and purposes, slowly filled a power vacuum. Then there was the problem of sustenance, particularly if the group was sizable. If we knew the precise situation underlying the lists in Ezra ii and Nehemiah vii, we might be able to evaluate better how many Jews returned in the time of Sheshbazzar and Zerubbabel.[19]

Evidence seems to indicate that the people who returned were poor and not very well organized, though doubtless invested with religious zeal. They appear to have rebuilt the altar first (Ezra iii 2, 3) so as to carry on at least a modicum of worship, such as the

[19] See discussion on Ezra ii and Neh vii in COMMENTS.

celebration of the regular festivals and the daily sacrifices (Ezra iii
4–6a). Then they made preparations to carry out the main provision of the Cyrus decree—the rebuilding of the temple. Timber
was brought in from Lebanon, supplies collected for the workmen
and skilled craftsmen appointed. The actual work began (Ezra iii
8) in the second year of the return—laying the foundation of the
temple with proper ceremony.[20] Then they hit an obstacle: they
were opposed by the people from Samaria, because they refused to
give them permission to participate in the construction of the temple
and its worship. It would not have been denial of permission to
participate in the reconstruction that occasioned offense but the exclusion of the people of the land from worship on the grounds that
they were regarded as unclean and their worship unacceptable to
the golah. For the latter to have permitted participation in worship
of the people of the land—a technical term for the ruling classes—
would have meant a compromise of their faith; their stand naturally
produced friction with those excluded. Indecision in rebuilding the
temple could very well have been due, at least in part, to that
friction (cf. Ezra iii 3, iv 4, 5; Hag ii 4; Zech viii 10), though the
usual reason given is that the populace was occupied with building
homes, crop failure, or general indifference.

[20] There are two apparently contradictory statements about the laying of
the foundations of the temple. One (Ezra v 16) says Sheshbazzar did it; the
other (Zech iv 9) attributes it to Zerubbabel. I Esdras vi 20 states that
Sheshbazzar laid the foundation of the house of Yahweh and that even though
building operations had continued it had not yet been completed. Earlier in
the same chapter (vi 2) it was noted that Zerubbabel and Jeshua began to build
the temple in the second year of Darius. This tradition persisted down to the
time of Sirach (Sirach xlix 11–12). Several observations are in order. There is
no doubt that royal permission for the return of the Jews to reactivate their
worship at Jerusalem was granted by Cyrus to Sheshbazzar. The legal document affirming that order was the one referred to in the Ezra passage; its
authority was basic for the continuance of the work under Zerubbabel. The
part played by Sheshbazzar is the problem. He could have initiated preparations
for building the temple by gathering the requisite materials and clearing away
the debris from the site (David had arranged the site and provided materials
for the first temple). Or he might actually have laid the lower courses of the
substructure ('šyy', "lower base or foundation") upon which the first or
foundational courses of the superstructure rested. Or his work was so insignificant it may have crumbled during the intervening years so that Zerubbabel
had virtually to begin all over again. See further K. Galling, "Serubbabel und
der Wiederaufbau des Tempels in Jerusalem," in VuH, pp. 67–96, and COM-
MENT on Ezra v.

Activity in the time of Darius (522–485)

The main sources of information on this period are the prophecies of Haggai and Zechariah and the account in Ezra v–vi.

According to the sources, the work of rebuilding remained in abeyance from the time of its cessation (?) until the second regnal year of Darius (520). In 520 Haggai and Zechariah began to agitate for the resumption of work. In a series of fiery addresses, Haggai[21] demanded immediate action. He placed the blame for the poverty and the ills of the community on their failure to attend to the project for which they had returned and for which they had obtained permission from the authorities. He and Zechariah succeeded in goading the leaders—Zerubbabel and Joshua—into action. It is not inconceivable that the Jewish authorities were at first loath to move forward because of the uncertainties attendant upon events at the Persian court. Both Zerubbabel and Joshua seem to have been responsible and cautious persons whose aim was to make haste slowly in view of unsettled conditions on all sides. But the prophets apparently succeeded in arousing the people to the point where the leaders were compelled to act.

As they probably suspected, the resumption of building activity precipitated immediate reaction from the local Persian authorities, who appeared personally on the spot and demanded to see the building permit and a roster of names of those responsible for the work (Ezra v 3, 4). The eruptions connected with the accession of Darius[22] may have made the governor and his associates more sensitive to movements that might be misconstrued. Perhaps the Persian officials were motivated in their investigation by the reports of the local authorities from Samaria, whose suspicions were aroused by Haggai's declarations (Hag ii 22, 23), prophesying the downfall of Persia and signaling the investiture of Zerubbabel. Building operations were allowed to proceed (Ezra v 5) pending the arrival of a reply from Darius to the report sent to him by Tattenai. Investigation exonerated the Jews and Darius issued a further decree to his

21 See COMMENT on Ezra v.
22 A. T. Olmstead, HPE, pp. 110–16; Albright, BP, pp. 49 f. A new governor of Across the River by the name of Ushtani was appointed in 520. Tattenai was his assistant and Shethar-bozenai was his secretary. The local friends of the king were doubtless his "eyes and ears" reporting to him everything he needed to know (cf. Xenophon Cyropaedia viii.ii.10–12).

officials permitting the work to continue, even providing for support of the project from the royal treasury.

There is nothing improbable in Darius' decree, for Darius, like Cyrus, was benevolently inclined toward the religions of the peoples in his vast empire. For example, he reversed the policy of Cambyses in Egypt; he restored the income for the temples which he rebuilt.[23] In fact, Darius was regarded as a protector and darling of the gods.[24] He sent a mission to Egypt in 519 to recodify the laws of the country. His interest in religious affairs is demonstrated further by a decree directing Pherendates the satrap in 492/1 B.C. to appoint administrative heads for the temples from a list of priests submitted to him by the priests of Khnum.[25] The concern of the Persian kings for the temples and gods of the peoples under their rule was probably due to political reasons, though some of them may have been intrigued by the Hebrew conception of Yahweh, especially the Zoroastrians.

No further impediments appear to have developed and the Jerusalem temple was completed in 515 B.C. It was dedicated with proper ceremonies (Ezra vi 16–18), though not so elaborate as one might expect in view of the normal exaggeration of the Chronicler. Whether Zerubbabel was still alive and present is not stated, though Zechariah had prophesied that he would bring the building of the temple to its consummation (Zech iv 9). The much tampered with passage of Zech vi 9–15,[26] as it now stands, describes the high priest Joshua receiving the crown which may originally have been intended for Zerubbabel. The plural "crowns" in Zech vi 11 (MT, LXX, Vulg.) points to an earlier version of this prophecy in which leadership of the community rested with both governor and high priest. But the passage in Ezra suggests that such leadership was in the hands of the latter alone. Whether Zerubbabel was removed from office by the Persian authorities prior to his death is uncertain; he seems to have conducted himself quite properly so far

---

[23] See Kienitz, GÄJZ, pp. 61 f., and R. de Vaux, "Les décrets de Cyrus et de Darius sur la reconstruction du temple," RB 46 (1937), 38 ff., and the references cited there. Among the Egyptian building enterprises of Darius were the temple of Anum in the oasis of El-Khargeh, other buildings at Abusir and possibly at El-Kab.

[24] Kienitz, GÄJZ, p. 63.

[25] Olmstead, HPE, p. 225.

[26] See K. Elliger, Das Buch der zwölf Kleinen Propheten II: Die Propheten: Nahum, Habakuk, Zephanja, Haggai, Sacharja, Maleachi (Das Alte Testament Deutsch, XXV), 1950, 119–23.

as we can tell from the present sources and may have simply returned to Babylon when his work was finished. Something must have happened to the Jewish community in those early years of Darius to dampen its ardor. The Persians were aware of the political fortunes of Jerusalem (cf. Ezra iv 12, 13, 15) and may have nipped the messianism of the prophets in the bud. In any case, the first series of returns failed to achieve significant results and the Jews became further discouraged, as may be seen from the reports which reached Nehemiah at the Persian court more than half a century later.

From Darius to Artaxerxes I (485–425)

The early part of this period for Judah is obscure. The last years of the reign of Darius were especially marked by unrest; Egypt rebelled.[27] Some unrest may have been created in Judah, though it probably was stirred up by the local enemies of the Jews (Ezra iv 6) rather than by the Jews themselves. Such seems to have been the case especially at the beginning of a new regime. A Jewish revolt of major proportions in 485 B.C.[28] does not appear probable. Rather, despite every encouragement from the Persian authorities,[29] matters do not seem to have improved after the completion of the temple. Much of the trouble was due, in all probability, to the lack of dynamic leadership in the community after the disappearance of Zerubbabel. The relationship of the returnees to the people of the land—both the Jews who remained after 586 and the Samaritans—was never quite clear until the coming of Nehemiah. The territory

[27] Olmstead, HPE, pp. 227–29.
[28] J. Morgenstern thinks there was a major nationalistic rebellion in 486/5 in which the Jewish community suffered catastrophe and that after the rebellion was put down by Xerxes (485–465) it endured oppression throughout his reign. Ezra then built the third temple ("Jerusalem—485 B.C.," HUCA 27 [1956], 101–79; 28 [1957], 15–47; 31 [1960], 1–29). Cf. also S. A. Cook in The Apocrypha and Pseudepigrapha of the Old Testament, ed. R. H. Charles, 1913, I, pp. 13 f., and older literature noted there. He thinks conditions referred to in Neh i 3 were brought about by Edomite activity after the time of Zerubbabel. F. Heichelheim (Zeitschrift für Religions- und Geistesgeschichte 3 [1951], 251–53) thinks of Ezra as leading to Jerusalem a well-equipped group of Jewish volunteers to help stabilize affairs in Palestine during the Periclean intervention in Egypt by way of Phoenicia. Ezra promised Artaxerxes divine protection, presumably in exchange for the privilege of rebuilding the Jewish institutions in Judah.
[29] Cf. fn. 23 and Herodotus iii.91; Ezra vi 6–12—Darius even added to the decree of Cyrus, liberalizing it.

occupied by the returned Jews was at best small—the area of Jerusalem and its environs as far as Mizpah and Jericho toward the north and east, and Keilah, Beth-zur, and Tekoa toward the south; the valleys toward the west remained in other hands.[30] Lack of clear-cut title to the land must have been discouraging, making for a half-hearted life and provoking just enough concern to eke out the barest existence for the majority of people. The upper classes manipulated their way to much better situations, especially after the voices of Haggai and Zechariah had been quieted.[31] Stubborn opposition on the part of a hard core of zealous devotees made for continued tension between them and the people of the land, perhaps also with the less legalistically minded of their own brethren, in cultic matters. On the other hand, economic circumstances may have forced them into marriage with the people of the land.[32] Could some have followed the advice of Zech vii and regarded the old prophetic principles as more significant than cultic purity? If we could be certain of the date and provenance of some of the postexilic prophecies, we would be in a better position to describe this obscure period from 515 B.C. to the coming of Nehemiah and Ezra.

Verifiable data about the Jews in the reign of Xerxes (485–465) is at present unavailable; we know nothing with certainty. Ezra iv 6 has preserved a notice of a complaint made by the opponents of the Jews at Jerusalem to Ahasuerus (Xerxes). Presumably it was of the same character as those sent at the beginning of the reigns of Darius and Artaxerxes. As is well known, the legend of the Book of Esther is placed in the time of Ahasuerus. The tale itself may be pure romance, but the book does reflect some knowledge of Persian history and customs.[33] The persecution story may well be true in a general way. Xerxes was not so politic in his dealings with the religious practices of his subject peoples as his father had been, though there is nothing in the records to spell out his reaction to them in specific instances except in the case of Egypt and Babylonia.[34] Little credence may have been given to complaints lodged

---

[30] E. Meyer, *Geschichte des Altertums* (Darmstadt: 1953–58), IV, Pt. I, p. 180.

[31] E. Würthwein, *Der 'amm ha'arez im Alten Testament*, 1936, pp. 51–71.

[32] The prophecy of Malachi (Mal ii 10–16) against divorce may be connected with such a practice; they divorced the wives of their youth to marry the daughters of the people of the land.

[33] L. B. Paton, *The Book of Esther*, 1908, pp. 64 f.

[34] Olmstead, HPE, pp. 234–37.

against the Jews in Palestine by virtue of demands laid upon the authorities elsewhere.

However, complaints reaching the Persian court in the reign of Artaxerxes I were more serious and detailed (Ezra iv 7–23). There was apparently more than one communication with the king. The first may date from the beginning of a reign marked, as usual, with unrest, particularly at the extremities of the empire—Bactria and Egypt. If so, the second must have followed soon afterward, perhaps because, due to matters of succession, revolts in provinces, etc., which occupied the new king, there was no immediate response to the first. Since the last days of Darius there had been a gradual weakening of control in the west and the ruthless action of Xerxes in Egypt tended to arouse resentment there. In Palestine conditions must have been anything but stable. There was a continuation of petty bickering between various groups. To the south and east Arab pressure was manifesting itself, which in turn created turmoil in Edom, whose impact was increasingly felt in Judah. Persia could not effectively control the vast area of the Arabs, as may be seen from the fact that no tribute had been collected from them (Herodotus III.88). They were said to have contributed a huge quantity of spices yearly (Herodotus III.97) and their country was nominally a part of the province Across the River.

Thus interest in the west and the continued menace of foreign powers to the south may have inspired the Jews to do what they could to protect themselves (cf. Josephus *Antiquities* XI.v). To that end they undertook to raise the walls of Jerusalem and provide some measure of security against the threatening pressures all around. The leaders of Samaria regarded these activities as a hostile move toward them, constituting, in view of their position vis-à-vis the Persian empire, an act of rebellion. The response of the Persian government to the second letter of Rehum and Shimshai was decisive. The order to cease and desist was issued and forwarded to Samaria where the authorities lost no time in enforcing it. They appeared in Jerusalem with a police force (Ezra iv 23) and brought the work to a halt. It may be that Hanani, Nehemiah's brother, was sent to investigate the situation at Jerusalem or that he had been one of a group who fled to Susa afterward, perhaps to lay the matter before the king.

In any event, Nehemiah learned from Hanani the sorry condition of Jerusalem sometime after the people there had been forced to bring their work to a halt. Nehemiah was unable to hide his distress and anxiety from the king. And the king would naturally want to know what had upset one of his most important officials.[35] His interest enabled Nehemiah to inform him about the sad state of the city of his fathers and suggest a plan for restoring it. That was in the twentieth year of Artaxerxes (445 B.C.). The mission either materialized at once or was delayed while the king deliberated the necessity for careful preparation, as Josephus suggests (*Antiquities* XI.v.7.168—Josephus says Nehemiah came to Jerusalem in the twenty-fifth year of the king). He may well be right because the biblical narrative appears to telescope materials in the direction of the author's purpose—the rebuilding of the walls and the security and activity of the city.[36]

Invested with royal authority, carrying directives to the governor and commissars of Across the River, and accompanied by an imperial escort, Nehemiah made his way to Judah. Apparently everything went well until the officials at Samaria heard about it. They confronted Nehemiah with the same charge leveled against the colony on numerous earlier occasions—sedition first and then rebellion. The unholy alliance against Judah consisted of Sanballat, Tobiah, and Geshem—the commissars of three districts who claimed jurisdiction over it. Nehemiah's reply to their charges was, strictly speaking, accurate—"you have no share or right or memorial in Jerusalem" (Neh ii 20b)—from the Jewish point of view. On the other hand, Sanballat's claim at least was based on the old Babylonian arrangement under which Jerusalem and a part of Judah were added to the province of Samaria.[37] The exiled Jews, however, seem not to have accepted that interpretation of the situation, especially in view of the appointment of Nehemiah to the governorship.

Evidently Nehemiah had thought through his course of action; it was based on firm grounds, and he refused to be intimidated or diverted from it. And his enemies never appealed to the Persian court; rather, they chose ridicule, threats, and all sorts of stratagems to undermine the building of the walls. They received some support from the nobles of Judah related to Tobiah (Neh vi 17–19) and unscrupulous prophets (vi 10–14).

[35] HPE, pp. 217 f.
[36] See Albright, BP, pp. 51 f.
[37] Cf. Alt, KS, II, pp. 327–29.

After a survey of the ruined walls, a procedure for repairing them was worked out and put into effect (Neh iii). It appears almost incredible that such an enormous task could be completed with volunteer workers, despite unparalleled harassment, in fifty-two days (Neh vi 15)! Josephus (*Antiquities* XI.v) may be more nearly right when he says it took two years and four months.[38] Presumably this included the time required for the construction of the towers and the hanging of the gates. How soon afterward the service of dedication took place is not specified (Neh xii 27–43), but it could not have taken place until sometime later if Ezra participated (xii 36) (though this is not beyond doubt).

Nehemiah did more than build the walls of Jerusalem. He was also governor (*pḥh,* Neh v 14, xii 26; *htršt',* viii 9, x 2) of Judah. The organization of building operations reflects his ability as well as the character and extent of the provincial government. The corrected census list of Neh vii exhibits some interesting data. The citizenry of Judah was made up of families bearing old and new names. Some had doubtless returned only recently, since their names point to long residence elsewhere, for example, Bigvai, Elam, Pahath-moab. They occupied old villages and towns from Lod in the west to Jericho in the east and from Bethel and Ai in the north to Bethlehem in the south.[39] From Neh iii we learn that a district (*plk*) organization prevailed. Five districts are mentioned—Jerusalem, Beth-haccherem, Mizpah, Beth-zur, and Keilah.[40] Nehemiah, more than a political official of the Persian government, was a student of history, the history of his own people, and knew that no people could continue to exist without a concern for their historical past. In the kind of world in which he lived, tradition and community were important, perhaps matters of life and death; hence Nehemiah's attitude toward Sanballat, Tobiah, and Geshem and his determination to institute social reforms (Neh xiii 23 ff.). His recognition of the religious basis for those reforms is everywhere apparent (xiii 8–22, 28–31).

[38] Sequence of dates for Nehemiah according to Bible and Josephus: 445 B.C., in the month of Kislew, Nehemiah receives word of ruinous state of Jerusalem (Neh i 1 f.); 445 B.C., in the month of Nisan, he requests permission to go to Jerusalem (Neh ii 1 ff.); 440 B.C., in twenty-fifth year of the king, he arrives in Jerusalem (Josephus *Antiquities* XI.v.7.168); 437 B.C., in twenty-eighth year of the king, the wall is complete (Josephus *Antiquities* XI.v.8.179); 433 B.C., in thirty-second year of the king, he returns to Susa (Neh xiii 6); *after some time* he comes back to Jerusalem (Neh xiii 6, 7).

[39] Cf. Albright, BP, pp. 52 f.

[40] See M. Noth, *The History of Israel,* 1958, p. 324.

Whether there were governors between Zerubbabel and Nehemiah is not certain though unlikely. After the disappearance of the former, control of the community seems to have been in the hands of the high priest (cf. Zech vi 9–14).[41] With the coming of Nehemiah, the dual leadership of the Jewish community was resumed. He seems to have dealt with only one high priest, Eliashib (Neh iii 1, 20, 21, xiii 4, 7, 28), who in some respects co-operated well with the governor but who also seems to have been on good terms with both Sanballat and Tobiah (xiii 4 ff., 28). Nehemiah's first term as governor ended when he returned to Susa in 433 B.C. It may be that his brother Hanani was left in charge (vii 2), but if so he was either unwilling or unable to hold matters in check. Tobiah moved into the temple chamber (xiii 4 ff.), the Levites, neglected, returned to their farms (xiii 10), commercialization was taking over at the expense of the cultic institutions (xiii 15 ff.), and intermingling with foreign elements was threatening to undo still further the efforts of those who wanted to maintain the identity of the community. That is what Nehemiah found when he came back to Judah "after some time" (xiii 6 f.). How long a time we do not know, nor is there any indication as to the length of his second term. In 411 B.C. Bigvai was governor[42] (just when he assumed authority is unknown), which was after the time of Nehemiah. Perhaps it is possible to go further: *if* the Hananiah of the famous Passover letter containing Darius II's directions to the Jews at Elephantine in 419 B.C. was the brother of Nehemiah and was in charge of affairs in Judah at the time, then Nehemiah would, presumably, have already left.[43]

[41] List of high priests after the Exile (cf. Neh xii 10–11): Jeshua, Joiakim (Neh xii 22), Eliashib, Joiada (Neh xii 22, xiii 28), Johanan, Jaddua. Cf. Galling, VuH, p. 95; he thinks no governor followed Zerubbabel.

[42] AP, Letter 30, lines 17–22. Cf. E. Auerbach, *Congress Volume, Bonn, 1962,* VTS, IX (Leiden, 1963), p. 247.

[43] See Bright, *A History of Israel,* p. 390; Albright, BP, pp. 53 f.; A. Lods, *The Prophets and the Rise of Judaism,* 1937, p. 309; but cf. Cowley, AP, p. 62. That Hananiah was a powerful official is plain from his position in AP, No. 21, and from the repercussions of his visit reflected in No. 38, line 7. But that does not prove that he was governor of Judah.

The Period of Ezra

One of the most troublesome, possibly insoluble, problems is that of the relationship between Nehemiah and Ezra.[44] It has been observed that nowhere in the memoirs of Ezra is Nehemiah mentioned or even alluded to. And only once does the name of Ezra appear in the memoirs of Nehemiah (xii 36), as distinguished from the Ezra material in the Book of Nehemiah, and that may be a later insertion.[45] Each performed a unique function and hence may not have been directly involved in the other's work. It is, of course, certain that Ezra did his work in the reign of Artaxerxes but which Artaxerxes? There were three kings of Persia bearing that name (Longimanus, 465–425 B.C., Mnemon, 405–359, and Ochus, 359–339). As the text now stands, it simply says that Ezra came to Jerusalem in the seventh year of Artaxerxes (Ezra vii 7, 8). If Artaxerxes I is intended the date would be 458 B.C. If Artaxerxes II, then it would have to be 398 B.C. I Esdras (viii 1, 6) is based on canonical materials and adds nothing. Nor does Josephus, since he follows the biblical sources except that he has Xerxes in place of Artaxerxes. He does locate the activity of both Nehemiah and Ezra in the reign of his "Xerxes" (*Antiquities* XI.v.5). He quotes Ezra x 6, though the passage does not agree with what he says elsewhere about the reigning high priest. It is all but certain that the only high priest named in connection with Ezra is Jehohanan, the grandson of Eliashib (x 6),[46] to whose chamber the scribe retired after his prayer of confession offered in connection with the disclosure of numerous intermarriages between important Jewish families and those of the people of the land. According to Neh xiii 28 a grandson of Eliashib had married a daughter of Sanballat, which must have occurred while Eliashib was still living; otherwise the name of the

---

[44] See J. Bright, "The Date of Ezra's Mission to Jerusalem," *Yehezkel Kaufmann Jubilee Volume*, 1960, pp. 70–87, and literature cited there; and H. H. Rowley, "The Chronological Order of Ezra and Nehemiah," *Ignace Goldziher Memorial Volume*, 1948, Pt. I, pp. 117–49.

[45] Cf. R. de Vaux, *Supplément au Dictionnaire de la Bible*, IV, 1938, col. 765.

[46] For a list of high priests in the Persian period with suggested dates see W. F. Albright, "The Date and Personality of the Chronicler," JBL 40 (1921), 122. Joiada could not have served very long, though it is not known when Jehohanan assumed office nor how long he continued; he was high priest in 411 and still in 408 B.C. (Cowley, AP, No. 30).

reigning high priest would have been given. Josephus (*Antiquities* XI.vii.1) records the names of three sons of Joiada, the son of Eliashib: Jehohanan, who himself became high priest, Jeshua, and Manasseh. The last named was the son-in-law of Sanballat, whose name, incidentally, does not occur in Ezra or I Esdras. It is interesting to note that Jedoniah, who communicated with both the Jews at Jerusalem and the authorities at Samaria in 408 B.C., addressed the appeal to the Samarians to Delaiah and Shelemiah, the sons of Sanballat (Cowley, AP, No. 30, line 29). Sanballat was doubtless still governor but may have been too old to deal with such matters himself. These observations do not permit us to fix a specific date for Ezra, but they do seem to suggest that Ezra came after Nehemiah, or at least subsequent to the first period of Nehemiah's governorship. Albright has suggested[47] that "thirty" may have dropped out of the text of Ezra vii 7, 8, which originally read "in the thirty-seventh year of Artaxerxes." That would put the beginning of Ezra's mission in 428 B.C.

We know virtually nothing about the Jewish community in Palestine in the fourth century because there are few verifiable sources. All indications are that the good relations between the Jews and Persians in the time of the Second Isaiah continued throughout the period of Persian control of the west. Certainly Nehemiah and Ezra were on good terms with them. To judge from archaeological remains, the Jews were at least making progress toward their goal of district home rule directly under the Persian authorities of Across the River. The population was increasing and local autonomy was apparently the rule. The Jews conducted their own fiscal affairs as the *yhd* stamps show.[48]

[47] BP, p. 64, n. 133.

[48] Cf. W. F. Albright, JPOS 6 (1926), 93–102. Cf. N. Avigad, "A New Class of *Yehud* Stamps," IEJ 7 (1957), 146–53, with references cited there; IEJ 9 (1959), 55 f. A Jewish community at En-gedi dating from the Persian period has been uncovered recently (*The Israel Digest*, May 11, 1962, p. 7). Y. Aharoni's reading of *pḥwa* on the Ramat Rahel stamps (*Excavations at Ramat Rahel: Seasons 1959 and 1960* [Roma: Università degli Studi Centro di Studi Semitici, 1962], pp. 7–10) has been questioned and thus cannot be used for evidence on this point. The term *pḥh* does occur as late as the second century B.C. in an Arabic inscription, *fḥt ddn* "governor of Dedan." See W. Caskel, *Lihyan und Lihyanisch* (Arbeitsgemeinschaft für Forschung des Landes Nordrhein-Westfalen, Heft 4. Abhandlung [Köln und Opladen: Westdeutscher Verlag, 1954]), pp. 101 f.—it is No. 349 in RR. PP. Jaussen et Savignac, *Mission archéologique en Arabie*, II. El-'Ela, d' Hégra a Teima Harrah de Tebouk (Paris: Geuthner, 1914).

LITERARY AND HISTORICAL ORDER

Before entering upon a detailed discussion of the problems reflected in the title to this section, it may be helpful to present a brief statement on the canonical position and content of Ezra-Nehemiah.

The summary at the end of Nehemiah shows that Ezra-Nehemiah was once regarded as a single book under the title of Ezra. The earliest canonical lists (Baba Bathra, 15a, and Melito of Sardis) refer to our books of Ezra and Nehemiah as Ezra. Sirach (xlix 13) praised the memory of Nehemiah but does not even mention Ezra, which points to an awareness of the work of Nehemiah though apparently contained in the book attributed to Ezra. In the margin of MSS used by Kittel in *Biblia Hebraica,* at the beginning of Nehemiah, are the words "book of Nehemiah." Though of late origin, it may represent the persistence of an early tradition that regarded Nehemiah as a separate source appended to or incorporated in the book of Ezra. From the time of Origen, there has been a definite division of material into two books—First and Second Ezra. The Second book of Ezra was called Nehemiah by Luther on the basis of Neh i 1.

Both LXX and Vulgate have transmitted a wider Ezra literature than that reflected in our English Bibles. The following table illustrates the situation:

LXX	*Vulgate*	*English*
Esdras A	Esdras III	First Esdras (Apocryphal book)
Esdras B	Esdras I	Ezra
Esdras C	Esdras II	Nehemiah
Esdras (the Prophet)	Esdras IV	II Esdras (Apocalypse, sometimes referred to as IV Ezra.)

Ezra i–vi relates the events leading to the first return and the story of the rebuilding of the temple. The section begins with a repetition of the two last verses of Chronicles (II Chron xxxvi 22–

23 || Ezra i 1–2), reproduces the edict of Cyrus (i 2–4), and outlines the acceptance and conditions of the edict (i 5–11). Chapter ii lists the men of Israel (3–35), the priests (36–39), the Levites (40–42), temple servants (43–54), royal servants (55–58), and those who could not furnish a legal record of their families (59–63); vss. 64–70 give the number of those returned, an inventory of transport animals, and the contribution of voluntary services and gifts for the house of Yahweh. The erection of the altar and the commencement of worship (iii 1–6) is followed by the laying of the foundation of the house with festival joy (iii 7–13). The religious activity of the returnees was attended by opposition from the people of the land that required considerable negotiation (iv 1–24). Inspired by the prophets Haggai and Zechariah, the returnees began the work of rebuilding, though permission to proceed had once more to be verified (v 1–17); when a copy of the decree of Cyrus was located, Darius issued a confirmatory decree (vi 1–12). The troubles thus ended for a time, the work was completed, the structure dedicated, and a Passover celebrated (vi 13–22).

Ezra vii–x; Neh viii–x recount the work of Ezra the scribe. Ezra vii 1–10 relates Ezra's ancestry and the journey to Jerusalem; he was provided with a royal memorandum from Artaxerxes (vii 11–26), for which he gave praise to Yahweh (vii 27, 28). viii 1–20 contains the list of families of those who returned with Ezra, together with the Levites he prevailed upon to join him. Requesting divine protection and placing the precious objects in the hands of the Levites, they set out for Jerusalem, where they finally arrived (viii 21–36). The remainder of Ezra deals with the problems of mixed marriages and tells how the scribe handled them (ix 1–x 17); then comes the list of the men who were guilty (x 18–44). The Ezra material in Neh viii–x includes the reading of the law (viii 1–12), a celebration of the Feast of Tabernacles (viii 13–18), observance of a day of fasting concluding with a lengthy, fervent prayer by Ezra (ix 1–37), and the ratification of a written covenant subscribed by Nehemiah and the other heads of families (ix 38–x 27). The content of that document itemizes the pledges of the people of the Jerusalem community.

Neh i–vii contains the first part of the memoirs of Nehemiah. Informed of the plight of Jerusalem (i 1–3), Nehemiah offers a prayer imploring Yahweh to alter the situation (i 4–11).

When the king notices his dejection and discovers the cause of it, he grants him permission to go to Jerusalem to set things right (ii 1–8). Sanballat and Tobiah are irritated by his arrival (ii 9–10). Soon after his coming, he secretly inspects the walls and then summons the people to the task (ii 11–18), which immediately draws ridicule from his opponents (ii 19–20). Undaunted by their attitude, Nehemiah apportions the work to those who were to participate (iii 1–32). Despite continuing derision (iv 1–3), the work continues with prayer (iv 4–9); a system of defense and protection was devised (iv 10–23). Internal difficulties involving oppression of the poor by the affluent are resolved in assembly (v 1–19). All attempts to frustrate the work of rebuilding and repairing the wall are finally overcome and the task completed (vi 1–19). Guards are then stationed at the city gates (vii 1–3). The assembly called by Nehemiah (vii 4–5a) is described later. The list of returnees repeats, with few changes, that of Ezra ii and may be a later addition to the memoirs.

Neh xi–xii deal with the assembly, the notice of its convocation having been given in vii 4–5a (xi 1–xii 26), and the dedication of the wall (xii 27–47).

Neh xiii reports the reform measures of Nehemiah taken in connection with his second visit to Jerusalem. In accordance with Deut xxiii 3 f., Tobiah was ejected from the temple (1–9). The mishandling of the Levites was remedied (10–14), desecration of the Sabbath stopped (15–22), and the problem of mixed marriages resolved (23–31).

Ezra was intended from the start as an integral part of Chronicles, as is shown by the connecting verses between II Chronicles and Ezra (II Chron xxxvi 22–23 ‖ Ezra i 1–3a) and the content of Ezra i 5–vii 26, which deals with Jewish activity in Palestine from the time of Sheshbazzar to Ezra. The aim of the Chronicler seems to have been to portray the cultic community of his people from David to Ezra—to show how it was oriented, maintained, and perpetuated amid the varied fortunes of the people. He tried to show the essential character of the cult through the nation's history, that the cult was the stabilizing institution responsible for the survival of the people as such. In his time, when so many hostile forces threatened to sabotage every endeavor to reconstitute the community in Jerusalem and Judah, the writer believed that a virile cultus

alone could prevent its extinction. That accounts for the order of
Ezra-Nehemiah in our present Bibles. It was not a downgrading of
Nehemiah and his work; it was rather the exigencies of the situation
that dictated the interests and form reflected in the writer's composition. The memoirs of Nehemiah thus were added as an appendix
to the larger corpus of the Chronicler, though the coming of Nehemiah may have antedated that of Ezra.

THE PRESENT ORDER OF EZRA-NEHEMIAH

As they stand, these books deal with two significant periods in
the postexilic history of the Jews. Ezra i–vi is concerned with the
edict of Cyrus and its execution by the first repatriates, that is, the
period from ca. 538 to 515 B.C. Chapter iv, however, is a summary
of oppositions experienced by the Jews under Cyrus, Darius, Ahasuerus (Xerxes), and Artaxerxes; it appears to have been given for
illustrative purposes. Ezra vii–Neh xiii is devoted to the work of
Ezra and Nehemiah in the reign of Artaxerxes.

The major problem is, of course, the order and arrangement of
this large block of material. Ezra vii–x contains the so-called
memoirs of Ezra, giving us the story of his achievements as they
relate to the group he led from Babylon to Jerusalem and his
handling of the problem of mixed marriages. Neh i–vii 5 are Nehemiah memoirs recounting the reaction of this great layman to news
of the situation in Jerusalem, his appeal to the king and the latter's
reaction, the trip to Judah, the survey of the ruins, disclosure of his
purpose to the local citizens and the hostile reaction of their neighbors, a detailed description of the work of rebuilding the walls, the
attempts of the enemies of the Jews to thwart the builders and how
they were met, the problem of debts and its resolution, numerous
endeavors to entrap Nehemiah but without success, and the operation of the security system of the city. vii 6–72 is a revised census
list. Chapters viii–ix describe Ezra's reading of the law and prayer
of confession; ch. x presents a list of the obligations the community imposed upon itself at the suggestion of the scribe and the
signatories to the formal agreement. Chapter xi contains a list of
those who resided in Jerusalem and of the towns occupied at the
time. Chapter xii begins with a series of lists of clerical and lay

families, probably as a prelude to the account of the dedication of the wall which follows; the chapter ends with appointment of officials for various functions in accordance with the practices established by David and Solomon. The last chapter (xiii) is confined to the reforms of Nehemiah brought about during the second period of his governorship.

ATTEMPTS TO REARRANGE THE LITERARY MATERIALS OF EZRA-NEHEMIAH

The confusion of the materials in these books is abundantly clear to any observant reader in our present arrangement. Earlier students of the Bible recognized it: they tried to rearrange the various episodes into what appeared to them to be the proper order. Probably the first serious attempt to do so was made by the compiler of I Esdras, whose main interest seems to have been in the law—for he begins his work with the Josian reformation and concludes with Ezra's reading of the law.[1] His special concerns could have been responsible for the order he imposed upon his document. Yet it is difficult to see how that could have been done so lightly if the tradition was thoroughly fixed. I Esdras is not an independent work; it is a composition and, in part, a translation into Greek of the canonical materials involved.[2] For the moment, there need be no concern for the additions; only the *order* in which these canonical elements are presented is noteworthy.

The second witness to the historical sequences of events in the period involved is Josephus (*Antiquities* XI.i–v). It has often been observed that he follows the same order, in general, as prevails in I

---

[1] The following table shows the order suggested by the compiler of I Esdras:

I Esdras i 1–20 ‖ II Chron xxxv 1–19
       i 21–22 ‖ ——————
       i 23–55 ‖ II Chron xxxv 20–xxxvi 21
       ii 1–3a ‖ II Chron xxxvi 22–23 ‖ Ezra i 1–3a
       ii 3b–11 ‖ Ezra i 3b–11
       ii 12–26 ‖ Ezra iv 7–24
       iii 1–v 6 ‖ ——————
       v 7–71 ‖ Ezra ii 1–iv 5 (for comparison of lists see Appendix).
       vi 1–ix 36 ‖ Ezra v 1–x 44
       ix 37–55 ‖ Neh vii 22–viii 13a

[2] Cf. C. C. Torrey, ES, pp. 18 ff.; O. Eissfeldt, EAT, 3d ed., 1964, pp. 779 f.; R. H. Pfeiffer, *History of New Testament Times*, 1949, pp. 233–57.

Esdras. For purposes of comparison, a brief outline of Josephus' story may be useful here.

1. The decree of Cyrus and the first return.
2. People of Samaria complain to Cambyses about the work of the Jews. He orders a suspension of the work of rebuilding Jerusalem.
3. Accession of Darius. The story of the three guards, one of whom was Zerubbabel who, because of his wisdom, was granted permission to lead a group of Jews to Jerusalem.
4. Experiences of Zerubbabel in connection with the rebuilding of the temple.
5. Accession of and Jewish activity under Xerxes (Artaxerxes).
   a. Ezra is well known to the king, who issues a rescript permitting him to return to Jerusalem with a company of Jews. Story of Ezra's return, the problem of mixed marriages, Ezra's reaction, his prayer, his confession, and his resolution of the problem. People request a reading of the law at the Feast of Tabernacles in the seventh month. Death of Ezra.
   b. Story of Nehemiah, the cupbearer of the king. He goes to Jerusalem via Babylon. Rebuilds the wall of Jerusalem in two years and four months. Feast of eight days. Plan to occupy the city. Order for tithes for support of temple. Constitutions of Nehemiah. The wall of Jerusalem is an eternal monument to Nehemiah.

Two points may be noted here. The first is Ezra's reading of the law in the seventh month—as in Neh viii and I Esdras ix 37 ff. The second is the complete separation of Ezra and Nehemiah; neither is mentioned or even alluded to in the story of the other.[3] Josephus ends his story of Ezra's mission with the ceremony of reading the law, followed immediately by the notice of the death of Ezra at a very great age. He does not appear to have used Neh ix–x but does refer to the bringing into Jerusalem of people from the outlying areas, though not for the reason given in Neh xi 1–2. However, Josephus seems to have telescoped the story of Nehemiah in

[3] Nehemiah is nowhere mentioned in I Esdras, though the author does refer to a statement (ix 49) by the governor (*attarate*), who is not named, to Ezra. For a possible explanation see H. Cazelles, "La mission d'Esdras," VT 4 (1954), 113–40, especially pp. 131 ff.

a way that gives the impression he knew more than he was disposed to relate.[4]

The most far-reaching recent attempt to solve the problem of dislocation was undertaken by C. C. Torrey.[5] He suggests the following order: Ezra i; I Esdras iv 47–v 6; Ezra ii 1–viii 36; Neh vii 70–viii 18; Ezra ix 1–x 44; Neh ix 1–x 39; Neh i 1–vii 69; Neh xi 1–xiii 31. The basic dislocation is due to a scribal error in copying the text. The scribe knew that Ezra ii was a duplicate of Nehemiah vii and, having gotten as far as Ezra viii 36, observed the similarity between Ezra ii 68–iii 1 and Neh vii 70–73; he regarded Ezra ii 68–iii 1 as the sequel of Neh vii. Then he simply went on to copy Ezra ix–x, and when he came to the end of Neh vii, in the proper sequence of his material, he followed it up with the chapter held in reserve from Ezra viii.[6]

A. Gelin is of the opinion[7] that, since the whole difficulty lies in the realm of the Ezra material, the dates mentioned therein may help us toward a solution. The time sequence is as follows:

1. Ezra vii 9: first day of the first month (preparations for journey);
2. Ezra viii 31: twelfth day of the first month (departure from the Ahava river in Babylon);
3. Ezra vii 8, 9: first day of the fifth month (arrival at Jerusalem);
4. Neh vii 72b–Neh viii 2, 18: first day of the seventh month to eighth day of the seventh month (reading of law during a feast);
5. Ezra x 9: twentieth day of the ninth month (assembly at Jerusalem);

[4] Cf. *Antiquities* XI.v.8.183 ". . . Nehemiah had done many other excellent things, and things worthy of commendation in a glorious manner. . . ." For an evaluation of Josephus' story of Nehemiah, see C. C. Torrey, *The Apocryphal Literature*, 1945, pp. 44 f., and H. H. Rowley, "Sanballat and the Samaritan Temple," BJRL 38 (1955), 166–98.

[5] In *The Composition and Historical Value of Ezra-Nehemiah*, 1896; the more elaborate and rigorously argued work, ES, 1910, especially pp. 252–84; and CHI, 1954, where he has printed the Hebrew text, with translation, in the order he proposes.

[6] Torrey, CHI, p. xxix, and ES, pp. 255–58.

[7] *Le Livre de Esdras et Néhémie*, p. 14 (see Gelin, Selected Bibliography, Commentaries). For a discussion of the Ezra sources see F. Ahlemann, "Zur Esra-Quelle," ZAW 59 (1942/43), 77–98.

6. Ezra x 16: first day of the tenth month to first day of the first month (period of examination of cases of mixed marriages);

7. Neh ix 1: twenty-fourth day of the same (1st) month (confessional service).

The resultant order then would be:

Ezra vii–viii: events relating to Ezra's return to Jerusalem;
Neh vii 72–viii 18: the law-reading ceremony;
Ezra ix–x: the problem of mixed marriages and its resolution;
Neh ix: the confessional service.

This appears to be a realistic approach to the problem of order and emphasizes the over-all impression one gets of the mission of Ezra from a perusal of the sources. If he was the secretary for Jewish religious affairs at the Persian court, as H. H. Schaeder has suggested,[8] he must have been invested with legal authority on two levels—that of the court and that of Jewish law (torah). And if the surmise is correct that he came after Nehemiah, it follows that he acted with dispatch. Nehemiah had already established a modus vivendi; Ezra gave it legal sanction by applying to the reforms the principles of the law of Moses which he brought along from Babylon and promulgated in Jerusalem and Judah. This is what the Persian king sent him to do (Ezra vii 25–26). Ezra seems to have gone further in resolving the matter of mixed marriages than Nehemiah; he demanded divorce of the guilty parties. Nehemiah forbade only the intermarriage of the youth.

These studies are, of course, only concerned with the achievements of Ezra which—significant as they are—occupy only about one fourth of the chapters in our present books of Ezra and Nehemiah. On the order and arrangement of the original sequence of events in the entire complex, W. Rudolph[9] goes perhaps as far as it is possible to do now. He follows Torrey in substance, though

---

[8] EdS, pp. 42–55.

[9] *Esra und Nehemia*, p. XXII (see Rudolph, Selected Bibliography, Commentaries). He postulates this order: Ezra i–viii; Neh vii 72b–viii 18; Ezra ix 1–x 44; Neh ix 1–x 40; Neh i 1–vii 72a; Neh xi 1–xiii 31. He suggests that Neh x 2–28 and xii 1–26, and possibly other minor sections, were later additions; and that Neh vii 72b–viii 18 and ix 1–x 40 found their way into the Nehemiah memoirs later. Bowman (*Introduction and Exegesis to the Book of Ezra and the Book of Nehemiah*, pp. 560 f.) appears to follow Rudolph substantially (see Bowman, Selected Bibliography, Commentaries).

he does not include anything of I Esdras. He thinks that the whole work was originally grouped around three periods: (a) Ezra i–vi (538–515 B.C.), (b) Ezra vii–viii; Neh viii; Ezra ix–x; Neh ix–x (458–457 B.C.), (c) Neh i–vii, xi–xiii (446 till after 433 B.C.). The Chronicler, in his review of Israel's history, stressed the great work of David which was nullified by the nation's subsequent deviation from the will and purpose of the Lord. The story of Ezra (and Nehemiah) then is one of thanksgiving to God for his gracious guidance and direction and for his inspiration of the Persian authorities in their sympathetic treatment of the Jews' successful efforts at rehabilitation. The work of re-establishing their institutions at Jerusalem centers about personalities, so that Ezra-Nehemiah is essentially a narrative of the experiences of the two or three great men who served as leaders.

One further contribution toward a solution of the enigma must be considered briefly[10]—that of Father Pavlovsky,[11] based on the theory that Ezra followed Nehemiah in time. His work is a thoroughgoing study of the issues involved and grounded on the most recent

[10] Batten's order (*Ezra and Nehemiah*—see Selected Bibliography, Commentaries) is as follows: Ezra i 1–iv 3, iv 24b–vi 22, iv 4–24a; Neh i–vii, xi–xiii; Ezra vii–x; Neh viii–x. N. H. Snaith (ZAW 63 [1951], 53–66) proposes this order: Ezra i, iv 7–24, ii 1–iv 5, v 1–vi 22; Neh i 1–vii 72, ix 1–xiii 31; Ezra vii 1–10, viii–x; Neh vii 73–viii 18. Galling (*Die Bücher der Chronik, Esra, Nehemia*—see Selected Bibliography, Commentaries) postulates two hands responsible for the work of the Chronicler. To the original hand he ascribes most of Ezra i–x and the original parts of Neh viii. To the second he attributes Ezra iii (except vss. 2, 3, 8, 10a, 12), vi 19–22, vii 1b–10, 24–25, viii 35–36, ix 1b, 3–x 1; additions to memoirs of Nehemiah: i 5–11, ii 10, 19–20, vii 5b–72, viii 2b, 4–8, 11, 13–18, ix 1–37, x 1–30, 34, 35, 37a, 38b–40, xi 1, 2, 3b–4a, 17b, 21–23, 36, xii 1–26, 27b–30, 33–36, 41–47, xiii 1–3, 16–18, 22a, 26, 27, 29–31a. For other orders see R. H. Pfeiffer, *Introduction to the Old Testament*, 1941, pp. 830–38; cf. A. Lods, *Histoire de la littérature hébraique et juive*, 1950, p. 630. S. Mowinckel summarizes his view briefly in his article in VuH, p. 212. He thinks that the original history of the Chronicler did not contain the Nehemiah memoirs; only the Ezra history was included, as a continuation of Ezra i–vi. The arrangement of Ezra-Nehemiah and the confused material of Neh vii–xii is not the work of the Chronicler but that of a post-Chronicler redactor. Neh viii–x has nothing to do with either the Ezra history or the memoirs of Nehemiah. Neh viii (apart from chs. ix–x) originally followed Ezra x and thus served as the conclusion of the Ezra history. Neh viii does not contain the account of new law authored and promulgated by Ezra but has to do with a New Year's celebration related through the events to which it joined.

[11] "Die Chronologie der Tätigkeit Esdras: Versuch einer neuen Lösung," *Biblica* 38 (1957), 275–305, 428–56.

archaeological and historical investigations. He believes that the
original work of the Chronicler included only I and II Chronicles
and Ezra i–vi 22. The structural elements reflected in that portion of the Chronicles-Ezra-Nehemiah complex are totally lacking
in the subsequent chapters—Ezra vii to Neh xiii. Since Pavlovsky's
conception of the situation is somewhat more detailed than those
already noted, it may be well to present his outline of what he
thinks is the proper sequence of events recorded in Ezra-Nehemiah.

1. Ezra i–iii: return from exile and the beginning of temple
reconstruction under Cyrus (537/6 B.C.).
2. Ezra iv 1–5, 24: cessation of the project due to local complaints (536).
3. Ezra v–vi: continuation and completion of work on temple
under Darius (520–515).
4. Ezra iv 6: accusations directed against the Jews in the time
of Xerxes (486/5).
5. Ezra iv 7–23: unsuccessful attempt of returnees to repair
the walls of Jerusalem in the time of Artaxerxes (448/7).

FIRST PERIOD OF NEHEMIAH'S GOVERNORSHIP (445–433)
6. Neh i 1–vii 3: reconstruction of the walls.
7. Neh vii 4–72: preparation for the expansion of the population of Jerusalem.
8. Neh xi 1–xii 26: steps to bring country residents into the
city.
9. Neh xii 27–43: dedication of the walls.
10. Neh xii 44–47, v: provisions for support of temple and re-
mission of debts. Nehemiah's return to Persia.

SECOND PERIOD OF NEHEMIAH'S GOVERNORSHIP (430)
11. Neh xiii 4–31: Nehemiah's return to Jerusalem (unoffically
accompanied and influenced by Ezra); abolishes religious
abuses.
12. Neh xiii 1–3, 8–9: Ezra's reading of the law (7th month);
exclusion of foreigners from the congregation of Israel; day
of penitence.
13. Neh x: People pledge obedience to the law (renewal of the
covenant. Nehemiah and Ezra return to Susa).

OFFICIAL ACTIVITY OF EZRA (428/7–?)

14. Ezra vii–viii: (At the instigation of Nehemiah) Ezra is vested with authority by Artaxerxes. Journey to Jerusalem.
15. Ezra ix–x: Resolution of the mixed marriages (continuity of the reform).

Pavlovsky's major contribution is his conjecture that Ezra accompanied Nehemiah unofficially on his second tour of duty in Jerusalem[12] and was the prime mover in the latter's reforms. Later, at the behest of Nehemiah, Ezra returned to Jerusalem invested with royal authority. He led a caravan of exiles from Babylon. After his arrival he took some time to settle those who came with him and then set to work dealing finally with the problem of the mixed marriages. When that had been resolved, he composed a history of Israel for the new community (Chronicles and Ezra i–vi). Later one of his disciples added the chapters on the work of Ezra and Nehemiah from memoirs, official documents, and papers deposited in the temple archives.[13]

H. Schneider remarks that the "Urform" (i.e., original form) theory is unsatisfactory and that the transpositions required are not so convincingly proven as to suggest preference for such an attempted solution of the problem.[14] Perhaps he is right but his theory is not conclusive. At best any solution can only be probable and as such Pavlovsky's may be preferable to others. The COMMENTS reflect the present writer's views at the moment; they appear to him to explain best—in a broad, general way—the evidence in the case.

THE SOURCES

Though there are not as many sources in Ezra-Nehemiah as in I and II Chronicles, those there are are further obscured by the nature of the material. To begin with, there are the large sections, designated as the memoirs of Ezra and the memoirs of Nehemiah, which account for more than half of the books. Yet even within those tightly constructed documents sources are still discernible.[15]

[12] Biblica 38 (1957), 448.
[13] Ibid., 449 ff.
[14] Die Bücher Esra und Nehemia, p. 60 (see Schneider, Selected Bibliography, Commentaries).
[15] Cf. A. R. Burn, Persia and the Greeks, 1962, p. 56, n. 25.

Following the order of our present books of Ezra-Nehemiah, the following sources may be noted.

THE PRE-EZRA-NEHEMIAH PERIOD (Ezra i-vi)

1. The edict of Cyrus (i 2–4).
2. List of temple vessels returned to Sheshbazzar (i 9–11).
3. List of returnees with Zerubbabel (ii 1–70).
4. Letter of Rehum and Shimshai to Artaxerxes (iv 11–16).
5. Reply of Artaxerxes to Rehum, Shimshai, and their partners (iv 17d–22).
6. Letter of Tattenai and Shethar-bozenai to Darius (v 7b–17).
7. Memorandum of Cyrus located from the archives at Ecbatana (vi 2c–5), prefixed to
8. The reply of Darius to Tattenai, Shethar-bozenai and their partners (vi 6–12).

THE MEMOIRS OF EZRA (Ezra vii–x)[16]

1. Rescript of Artaxerxes to Ezra (vii 12–26).
2. List of family heads of those returning with Ezra (viii 1–14).
3. Inventory of vessels and bowls (viii 26–27).
4. Ezra's prayer (ix 6–15).
5. List of those who had married foreign wives (x 18–44).

THE MEMOIRS OF NEHEMIAH (i 1–vii 72a, xi 1–2, xii 27–43, xiii 4–31)

1. Prayer of Nehemiah (i 5–11).
2. List of builders (iii 1–32).
3. Complaint of Sanballat against Nehemiah (vi 6–7).
4. Note of Nehemiah to Sanballat (vi 8).
5. Census list (vii 6–72a).
6. Ceremony of dedication of walls (xii 27–43).

OTHER MATERIAL IN THE BOOK OF NEHEMIAH (vii 72b–x 40, xi 3–36, xii 1–26, xiii 1–3)

1. Law reading ceremony (?) (vii 72b–viii 18).
2. Ezra's prayer (ix 6–37).
3. Signatories to agreement (x 1–28).
4. The code of "Nehemiah" (x 31–40).
5. List of residents of Jerusalem (xi 3–24).
6. List of towns occupied in Judah and Benjamin (xi 25–36).
7. List of priests and Levites (xii 1–26).

---

[16] On the problem of the "I" and "He" sources, see Mowinckel's article in VuH, pp. 211–33.

Many of these sources undoubtedly came from the temple archives; others may have come from the Persian national archives through someone who had access to them. Some are probably constructions of the Chronicler, or a somewhat later hand, from floating (?) tradition or from scattered written fragments. The specific documents mentioned in the memoirs themselves seem to form an integral part; they were not insertions by the Chronicler.

THE USE OF THE SOURCES

The Return and Rebuilding of the Temple (Ezra i–vi)

Chapter i: The decree of Cyrus (cf. I Esdras ii 1–12). This is substantially the decree as issued by the Persian king pemitting the Jews to return to Babylon.[17]

Chapter ii: List of returnees (cf. I Esdras v 7–45; Neh vii 6–72), probably taken from the Nehemiah memoirs because of the confusion of Sheshbazzar with Zerubbabel. The list may itself be a compilation from several sources.[18]

Chapters iii–vi: The reconstruction of worship facilities. (a) The building of the altar (iii 1–3; cf. I Esdras v 47–50). (b) Offerings (iii 4–6; cf. I Esdras v 50b–53). Source is uncertain but that portion pertaining to the altar is substantially correct; offerings are also probable where there is an altar. (c) Laying the foundation of the temple (iii 7–13 || I Esdras v 54–65; cf. Zech iv 9). Note emphasis on the Levites. (d) Temple built despite opposition (iv 1–vi 22; cf. I Esdras v 66–73, ii 16–30, vi 1–34, vii 1–15). The Aramaic source (iv 7–vi 18) with its introduction and conclusion in Hebrew represents authentic material.[19]

The Ezra Memoirs (Ezra vii–x)

Chapter vii 1–20 || I Esdras viii 1–24; viii 1–36 || I Esdras viii 28–67; ix 1–x 24 || I Esdras viii 68–25. This is in all proba-

[17] See E. J. Bickermann, "The Edict of Cyrus in Ezra 1," JBL 65 (1946), 247–75; De Vaux, RB 46 (1937), 29–57; Albright, BP, pp. 49 f.

[18] K. Galling, "The Gola-List according to Ezra 2 / Nehemiah 7," JBL 70 (1951), 149 ff.

[19] Cf. Lods, Histoire de la littérature hébraique et juive, p. 543; on the Cyrus memorandum see note [17].

bility the work of the Chronicler himself, composed from notes and oral sources. It may be out of place and should follow Nehemiah.[20]

The Nehemiah Material

Chapters i 1–vii 72a, xi 1–2, xii 27–43, xiii 4–31 are the memoirs of Nehemiah and remain virtually unchanged.

Chapters vii 72b–ix 5a is part of the Ezra story.

Chapter ix 5b–37 is a psalm.

Chapters ix 38–x 39 is misplaced material but drawn from temple archives and related to the Nehemiah memoirs.[21]

Chapter xi 3–24; cf. I Chron ix 2–34. Related but it is difficult to say how.

Chapter xii 1–26. xii 1–7 has a list of priests almost identical with that in x 2–8. xii 8–9 is composite. On list of high priests, cf. I Chron vi 115.

Chapter xii 27–33, dedication of the wall.

Chapters xii 44–xiii 3, the ideal community.

It has been shown fairly conclusively that the Ezra memoirs present the same linguistic and literary characteristics found elsewhere in the work of the Chronicler.[22] The memoirs of Nehemiah, on the other hand, reflect quite different characteristics.[23] The Chronicler must have received them and used them substantially in the (written) form in which they now appear. In view of stylistic considerations it is difficult to dissociate the Ezra materials (Ezra viii–x, including Neh viii–x), from the work of the Chronicler. It looks more and more as though the putting together of the whole complex of Chronicles-Ezra-Nehemiah, [with the exceptions noted in the Introduction to *I Chronicles*], was the product of a single hand. It seems almost certain, in as much as chapters xi to xiii of Nehemiah bear evidence of the same type of treatment employed by the author in his handling of other materials utilized by him.[24] Sometimes he

[20] G. E. Wright, *Biblical Archaeology*, 1957, p. 208.
[21] Cf. Rudolph, pp. 173–74. Eissfeldt, EAT, pp. 744 f.
[22] Cf. Torrey, ES, pp. 231–48; A. S. Kapelrud, QAEN; S. R. Driver, *Introduction to the Literature of the Old Testament*, 1913, pp. 544, 549. But see De Vaux, *Supplément au Dictionnaire de la Bible*, IV, col. 764.
[23] Kapelrud, QAEN, pp. 956 f.; W. Bayer, *Die Memoiren des Statthalters Nehemia*, 1937, pp. 6 ff.
[24] Cf. Torrey, ES, pp. 248–50; Eissfeldt, EAT, pp. 742 f.

copied the sources much as he found them, sometimes he rewrote them, and sometimes he doubtless composed freely (in the case of speeches and prayers). He may have confused the historical order (as in Ezra iv and the placing of Ezra before Nehemiah), but that may have been dictated by his purpose. Some of the inner confusion (e.g., the dislocation of Neh vii 70–viii 18) may be due to copyists.

The purpose of the Chronicler was to present the history of Israel (Judah) from a cultic point of view, showing how the nation prospered when the cultus was maintained in purity and vitality and how it fared when that was not the case. Difficulties in the post-exilic community were due, very largely, to the failure to support the cultus and keep it pure. The rehabilitation and survival of Israel was utterly and unquestionably dependent upon the maintenance of a vigorous and healthy religious institution. That was the un-mistakable lesson of its history. And Ezra and Nehemiah devoted all their energy and means to the revitalization of the cult so that Israel might live. The Chronicler's intentions may account for the present order of Ezra-Nehemiah.

THE ACHIEVEMENTS OF NEHEMIAH AND EZRA

Numerous scholars[1] have discussed this subject and not much can be added, in the present state of our knowledge, to what they have said. Nevertheless, a recapitulation of what the biblical tradition affirms is essential.

NEHEMIAH

When Nehemiah learned of the sad state of affairs in Judah and Jerusalem—"the city, the site of the graves of my fathers, is in ruins and its gates destroyed by fire" (Neh ii 3)—he requested the king to send him "to Judah, to the city of the graves of my fathers, that I may rebuild it" (ii 5). When the king agreed, he solicited an official pass to traverse the province Across the River and a royal order for "the keeper of the king's forest" directing him to supply "timber for the beams of the gates of the citadel guarding the house and for the wall of the city and for the house which I am to occupy" (ii 8). Nehemiah's inspection tour had to do only with the physical ruins of the city, more especially with its walls, which, to judge from his report to the Jewish officials and his subsequent activity, were certainly his paramount interest and concern. The chief purpose of his coming to Jerusalem was to provide for its security and security, in the world of his time, usually meant building a wall. A major project like the one contemplated required planning and organization, the details of which are not given in our sources.

But there was something more which is sometimes minimized. Nehemiah was an official of the king, limited, to be sure, by his firman, yet invested with power to carry out his mission. There was

---

[1] Cazelles, VT 4 (1954), 113–40; H. H. Rowley, "Nehemiah's Mission and Its Background," BJRL 37 (1955), 528–61, and relevant discussions in the various introductions and commentaries.

probably more to the local opposition than appears on the surface. Though Nehemiah took that opposition quite seriously, there is not the slightest hint that he consulted or conferred with Sanballat, Tobiah, and Geshem. Some indication of his position is given in the unobtrusive statement "the house which I am to occupy" (ii 8). Was that the governor's house?[2] If so, it throws considerable light on his mission as well as on the resistance of the local district governors, who assumed jurisdiction either by default or by appointment of the provincial authorities, whenever a vacuum in political control occurred. It should be recalled that the reconstruction of the wall took, at best, only two years and four months (Josephus, *Antiquities* XI.v) of his first period of service, which lasted for twelve years (v 14). The provincial officials are referred to as governors (*phwwt*) in the memoirs (ii 7, 9, iii 7); so are those who were over Judah before Nehemiah (v 15), whether the reference is to Sheshbazzar and Zerubbabel (Hag i 1, 14, ii 2, 21) or to the authorities at Samaria.[3] The clincher, however, is Neh v 14 where Nehemiah refers to himself as having been appointed as governor (*phm* "their governor") in the land of Judah. Neh xii 26 also speaks of him as the governor (*hphh*). In the Ezra section, Nehemiah is called the *tirshata* (*htršt'* "the governor," viii 9, x 2).[4] From these references it would appear that Nehemiah had come to Jerusalem not only to build the city's walls but as governor of the district of Judah. As such he was responsible for setting things in order in the community, which must have been in a pretty chaotic state as may be seen from the report that the people were "in dire straits and in disgrace" (i 3) and from the situation reflected in the book of Malachi.

That Nehemiah went to Jerusalem with great authority is apparent from his reaction to the problems that arose in carrying out his building project. When the poor of the community complained of the treatment they were receiving from their brethren (Neh v), he acted with firmness. Not only did he know the law (Exod xxii 25; Lev xxv 35–37; Deut xxiii 19–20); he also exhibited a deep sense of what is right. He seems to have appealed privately to the violators of the law but without success. His cautious course of

---

[2] Cf. Xenophon *Cyropaedia* VIII.vi.4, 5.

[3] Cf. Alt, KS, II, p. 333, n. 2.

[4] See textual note and NOTES on Ezra ii 63 and on passages indicated.

action may be attributable, in part, to the fact that he was a eunuch, a serious handicap in dealing with cultic matters (the reference to the position of eunuchs in the new age in Isa lvi 3–5, reflects their low status at that time). Then he called a mass meeting of the citizens and presented his case. In so doing he discreetly used his authority as governor, which he played down somewhat by calling attention to the personal contributions he and his party had made and were making to the community. His ability to force the guilty to take an oath before the priests is further testimony to his influence. Then there is the manner in which he dealt with political pressure from the outside (Neh vi 1–9) and subversion from within (vi 10–14). One without royal authority as governor could not have handled the affair as Nehemiah did; his opponents would not have been content with diplomatic measures. They would have used force to gain their objectives. One other aspect of his work reveals his diplomacy—the organization of the community. After the completion of the walls, he set up regulations for the life of the city (vii 1–3) and took a census of the people preparatory to providing housing for them in the spaces within the now secure city (vii 5, xi 1 ff.). Such actions alone reveal a broader mission than that of a building contractor.

Nehemiah's official capacity is delineated even more clearly in the reforms[5] undertaken during the second visit to Jerusalem. The compromising position of the religious leaders is shown by the priest's granting Tobiah permission to occupy space in the precincts of the temple (Neh xiii 4–9). The summary way this infringement of the temple's sanctity was dealt with underscores both the interest and authority of the governor. So does his handling of the injustices suffered by the Levites (xiii 10–14), though some aspects of this story may reflect the interests of the compiler. The Deuteronomic injunctions not to forsake the Levites (Deut xii 19, xiv 27, xxvi 13) were pointed; those of the priestly writer (Num xviii 21 ff.), while emphasizing the tithe for the Levites, are not so insistent. Nehemiah's concern for the Sabbath may have been inspired by

---

[5] Bright's remarks (*Yehezkel Kaufmann Jubilee Volume,* p. 74) are very much to the point. He thinks they may have been *ad hoc* measures demanded by the exigencies of the situation. While based on Deuteronomic laws, they do not seem to have been in any way connected with a legal reformation or the introduction of a formal code. What happened in Egypt during the absence of Arsames (AP, Nos. 27, 30) illustrates what took place during Nehemiah's absence—internal conflict and breakdown of order.

his knowledge of the observations of Jeremiah (xvii 19–27)[6] and Ezekiel (xx 12–24), who both regarded the misfortunes of Judah as due, in part, to the violation of the Sabbath law. Nehemiah wanted, in the new venture, to avoid the mistakes of the past. His experiences had opened his eyes to the dangers of too close identification with the peoples of the land. The basis for the exclusion of Moabite and Ammonite wives was Deut xxiii 3. Though Moabites are mentioned only here (Neh xiii) and in Ezra ix 1, Ammonites are frequently referred to, probably because of Tobiah. Ashdodites were among those incensed by Nehemiah's success in repairing the walls of Jerusalem (iv 7) and were looked upon according to Zech ix 6, as "a mongrel people." So it may be that these groups are singled out because of Nehemiah's difficulties with them and because of the Deuteronomic proscription. But the principle involved was the important thing. The land and people could not rest secure so long as foreign elements remained to bore from within. And Nehemiah's heart was set upon the welfare and success of Judah and Jerusalem.

Political and religious aspects of the community life cannot be separated. As a matter of fact, religion was its heart and the external political structure its body. Judaism was a religious state. Nehemiah was motivated primarily by religious interests, as may be seen from the dedicatory formulas occurring throughout his memoirs (v 19, vi 14, xiii 14, 22, 31). The depth of his faith appears in his frequent engagement in prayer (i 5–11, ii 5, iv 4–5, 9, vi 9) and the ascription of success to "the good hand of my God" (ii 8, 18). Profoundly concerned about the faith of his fathers, Nehemiah set out to do what he could for its security, its activity, and its effectiveness in the land the Lord had given to them. His great achievement was the reconstruction of the walls of Jerusalem. But along with it, and perhaps of equal or greater significance, went new inspiration and direction for the proper functioning and well-being of the people of God.

---

[6] While the passage as it now stands is Deuteronomic in character, it may contain a kernel of Jeremian material. See W. Rudolph, *Jeremia* (Handbuch zum Alten Testament), 1947, pp. 101–3; A. Weiser, *Das Buch des Propheten Jeremia* (Das Alte Testament Deutsch, XX), 1955, pp. 155 f.

EZRA

The Bible connects the mission of Ezra with that of Nehemiah. But there was a significant difference. Nehemiah's activities centered, for the most part, in political aspects of the community, specifically in building projects designed to make the position of the Jews more secure against hostile encroachments from their neighbors. There was also some social reform, as we have seen. But, though Nehemiah was a deeply religious man, he was not a recognized authority in matters of Jewish law as Ezra was. He could not —his ability and power were limited—do everything that needed to be done for the people of Judah. Among the tasks he was not up to was the reorganization and revitalization of the cult.

The fulfillment of the congregation in its cultic sense was basically the purpose of Ezra's coming.[7] The royal directive (Ezra vii 12–26) was far-reaching in its implications. Among other things called for was "an investigation about Judah and Jerusalem in harmony with the law of your God" (vs. 14), manifestly to bring the local practices into conformity with that law. We know from other sources that the Persian kings were concerned about the religion of their subject peoples,[8] no doubt to keep them content with their lot and to serve the purposes of the central government. Yet the religious interest of some of the Persian kings seems to have been genuine,

[7] The term *qhl*, "congregation," occurs almost exclusively in the Ezra sections of Ezra-Nehemiah (Ezra x 1, 8, 12, 14; Neh viii 2, 17; elsewhere only in Neh vii 66 ‖ Ezra ii 64; Neh v 13, xiii 1). While the term is applied to other assemblies, it is generally used in a cultic sense. It is especially prominent in Deuteronomic literature (where *'dh*, "congregation," rarely occurs) and in Chronicles (some thirty-two times). *'dh* does not occur in Ezra-Nehemiah and only once in II Chron v 6 ‖ I Kings viii 5. Cf. B. Luther, ZAW 65 (1938), 44–63.

[8] Cf. Cyrus barrel inscription in ANET, pp. 315 f. Xerxes was an ardent devotee of Ahuramazda, *ibid.*, pp. 316 f. Of particular significance was Darius I's codification of the laws of Egypt (519–503 B.C.) in reference to which the Persian word *dt* "law" occurs for the first time (Olmstead, HPE, pp. 119 ff.; W. von Soden, ZA 10 [1938], 181–83). Interestingly enough this is precisely the term used in the royal rescript issued to Ezra (vii 12, 14, 21, 25, 26). The Darius precedent may have been the pattern followed by Artaxerxes I (cf. Alt, KS, I, p. 283). Further evidence is the famous Passover letter sent to the Elephantine community in the fifth year of Darius II (424–405 B.C.), in which the king is represented as giving specific directions for the celebration of the Passover (see Cowley, AP, No. 21).

as may be seen from their handling of Jewish affairs and the changes that evidently took place in their religious outlook. Nehemiah himself may have been instrumental in bringing Ezra to Jerusalem because of the need for making order out of the social confusion and consequent cult laxity, with which he endeavored to deal in piecemeal fashion.

The specifics of the official document carried by Ezra called for (a) permission to accompany the mission to Jerusalem for any one who desired to do so, (b) an investigation of conditions in Judah and Jerusalem, (c) provision for the transportation to Jerusalem of the cult offerings, (d) the proper application of the funds contributed for the offerings, (e) the availability of royal funds for further, unforeseen expenses, (f) notice of orders issued to the officials of the province Across the River, (g) tax exemption for cult personnel, (h) authority for the appointment of magistrates and judges competent to apply the law of Ezra, and (i) penalties for those who failed to comply with that law. All this presupposes a fairly definite legal document embodying the law to become the standard of cultic life and practice in the land. If Ezra was, as Schaeder contends,[9] a Persian official in charge of Jewish affairs in Babylon, he undoubtedly had worked for a long time on "the law of your God." The Persian government was well aware of conditions in the various provinces of the empire and not the least of those in the district of Judah. As we know from the correspondence mentioned in Ezra (iv–vi) and the Elephantine letters, communication was almost constant, so that what transpired locally was soon known in governmental centers. Moreover, much unofficial information came by way of travelers or refugees (Neh i 1–3). Therefore, far-sighted Jews such as Ezra certainly could not remain indifferent and unresponsive to contemporary needs. From other sources, it is evident that literary and cultic activity was being carried on apace in the Jewish centers of Babylon. This is to be expected—the religious leaders and the elite had been there since the days of the destruction of Jerusalem. Even after the early returns, little of positive cultic significance, except the reconstruction of the temple, came out of Jerusalem.[10]

It was no accident that Jewish torah activity focused upon Ezra

[9] EdS, pp. 39–59; cf. M. Noth, *Gesammelte Studien zum Alten Testament*, 2d ed., 1960, pp. 99–101.

[10] Jeremiah was right (xxiv 1–9).

who, in the fullness of time, revitalized and gave direction to the religion of the fathers; for it was he who saw clearly that without a firm cultic structure the hopes of the prophets could never be realized. Without his work the religion of Israel might have disintegrated. Something more than a Jewish ghetto in Babylon was required. Unless the achievements of pious Jewish teachers there could somehow be transplanted into the old garden of Israel's faith they would remain merely a blueprint in the archives of time. The "law of your God" represented in substance the legal (cultic) material transmitted in the Pentateuch. That this is so may be seen on almost every page of the Chronicler's work.[11]

Just what is meant by "the book of the law of Moses" (Neh viii 1), "the book of the law" (viii 3), "the book of the law of God" (viii 8, 18), "the words of the law" (viii 9, 13), "the book of the law of Yahweh their God" (ix 3), "the book of Moses" (xiii 1; Ezra vi 18), "the law of Moses" (Ezra iii 2, vii 6) is not quite certain.[12] That it was a body of written material may be seen from the frequent qualification *ktb* ("write, written") in connection with it (Ezra iii 2, 4; Neh viii 14, 15, x 35, 37, xiii 1) and the references in which Ezra "opened the book" (Neh viii 5) and he (they) read in (from) it (Neh viii 3, 8, 18, ix 3, xiii 1). The question is whether Ezra brought along only the *P* code or the whole Pentateuch. The over-all picture presented in Chronicles, Ezra-Nehemiah seems to point pretty decisively to the latter—that it was a written document embodying substantially the content of our present Pentateuch. This may be seen both in the general orientation of the community of the restoration as well as in specific points. The community organization follows, on the whole, that posited in Deuteronomy—that is, it revolves around Jerusalem and the temple ("the place which Yahweh your God will select out of all your tribes to put his name," Deut xii 5). Jerusalem occurs about eighty-six times in Ezra-Nehemiah; temple, the house, the house of Yahweh, and the house of God about fifty-three times. The law of tithes in

---

[11] For a summary of scholarly opinion on the Chronicler's attitude toward and use of the various codes, see N. H. Snaith in *The Old Testament and Modern Study*, ed. H. H. Rowley, 1951, pp. 109 ff. For a general statement of the significance of the *torah* for the Chronicler see my Introduction in *I Chronicles* (The Anchor Bible, vol. 12), 1965.

[12] Cf. Noth, *Gesammelte Studien zum Alten Testament*, pp. 11 f., n. 2.

Deut xii 6, 11, 17, requires them to be brought to the central sanctuary where they are to be used (Deut xiv 23); a third year tithe is
apparently to be eaten in the local towns (Deut xiv 28, xxvi 12).
The regular tithe is a yearly requirement (Deut xiv 22). Numbers
(xviii 21–28) gives the tithe to the Levites who in turn give a
tenth of it to Yahweh, for the sons of Aaron. According to Lev xxvii
30–32 the tithe is holy and therefore belongs to Yahweh; it cannot be redeemed. Neh x 37b–39 has the Levites collecting the
tithes locally but bringing them to the house of God; in Neh xiii 12
"all Judah" is said to have brought them to the storehouses in Jerusalem. The law of Nehemiah thus seems to be a combination of D
and P (H, or Holiness Code) adapted to the new situation. To the
seventh year Sabbath of the land (Exod xxiii 11; Lev xxv 4–7),
Nehemiah (x 32) adds the Deuteronomic provision for the release
of debts (Deut xv 12). The regulation appealed to in order to justify renunciation of foreign marriages (Neh xiii 1–3) was Deut
xxiii 3–6, but the observation that foreigners defiled the land
(Ezra ix 11) is based on Lev xviii 25 ff. (cf. Lev xx 22 ff.). Again
both D and P are involved. Tabernacles was celebrated at Jerusalem (Neh viii 14 ff.) as prescribed by Deuteronomy (xvi 13–
15).[13] While the passage does not specifically say so, the context
of Ezra vi 19–21 implies that the Passover was celebrated in Jerusalem—another Deuteronomic injunction (Deut xvi 1–3). Much is
made of the law of firstlings, first fruits (Neh xii 44, xiii 31) and
the best of other produce (x 36–38). The requirement to bring
them to the house of God is the same as in the old law (Exod xxiii
19, xxxiv 26), but it is not specified that they are for the priests
as in Num xviii 12, 15; Deut xviii 4; cf. Lev xxiii 20, though
it is doubtless implied (cf. Neh x 38). Nothing is said about
their presentation as a wave offering, as in Lev xxiii 10 f., 17, 20.[14]

Another doctrine of importance for the Chronicler was that of

[13] Neh viii 15 prescribes the use of "olive branches, pine branches, myrtle
branches, palm branches and (branches of) other leafy trees" for the making
of booths; this may be a reminiscence of Lev xxiii 40, though it is certainly not
a close one, as Rudolph, pp. 150 f., has shown. "As it is written" seems to
require a more specific reference. If, however, it is based on the Leviticus
passage, it would mean the combination of D and P (H). See Y. Kaufmann,
The Religion of Israel, 1960, p. 209.

[14] On the whole matter of the firstlings, first fruits, and the tithes see
O. Eissfeldt, Erstlinge und Zehnten (Beiträge zur Wissenschaft vom Alten
Testament, Heft 22), 1917.

separation (Habdalah), in which he follows the *P* code.[15] The term occurs almost exclusively in exilic and postexilic literature, just when the idea of separateness or apartness received its greatest stress by virtue of the exigencies of the situation. It is a characteristic conception of the priestly writings. *P*'s separation of the Levites (Num viii 14) is an article of cultic faith for the Chronicler, whose bias in their favor has been referred to elsewhere. As in *P,* the Levites throughout are clearly distinguished fom the Aaronites, however highly they may have been regarded. Perhaps the best illustration of the Chronicler's use of both *D* and *P* is his combination of the basic ideals of both in his attempt to provide a cultic framework for the religious state of his time. Thus *D*'s emphasis on Jerusalem and the temple and *P*'s on Moses, the tabernacle, and the law are forged into the conception of Jerusalem, the temple, the law. The Sabbath law applied to a specific situation (Neh x 32, xiii 15–22—the latter an application by Nehemiah of the Sabbath law to abuses on the part of local manufacturers and retailers and foreign hucksters) rests on the prescription of the decalogue and may be based, in part, on the injunctions of *P* in Exod xxxv 3 and Num xv 32–36. But the observations of the prophets (Amos viii 5; Isa lviii 13–14; Jer xvii 19–27) may have been associated with the untoward experiences of the nation when it violated the law (the view of *D,* followed by the Chronicler). The pledge to furnish wood for offerings (Neh x 35, xiii 31) may have been based on Lev vi 5–6 (vi 12–13E[16]), though "as prescribed in the law" (Neh x 35) could refer to the other precedents of the section too.[17] What we have here is possibly a specific application of the broader principle of Leviticus, again tailored to fit the local situation and time.

The Chronicler carried on in the tradition of *D* and *P,* each of which represents the application of the law of Moses to the needs of the time as its author saw them. Ezra, too, faced a situation fraught with problems. These he met in the light of past experience. He

[15] N. H. Snaith, *The Jews from Cyrus to Herod,* 1949, pp. 76–78. Statistics must be used with caution but the following distribution of the usage of the root (*bdl*) is interesting: 13 times in Chronicles, Ezra, and Nehemiah, 3 in Numbers, 5 in Deuteronomy, 8 in Leviticus, 1 in Exodus, 3 in Ezekiel, 1 in I Kings, 3 in Isaiah (lvi–lix) and 5 in Genesis (all in ch. i)—in all, 42 times.

[16] E denotes English text; where biblical citations are followed by H, the Hebrew text is meant.

[17] Rudolph, p. 180, thinks the wood-offering law may have been present in a law no longer extant in our OT.

brought with him from Babylon a large body of material (the Pentateuch) which he endeavored to expound to the community of Jews in Judah and whose principles he appealed to as occasion and need dictated. He manifestly began where the community was when he arrived. What its condition and circumstances were may be seen from the memoirs of Nehemiah. What the latter attempted to do for the cult on a hit or miss basis, Ezra undertook in a planned program drawn from the law of Moses.

From the above illustrations *it is apparent* that Ezra's lawbook, so far as it can be checked, seems to have corresponded closely to the legal materials in our present Pentateuch. G. von Rad observes that stipulations from all sources of the Pentateuch are present in the lawbook, some are to be found only in *P,* some only outside of *P,* and others nowhere else.[18] To judge from the Ezra material, it appears fairly clear that the great religious leader was concerned primarily with the reorganization of the cult on the basis of the Pentateuchal legislation. While he had credentials from the Persian court for that purpose and there is evidence that priests carried out local as well as central administrative duties (cf. NOTE on Neh iii 4), it is becoming increasingly certain that Ezra did not function as governor. What he came to do was more significant in the long run—laying the foundations of Judaism that was to make an incalculable impact upon the world in the following centuries. It withstood the hostile and angry forces beating against its fortifications of Torah, whose positive qualities are as evident in Western history as in the resurgence of Judaism today. It became the mother of two great faiths destined to transmit something of its blessing to every corner of the world.

Nehemiah thus provided the physical structure for the Jewish community in the Palestine of his time. He brought security to a disorganized, oppressed, and abused people. He gave them leadership on a sound, official basis. Ezra, on the other hand, furnished the program for the development of a virile cultus that brought encouragement and religious unity to the Jews in Judah. It is perhaps not too much to say that what Nehemiah did for the body of Judaism, Ezra did for its soul.

[18] *Das Geschichtsbild des Chronistischen Werkes* (Beiträge zur Wissenschaft vom Alten und Neuen Testament), 1930, p. 39. For the first he cites Neh x 32b; for the second, Neh x 33; for the third, Neh x 31; for the fourth, Neh x 35.

TEXT AND RELATED MATTERS

THE HEBREW TEXT

The Hebrew text is, on the whole, fairly well preserved, though there are lacunae here and there (cf. Ezra v 8, vi 3, 15; Neh x 32, xii 46). Some passages are obscure and difficult (e.g., Ezra x 44; Neh iii 34, iv 6, 10, v 2, xii 46) but not more so than certain ones in other prose books of the Bible. The peculiarities of syntax and structure are, in general, those of late postexilic Hebrew (e.g., the use of *'šr* for *ky*). In Ezra i 9, 10, marginal notes intended to explain the discrepancy have crept into the text. The Aramaic of Ezra (iv 8–vi 18, vii 12–26) is that prevailing in the official documents of the Persian empire as may be seen from the Elephantine correspondence and other documents.[1] So far only one manuscript has turned up at Qumran.[2]

There is not nearly so much plene (full) spelling as might be expected, though there seems to be a stronger tendency in this direction in Nehemiah than in Ezra. The *w* of the feminine plural (*wt*) is more frequently omitted than expressed in both Ezra and Nehemiah. There are a few omissions of the *y* of the plural masculine before suffixes, and several times in the *hiphil*. The *w* of the plural termination of verbs before suffixes is almost always retained. The *w* (*ō*) in the infinitive construct of *lamed he* verbs is frequently not written (Ezra vii 10; Neh viii 15, xii 27, xiii 27); but is written in the *qal* participle (Ezra iv 5, vii 28; Neh ii 6, iii 33, 35, 37, iv 11, 12, v 12, vi 6, 8, vii 5, viii 9, etc.). The interrogative negative (*hlw'*) is always spelled plene; the simple negative (*l'*), never. The first

---

[1] See H. H. Schaeder, *Iranische Beiträge*, I, 1930, pp. 27–56; E. Meyer, EJ, pp. 8–12; F. Rosenthal, *Die aramäistische Forschung*, 1939, pp. 63–65, 67–51, and *A Grammar of Biblical Aramaic*, 1961, pp. 5 f.; H. H. Rowley, *The Aramaic of the Old Testament*, 1929, passim.

[2] F. M. Cross, Jr., BA 19 (1956), 85. The manuscript contains a portion of Ezra iv–v.

person singular imperfect of *'mr* with *waw* consecutive is written three times as *w'wmr* (Neh ii 7, 17, 20).

The vocabulary is similar to that of other postexilic writings though some of the meanings of words are far from clear. Most of the hitherto obscure words and phrases can now be understood in the light of usage reflected in the growing accumulation of inscriptional materials from all over the Near East[3] and a thorough study of the versions and their variants. There are numerous Persian words or expressions, as may be seen from the following list:[4]

'grṭl, "dish?" (Ezra i 9).

'drzd', "diligently" (Ezra vii 23).

'prsky', "partners, investigators" (Ezra v 6). See R. G. Kent, *Old Persian: Grammar, Texts, Lexicon,* 2d ed., rev. 1953, p. 198.

'ptm, "storehouse" (Ezra iv 13). But see F. Rosenthal, *A Grammar of Biblical Aramaic,* 1961, p. 59.

'sprn', "precisely, exactly" (Ezra v 8, vi 8, 12, 13, vii 17, 21, 26).

'štdwr, "stir up revolt, break the peace" (Ezra iv 15, 19).

'šrn', "woodwork?" (Ezra v 3, 9).

gzbr, "treasurer" (Ezra i 8, vii 21).

gnzy', "treasuries" (Ezra v 17, vi 1, vii 20).

dt, "law" (Ezra vii 12, 25, 26).

htršt', "the Tirshata," title of the Persian governor (Ezra ii 63; Neh vii 65; cf. I Esdras v 40). The word means "the one to be respected or feared."

zmn, "time" (Ezra v 3; Neh ii 6).

nštwn, "text of letter" (official order) (Ezra iv 7, 18, 23, v 5, vii 11).

pršgn, "copy" (Ezra iv 11, 23, v 6, vii 11).

ptgm, "message, document, matter" (Ezra iv 17, v 7, 11, vi 11).

šršw, "corporal punishment?" (Ezra vii 26).

Then there are the Persian names of the kings, of Bigvai, of Mithredath (Ezra i 8, iv 7), and of the family of Elam.

[3] Cf. C. F. Jean and J. Hoftijzer, *Dictionnaire des inscriptions sémitiques de l'Ouest* (Leiden, 1960).

[4] For discussion and references see COMMENTS on verses indicated.

THE VERSIONS

It is impossible here to go into critical matters dealing with the various recensions of the Greek text[5]—imperative for a demonstrably accurate assessment of the Greek textual tradition so far as Ezra and Nehemiah are concerned—because of the apparently wide variation between the two great codices B and A (*Vaticanus*, LXX[B] and *Alexandrinus*, LXX[A]) and the question of the relationship of our present Greek text to Theodotion. C. C. Torrey thought it represents a development from Theodotion. He believed that *Sinaiticus* (LXX[ℵ]) is the best text so far as it has been preserved and that B, contrary to Kittel, is the worst.

On the whole, LXX is shorter than MT—especially Codex B and its supporters. Codex A fills in many of the omissions. A few examples may be given to illustrate the situation.

Ezra i 2a

Heb. " 'Thus has Cyrus the king of Persia said: *Yahweh* God of the heavens has given me all the kingdoms *of the earth. . . .*' "
LXX[A] follows Hebrew exactly.
LXX[B] omits the italicized words.

Ezra iii 2

Heb. "Then Jeshua, the son of Jozadak, and his brothers, *the priests and Zerubbabel, the son of Shealtiel, and his brothers* arose. . . ."
LXX[A] follows Hebrew but reads "Salathiel" for "Shealtiel."
LXX[B] omits italicized words.

[5] See Torrey, ES, pp. 62–114; J. A. Bewer, *Der Text des Buches Esra*, 1922; Jahn, *Die Bücher Esra (A und B) und Nehemja* (see Selected Bibliography, Commentaries); P. Katz's review of *The Old Testament in Greek*, eds. A. E. Brooke and N. McLean, II, 1935, Pt. 4, in TLZ 62 (1937), cols. 341–45; A. Allgeier, "Beobachtungen am Septuagintatext der Bücher Esdras und Nehemias," *Biblica* 22 (1941), 227–51; A. Klostermann, "Esra und Nehemia" in *Realencyklopädie für protestantische Theologie und Kirche*, ed. A. Hauck, 1898, V, pp. 507–13.

Ezra vi 5

Aram. ". . . from the temple at Jerusalem *and brought to Baby-lon be returned and brought back to the temple at Jerusa-lem.* . . ."
LXX[A] follows Aramaic.
LXX[B] omits italicized words.

Neh ii 16

Heb. ". . . the priests, the nobles, *the local officials,* and the other participants in the task."
LXX[A] follows Hebrew.
LXX[B] omits italicized words.

Most omissions occur in the lists of Nehemiah (iii 7, 37b–38, viii 4 [B], 7, x 11 [B], much of xi 15–31, xii 3–7, and many names from xii 14–42, especially B). The lists in Ezra have come down pretty much as they are in MT. While some of the omissions are to be explained by homoioteleuton or homoioarkton and inner Greek corruption, others cannot. There are also a number of transliterations from Hebrew to Greek: e.g., Ezra i 10, *Kephphoure(s)*; viii 17, silver for *Kasiphia;* Neh ii 13, *golela* for valley (by) night; iii 5, *adoreem* for their nobles; iii 11, *thannoureim* (A), *nathoureim* (B) for furnace (tower); iii 16, *beththagaareim* (A), *Bethabareim* (B) for the House of the Mighty Men; iii 22, *achechar* for the district; iii 31, *maphekad* for Muster (gate); vii 7, *Masphar* for number. LXX is often helpful in the determination of proper names and of-fers minor corrections of MT elsewhere (e.g., Ezra viii 10 "Bani," with LXX[A]; Neh ii 1 "I had charge of the wine"; iii 11 "as far as"; viii 15, the addition "and Esdras said"; so also in ix 6; ix 17 "in Egypt").

The Vulgate follows MT quite closely. Sometimes, however, it evidences a preference for LXX (Ezra i 8, v 2, vii 8; Neh iii 8, 30, vi 2, 9). Several times it diverges from both (Ezra i 9, 10, v 3; Neh v 15, vi 13, vii 1, xi 36 with Syr.).

The Syriac does not add much to our knowledge of Ezra-Ne-hemiah, though it does assist in confirming the Hebrew text which it follows most closely. Divergences from LXX and MT are usually thought to be due to interpretation and not to the presence of another text tradition.[6] However, the Qumran texts appear to point in another direction for Samuel, Kings, and Chronicles, and may follow the same tendency here, but there is not yet enough evidence to establish a firm conclusion.[7]

[6] Cf. Klostermann, *ibid.,* pp. 504–7, where numerous illustrations are given in the categories discussed by the author.

[7] See F. M. Cross, Jr., BASOR 132 (December 1953), 15–26; JBL 74 (1955), 165–72.

AUTHORSHIP AND DATE

In arriving at an approximate date for Ezra-Nehemiah, which is part of the Chronicler's work, several factors must be taken into consideration. First is the matter of authorship. II Maccabees (ca. 50 B.C.) speaks of the records and memoirs of Nehemiah (ii 13) and his collection of books and documents for a library. The writer may have meant to attribute to him the authorship of materials beyond the memoirs.[1] The Talmudic tradition (*Baba Bathra,* 16a) credits Ezra with the authorship of Chronicles, which it says was completed by Nehemiah (*ibid.,* 15a). Torrey[2] and Kapelrud[3] have shown that the person responsible for the Ezra memoirs also penned Chronicles. Bayer's study[4] indicates that the Nehemiah memoirs are characteristically different from the writings of the Chronicler. Whether they were utilized by the Chronicler directly or attached to and incorporated into his work by a later hand is not clear. The argument presented in my Introduction to *I Chronicles* (The Anchor Bible, vol. 12) need not be repeated but, after further study and the weighing of possibilities at hand, Ezra appears a more and more likely candidate for authorship.

The identification of the author has, of course, a significant bearing on the date of Ezra-Nehemiah. But the following points must be kept in mind in any resolution of the problem of date:

1. The postexilic list of the Davidic family, which ends with the sons of Elioenai whose youngest son was, in all probability, born around 405 B.C.[5]
2. The last functioning high priest seems to have been Jehohanan (Ezra x 6). The lists in Neh xii 10–11, 22, contain also the name of Jehohanan's son and successor (Jaddua), but there is

[1] Cf. Torrey, CHI, p. xiii, and references cited there to his own articles on the subject.
[2] *The Composition and Historical Value of Ezra-Nehemiah,* ES, pp. 240 ff.
[3] QAEN.
[4] *Die Memoiren des Statthalters Nehemia.*
[5] See my *I Chronicles,* COMMENT on iii 17–24.

nowhere a hint that he officiated as high priest.[6] Nor do we know when he did take over. Jehohanan was still in office in the fourteenth year of Darius II (i.e., in 411 B.C.)[7]; when he became high priest is also unknown. Though the name of Joiada, the father of Jehohanan, occurs in both lists there is no reference to his term of office or any act of his—perhaps because he died prematurely.[8]

3. The last Persian king mentioned is Darius II (424–405 B.C.)—Neh. xii 22; unless the references to Artaxerxes are to Mnemon (405–359) rather than to Artaxerxes Longimanus (465–425), in which case Mnemon would be the last.

4. The name of Bigvai, who was governor of Judah in 408 B.C., does not occur in Ezra-Nehemiah,[9] though this may be because the events related there occurred earlier and hence did not involve him. Josephus (*Antiquities* XI.vii.1) does refer to him as a friend of Judas, the brother of Jehohanan, and as "the general of another army of Artaxerxes," who became involved in the struggle of the brothers for the office of high priest. According to the story, Judas was slain in the temple by John (Jehohanan).

5. We hear little about Samaritan opposition after Nehemiah. It is not mentioned in the Ezra memoirs. The Samaritans are not among the foreigners named in connection with intermarriage in either Nehemiah or Ezra, except in Neh xiii 28 where we are informed that a son of Joiada married a daughter of Sanballat.[10] Just why there are no Samaritans mentioned as wives cannot be ascertained at present. The trouble may have been more political and economic than religious, at least from

---

[6] Albright (JBL 40 [1921], 112) thinks the Chronicler completed his work during the official occupancy of Jehohanan, though Jaddua was recognized as his legitimate successor.

[7] AP, No. 30.

[8] Josephus says simply that "When Eliashib the high priest was dead, his son Judas succeeded to the high priesthood; and when he was dead, his son John took that dignity" (*Antiquities* XI.vii.1.297).

[9] AP, No. 30.

[10] Josephus (*Antiquities* xi.vii) has an expanded notice of the same event. He says the name of Joiada's son was Manasseh and the daughter of Sanballat was Nikaso. When Manasseh refused to divorce his wife he was unfrocked. Complaining to his father-in-law that though he loved his wife he did not want to lose his office, he was promised not only a priestly rank but that of the high priest of a (new) cult with a temple on Mount Gerizim.

the point of view of the Samaritans. However, the Chronicler's interpretation of those difficulties was quite different.[11]

6. While Sanballat was probably still alive in 408 B.C., he was no longer active, since the Elephantine request was addressed to his sons. Bigvai and Delaiah replied in a joint memorandum[12] which does not mention Sanballat.

All signs point to a date around 400 B.C. for the completion of the main work of the Chronicler. There is no evidence that demands a later date.[13] To judge from archaeological remains, life did not stand still in the fourth century B.C., and had the author compiled his work in that period there would doubtless have been clear hints, if not overt reference, to some conspicuous events. The most telling factor is that of the royal genealogies of I Chron iii 17–24 and the list of high priests in Neh xii. If there had been further names they would surely have been included, especially of high priests.[14] The reason the lists end where they do is that they represent the situation at the time of writing (ca. 400).

Note on Samaritan Pentateuch

The Samaritans of Ezra's time were an unorthodox, syncretistic group reflecting affinities with the Elephantine community and the diaspora Jews of the Northern Kingdom. While the Samaritans and

[11] Cf. W. F. Albright, *The Biblical Period from Abraham to Ezra*, 1963, pp. 91 f. While the exigencies of the situation may have forced Ezra to play down somewhat his overt opposition to the authorities at Samaria, there could be no compromise on cult matters. Could the underlying reason for ignoring the religious community of Samaria have been the same as that for disregarding the Northern Kingdom in Chronicles, except where it impinged directly upon the interests and movements of Judah? The impression created by a rapid reading of Chronicles, Ezra, Nehemiah, at one sitting, is that the writer or compiler was really offering an *apologia pro* Jerusalem and its now continuing worship, his intention being to demonstrate that there could be no rapprochement with the syncretistic cults to which Sanballat and Tobiah adhered, while making, at the same time, a subtle appeal to them to accept the true faith of the fathers. Cf. II Maccabees (ca. 50 B.C.); Rowley, BJRL 38 (1955), 184 ff.; Alt, KS, II, pp. 357 f.

[12] AP, Nos. 30, 32.

[13] See W. F. Albright, "The Judicial Reform of Jehoshaphat," *Alexander Marx Jubilee Volume*, English Section, ed. S. Lieberman, 1950, pp. 71 f.

[14] On the confused situation in Josephus (*Antiquities* XI.viii) see Rowley, BJRL 38 (1955/56), 166–98. Preliminary study of the Samaria papyri, recovered from Wadi Daliyeh by Frank M. Cross, Jr., throws new light on the situation following the Ezra-Nehemiah period; for details, see his article in BA 26 (1963), 110–21. The documents date from ca. 375 to 335 B.C.

Tobiah were Yahwists, they were clearly regarded as heretical by the orthodox Jews who returned from Babylon.[15]

The Pentateuch was completed before the time of the Chronicler and was utilized by him, but there was as yet no standardized recension.[16] The Samaritan Pentateuch dates from the second–first centuries B.C., since it reflects essentially the Palestinian text of that period which has turned up at Qumran.[17] There was an "official" Palestinian text, adopted by the Maccabees, as well as the Egyptian Vorlage—the Egyptian text represented by the oldest LXX MSS—which goes back to the third century B.C. The Vorlage of MT appears to have been imported from Babylon between the third and first centuries B.C.

The Samaritans were brought under Maccabean rule by compulsion; their religious beliefs and practices were presumably made to conform, in large measure, to the official Maccabean Pentateuch which then became their Bible. It may be that the Maccabees officially adopted the Palestinian version of the Pentateuch, which they then imposed upon the Samaritans and Idumeans. From the time of the Maccabees on the official Jewish Pentateuch became their Scripture, though there may have been some survivals of their older religious practices.

The Samaritans of the fifth–fourth centuries must be separated from those of the second–first centuries and of the New Testament. The reformation in Samaritan religion took place in the days of John Hyrcanus (134–104 B.C.), who destroyed the temple on Mount Gerizim and brought its devotees under Jewish control.

---

15 Cf. Albright, *Archaeology and the Religion of Israel*, pp. 168–75.

16 See W. F. Albright, *From the Stone Age to Christianity*, Anchor ed., 1957, pp. 345 f.

17 Cf. P. W. Skehan, "Exodus in the Samaritan Recension from Qumran," JBL 74 (1955), 182–87; F. M. Cross, Jr., *The Ancient Library of Qumran*, Anchor ed., 1961, pp. 172 ff., 186; *Harvard Theological Review* 59 (1966), 201–11.

EVALUATION OF EZRA AND NEHEMIAH

The host of problems associated with almost every aspect of the lives, work, and personalities of Ezra and Nehemiah does not in any way diminish their importance in and influence on Jewish history. In fact they may have accentuated the study of their character and contributions thereto.

EZRA

Doubtless many of the qualities and activities attributed to Ezra are apocryphal but they are, at the same time, powerful testimony to his achievements and his place in Jewish religious history. His name is attached not only to the biblical books of Ezra-Nehemiah (II Esdras) and the apocryphal book of I Esdras, but also to the pseud-epigraphic IV Ezra, portions of which circulated independently as fifth and sixth Ezra. There is also the Revelation of Ezra,[1] a Christian imitation of IV Ezra. While Ezra does not appear in Sirach's list of worthies (Sirach xliv–xlix) nor in the New Testament, he occupies a prominent place in Josephus and in the Talmud. Josephus[2] praises him as the principal priest of the people, skilled in the law of Moses, and affirms his personal acquaintance with Xerxes. He states further that Ezra reached a ripe old age, died, and was buried in Jerusalem.[3]

References to Ezra abound in the Talmud. Only a few can be recalled here. Of course he is connected with the law. *Sukkah* (20a) credits him with re-establishing the law after it had been forgot-

---

[1] *The Ante-Nicene Fathers: Translations of the Writings of the Fathers down to A.D. 325.* The Rev. Alexander Roberts, D.D., and James Donaldson, LL.D., Editors. American Reprint of the Edinburgh Edition (Buffalo: The Christian Literature Company, 1886). VIII, pp. 571–74.

[2] *Antiquities* XI.v.

[3] There is an Arab tradition to the effect that he died and was buried in Babylon.

ten by Israel. *Megilla* (16b) says Ezra and the Torah surpassed in importance the building of the temple. Certain regulations with respect to the reading of the curses in Leviticus (before Pentecost) and in Deuteronomy (before the New Year) were attributed to Ezra by Rabbi Simeon ben Eleazar (*Megilla* 31b).[4] *Baba Ḳamma* (82a) ascribes to him ten legal enactments. According to *Sanhedrin* (21b, 22a) Rabbi Jose affirmed that Ezra would have been worthy of receiving the Torah had Moses not preceded him. To be a descendant of Ezra was preferable to any other qualification (*Berakoth* 27b) and to be a disciple of his a crowning honor (*Soṭa* 48b, *Megilla* 15a). Some manuscripts of the Targum ascribe the authorship of Malachi to Ezra.[5] *Baba Bathra* (16a) says Ezra wrote Chronicles.

The curious stories of the Koran[6] appear to be distortions based on the Nehemiah story of the nocturnal survey of the ruins of Jerusalem and the beliefs of a heretical group which referred to Ezra as the son of God. Ibn Khaldun thinks of Ezra as a prophet and imputes to him the rebuilding of the temple.[7] The postapostolic writings speak of him as a servant of the Lord[8] and prophet.[9] The Church Fathers refer to him as priest and Levite, scribe (cf. Ezra vii 21) and prophet. Origen thought "Ezra, who was most learned in the law (cf. Ezra vii 25) and repeated orally the whole Old Testament, wrote the law and some other things that happened and were revealed."[10] In his various commentaries he quotes Ezra a number of times. Wing Panel III of the central group on the north half of the west wall of the synagogue at Dura-Europas in all probability represents Ezra reading from a Torah scroll.[11] That would indeed be appropriate, both geographically and ideologically.

The over-all impression one gets from the biblical story of Ezra

[4] Cf. also *'Arakin*, 32b, which mentions Ezra in connection with booths and jubilees.

[5] See A. Sperber, *The Bible in Aramaic*, III (Leiden: Brill, 1962), p. 500—adding to vs. 1 *dytqry šmyh 'zr' spr'* "whose name is Ezra the scribe."

[6] Sura II and IX.

[7] *The Muqaddimah*, IV.2 (Franz Rosenthal edition, 1958, II, p. 260).

[8] *The Ante-Nicene Fathers* . . . , VII, p. 493, *Apostolic Constitutions*, 8:3:22.

[9] *The Ante-Nicene Fathers* . . . , VII, p. 109, *The Divine Institutes*, 4:11.

[10] *Library of the Greek Fathers and Ecclesiastical Historians* (Athens), XV, 1958, p. 203.

[11] See Comte du Mesnil du Buisson, *Les Peintures de la Synagogue de Doura-Europes* (Roma, 1939), pp. 92–94, with references, and *The Excavations at Dura-Europas: Final Report*, VIII, Pt. I: *The Synagogue*, by Carl H. Kraeling, 1956, pp. 232–35, and Pls. XIX and LXXVII.

is that he was a very humble man,[12] possessed of genuine piety and concern for his people. His ultimate concern was for Israel and the Torah, which was God's revelation for her welfare. However, contrary to the commonly expressed opinion, he looked upon the Torah as an instrument for the salvation of Israel rather than as an end in itself. Individuals as well as the community or congregation of Israel found therein guidance for the proper relationship to Yahweh and to one another, and for the maintenance of the covenant so essential for true happiness and well-being.

The Tractate Aboth (Fathers) begins as follows: "Moses received Torah from Sinai and transmitted it to Joshua, and Joshua to the elders, and the elders to the prophets, and the prophets to the Men of the Great Assembly" (1:1). On the basis of Neh viii–x Jewish tradition regards Ezra as the prime mover in the activity of the Great Assembly.[13] The prominence accorded him by the great rabbis attests his part in the development of the Jerusalem cult in the period following the building and organizational activity of Nehemiah. It is highly probable that Ezra was responsible for the editing and introduction of the Pentateuch in its present form. The latter aspect of his work is demonstrated by the events related in Nehemiah viii–x. Little political activity is ascribed to him—his work is centered about the Torah and its application to the life of the community. As such Ezra presents a pattern of approach to community life worthy of emulation today. His basic concern was with the soul of his people, realizing, as perhaps no one else had since Moses and the prophets, that man cannot live by bread alone, only by and through the words that proceed from the mouth of God.

NEHEMIAH

Though Sirach[14] does not include Ezra in his list of heroes of the faith he speaks glowingly of Nehemiah:

> Nehemiah, glorious is his memory!
> Who raised up our ruins,
> And healed our breaches,
> And set up doors and bars. (xlix 13)

[12] Cf. Kapelrud, QAEN, p. 17.
[13] See G. F. Moore, *Judaism*, I, 1926, pp. 29–36; R. T. Herford, *Pirke Aboth*, 3d ed., 1945, pp. 19–22.
[14] Ca. 180 B.C.

II Maccabees[15] credits him with the reconstruction of the temple and altar and the offering of sacrifices (i 18). Later he is said to have been commissioned by the king of Persia and retrieved the sacred fire hidden by the priests when the fathers were exiled to Persia (i 20–36). The same source attributes to him the founding of a library (ii 13).[16] Some of this is apocryphal but the source is quite right in speaking of records and memoirs of Nehemiah. There is probably only one allusion to Nehemiah (ix 6) in the New Testament (Acts iv 24).

Josephus (*Antiquities* XI.v) devotes somewhat less space to Nehemiah than he does to Ezra. Interestingly enough he says absolutely nothing about a meeting between the two men, nor does he offer the slightest hint of their possible co-operation in Jerusalem. The only indication of their contemporaneity is his affirmation that both lived and worked under the Persian king Xerxes (Artaxerxes). He places Nehemiah after Ezra and separates their arrival at Jerusalem by about eighteen years.[17] Nothing, in general, is added beyond what the Bible tells us, though some details are filled in that are either missing in, or at variance with, it.

As might be expected, the Talmud has fewer references to Nehemiah than to Ezra. *Berakoth* (13a) speaks of him as a prophet. *Sanhedrin* (38a) says his real name was Zerubbabel. He is further credited with having narrated the subject matter of the book of Ezra (*Sanhedrin* 93b); the only reason the book does not bear his name is because he claimed merit for himself (Rabbi Jeremiah ben Abba) or because he spoke disparagingly of his predecessors (Rabbi Joseph). At a number of places there are, of course, quotations from his book dealing with specific points in which the rabbis were interested or which they summoned to establish their position in connection with some argument or other.

The references to Nehemiah in the Church Fathers are not too abundant though there are a few interesting observations. Julius Africanus in a letter to Origen says Nehemiah sought permission from Artaxerxes to build Jerusalem and that he received a favorable

---

[15] Date is uncertain, but it was known to Philo of Alexandria (ca. A.D. 40).

[16] On this claim see C. C. Torrey, JAOS 70 (1950), 118, and CHI, pp. xiii f.

[17] Ezra came to Jerusalem in the seventh year of Xerxes, Nehemiah in the twenty-fifth year.

response. Acting on that response he came to Jerusalem, in the 115th year of the Persian empire. At Jerusalem he superintended the work of building the plaza and the wall.[18] Origen (A.D. 182–251) in a letter to Africanus apparently combines the texts of LXX[A] and LXX[B] because he says Nehemiah was "the cupbearer of the king and his eunuch."[19] M. Hadas[20] thinks the framework of Aristeas may be due to Ezra-Nehemiah. The Latin section of the Hippolytus Chronicle[21] goes so far as to attribute Davidic descent to Nehemiah. Other writings such as the Apostolic Constitutions (7:3:37) repeat the biblical tradition about his Jerusalem activity, notably the rebuilding of the walls of the city.

Like Ezra and some other famous Jews, Nehemiah enjoyed the confidence and respect of the Persian king, as may be seen from the latter's response to the several requests for assistance in the rehabilitation of Jerusalem. His concern for his people and their welfare is shown by his inquiry of Hanani about conditions in Jerusalem (Neh i 2 ff.) and the effect upon him personally of what he learned (ii 3). Further demonstration of his seriousness of purpose may be seen from his reaction to injustices and unbrotherliness in the Jerusalem community itself (ch. v) and to its treatment of the Levites during his absence (xiii 10–13). His superb leadership qualities are clear from the way he organized the community for the work he came to do (ch. iii) and the way he handled the impending threats of disruption to that work (iv 15 ff.). The resolute way he dealt with those who tried to undermine his work is sign of an iron will and invincible determination to accomplish what he believed to be the will of God (ii 20). It took tremendous courage for a layman to withstand the compromising tendencies of the high priest Eliashib (xiii 4–9) and to hold in check the commercial interests that threatened to undermine the religious obligations of the new community (xiii 15–22). If our position on the date of Nehemiah is correct, he was the first to take measures against mixed marriages, many of which had been contracted for social and economic advantage (xiii 23–28), a situation deplored by Malachi (Mal ii 10–16).

[18] *Library of the Greek Fathers and Ecclesiastical Historians,* XVII, 1958, p. 179. Both Eusebius (*ibid.,* XXVII, 1961, pp. 335 f.) and Syncellus (*ibid.,* XVII, p. 183) report the same sentiment.

[19] *Ibid.,* XVI, 1958, p. 360.

[20] *Aristeas to Philocrates,* 1951, pp. 38–40.

[21] *Library of the Greek Fathers and Ecclesiastical Historians,* VI, 1956, p. 260.

Nehemiah's strong will and singlemindedness of purpose were the result of a deeply religious nature. So much is evident from his prayers (i 5–11, ii 4, iv 4–5, 9) and his genuine piety. His memoirs are shot through with ejaculations calling upon God to remember him for the good he did at the time (v 19, vi 9c, 14, xiii 14, 31) —and these are far from sentimental explosions or expressions of religious affectation. They are graphic utterances, characteristic of all truly devout persons when subjected to great crises in the task or work to which they have felt themselves called by God. If, as some think,[22] the memoirs of Nehemiah were dedicatory inscriptions deposited in the temple, they assumed the character of monumental collects invoking the blessing of God upon his work and continual prayers of thanksgiving for what he had been able to achieve by the help of Yahweh. At the same time they were ever present invocations to Yahweh soliciting his remembrance of his servant in life and death. They may have been composed for that purpose because as a eunuch and layman[23] he could not himself appear before Yahweh in the temple (cf. vi 10 ff.). Nehemiah was far from the proud and selfish man he is sometimes said to have been; this aspect of his character is apparent from the form of his prayers (cf. i 6, iv 4)—"we have sinned," "we are despised." Whatever there was in him of sternness or tyranny was called forth by the nature of the forces confronting him and the times in which he lived. He combined in his person the qualities of firmness, love of and zeal for God, land, and people, and a fierce dedication to the proposition that his was the only way to achieve the immediate ends to which he had committed himself and for which he had received the mandate of the Persian king. And he was right.

[22] Bayer, *Die Memoiren des Statthalters Nehemia*, pp. 1 ff.
[23] See above, p. LXXVI.

SELECTED BIBLIOGRAPHY

COMMENTARIES

Batten, L. W., *A Critical and Exegetical Commentary on the Books of Ezra and Nehemiah* (International Critical Commentary). New York: Scribner, 1913.

Bertheau, Ernst, and Ryssel, Victor, *Die Bücher Esra, Nehemia und Esther* (Kurzgefasstes exegetisches Handbuch zum Alte Testament). Leipzig: Hirzel, 2d ed., 1887.

Bertholet, A., *Die Bücher Esra und Nehemia* (Kurzer Hand-Commentar zum Alten Testament). Tübingen: Mohr, 1902.

Bowman, R. A., *The Book of Ezra and The Book of Nehemiah. Introduction and Exegesis* (IB, III, pp. 549–819). New York and Nashville: Abingdon Press, 1954.

De Fraine, J., *Esdras en Nehemias* (De Boeken van Het Oude Testament). Roermond en Maaseik: J. J. Romen & Zonen, 1961.

Galling, K., *Die Bücher der Chronik, Esra, Nehemia* (Das Alte Testament Deutsch, XII). Göttingen: Vandenhoeck & Ruprecht, 1954.

Gelin, A., *Le Livre de Esdras et Néhémie* (La Sainte Bible). Paris: Les éditions du Cerf, 2d ed., 1960.

Haller, M., *Das Judentum* (Die Schriften des Alten Testament). Göttingen: Vandenhoeck & Ruprecht, 2d ed., 1925.

Hölscher, G., *Die Bücher Esra und Nehemia* (Die Heilige Schrift des Alten Testaments, eds. E. Kautzsch and A. Bertholet). Tübingen: Mohr, 4th ed., 1923.

Jahn, Gustav, *Die Bücher Esra (A und B) und Nehemja*. Leiden: Brill, 1909.

Kahana, A., *Sifre Ezra weNehemiah Miporašim* (in Hebrew). Tell Abib, 1930.

Noordtzij, A., *Esra-Nehemia*. Kampen: J. H. Kok, 1951.

Oettli, S., *Die Bücher der Chronik, Esra und Nehemia* (Kurzgefasstes Kommentar zu den heiligen Schriften Alten und Neuen Testaments). Nördlingen, 1889.

Rehm, M., *Esra-Nehemias* (Echter-Bibel). Würzburg: Echter Verlag, 1956.

Rudolph, Wilhelm, *Esra und Nehemia* (Handbuch zum Alten Testament). Tübingen: Mohr, 1949.

Ryle, H. E., *The Books of Ezra and Nehemiah* (The Cambridge Bible for Schools and Colleges). Cambridge University Press, 1901.

van Selms, A., *Ezra en Nehemia* (Tekst en Uitleg). Groningen, Batavia: J. B. Wolter, 1935.

Schneider, H., *Die Bücher Esra und Nehemia* (Die Heilige Schrift des Alten Testamentes). Bonn: Peter Hanstein Verlag, 1959.

Siegfried, C., *Esra, Nehemia und Esther* (Handkommentar zum Alten Testament, ed. W. Nowack). Göttingen: Vandenhoeck & Ruprecht, 1901.

Slotki, J. J., *Daniel, Ezra and Nehemiah*. London: The Soncino Press, 1951.

Zer-Kabod, M., *Sifre Ezra weNehemia* (in Hebrew). Jerusalem, 1948.

OTHER BOOKS

Abel, F. M., *Géographie de la Palestine* (abbr. AGP). Paris: Gabalda, 1933, 1938.

Albright, W. F., *The Biblical Period from Abraham to Ezra*. New York: Harper, 1963.

Alt, A., *Kleine Schriften zur Geschichte des Volkes Israel* (abbr. KS). Munich: Beck, 3 vols., 1953–59.

Avi-Yonah, M., *Sepher Yerushalayim* (abbr. SY), I. Jerusalem and Tell Abib: The Bialik Institute and Dvir Publishing House, 1956.

Bayer, W., *Die Memoiren des Statthalters Nehemia*. Speyer a.Rh: Pilger Druckerei, 1937.

Cowley, A., ed. and tr., *Aramaic Papyri of the Fifth Century B.C.* (abbr. AP). Oxford: Clarendon Press, 1923.

de Vaux, R., *Les Institutions de l'Ancien Testament* (abbr. IAT), I, II. Paris: Les éditions du Cerf, 1958, 1960.

Eissfeldt, O., *Einleitung in das Alte Testament* (abbr. EAT). Tübingen: Mohr, 3d ed., 1964.

Gerleman, G., *Studies in the Septuagint*. II: *Chronicles*. Lunds Universitets Årsskrift, 1946.

Guthe, H., and Batten, L. W., *The Books of Ezra and Nehemiah* (The Sacred Books of the Old Testament). Leipzig: Hinrichs, 1901.

James, F., *Personalities of the Old Testament*. New York: Scribner, 1939.

Junge, P. J., *Dareios I, König der Perser*. Leipzig, 1944.

Kapelrud, A. S., *The Question of Authorship in the Ezra-Narrative* (abbr. QAEN). Oslo: Dybwad, 1944.

Kegel, M., *Die Kultusreformation des Esra*. Gütersloh: Bertelsmann, 1921.

Kienitz, F. K., *Die politische Geschichte Ägyptens vom 7. bis zum 4. Jahrhundert vor den Zeitwende* (abbr. GÄJZ). Berlin: Akademie Verlag, 1953.

Kittel, R., *Geschichte des Volkes Israel* (abbr. GVI). Three vols., 1923–29: Vols. I, II (Gotha: Leopold Klotz Verlag, 1923, 1925); Vol. III (Stuttgart: W. Kohlhammer, 1927, 1929).

———, *Great Men and Movements in Israel*. New York: Macmillan, 1929.

Kraeling, E. G. H., ed., *The Brooklyn Museum Aramaic Papyri* (abbr. BMAP). Yale University Press, 1953.

Kuschke, A., ed., *Verbannung und Heimkehr: Festschrift für Wilhelm Rudolph* (abbr. VuH). Tübingen: Mohr, 1961.

Leuze, O., *Die Satrapieneinteilung in Syrien und im Zweistromlande von 520 bis 320*. Halle: Max Niemeyer Verlag, 1935.

Liver, J., *The House of David* (in Hebrew). Jerusalem: Magnes Press, 1959.

Meyer, E., *Die Entstehung des Judenthums* (abbr. EJ). Halle a. S.: Niemeyer, 1896.

Mowinckel, S., *Esra den Skriftlaerde*. Studier til den jødiske menighets litteratur. Annen samling. Kristiania, 1916.

———, *Statholderen Nehemia*. Studier til den jødiske menighets litteratur. Første samling. Kristiania, 1916.

———, *Studien zu dem Buche Ezra-Nehemia*. I: *Die nachchronische Redaktion des Buches. Die Listen*. II: *Die Nehemia-Denkschrift*. Oslo: Universitetsforlaget, 1964.

Nikel, J., *Die Wiederherstellung des jüdischen Gemeinwesens nach dem babylonischen Exil*. Freiburg im Breisgau: Herder, 1900.

Noth, M., *Die israelitischen Personennamen im Rahmen der gemeinsemitischen Namengebung* (abbr. IPN) (Beiträge zur Wissenschaft vom Alten und Neuen Testament). Stuttgart: Kohlhammer, 1928.

———, *Überlieferungsgeschichtliche Studien* (abbr. ÜS). Tübingen: Niemeyer Verlag, 2d ed., 1957.

Olmstead, A. T., *The History of the Persian Empire* (abbr. HPE). University of Chicago Press, 1948.

Pritchard, J. B., ed., *Ancient Near Eastern Texts Relating to the Old Testament* (abbr. ANET). Princeton University Press, 2d ed., 1955.

Schaeder, H. H., *Das persische Weltreich*, O.J. (Vorträge d. Fried. Wilh. Universität zu Breslau im Kriegswinter 1940/41).

———, *Esra der Schreiber* (abbr. EdS) (Beiträge zur historischen Theologie). Tübingen: Mohr, 1930.

———, *Iranische Beiträge*, I. Halle: Niemeyer, 1930.

Snaith, N. H., *The Jews from Cyrus to Herod*. Wallington, England: Religious Education Press, 1949.

Steuernagel, C., *Lehrbuch der Einleitung in das Alte Testament*. Tübingen: Mohr, 1912.

Tallquist, K. L., *Assyrian Personal Names* (abbr. APN). Helsingfors: Acta Societalis Scientiarum Fennicae, Tom. XLIII, No. 1, 1914.

Torrey, C. C., *The Chronicler's History of Israel* (abbr. CHI). Yale University Press, 1954.

——, *Ezra Studies* (abbr. ES). University of Chicago Press, 1910.

Weissbach, F. H., *Die Keilinschriften der Achämeniden* (Vorderasiatische Bibliotek, III). Leipzig, 1911.

Welch, Adam C., *Post-Exilic Judaism*. Edinburgh and London: William Blackwood, 1935.

Wright, J. S., *The Date of Ezra's Coming to Jerusalem*. London: Tyndale Press, 1958.

ARTICLES

Ackroyd, P. R., "Two Old Testament Historical Problems of the Early Persian Period," JNES 17 (1958), 13–27.

Ahlemann, F., "Zur Esra-Quelle," ZAW 59 (1942/43), 77–98.

Albright, W. F., "The Biblical Period" (abbr. BP), in *The Jews: Their History, Culture, and Religion*, ed. L. Finkelstein, I, pp. 3–69. New York: Harper, 1949.

Allrik, H. L., "Lists of Zerubbabel—Neh. 7–Ezr. 2," BASOR 136 (1954), 21–27.

——, "I Esdras According to Codex B and Codex A," ZAW 66 (1954), 272–92.

Alt, Albrecht, "Die Rolle Samarias bei der Entstehung des Judentums," KS, II, pp. 316 ff.

——, "Judas Nachbarn zur Zeit Nehemias," KS, II, pp. 338–45.

Avi-Yonah, M., "The Walls of Nehemiah," IEJ 4 (1954), 239–48.

Bentzen, A., "Priesterschaft und Laien in der jüdischen Gemeinde des 5. Jahrhunderts," AfO 6 (1931), 280–86.

——, "Sirach, der Chronist und Nehemia," *Studia Theologica* 3 (1949), 158–61.

Bickerman, E., "The Edict of Cyrus in Ezra 1," JBL 65 (1946), 247–75.

Bright, J., "The Date of Ezra's Mission to Jerusalem," in *Yehezkel Kaufmann Jubilee Volume*, pp. 70–87. Jerusalem: Magnes Press, 1960.

Cazelles, H., "La mission d'Esdras," VT 4 (1954), 113–40.

Cook, S. A., "The Age of Zerubbabel," in *Studies in Old Testament Prophecy*, ed. H. H. Rowley, pp. 19–36. Edinburgh: T. and T. Clark, 1950.

de Vaux, R., "Les décrets de Cyrus et de Darius sur la reconstruction du temple," RB 46 (1937), 29–57.

Galling, Kurt, "Denkmäler zur Geschichte Syriens und Palästinas unter Herrschaft der Perser," PJB 34 (1938), 77 ff.

————, "The Gola-List According to Ezra 2 and Nehemiah 7," JBL 70 (1951), 149–58.

————, "Kronzeugung des Artaxerxes," ZAW 63 (1951), 66–74.

————, "Syrien in der Politik der Achämeniden," Der Alte Orient 36 (1937), Heft 3/4.

————, "Der Tempelschatz nach Berichten und Urkunden im Buche Esra," ZDPV 60 (1937), 177–83.

————, "Von Naboned zur Darius," ZDPV 69 (1953), 42–64; 70 (1954), 4–32.

Gelin, A., "Les premiers Sioniens," Lumen Vitae 7 (1952), 95–104.

Gordis, R., "The Biblical Edah," in Alexander Marx Jubilee Volume, English Section, ed. S. Lieberman, pp. 369 ff. New York: The Jewish Theological Seminary of America, 1950.

Grosheide, H. H., "Twee Edicten van Cyrus ten Gunste van de Joden," Gereformeerd Theologisch Tijdschrift 54 (1954), 1–12; "Juda als onderdeel het perzische Rijk," ibid., 65–76.

Haupt, P., "Nehemiah's Night Ride," JAOS 39 (1919), 143.

Heichelheim, F., "Ezra's Palestine and Periclean Athens," Zeitschrift für Religions- und Geistesgeschichte 3 (1951), 251–53.

Jepsen, A., "Nehemiah 10," TLZ 79 (1954), cols. 305 f.

————, "Nehemiah 10," ZAW 66 (1954), 87–106.

Kamil, M. M., "The Aramaic Papyri Discovered at Hermopolis-West," in Actes du XXIᵉ Congrès International des Orientalistes, Paris: Imprimerie Nationale, 1949, pp. 106 f.

Klostermann, A., "Esra und Nehemia," in Realencyklopädie für protestantische Theologie und Kirche, ed. A. Hauck, V, pp. 500–23. Leipzig: Hinrich, 1898.

König, F. W., "Älteste Geschichte der Meder und Perser," Der Alte Orient 33 (1934), Heft 3/4.

Lambert, G., "La Restauration juive sous les rois Achemenides," Cahiers Sion 1 (1947), 314–37.

Liver, J., "The Return from Babylon: Its Time and Scope," in Eretz Israel, V, pp. 114–19. Dedicated to Professor Benjamin Mazar on his fiftieth birthday. Jerusalem: Israel Exploration Society and the Hebrew University, 1958.

Mazzacasa, F., "Esdras, Nehemias y el Ano Sabático," Revista Biblica 23 (1961), 1–8; see also review in ZAW 74 (1962), 91.

Meissner, B., "Die Achämenidenkönige und das Judentum," Sitzungsberichte der preussischen Akademie der Wissenschaften (phil.-hist. Klasse), 1938, pp. 6–26.

Neufeld, E., "The Rate of Interest and the Text of Neh. 5:11," JQR 44 (1953/54), 194–204.

Olmstead, A. T., "Tattenai, Governor of Across the River," JNES 3 (1944), 46.

Pavlovsky, V., "Die Chronologie der Tätigkeit Esdras: Versuch einer neuen Lösung," *Biblica* 38 (1957), 275–305, 428–56.

Rabinowitz, I., "Aramaic Inscription of the 5th Century B.C.E. from a North Arab Shrine in Egypt," JNES 15 (1956), 1–9.

Rehm, M., "Nehemia 9," *Biblische Zeitschrift* N. F. 1 (1957), 59–69.

Rowley, H. H., "The Chronological Order of Ezra and Nehemiah," in *Ignace Goldziher Memorial Volume*, eds. S. Löwinger and J. Somogyi, pp. 117–49. Published by the editors in Budapest, 1948.

——, "Nehemiah's Mission and Its Background," BJRL 37 (1954/55), 528–66.

——, "Sanballat and the Samaritan Temple," BJRL 38 (1955/56), 166–98.

Snaith, N. H., "The Date of Ezra's Arrival in Jerusalem," ZAW 63 (1951), 53–66.

Ungnad, A., "Keilinschriftliche Beiträge zum Buch Esra und Ester," ZAW 58 (1940/41), 240.

EZRA

1. CYRUS RELEASES THE JEWS
(i 1–11)†

The edict of Cyrus

I 1 And in the first year of Cyrus the king of Persia—to fulfill the word of Yahweh from Jeremiah—Yahweh aroused the spirit of Cyrus the king of Persia who made the following proclamation throughout all his kingdom and which he also posted officially in writing: 2 "Thus has Cyrus the king of Persia said: *Yahweh* God of the heavens has given me all the kingdoms *of the earth* and he has appointed me to build him a house in Jerusalem which is in Judah. 3 Who is among you of all his people? May his God be with him, let him go up to Jerusalem *which is in Judah and build the house of Yahweh God of Israel who is the God that is in Jerusalem*; 4 and every one who remains wherever he may sojourn, the men of his place, shall support him with silver, gold, equipment, and riding beast in addition to voluntary offerings for the house of God which is in Jerusalem."

The response

5 Then the heads of the families of Judah and Benjamin, the priests and the Levites arose—indeed, everyone whose spirit God had aroused—to go up to build the house *of Yahweh* which was at Jerusalem, 6 and all their neighbors supported them vigorously with vessels of silver, with gold, with goods, with cattle and with [other] choice gifts, in addition to all [they] contributed voluntarily. 7 King Cyrus also handed over the articles

† Ezra i 1–4: cf. II Chron xxxvi 22–23, I Esdras ii 1–7.

*–*Omitted by LXXᴮ.

of the house *of Yahweh* which Nebuchadnezzar had brought away from Jerusalem and placed in the house of *his gods*. 8 Cyrus the king of Persia handed them over to Mithredath the treasurer* who enumerated them to Sheshbazzar the prince of Judah; 9 and this was their number: thirty gold dishes, a thousand *[to be changed]* and twenty-nine silver dishes, 10 thirty gold bowls, four hundred and ten *[to be changed]* silver bowls, and a thousand other articles. 11 All the gold and silver articles numbered five thousand and four hundred. Sheshbazzar brought all those along when he brought up the exiles from Babylon to Jerusalem.

b–b LXX "his god."
c Heb. *gizbar*, which is derived from the Persian loanword *ginzabara*. See Schaeder, *Iranische Beiträge*, I, p. 47, n. 3. LXX*B* *Tasbarenos*, LXX*A* *Garbarenos*, LXX*L* *ganzambraios*.
d–d Omitted by LXX and Vulg. See NOTE.

NOTES

i 1–4. For a translation and discussion of this decree and the Aramaic record, see Bickerman, JBL 65 (1946), 247–75.

1. *Cyrus the king of Persia*. Occurs as title as early as Nabonidus Chronicle (ANET, p. 306).

proclamation. The royal proclamation was promulgated by official heralds in all Jewish communities in Babylon. Cf. x 7; Neh viii 15 for examples of proclamations issued by Ezra and Nehemiah.

in writing. *mktb* occurs only seven times in OT and is a technical term meaning "inscription" or "official document." For written and oral proclamation see also II Chron xxx in Sec. 32 of *II Chronicles*.

2. *God of the heavens*. A postexilic expression found frequently in the Elephantine correspondence.

has given me . . . of the earth. Cf. C. J. Gadd and L. Legrain, *Ur Excavation Texts: Royal Inscriptions*, 1928, p. 58, No. 194, which affirms that "the great gods have given all the lands into my hands."

3. *Who . . . ?* It is perhaps better to retain the interrogative form. See Bowman, p. 572.

4. For the rendering of this verse see H. L. Ginsberg, JBL 79 (1960), 167–69.

riding beast. Cf. I Esdras ii 6 "horses" (*'ippōn*).

6. *all their neighbors*. Literally "all those around them."

with vessels. Cf. I Esdras ii 9 "in everything, silver . . ." (*en pasin*).
cattle. Perhaps "riding animals." Cf. above vs. 4 and I Esdras ii 6.

8. *Sheshbazzar.* So spelled here, vs. 11 and v 14, 16. Possibly a corruption of *šn'ṣr* (by haplography from *šn'b'ṣr*, "Sin, protect the father"); a Babylonian name. See M. Lidzbarski, *Ephemeris für semitische Epigraphik,* III, 1909, p. 128, and Albright, JBL 40 (1921), 108–10, and BASOR 82 (April 1941), 17.

9. *dishes.* Used only here in the Bible; probably of Persian origin. On meaning, cf. Syr. *'agunâ* "small dish or other container"; Vulg. *phiala,* "small drinking bowl" or "saucer"; see further C. Rabin, *Orientalia* 32 (1963), 126 ff.

[*to be changed*]. K. Galling ("Der Tempelschatz nach Berichten und Urkunden im Buche Esra," ZDPV 60 [1937], 180 f.) is probably correct in pointing *mḥlpym* as hophal participle, but, as Rudolph, p. 5, points out, the word is to be translated "to be changed." It slipped into the text from the margin, where it originally stood as a scribal note of one who observed that the total in vs. 11 did not correspond with the sum of all the individual items.

10. [*to be changed*]. To be taken, with Galling and Rudolph, as pual participle of *šnh.*

11. *All . . . numbered five thousand and four hundred.* It is futile to attempt to reconcile the figures because it is impossible to determine where the error, if any, lies—in the individual items or in the total. Perhaps not all of the items contributed were recorded individually.

when he brought up. Reading hiphil with *Biblia Hebraica,* ed. R. Kittel, 3d ed., 1937. MT has niphal. Literally "with the golah [exiles] journeying from Babylon to Jerusalem."

COMMENT

[Introduction, i 1]: There are two accounts of the edict of Cyrus, one here in Hebrew and the other in vi 3–5 in Aramaic. Bickerman JBL 65 [1946], 250–53) is doubtless right in inferring that they are not variants of the same record but independent documents having to do with the same case. (See also De Vaux, RB 46 [1937], 29–57, especially pp. 56–57, and L. Rost, "Erwägung zum Kyroserlass," in VuH, pp. 301–7. Cf. Burn, *Persia and the Greeks,* p. 56, n. 25.) The account in Ezra i represents the Jewish version promulgated in their communities at the time of the issuance of the decree. The Cyrus cylinder (ANET, p. 316) records similar acts of amnesty and favor shown to the peoples and deities of other countries fol-

lowing his conquest of Babylon in 538 B.C., which marked the first
year of Cyrus' hegemony over the Jews—not the first year of his
reign as king of Persia (ca. 557 B.C.).

The beneficent act of the king is linked to the prophecy of
Jeremiah that Jerusalem will be rebuilt (Jer xxxi 38) and there
will be a return from captivity after a sabbath of seventy years
(xxv 11, 12, xxix 10). See C. F. Whitley, "The Term Seventy
Years Captivity," VT 4 (1954), 60–72; he thinks the reference is
to the destruction and rebuilding of the temple and thus involves
and exact date from 586 to 516 B.C. See also my *II Chronicles* (The
Anchor Bible, vol. 13), COMMENT on Sec. 42, xxxvi 21. (Cf. the
inscription of Esarhaddon in R. Borger, "Die Inschriften Asarhad-
dons Königs von Assyrien," AfO Beiheft 9 [1956], 15, and discussion by Galling, VuH, pp. 68 f. Cf. also Borger's note in JNES
18 [1959], 74.) The Chronicler regarded the whole matter of
captivity and exile as being under the control of Yahweh who in
due time will act in behalf of his people as he had done before
(cf. II Chron xxxvi 20 f.). Hence it was that he had aroused the
spirit of Cyrus who is depicted elsewhere as Yahweh's anointed
(Isa xlv 1) and who, Yahweh says, "is my shepherd and he will
fulfill all my purpose, saying of Jerusalem, 'She shall be built', and
of the temple, 'Your foundation shall be laid' " (Isa xliv 28).

Proclamations by official heralds or messengers are mentioned in
connection with Hezekiah's Passover (II Chron xxx 5) and the
summons of the returnees to Jerusalem to settle the problem of
mixed marriages (Ezra x 7). Ezra's call for reinstitution of the Festival of Booths (Neh viii 15; cf. Exod xxxvi 6=P) was also proclaimed in the same way (for other references to heralds see
Bickerman, JBL 65 [1946], 252). But the proclamation was supported in writing, that is, by an official posting in the meeting place
of the Jewish community in Babylon (*ibid.,* pp. 272 f.). A kind of
bulletin board from the time of Antiochus III (223–187 B.C.)
turned up in Jezreel. (Cf. *The Israel Digest,* December 9, 1960,
p. 7.)

Accordingly, the decree of Cyrus was heralded throughout the
community and then posted at the accustomed place for such notices
for all to read. Such double notification of an official decision
occurs also in II Chron xxx.

[The proclamation, 2–4]: The proclamation harmonizes with
what is known from other sources of the Persians' magnanimity

toward displaced peoples. They were the liberators of the captives from other lands brought to Babylon by Nebuchadnezzar (cf. Weidner texts in *Mélanges Syriens offerts à Monsieur René Dussaud,* II, 1939, pp. 923-35). The divine command to build the house of Yahweh in Jerusalem attributed by Cyrus to "Yahweh God of the heavens" must be interpreted in the light of the Cylinder Inscription that speaks of Marduk's communications with the Persian king (ANET, pp. 315 f.). It is not impossible that Cyrus came in contact with Jews in the course of his conquest of Babylon—some of them evidently occupied positions of influence in the Neo-Babylonian regime—who conveyed to him some views of the prophets, notably those of Jeremiah, Ezekiel, and the Second Isaiah. As might be expected, the thrust of the edict is in the direction of the reconstruction of the temple. The announcement itself says nothing about the cultic objects mentioned later (vs. 7). But it does specifically include permission to return for those who desire to do so, possibly with the intent of carrying out the order to build the house of Yahweh, as suggested in vs. 3. Galling thinks there were two edicts, one having to do with the return and the other with the building of the temple (ZDPV 70 [1954], 11 ff.), which fell together here. On the basis of v 14-16 and vi 3-5, Sheshbazzar was delegated to return the cult objects Nebuchadnezzar had taken and initiate work on the building of the house of God. But the Chronicler could not conceive of an institution without the people of Yahweh, hence his amalgamation of the two edicts. But J. Liver (*Eretz Israel,* V, 1958, pp. 114-19) points out that the decree of Cyrus relates specifically to the building of the temple, and that permission for the exiles to return is incidental thereto. No royal rescript was necessary for the return because the status of Judah did not change after the Persian conquest of Babylon—it remained a tributary state, now, however, of Persia.

It must be remembered that the decree as we have it here was either the work of a Jewish secretary (cf. De Vaux, RB 46 [1937], 48) or the Chronicler's phrasing of it, in which case it would naturally embody something of his own thought. This appears in the use of the word *kol,* "all," "every," in vss. 3-4 (see Introduction in *I Chronicles*), which emphasizes that all Yahweh's people were involved "in every place where he sojourns," that is, the Assyrian as well as the Babylonian golah (cf. the Chronicler's concern for the North Israelites as shown in I Chron ix 3; II Chron

xi 16, xxx 11, 21, xxxi 6 and his hope for their release in II Chron
xxx 9). That was, of course, idealistic as the later reference to
Judah and Benjamin indicates (vs. 5). The association of the return
from Babylon with the Exodus from Egypt was made by the prophet
of the Exile (e.g., Isa xli 17 ff., xliii 16 ff., xlviii 21) and is here
accentuated by the injunction that "the men of his place" provide
contributions for those undertaking to return (cf. Exod iii 21, xi
2–3, xii 35–36). There is more than a hint here that many of the
enterprising Jews had taken Jeremiah's advice (Jer xxix) and had
become exceedingly successful in their undertakings. Hence they
were reluctant to return to the land of their fathers. These were
the ones to whom the appeal was made to support those who did
desire to take advantage of the edict. While the writer may have
meant the edict to apply to Babylonians, that can hardly have been
the case in the original document; for Cyrus would hardly have
claimed that Yahweh had given him all the kingdoms of the earth.
It may be that it represents an interpretation of Darius' order to
the effect that the rebuilding and the operation of the cultus were
to be financed from the royal revenues accruing from the local province (Ezra vi 8–10). In any case, there is no mention of the edict
of the cult vessels (vi 5) in this version, though the original manifestly referred to them but said nothing about the matters dealt with
in vss. 3, 4.

As it stands, the Hebrew version of the edict makes the following
points: (a) Cyrus' declaration that Yahweh has given him "all the
kingdoms of the earth," (b) that he has ordered the reconstruction
of the temple, (c) that all Yahweh's people who so wish may return to assist in the carrying out of the order, and (d) those who
remain are to support them in tangible ways.

[The response, 5–11]: Though the Chronicler may have had,
ideally, a wider hope in mind, he has come to grips with realities
here. As so frequently, he uses the term Judah and Benjamin
(I Chron xii 16; II Chron xi 1, 3, 10, 12, 23, xv 2, 8, 9, xxv 5,
xxxi 1, xxxiv 9; Ezra i 5, iv 1, x 9; Neh xi 4, xii 34) for those
he regards as the true representatives of the people of God—the
cream of the nation who had gone into exile in 597 and 587.
Yahweh also aroused the spirit of the priests and Levites—without
whom there could have been no authentic community of Israel—
to accompany them on their state-appointed mission. Because of
their position, the family heads took the initiative in the project.

According to the writer, they received support not only from "every one who remains wherever he may sojourn" (vs. 4) but from "all their neighbors," (vs. 6) which appears to include other persons than Jews; again probably on the basis of the Exodus precedent, which emphasizes the contributions of the Egyptians as pay for the services of the Hebrews.

Cyrus also released the cult objects taken away by Nebuchadnezzar (II Kings xxiv 13, xxv 13–16; II Chron xxxvi 10, 18; Jer lii 17–19) and delivered to the governor through official channels, as the reference to Mithredath the treasurer indicates. The whole transaction thus became a matter of official record from which the present account was manifestly taken. A copy was given to the recipient, the so-called Sheshbazzar, the fourth son of Jehoiachin (I Chron iii 18), here rightly referred to as the prince (han-nāsī'), who was charged with the delivery of the treasures for Yahweh's house. He deposited the copy in the temple archives and entered into negotiations with the Persian officials. He is referred to as governor (peḥā) in v 14 (Meyer, EJ, pp. 75–79; Kittel, GVI, III, pp. 349 ff.). The tradition that as governor he led back a contingent of returnees and had something to do with laying a foundation of the temple is too strong to be disputed (cf. Ezra v 14–16), though attempts have been made to do so. In any case he appears to have been succeeded by Zerubbabel. All that can be said positively is that Zerubbabel and Sheshbazzar were different persons and that both are referred to as Persian governors of Judah and were Jews with Babylonian names.

Not much can be made of the figures given for the number of cult vessels returned. It is possible that the numbers given in vss. 9, 10, approximate the truth and that the total given in vs. 11 represents a typical exaggeration of the Chronicler. The list itself is basically authentic, as the language indicates (see Galling, ZDPV 60 [1937], 177–83; and cf. the inventory of Elephantine in Cowley, AP, No. 61, pp. 164 f.). Galling thinks vss. 8–11 represent a defective inventory of vessels taken from the temple by Nebuchadnezzar in 587 B.C. (cf. VuH, p. 68, n. 7).

2. THE RETURN TO JERUSALEM
(ii 1–70)†

Introduction

II 1 These were the constituents of the province [of Judah] who went up from the captivity of the Exile—those whom Nebuchadnezzar the king of Babylon had exiled to Babylon—and who returned to Jerusalem and Judah, each one to his own city. 2 They were the ones who came with Zerubbabel, Jeshua, Nehemiah, Seraiah^a, Reelaiah, Mordecai, Bilshan, Mispar, Bigvai, Rehum, Baanah.

The list of returnees

The number of the men of the people of Israel: 3 the sons of Parosh, 2172; 4 the sons of Shephatiah, 372; 5 the sons of Arah, 775; 6 the sons of Pahath-moab, that is, the sons of Jeshua and Joab, 2812; 7 the sons of Elam, 1254; 8 the sons of Zattu, 945; 9 the sons of Zaccai, 760; 10 the sons of Bani, 642; 11 the sons of Bebai, 623; 12 the sons of Azgad, 1222; 13 the sons of Adonikam, 666; 14 the sons of Bigvai, 2056; 15 the sons of Adin, 454; 16 the sons of Ater, that is Hezekiah, 98; 17 the sons of Bezai, 323; 18 the sons of Jorah^b, 112; 19 the sons of Hashum, 223; 20 the sons of Gibbar^c, 95; 21 the sons of Bethlehem, 123; 22 the men of Netophah, 56; 23 the men of Anathoth, 128; 24 the sons of Azmaveth, 42; 25 the sons of Kiriatharim, Chephirah and Beeroth, 743; 26 the sons of Ramah and Geba, 621; 27 the men

† **Ezra ii 1–70** ‖ Neh vii 7–69, I Esdras v 9–43.

^a LXX^B "Araias"; LXX^A "Saraias." Neh vii 7 "Azariah."
^b LXX^B "Oura." "Hariph" in Neh vii 24.
^c See NOTE.

of Michmas, 122; 28 the men of Bethel and Ai, 223; 29 the sons of Nebo, 52; 30 *the sons of Magbish, 156;* 31 the sons of Elam, the other one, 1254; 32 the sons of Harim, 320; 33 the sons of Lod, Hadid, and Ono, 725; 34 the sons of Jericho, 345; 35 the sons of Senaah, 3630. 36 The priests: the sons of Jedaiah, of the house of Jeshua, 973; 37 the sons of Immer, 1052; 38 the sons of Pashhur, 1247; 39 the sons of Harim, 1017. 40 The Levites: the sons of Jeshua and Kadmiel, of the sons of Hodaviah, 74. 41 The singers: the sons of Asaph, 128. 42 The sons of the gatekeepers: the sons of Shallum, the sons of Ater, the sons of Talmon, the sons of Akkub, the sons of Hatita, and the sons of Shobai, total 139. 43 The temple slaves: the sons of Ziha, the sons of Hasupha, the sons of Tabbaoth, 44 the sons of Keros, the sons of Siaha, the sons of Padon, 45 the sons of Lebanah, the sons of Hagabah, the sons of Akkub, 46 the sons of Hagab, the sons of Shamlai, the sons of Hanan, 47 the sons of Giddel, the sons of Gahar, the sons of Reaiah, 48 the sons of Rezin, the sons of Nekoda, the sons of Gazzam, 49 the sons of Uzza, the sons of Paseah, the sons of Besai, 50 the sons of Asnah, the sons of the Meunim, the sons of the Nephisim, 51 the sons of Bakbuk, the sons of Hakupha, the sons of Harhur, 52 the sons of Bazluth, the sons of Mehida, the sons of Harsha, 53 the sons of Barkos, the sons of Sisera, the sons of Temah, 54 the sons of Neziah, the sons of Hatipha. 55 The sons of Solomon's servants: the sons of Sotai, the sons of Hassophereth, the sons of Peruda, 56 the sons of Jaalah, the sons of Darkon, the sons of Giddel, 57 the sons of Shephatiah, the sons of Hattil, the sons of Pochereth-hazzebaim, the sons of Ami; 58 the total of the temple slaves and the sons of Solomon's servants, 392.

59 These are the ones who came up from Tel-melah, Tel-harsha, Cherub, Addan, Immer, though they were unable to say whether their families or their origin were Israelite: 60 the sons of Delaiah, the sons of Tobiah, the sons of Nekoda, 652. 61 And of the sons of the priests: the sons of Hobaiah, the sons of Hakkoz, the sons of Barzillai—who had married one of the daughters of Barzillai the Gileadite and was named after

a–a Omitted in Neh vii between vss. 33 and 34 but added there in LXXᴬ.

them. 62 These had sought their register in the official genealogies, but because they were not found [enrolled there] they were disqualified from the priesthood. 63 Therefore the governor ordered them not to eat any of the consecrated food until a priest*e* arose [to consult] Urim and Thummim. 64 The total number of the whole congregation was 42,360, 65 besides their male and female slaves; these numbered 7337, and they also had 200 male and female singers. 66 They had 736 horses, 245 mules, 67 435 camels and 6720 asses.

Temple contributions

68 Some of the family heads, when they arrived at the house of Yahweh which was at Jerusalem, contributed voluntarily toward the house of God, for its restoration on its site. 69 They contributed, as they were able, sixty-one thousand drachmas of gold, five thousand minas of silver, and a hundred priestly vestments for the fund for the work. 70 The priests, the Levites, and some of the people lived in *f*Jerusalem and its environs*f*, the singers, the gatekeepers, and the temple slaves in their cities, and all [the other] Israelites in their cities.

e Syr. has "high priest," which is probably correct. See NOTE.
f–f So with I Esdras v 45.

NOTES

ii 2. *Reelaiah.* Neh vii 7 "Raamiah," followed by "Nahamani," which probably ought to be added here to fill the number of twelve, the full complement of the tribes of Israel.

Rehum. Neh vii 7 "Nehum." Also occurs in Ezra iv 8, 9, and Neh iii 17, x 25, xii 3; in BMAP, 10:19, 11:14, 12:34; see also seal impressions from Lachish, O. Tufnell, *Lachish III: The Iron Age,* 1953, p. 341, Pls. 47A, B.

Mordecai, Bilshan, Mispar, Bigvai. Three of the names are Babylonian—Zerubbabel, Bilshan, Mordecai—and one Persian—Bigvai. Mispar, "Mispereth" in Neh vii 7, is uncertain.

6. *Pahath-moab.* Pahath-moab is generally regarded as a tribal name. B. Mazar (IEJ 7 [1957], 232) thinks the sons of Pahath-moab were

descendants of those exiled by Tilgath-pilneser III (I Chron v 26) who returned after the Exile.

8. *Zattu. Aramaic Documents of the Fifth Century B.C.*, ed. G. R. Driver, 1955, 6:1, has *ztwhy.*

9. *Zaccai.* Cf. stamp with *zk'* in S. Moscati, *L'epigrafia ebraica antica, 1935–1950* (Roma: Pontificio Istituto Biblico, 1951), p. 75. Also C. F. Jean in *Studia Mariana*, ed. A. Parrot, 1950, p. 79.

12. *Azgad.* Occurs in AP, 81:31.

14. *Bigvai.* A Persian name. See AP, 30:1, 32:1.

16. *Ater.* AP, 13:3.

17. *Bezai.* BMAP, 3:2 has *bzw.*

20. *Gibbar.* Neh vii 25 has "Gibeon"; LXX^B "Taber"; which is correct cannot be determined at present, though it could be a personal name rather than the place name Gibeon. Cf. Akk. *gibbaru*, K. L. Tallquist, APN, 1914, p. 78. In the time of Nehemiah, Gibeon was under the jurisdiction of the Persian governor of the province Across the River (Neh iii 7) and not of the governor of Judah.

21. *the sons of Bethlehem.* Neh vii 26 has "men of Bethlehem and Netophah."

24. *the sons of Azmaveth.* Neh vii 28 has "men of Beth-azmaveth."

25. *the sons of Kiriatharim . . . Beeroth.* Neh vii 29 has "men of Kiriath-jearim."

Kiriatharim. The *y* has dropped out in Ezra.

26. *the sons of Ramah and Geba.* Neh vii 30 has "men" instead of "sons."

29. *the sons of Nebo.* Neh vii 33 has "men" instead of "sons."

33. Interchanged with vs. 34 in Neh vii 36–37.

35. *Senaah.* The number is extraordinarily large for a family; "Senaah" may be a place name, though Neh vii 38 apparently also regarded it as a family name.

38. *Pashhur.* Found on seals. See *Kedem: Studies in Jewish Archaeology*, II., ed. E. L. Sukenik, (Jerusalem, 1945), pp. 9 f., and Fig. 1, p. 8; A. Reifenberg, *Ancient Hebrew Seals*, 1950, p. 38, No. 24.

40. Possibly verse is corrupt and ought to be read "of the sons of Jeshua, Kadmiel, Binnui, and Hodaviah" (cf. I Esdras v 26).

Hodaviah. Occurs frequently in Elephantine papyri. See index in AP.

42. *Shallum.* Also at Elephantine and in Lachish Letter 3, line 20. *Akkub.* Cf. "Aqabnebo," AP, 54:10 and BMAP, 8:10.

Shobai. Occurs on a seal from Khirbet Huse, D. Diringer, *Le iscrizioni antico-ebraiche Palestinesi*, 1934, p. 201; also in a seventh-century B.C. ostracon letter from Yavneh Yam (J. Naveh, IEJ 10 [1960], 129–39).

43. *Ziha.* Egyptian; occurring frequently at Elephantine. Neh xi 21 makes him one of the leaders of the *nethinim* (temple slaves).

45. *the sons of Hagabah, the sons of Akkub.* Missing in Neh vii 48.

46. *Hagab.* Occurs in Lachish Letter 1, line 3.

49. *Besai.* Babylonian name.

50. *Asnah.* Egyptian name; missing in Neh vii 52.

Nephisim. Neh vii 52 reads *npwšsym.* Both Meunim and Nephisim were Arabic tribal groups taken captive at one time or another.

53. *Barkos.* Aramaic name.

Sisera. Cf. *ssr'l* on a seventh-century Aramaic seal (Reifenberg, *op. cit.,* p. 44).

57. *Ami.* Neh vii 59 has "Amon."

60. *Tobiah.* Occurs in Lachish Letter 3, line 19, and numerous times in the Bible.

61. *was named after them.* For the adopted one taking the name of the one adopting him see IEJ 9 (1959), 180 f.

63. *the governor.* The title of the Persian governor, Tirshata, means "the one to be respected or feared."

a priest. Note that the priest now takes the place of the prophet (Rost, VuH, p. 305).

Urim and Thummim. Occurs only five times in OT and marks a return to earlier oracular forms.

65. *female singers.* On women as singers (participants in the cult), see W. Eichrodt, *Theology of the Old Testament,* I, 1961, p. 131, n. 3. They may have been used for other than cultic occasions.

69. *sixty-one thousand drachmas.* If the Persian daric is meant, the total would be about 1132⁶⁄₇ lbs. (130 grains per daric); if the Median shekel (100 Median shekels equals 1 mina) is used as a base, the total amount would be about 6171³⁄₇ lbs.

five thousand minas. About 6296¼ lbs.

70. *the people.* The phrase *wmn-h'm* appears also in Neh vii 72. E. A. Speiser (IEJ 13 [1963], 70, and n. 8) translates it "natives," but does not further explain it.

COMMENT

No one has yet come up with a fully satisfactory explanation of the purpose of the list, of the place where it stood originally, or of the discrepancies between the two recensions, Ezra ii and Neh vii. The list in I Esdras v has, in all probability, been copied from the Ezra recension since it agrees more frequently with it where it diverges from Nehemiah. The list itself is doubtless a compilation of smaller lists, as is apparent from the shift from family to town and back again, though this does not necessarily imply a significant lapse of time in the process. It could be due to the character of the records themselves or the method of gathering the information available and herein relayed.

[Introduction, ii 1–2a]: The chief purpose of Ezra i–vi is to relate the progress of the community of the true Israel from the time the decree of Cyrus was issued to the completion of the temple. The situation prevailing between 538 and 520 B.C. is far from clear. The Chronicler appears to identify Sheshbazzar and Zerubbabel, since he attributes to both leadership during the return (i 11 and ii 2) and both are said to have laid the foundation of the temple (v 16; Zech iv 9); while it is easy to conjecture, the sources do not admit of an easy solution (see COMMENT on Sec. 1, i 5–11).

The introduction connects directly with the last verse of the preceding chapter, which asserts that Sheshbazzar brought along all the cult vessels with the golah he led from Babylon to Jerusalem. But the scene is shifted at once from the golah in motion to "the constituents of the province [of Judah] who . . . [had] returned to Jerusalem and Judah." They had come with Zerubbabel and Jeshua and their associates but were now in the homeland. The introduction sounds as if the writer was using a later list compiled for other purposes to magnify the first response of the golah to Cyrus' edict and to the preaching of the great prophet of the Exile. This seems clear from the shift to Zerubbabel from Sheshbazzar and the emphasis on the twelve tribe complement, a characteristic conception of the Chronicler. The subsequent leaders of the community, Zerubbabel and Jeshua, appear first. Note especially the order.

There is no way of knowing the original purpose of the list itself. In view of the situation just referred to, however, it is highly unlikely that it was compiled simply as a historical record of those who had returned from Babylon. Moreover, there is reason to believe that the response of the Babylonian Jews was not very great at first but may have increased between 538 and the beginning of the reign of Darius (cf. Albright, BP, p. 49), perhaps because of the comparative safety of travel to the west in the time of Cambyses. Various reasons have been given for the compilation of the list, notably by Hölscher (*Die Bücher Esra und Nehemia,* see Selected Bibliography, Commentaries), who thought it was a tax list drawn up by the Persians, and Alt, who suggested (KS, II, pp. 334 f.) that it was a list compiled by Zerubbabel for the purpose of determining land rights. Rudolph, p. 17, thinks it is a "genuine" list of returnees composed of different registers covering the period from 539/8 to 515. Torrey (ES, p. 250), on the other hand, following Bertholet (*Die Bücher Esra und Nehemia,* see Selected Bibliography, Commentaries), affirms it to be fictitious. The latest and most convincing explanation has been given by Galling, who thinks that it was originally a legitimation list detailing those who composed the true Israel in contradistinction to the Samaritans, and that it affirmed the Jews' willingness and ability to handle the situation at Jerusalem; for details see Galling, JBL 70 (1951), 149–58, noting especially the emphasis on the *qahal,* "congregation," a religious, not political term.

[Compilation of lists, 2b–67]: That this extensive accumulation of names and numbers is an amalgamation of lists is recognized by all students of the material and is clearly evident from the fact that some are oriented by families, others by localities, and still others by classes. This does not mean that the arrangement is haphazard, nor that the sections existed independently. It may indicate simply that the record was compiled from information as it was made available by those designated to gather it. Galling (JBL 70 [1951], 152), thinks 2b–20 are family names; 21–33, place names; 34–35, another family list; 36–37, place names; and 38, the family of Senaah. For an earlier view of the list, see J. Nikel, *Die Wiederherstellung des jüdischen Gemeinwesens nach dem babylonischen Exil,* 1900, pp. 71–80, and Schaeder, EdS, pp. 15 ff.

A few observations on the general character of the list as it stands here as over against Neh vii may be in order. In a general way it runs counter to the Chronicler's ideas. There is a substantial reduction in the numbers, though that may have been due to other causes (cf. H. L. Allrik, "Lists of Zerubbabel—Neh. 7–Ezr. 2," BASOR 136 [1954], 21–27). In only a few instances are they increased. One name has been added to lay families. The numbers of priests and of Levites is exactly the same, while the singers have been reduced by twenty and the porters have one added. The number of slave families has been increased by three. Solomon's servants have the same number in both lists but the total of those who could not prove their family relationship is increased by ten. The Chronicler has copied the list quite closely and accurately, even following the same order in most cases. Nor does he change the order, beginning with lay families, then continuing with priests,

Levites, singers, porters, temple slaves, Solomon's servants, and those who could not prove their identity specifically.

[1. Laymen identified by family relationship, 2b–19]: The introductory statement classifies the families referred to as "the men of the people of Israel," which fits in with the Chronicler's views. Though they were descendants of the exiles from Judah and Benjamin, they are classified under the old name prevalent in the days of David and Solomon. The term "people" here signifies the laity, in contradistinction to the religious officials, and although the idea of the twelve tribes appears in vs. 2a, the list itself makes no reference to it. Rather it is the conception of the families that forms the organizing basis for the writer. These families were well known in the postexilic period and could establish their identity without question, though they are designated simply as people of Israel. This may have a bearing on the significance of the list as proof of Israelite identity as separate from the Samaritans. All but four of the names, as they stand, are postexilic and mentioned only in Ezra and Nehemiah.

[2. Identification by place, 20–35]: Beginning with vs. 20, we often find it difficult to determine whether a name refers to a place or a family. It would appear that wherever it is limited by the word "sons" it ought to be a personal name; by the same token, limiting by "men" ought to indicate a place name. But there is no agreement between Ezra ii and Neh vii on this point; even LXX has disconcerting variants. MT has "men" before Netophah, Anathoth, Michmas, Bethel, and Ai in both Ezra and Nehemiah; but LXX has "sons" before Netophah and Anathoth in both Ezra and Nehemiah. The Nehemiah list (vii 25) has "sons of Gibeon" in Ezra ii 20—if "sons" is correct, then Ezra's "Gibbar" may be right, in which case it would belong to the preceding section—for place names would appear to be indicated from Bethlehem to Nebo, and personal names from Elam to Senaah (in Ezra x 31, 43, Harim and Nebo are referred to as families; Neh x 20 also has Magpiash (Magbish) and x 27 Harim as family names). However, no conclusion can be drawn along those lines. Certainly Lod, Hadid, Ono and Jericho are place names though both recensions speak of the sons of those places rather than the men. If all except Gibeon are to be identified as places, then there is a certain order to be observed, as well as a grouping that seems to stem from reports of investigating committees sent to the regions involved, for example,

in the order of the completion of work: Bethlehem and Netophah
to the south of Jerusalem, Anathoth and Azmaveth just to the north
of the city; Kiriath-jearim, Chephirah, and Beeroth to the northwest; Michmas, Bethel, and Ai farther north than Anathoth and
Azmaveth; Nebo, Magbish, Elam, and Harim in the southwest
corner of the province; Lod, Hadid, and Ono in the corridor to
Joppa; Jericho and Senaah to the northeast (see Abel, AGP, II,
Ch. 5 and Map VII; L. H. Grollenberg, *Atlas of the Bible*, 1956,
p. 96, Map 22; J. Simons, *The Geographical and Topographical
Texts of the Old Testament*, 1959, Ch. 23).

[3. The priestly families, 36–39]: The priestly list is given three
times by family names in Ezra (ii, x) and Nehemiah (vii) and
twice by personal names of contemporary priests (Neh x 2–8,
xii 1–7). This was a carefully controlled list, as is indicated by
the agreement of names, their order, and the numbers assigned to
each (Neh vii and Ezra ii). In Ezra x, the last two are interchanged. Undoubtedly they were somehow connected with the
priestly orders set forth in I Chron xxiv—Jedaiah was of the second
order, Immer of the sixteenth, Harim of the third; Pashhur may
have been a member of the fifth order, that of Malchijah (cf. Neh
xi 12; I Chron ix 12, but cf. Jer xx 1). The total number is interesting since it stands roughly in a ratio of one priest to ten to the
whole community.

[4. The Levites, 40]: The Levitical list is the smallest of all,
composed of only two (or three) representatives of a single family
—perhaps because they were a neglected group in the period of
the Exile and hence, by virtue of their talents, engaged in other
work. Their disengagement is why a special appeal had to be made
to them later to join in the task of rebuilding Jerusalem and its
temple institutions (Ezra viii 15 ff.). The Levite list seems to be
separate here, the singers and porters not yet having Levitical status
as in I Chron xxiii–xxvi. It is quite possible that the need for special
services in his time forced such recognition and was supported
and promoted by the Chronicler. The list here would therefore
antedate the work of the Chronicler.

[5. The singers, 41]: Only the sons of Asaph are mentioned.
They number 128 (148 in Neh vii and LXX[B]; LXX[A] has 128),
a very small number considering the emphasis the Chronicler placed
upon the service of song—another telling indication of the nature
of the list and the character of the local situation.

[6. The gatekeepers, 42]: The total for the six families was 139 (Neh vii 45 has 138), a relatively large number for the services required. It may have been due to the situation at the time. Four families are mentioned in I Chron ix 17—Shallum, Akkub, Talmon, Ahiman, with Shallum as the chief. A Shallum is said to have been the father of the threshold keeper in Jer xxxv 4.

[7. The temple slaves (*nethinim*), 43–54]: The institution of the temple slaves is far older than the use of the term, which occurs only in I Chron ix 2 and fifteen times in Ezra-Nehemiah. (See I. Mendelsohn, *Slavery in the Ancient Near East,* 1949, pp. 99–106, especially pp. 105 f. Cf. also Ugaritic administrative text 301, *ytnm.*) In the Bible it is attributed to Moses, Joshua, and David (cf. Num xxxi 30, 47; Josh ix 26 f.; Ezra viii 20) who presented captives to the Levites or for service at the altar of Yahweh. Most of them, if not quite all, were foreigners but they had become closely identified with Israel, as their inclusion in the total of all Israel indicates. Neh x 29 includes them among the other Israelite classes and "those who had separated themselves from the peoples of the land to the law of God." The list has thirty-five names as opposed to thirty-two in Neh vii.

[8. Solomon's servants, 55–58]: The origin of these slave families is traced to Solomon, but whether they were Canaanite captives handed over to the temple authorities for menial service (I Kings ix 20–21) or state slaves who were combined with the *nethinim* after the fall of the state is uncertain. (See Mendelsohn, *op. cit.,* pp. 96–99. Sennacherib presented forty-one persons to the god Zababa for the service of his temple. Cf. E. Ebeling, "Stiftungen und Vorschriften für assyrische Tempel," in *Deutsche Akademie der Wissenschaften zu Berlin Institut für Orientforschung,* No. 23, 1954, pp. 9–12, where the names of the persons and the number and type of relatives, when such are involved, are given.) The total number of families of temple slaves and Solomon's servants is forty-five, while the number of persons is 392 or between eight and nine persons per family group.

[9. Those without proof of ancestry, 59–63]: In the course of the Exile, it was to be expected that certain families lost sight of their ancestry, paticularly if they were proselytes, as seems to have been the case with some of them (vs. 59b). More zealous Jews kept their family records intact, while others doubtless devoted much time and effort to search out their genealogies, in view of eventuali-

ties such as the one under study (see references to the Talmud in
Bowman, p. 585). Ancestral property or family rights could be attested only through the maintenance of family registers (Neh vii 5)
that were kept up to date by the local officials so long as the state
remained (I Chron v 17). In addition to state records, there were
official family registers (I Chron v 7 f., ix 22) that had to be maintained by the family. The registers were now the only way to prove
family identity. The five localities mentioned in vs. 59 are otherwise
unknown. Only three lay families were involved. Nothing is said
about the fate of those families, though they were hardly excluded
from the community of Israel. Since we hear no more about them,
they evidently were restored to full rights in one way or another.
With the priestly families, matters were different, for failure to establish their identity meant disqualification for functioning in the
capacity of priests and with it the forfeiture of priestly rights. From
the community point of view the situation was even more serious
because it involved the possibility of ritual contamination. In any
event, these families were barred from exercising their priestly pre-
rogatives, though they were not required to withdraw from the community. The decision to set them aside fell upon the governor (in
this case Zerubbabel) who decreed that they must refrain from par-
taking of the consecrated food (Lev ii 3, vii 21–36) until such
time as their case could be disposed of properly, that is, by the use
of Urim and Thummim, which was committed to Levi (Deut xxxiii
8) but later restricted to the high priest (Exod xxviii 30; Lev viii 8;
Num xxvii 21). Urim and Thummim were oracular instruments for
ascertaining the will of God (see I. Mendelsohn, IDB, IV, pp.
739–40). Rabbinical tradition affirms that Urim and Thummim were
not used after the death of the former prophets (*Soṭa,* 48a), though
Josephus (*Antiquities* III.viii.9) seems to assume common knowledge of it in his time.

The reference to "a priest" here raises two possibilities: it may
be a reversion to early practice or the adjective "high" is to be
inserted before "priest" with the Syriac (Vulg. reads *sacerdos doc-
tus*) and I Esdras v 40 (according to LXXᴬ). If that is correct, the
date would be affected; as no high priest had yet been appointed,
our list would antedate 520, when Jeshua filled the office (Hag i 1).

[10. The totals, 64–67]: The total for the congregation is the
same in all recensions of the list, though I Esdras v 41 excludes
children under twelve. Needless to say, this figure is considerably

above the sum of the preceding numbers—Ezra ii has 29,818; Neh vii, 31,089; I Esdras v, 31,850. Various attempts have been made to interpret the discrepancies but none is quite satisfactory. The large number of slaves and the male and female singers (to be distinguished from the temple musicians; male and female singers were, among other things, accepted by Sennacherib from Hezekiah as tribute [cf. ANET, p. 288]) points to a certain affluence on the part of the returnees that is contrary to the general impression derived from other sources. It may be that the whole summary pertains to the situation around 520 rather than 538 and thus would include the people of Judah who joined the golah and the cumulative numbers of all who returned between the above-noted dates. The Nehemiah list omits the horses and mules and thus has only animals of travel (camels) and work or burden-bearing animals (asses). This point lends some weight to Galling's conjecture that the list is proof of ability to carry on the work of rebuilding the temple without assistance from outsiders (JBL 70 [1951], 155).

[Temple contributions, 68–69]: The influence of the Exodus is evident here (see COMMENT on Sec. 1, i 2–4). At Sinai the people were requested to contribute to the work of the ark, tabernacle, vestments, etc. (Exod xxv 2–7, xxxv 4–9), and the priestly writer of Numbers (vii) speaks of vast amounts of such donations, especially by family heads. The Chronicler has summarized his source here, which is given in detail in Neh vii. Rudolph, pp. 26 f., suggests that he gave round figures based on the source and figured the value of the bowls in terms of minas. Meyer in 1896 (EJ, pp. 197 f.) estimated their combined worth at 996,000 German reichsmarks, or about $238,000. For details see COMMENT on Sec. 10, Neh vii. These contributions were given for the building of the temple rather than the carrying on of the cultus; the reference to the priestly vestments, however, betrays the Chronicler's source, which he interpreted in line with his story as developed in the following chapter.

[Location of the golah, 70]: Obviously it was necessary for cultic and political officials to reside in or near the capital. Even before the construction of the temple there was an altar about which centered services of some kind that required the constant presence of cult personnel (iii 2 ff.). "Some of the people" probably involved the leaders of the community (the governor and his assistants) and perhaps others whose ancestral home had been at Jerusalem. The singers and porters served only on occasion or in relays, and hence did not need to reside in the city. It was clearly a gigantic undertaking to find dwelling places for the number of people involved. Most of them probably went to *their* cities, that is, the cities where their ancestors resided before the captivity. After all, the "province" of Judah was comparatively small and the people would be within easy reach of the capital.

3. RENEWAL OF RELIGIOUS INSTITUTIONS
(iii 1–13)†

The erection of an altar

III ¹ When the seventh month came, after the Israelites [had been located] in their cities, the people assembled as a body at Jerusalem. ² Then Jeshua, the son of Jozadak, and his brothers, the priests, and Zerubbabel, the son of Shealtiel, and his brothers arose and built the altar of the God of Israel to offer burnt offerings upon it as prescribed in the law of Moses, the man of God. ³ They set up the altar upon its bases—*ᵃfor they were afraid of the peoples of the lands*ᵃ—

The first worship services

and offered burnt offerings to Yahweh upon it morning and evening, ⁴ celebrated the festival of booths as prescribed, offered the [required] number of daily burnt offerings in accordance with the regulation for each day, ⁵ and afterward [in addition], offered the continual burnt offerings [for the Sabbaths], the new moons, and for all the sacred festivals of Yahweh, and for all who brought a voluntary offering for Yahweh. ⁶ From the first day of the seventh month on they began to offer burnt offerings to Yahweh, though the temple of Yahweh was not yet reconstructed.

† **Ezra iii 1–3a** ‖ I Esdras v 46–50a; **3b–6** ‖ I Esdras v 50b–53; **7** ‖ I Esdras v 54–55; **8–13** ‖ I Esdras v 56–65.

ᵃ–ᵃ Omitted by LXX^B.

Preparations for the building of the temple

7 They also contributed money for the masons and carpenters, and food, drink, and oil for the Sidonians and Tyrians [in payment] for bringing cedar lumber from Lebanon by sea to Joppa in accordance with the permit granted them by Cyrus the king of Persia.

Laying the foundation of the temple

8 So in the second month of the second year of their coming to the house of God at Jerusalem, Zerubbabel the son of Shealtiel, Jeshua the son of Jozadak and the rest of their brothers the priests and Levites, together with all those who came to Jerusalem from the captivity, began [operations] by appointing some of the Levites who were twenty years old and upward to direct the work of the house of Yahweh. 9 Then Jeshua and his sons and his brothers stood united with Kadmiel and his sons, the Judeans, and the sons of Henadad and their sons and their brothers, the Levites, to direct those who did the work on the house of God. 10 When the builders laid the foundation of the temple of Yahweh, the priests in their robes stood up[b] with trumpets, as did the Levites, the sons of Asaph, with cymbals, to praise Yahweh according to the order of David the king of Israel. 11 They sang antiphonally:

> Praise and give thanks to Yahweh
> For he is good
> Eternal in his devotion toward Israel.

Then all the people raised a mighty shout in praising Yahweh when the foundation of the house of Yahweh was laid. 12 Many of the older priests, Levites and family heads who had seen the first house wept very loudly when the foundation of this house was laid before their eyes, while many [others] shouted aloud

b Reading qal for hiphil, with LXX and a number of MSS.

with joy, [13] so that the people could not differentiate between
the sound of the joyful shout and that of the weeping of the
people, because the people shouted so loudly that the sound
could be heard from afar.

NOTES

iii 1. *the seventh month.* The month of Tishri (September/October),
earlier Ethanim (I Kings viii 2). I Esdras v 56 assumes the seventh
month to have been in the first year of Zerubbabel.

3. *its bases.* Really "foundations."

for they were afraid . . . On the explanation of this statement see I
Esdras v 50. For possible renderings see Ryle, *Ezra and Nehemiah* (see
Selected Bibliography, Commentaries), pp. 39 f. Just what is meant is
uncertain. It could be explained on the basis of iv 1. Possibly both religious and political fear are involved, the former growing out of the dis-
placement of the altar used by the peoples of the land, the possible demand for participation in the work of rebuilding the temple (iv 1), or a
fear of the consequences stemming from the use of a polluted altar. For
the latter (the political aspect) see Noordtzij, *Esra-Nehemia* (see
Selected Bibliography, Commentaries), p. 66.

the peoples of the lands. A technical term referring to the leaders
or leading citizens of the different districts at the time; it no longer has
the connotation of the *'am hā-'areṣ* of pre-exilic times when it signified
the upper classes of Judah. See Würthwein, *Der 'amm ha'arez im Alten
Testament,* pp. 55–57.

5. *[for the Sabbaths].* The basis for this addition is I Esdras v 51.

7. *money.* Literally "silver." Hardly coined money but rather the metal
itself. Payment was mostly in kind, as shown by the latter part of the
verse.

8. *the second month.* Iyyar (I Esdras v 57), which is April/May. Earlier Ziw (I Kings vi 37).

the second year. I.e., of the first return. See NOTE on vs. 12.

Zerubbabel the son of Shealtiel, Jeshua the son of Jozadak. Cf. Hag
i 1, 12, 14, ii 2; Ezra ii 2; Neh vii 7.

9. *his sons.* Cf. ii 40 and NOTE there. Probably read "Binnui" for "his
sons" (same consonants in Hebrew).

the Judeans. Perhaps a corruption of "Hodaviah," though a Judah is
mentioned among the Levites in Neh xii 8. Thus the combination would
read, "Kadmiel and Binnui and Hodaviah" (cf. ii 40).

the sons of Henadad. Appears to be a later addition, on basis of Neh

iii 18, 24, because the name of Binnui was omitted in the first part of the
list (9a).

11. *Praise and give thanks . . . toward Israel.* The title of a hymn,
with the addition "toward Israel." Cf. II Chron v 13, vii 3; Pss. cvi 1,
cxxxvi 1.

12. *Many . . . who had seen the first house.* This verse proves that
the date in question (vs. 8) is the second year of the return, rather than
any time later (e.g., the second year of Darius). In 536 there would still
have been a sizable number of people alive who had seen the first temple,
while by 520 the number would have been greatly reduced.

COMMENT

Chapter iii tells the story of the beginnings of the religious institutions at Jerusalem after the return. It deals with the construction of the altar, the worship services (offerings) conducted
upon that altar, preparations for the building of the temple and the
laying of its foundations, with the reaction of the people to the sight.

[The erection of an altar, iii 1–3a]: The Chronicler introduces
his account of the first congregational worship service after the
return with the same formula used in connection with the reading of
the Torah by Ezra (Neh vii 72b–viii 1a [vii 73b–viii 1aE]),
with the exception that this assembly takes place in "Jerusalem"
while that in Nehemiah centers at the water gate. The year of the
writer's seventh month is not specified. It could refer back to i 1 but
in view of vs. 8 more likely indicates the seventh month of the first
year of the return. The seventh month was traditionally an important one for Israel, religiously speaking (cf. Num xxix; Lev xxiii
23–43); moreover, and perhaps because of this tradition, the fes-
tivities connected with the dedication of Solomon's temple began
then (II Chron v 3). It marked the time for one of the three great
feasts when every Israelite was required to appear before Yahweh
(Exod xxiii 14–17, xxxiv 22–23; Deut xvi 16).

The service took place after the returnees had settled in their
villages and towns. Before there could be such a service, an altar
had to be provided. Jeshua and Zerubbabel, the representatives of
Zadok and David, acted to that end. Religious ceremonies had continued at Jerusalem after the destruction by the Babylonians (Janssen, *Juda in der Exilszeit,* pp. 94–104) not in reconstructed buildings but in the ruins (cf. Jer xli 5). Such offerings on the part of

the people who remained in the land required an altar which, more than likely, was erected with stones from the ruins and probably near them. The Chronicler, however, would not have regarded such an altar as legitimate because it was neither in the right place nor constructed by the right people, the golah (*ibid.*, pp. 102 f.). It would have been regarded as polluted. He emphasized that everything had to be done "as prescribed in the law of Moses" and that the altar was set up on its foundations, that is, on the original bases.

[The first worship services, 3b–6]: As Rudolph points out, p. 30, the Chronicler demonstrates the cultic zeal of the golah even before the building of the temple. The season of worship began with the regular daily offerings (*tamid*), then the festival of Sukkoth was celebrated, set for the fifteenth day of the seventh month (Lev xxiii 34; Num xxix 12 ff.). The offerings for Sabbaths, new moons, and festivals are emphasized elsewhere by the Chronicler (I Chron xxiii 31; II Chron ii 4, viii 13, xxxi 3), and provision was made for them by Nehemiah (x 33). Morning and evening offerings could begin as soon as there was an altar; likewise the great festival of Sukkoth, one of the three national festivals, could be carried out at the proper time. There is obviously no mention of the atonement because the temple was not yet in existence.

[Preparations for the construction of the temple, 7]: The main interest of the writer centered about the cult, but the center of the cult was the temple, for whose reconstruction the Cyrus edict had been issued. Hence the first thing to be done after due attention had been given to the functioning of the cult, as far as possible, was to initiate plans for carrying out the royal edict. The preparations, according to the Chronicler, parallel those made for the Solomonic temple. Stonecutters were employed (I Chron xxii 2), as well as wood carvers and carpenters (I Chron xxii 15). Arrangements were made with the Sidonians and Tyrians as David had done (I Chron xxii 4) and Solomon (II Chron ii 8 ff.). Payment was made in terms of food, drink, and oil (cf. II Chron ii 10). No permission from Sidon and Tyre was required since it belonged to the king of Persia. But cf. I Esdras iv 48, which may be an expansion of Ezra iii 7 and Neh ii 8; there the command to provide timber is attributed to Darius. Josephus (*Antiquities* XI.iv.1.78), however, says a shipment of timber had been received at the command of Cyrus at first and now at that of Darius. Josephus got his information from I Esdras. Local workmen were needed and had to

be hired directly. Evidently cedar from Lebanon was ferried by
sea to Joppa, as for the first temple (II Chron ii 16). There is
nothing inherently improbable in this procedure or its historicity.

[Laying the foundation of the temple, 8–13]: In line with the
initiation of building operations on the first temple (I Kings vi 1; II
Chron iii 2), the Chronicler places the beginning of activity for
the second temple in the second month—in the second year after
the return (for the activity in the time of Haggai and Zechariah, see
Ezra v 2; Hag ii 15; Zech iv 9. On the appropriate time, despite
the Solomonic precedent, see Kittel, GVI, III, pp. 428 f.). And,
taking Zerubbabel for Sheshbazzar the Chronicler attempted once
again to displace Sheshbazzar, perhaps because his attempts to rebuild the temple proved abortive while Zerubbabel succeeded.

However, other explanations are possible. For example, on the
reasonable assumption (in the light of the Weidner texts) that
Sheshbazzar was born before 593, he must have been an elderly
man when the return took place in 538 (at least fifty-five, possibly
nearer sixty); he may have been little more than a figurehead.
Zerubbabel was perhaps around forty and may well have been his
deputy actively in charge of affairs. Moreover, Sheshbazzar may
have relinquished active control soon after the return. Just why
Zerubbabel remained in the background from 538 to 520 (between
the time of the return and the building of the temple) is unknown.
Our information on actual conditions at the time is scanty. He may
have gone back to Babylon after a few years and then returned to
Jerusalem around 521. Whatever the case may be, by 522–515,
Zerubbabel was most certainly an old man; he may have died naturally toward the end of the period, which would explain why his
name then suddenly disappears from the account.

In any event, the governor, the priests and the Levites co-operated
in the planning and building of the temple. The first step was the
appointment of the Levites to direct the work. The age for the Levites
was twenty years in conformity with the Chronicler's conception
expressed in I Chron xxiii 24, 27; II Chron xxxi 17. The legal
prescription was thirty years and upward to fifty (Num iv 3, 23, 30;
I Chron xxiii 3) or twenty-five years (Num viii 24). This difference
in age requirements for Levitical service was due to the situation and
needs at the time. No time was lost in proceeding with the construction since the materials for the foundation were already to
hand. On the basis of vi 3 it is generally assumed that the rebuilt

temple was the same in size as the Solomonic one (I Kings vi 2) and hence the old foundation, once repaired, became the new. The original foundation stones were of enormous size (from twelve to fifteen feet, I Kings vii 10) and could hardly have been moved, at least not all of them. The laying of the foundation was accompanied by a religious service, somewhat like our cornerstone celebrations. The priests blew the trumpets (cf. I Chron xv 24, xvi 6; II Chron v 12) and "the sons of Asaph"—here definitely regarded as Levites—handled the cymbals in the order established by David (I Chron xxv 1, 6). They used the Chronicler's favorite hymn. The people's response was enthusiastic, though the writer's description is somewhat tempered by his later (vs. 13) observation that the shouts of weeping (for joy!) could not be distinguished from those of joy. The combined sound of weeping and joy shook the surrounding countryside. (Cf. Josephus *Antiquities* XI.iv for an interpretation of the weeping.) Verses 12–13 appear to be based on Hag ii 3. For a discussion of the entire chapter, see J. Goettsberger, "Über das 3. Kapitel des Esrabuchs," JSOR 10 (1926), 270–80.

4. WORK ON THE TEMPLE SUSPENDED BECAUSE OF SAMARITAN OPPOSITION
(iv 1–24)†

A proposal from the neighbors

IV ¹ When the opponents of Judah and Benjamin heard that the exiles were building the temple of Yahweh God of Israel, ² they approached Zerubbabel and the family heads and said to them, "Let us join you in building, for we seek your God, just as you do, and we have been offering sacrifices to him since the time of Esarhaddon who brought us here." ³ But Zerubbabel, Jeshua, and the rest of the family heads of Israel said to them, "You do not have the same purpose as we do in building a house for our God, for we alone shall build [a house] for Yahweh God of Israel as King Cyrus, the king of Persia, has commanded us."

Plots of the opponents

⁴ Then the people of the land undermined the morale of the people of Judah and deterred them from building; ⁵ they also hired counselors against them to frustrate their purpose throughout all the lifetime of Cyrus the king of Persia and even until the reign of Darius the king of Persia.

Communications with Ahasuerus and Artaxerxes

⁶ In the reign of Ahasuerus, at the beginning of his reign, they drafted an accusation against the citizens of Judah and Jerusalem. ⁷ In the days of Artaxerxes, Mithredath, Tabeel, and the rest of their partners wrote to Artaxerxes, the king of Persia, concerning Jerusalem; the text of the letter was written in Aramaic and translated [into Hebrew]. [This is the] Aramaic

† **Ezra iv 1–3:** cf. I Esdras v 66–71; **4–5** ‖ I Esdras v 72–73; **6–16:** cf. I Esdras ii 16–24; **17–22:** cf. I Esdras ii 25–29; **23–24** ‖ I Esdras ii 30.

[version]. 8 Then Rehum the commanding officer and Shimshai the scribe wrote a letter against Jerusalem to Artaxerxes the king as follows: 9 Then Rehum the commanding officer, Shimshai the scribe, and the rest of their partners, the judges, the emissaries, the consuls, officials, the Arkewites, the Babylonians, those of Susa, *that is* the Elamites, 10 and the rest of the peoples whom the great and honorable Osnappar took away into exile and settled in the towns of Samaria and the rest [of the province] Across the River, and now 11 this is the copy of the letter which they sent to him: To Artaxerxes the king, your servants, the men of [the province] Across the River, and now 12 let it be known to the king that the Jews who came up *from you* to us, have come to Jerusalem and are rebuilding the rebellious and evil city; they have begun [the task] of finishing the walls and are [already] laying the foundations. 13 Now, let it be known to the king that if that city is rebuilt and the wall is finished they will not pay tribute, tax, or duty and the royal treasury will certainly suffer loss. 14 Now because we are under obligation to the king, it is not fitting for us to look upon the affront to the king, therefore we have relayed the information to the king 15 that inquiry be made in record books of your fathers where you will discover in the record books and learn that that city is a rebellious city, damaging to kings and provinces, and the place where they have stirred up revolt in the past; therefore that city was laid waste. 16 We make known to the king that if that city is rebuilt and the walls are completed then you will have no portion Across the River.

Reply of Artaxerxes to Rehum

17 The king sent a message to Rehum the commanding officer, Shimshai the scribe, and the rest of their partners who lived in Samaria and the rest [of the province] Across the River. "Greetings! And now 18 the official document which you sent to

a–a See NOTE.
b–b LXXB "from Cyrus."

us has been translated clearly before me. 19 And an order has been issued by me, and they have inquired into and discovered that that city has indeed risen up against the kings in the past and that rebellion and revolt have been perpetrated in it. 20 Powerful kings have been over Jerusalem, governing over everything Across the River and tribute, taxes, and duty were paid to them. 21 And now, issue an order to make those men cease work; that city must not be rebuilt until the command is issued by me. 22 Beware of committing negligence concerning this [matter]; why should the damage increase to the injury of the kings?"

Suspension of the work

23 Then after a copy of the official document of Artaxerxes the king was read before Rehum, Shimshai the scribe, and their partners, they went at once to Jerusalem to the Jews and made them cease by force of arms. 24 At that time the work on the house of God at Jerusalem ceased and it was discontinued until the second year of the reign of Darius, the king of Persia.

NOTES

iv 2. *Zerubbabel.* I Esdras v 68 adds "and Jeshua."

4. *undermined the morale.* Literally "weakened the hands." Any type of activity leading to discouragement. Cf. Lachish Letter 6:6–7 discussed by Albright in BASOR 82 (April 1941), 22, and Jer xxxviii 4.

6. *Ahasuerus.* I.e., Xerxes.

at the beginning of his reign. Refers to the time of the actual assumption of power, rather than the first regnal year.

7. *Mithredath.* Occurs as name also in BMAP 3:23b.

Jerusalem. Generally read as a proper name—Bishlam. Rudolph, p. 34, reads "against Jerusalem." Galling, p. 194, may be right in reading *bšm yršlm* "on the Jerusalem affair." Rosenthal (*Die aramaistische Forschung,* p. 64) thinks the first communication was not a bill of indictment but an apology; his opinion is based on LXX "in peace," for *bšlm* (generally, "Bishlam").

translated. With Torrey, ES, p. 200. It was translated for the benefit of the exiles who had returned.

Aramaic. This is simply a note informing the reader that the following section is in Aramaic (cf. Dan ii 4).

8. *Rehum.* Occurs in BMAP, 10:19, 11:14, 12:34. Cf. Tallquist, APN, p. 185.

the commanding officer. b'l ṭ'm which means literally, "master of the order, then chancellor." Occurs only in Ezra iv 8, 9, 17. See BMAP, p. 33; Schaeder, *Iränische Beiträge*, I, p. 67; H. Bauer and P. Leander, *Grammatik des Biblisch-Aramäischen*, 1927, p. 312h.

9. *Shimshai.* On the form of the name see *ibid.*, p. 215.

the judges. Galling, p. 194, reads *dnw* for *dyny'* "passed judgment on." Cf. LXX *tade ekrinen.*

9–10. Galling renders: "Then [Rehum, the commander and Shimshai the scribe and the rest of their partners] judged the consular officials of TRPL and the reporters from Babylon and Susa [i.e., the Elamites] and the rest of the peoples whom the great and famous Ashurbanipal had deported and settled in the towns of Samaria and in the rest of the province Beyond the River [Ebirnari]."

the emissaries, the consuls, officials. On these meanings see K. Galling, "Kronzeugen des Artaxerxes?" ZAW 63 (1951), 66–74; Bowman, pp. 600 f.; Albright, JBL 40 (1921), 113 ff.

the Arkewites. Bowman thinks this term means "those of Erech (Uruk)."

that is. Reading *dy hw'* for *dhw'* (cf. LXXᴮ and Rosenthal, *A Grammar of Biblical Aramaic*, p. 21).

10. *Osnappar.* I.e., Ashurbanipal (669–627/6 B.C.); Josephus *Antiquities* XI.ii has "Shalmaneser." Ashurbanipal received the formal submission of twenty-two kings of the west (*Ancient Records of Babylonia and Assyria*, ed. D. D. Luckenbill, 1927, II, p. 340) but no settlement of peoples is mentioned. He did, however, continue the Assyrian policy, as may be seen from his exile of captives from Kirbit to Egypt (*ibid.*, pp. 326, 346, 351).

Across the River. Literally "Abar-Naharâ," the official name of the province on the west side of the Euphrates.

12. *they have begun. šyrw* added, with Rudolph, since obviously the walls were not completed; the addition requires the reading of an infinitive for the finite verb—*škllu.*

finishing the walls . . . laying the foundations. For this rendering see Bowman, pp. 602 f. Cf. Akk. uššu "lower part," "foundation." The meaning of the verse seems to be that the job of filling in the broken down portions of the wall had already begun with the laying of the lower courses (the foundations).

13. *tribute, tax, or duty.* The three terms occur in Akkadian: *mndh* <*mandattu* "tribute" (on this cf. *mndt hyl'* "colony tax" in AP, p. 318,

line 6); *blw*<*biltu* "tax" (sometimes from enemy country); *hlk*<*ilku* "income" (from labor).

the royal treasury. From Avestan *pathma* "storehouse." Cf. Albright, JBL 40 (1921), 114 f.

14. *we are under obligation to the king.* Literally "we eat the salt of the palace." Cf. H. C. Trumbull, *The Covenant of Salt,* 1899, especially pp. 19 f.

17. *a message.* From Pers. *patigama.* Cf. Albright, JBL 40 (1921), 115.

18. *has been translated.* See Sec. 11 of Nehemiah, NOTE on viii 8.

23. *official document.* For the origin and meaning of these terms see Rosenthal, *A Grammar of Biblical Aramaic,* pp. 58 f.

24. The second year of Darius II, whose reign is suggested by the present sequence of the chapter, was 422/1 B.C. That is obviously too late and the writer was influenced by Hag i 1. Rudolph, p. 44, is doubtless right in reading *kdnh* "so also, likewise," "in like manner," for *b'dyn* "thereupon," making the verse introductory to the following chapter.

COMMENT

The Chronicler has rearranged the historical records at his disposal in support of his main purpose, which is stated in vs. 24, itself a harmonistic verse. It is probable that iv 6–23 followed v 1–vi 18 in the original document, since that appears to be the historical order of events. See Eissfeldt, EAT, pp. 748 f.; Rudolph, pp. 40 f.; Galling, ZAW 63 (1951), 67; M. Noth, ÜS, p. 153. To conclude otherwise would mean the change of order of the Persian kings from Cyrus, Cambyses (who is not even mentioned here), Darius, Xerxes, and Artaxerxes to Cyrus, Xerxes, Artaxerxes, Darius. It is generally agreed that Ahasuerus means Xerxes. It has been suggested that *'hšwrš* means Cambyses and *'rthšst,* pseudo-Smerdis. On the traditional Jewish chronology see C. C. Torrey, "Medes and Persians," JAOS 66 (1946), 1–15. On the authenticity and value of the Aramaic records, see Rowley, BJRL 37 (1954/55), 528–66.

The first seven verses of the chapter are in Hebrew, but from there on it is Aramaic, as the note at the end of vs. 7 indicates, a part of the Aramaic chronicle of Jerusalem.

[A proposal from the neighbors, iv 1–3]: Having observed that the foundation of the temple was laid in the second month of the second year after the return (iii 8), the writer was forced to explain

the long interval between that time and the completion of the structure. Because of his view of the people of Yahweh, he could not,
like Haggai and Zechariah, see the reason for the delay in the
people's lethargy and indifference. The only reason that commended
itself to him was that opponents of the golah had interfered with
the work. Some such opposition as here reported unquestionably
took place, but that it occurred under Cyrus is doubtful. In any case
the residents of the land approached the leaders of the golah pro-
posing that they be given a share in the rebuilding of the temple.
They were the descendants of those whom Esarhaddon had settled
in Palestine. Nothing is known directly of such a resettlement in the
time of Esarhaddon (681–669 B.C.), though it may be hinted at
in Isa vii 8b. The inscriptions of the Assyrian king prove that he
undertook campaigns to the west. During a Syro-Palestinian campaign, he conquered Sidon and settled people there from the east
(see ANET, p. 290, and D. J. Wiseman, "An Esarhaddon Cylinder
from Nimrud," *Iraq* 14 [1952], 54–60). On the contrary, there
was no resettlement of outsiders to fill the vacuum left by the Neo-
Babylonian conquest of Judah. Hence the descendants of the Assyrian repatriates spilled over into Judah; it was doubtless about
such elements that the writer was concerned. (On the whole problem see Alt, KS, II, pp. 316–37 and Würthwein, *Der 'amm ha'arez
im Alten Testament,* pp. 57 ff.)

These residents of the land had some precedent for their claims
in the history of the Chronicler himself. Hezekiah had issued a
summons for the northerners to come to Jerusalem to celebrate the
Passover (II Chron xxx), and money was collected from "Ephraim
and Manasseh and from all the remnant of Israel" (II Chron xxxiv
9) to repair the temple in the time of Josiah; Israelites were also
said to have been present at his Passover (II Chron xxxv 18). After
the destruction of Jerusalem, offerings were still presented at the
holy place by devotees from Shechem and Shiloh (Jer xli 5). But
the returnees were charged with a royal mandate to construct the
house of Yahweh which they interpreted in the strictest terms because they looked upon themselves as the true community of Yahweh
who had maintained their purity whereas the peoples of the lands
had not; the latter were a mixed breed (cf. II Kings xvii 24–41). The
major reason for rejecting the proposal of the peoples of the lands
no doubt was that they were regarded by the returnees as mongrel
groups and hence not true worshipers of Yahweh. "So these na-

tions feared Yahweh and also served their graven images; their children too, and their grandchildren—just as their fathers did, they continue to do to this day" (II Kings xvii 41)—such was the observation of a later scribe contemplating the report of the Deuteronomist. The Deuteronomist was thoroughly skeptical of the North Israelites, as his constant refrain shows—"the sin of Jeroboam the son of Nebat who made Israel to sin." The attitude of the Chronicler is expressed in the speech of Abijah in II Chron xiii 4–12.

[Plots of the opponents, 4–5]: Interference with the religious project of the golah was the work of the people of the land (see Würthwein, *Der 'amm ha'arez im Alten Testament,* pp. 57 ff.). They operated in underhanded ways, discouraging the people of Judah. Just how that was done is not said but it probably took the form of casting doubt on their authority to proceed, inasmuch as Judah at the time was still a part of the province of Samaria (Alt, KS, II, pp. 328 f., thinks Jerusalem and Judah became part of the province of Samaria after the Babylonian conquest) and Jerusalem at least was so close to the border that the rulers of Samaria claimed authority over it. Whether there was overt harassment is uncertain. Josephus (*Antiquities* XI.ii) says officials of surrounding territories were hired to write complaints to Cambyses. From what appears later in the chapter, it is obvious that no confirmatory sources were available to explain the failure to follow through on the construction of the temple until the time of Darius.

[Communications with Persian kings, 6–16]: Wrenched from its historical position, this section of the Aramaic record is used by the author to bolster his view as to the reasons for the lack of progress on the work of reconstruction after its spectacular beginning. Here were illustrations from a later period drawn upon to show how the peoples of the land frustrated the efforts of the people of Yahweh. There can be no serious objection to the fundamental conclusion that the work on the temple did not progress. The attitude of the Chronicler appears to be that outside interference undermined the plans of the leaders by, among other things, protracted investigations of the position and authority of the golah in the land. And as such, it was spite work.

Nothing is known otherwise of such a communication from the leaders of Samaria to Xerxes (485–465 B.C.). I Esdras ii 16 mentions only a letter to Artaxerxes. If the section here has been displaced, then it is not difficult to believe that such a notice existed in the Chronicler's source and that he copied it. The time specified may be significant—the beginning of his reign—as that would normally have been the time for raising complaints. The draft of the complaint is not given (cf. Olmstead, HPE, pp. 234 f.). Morgenstern (HUCA 27 [1956], 101–79; 28 [1957], 15–47; 31 [1960], 1–29), following Hugo Winckler, argues for a rebellion of the Jews at the beginning of the reign of Xerxes in 485 B.C. that was quelled by turning loose their neighbors—Edomites, Moabites, Ammonites, Philistines, Tyrians, Sidonians, and Persians—against them.

Two complaints were lodged against Jerusalem in the reign of Artaxerxes. I Esdras ii 16 ff. has telescoped both communications into one as shown by a combination of the names appearing in vss. 7–8. For possible dates and reasons for Jewish activity at the time, cf. Bright, *A History of Israel,* p. 361, and Albright, BP, p. 50. As noted above, the first complaint is simply reported by the Chronicler in his own words. There is no further explanation except that it was "concerning Jerusalem." It was lodged through the Persian official, if not at his instigation, as the reference to Mithredath seems to show. Mithredath may have been the Persian consul at Samaria, and Tabeel the chief Samaritan representative of the people. The effect of that correspondence is not stated; it may not have been answered, at least not at once, because of the king's preoccupation with other affairs of state. Indeed it is possible that a second letter had to be sent with more authority behind it and that the response of the king (vss. 17–22) covers both communications.

The second accusation has more weight as is evident from the names attached to it. Our author has here reversed the normal order followed in the construction of such communications. The names usually appear at the end. In any event, this document carried the authority of the commanding officer, his scribe, and other officials, and the representatives of the people displaced in the time of Ashurbanipal. This item was taken from the writer's Aramaic source. A. Malamat ("The Historical Background of the Assassination of Amon, King of Judah," IEJ 3 [1953], 26–29) connects this reference with a resettlement of peoples taken captive by Ashurbanipal during a suppression of an Elamite revolt around 642 B.C. There may be some relation also between the rebellion of some of the subject peoples of Across the River ca. 640 and one of the two destructions suffered by Shechem in the seventh century B.C. The other (see G. E. Wright, *Shechem: The Biography of a*

Biblical City [New York, 1965], p. 166) may be connected with
Esarhaddon's activity noted in vs. 2 (cf. BA 26 [1963], 22 ff.).

The burden of the second complaint centers around political activity and—one of the enigmas of the whole episode—says nothing
at all about the reconstruction of the temple. It is possible that somewhere near the time indicated the populace was aroused by the
preaching of a prophet (Malachi?) or prophets and decided to take
some sort of protective action against their more aggressive neighbors whom the latter resented and endeavored to check. The al-
leged menace to the empire is patently fantastic. The complainants
refer to themselves as loyal and devoted servants of the central
Persian authorities and to the small Jewish community as potential
rebels who could do great injury to the imperial interests as well
as being an affront to the king (cf. vss. 13, 16). They were doubtless well informed about the past glories of the empire of David
and Solomon, but perhaps had in mind rather the more recent
events concerning the rebellion of Judah that led to the destruction
of Jerusalem by the Babylonians, as the last phrase of vs. 15 appears
to show. The phrase "from you to us" (vs. 12) points to a substantial migration of Jews to Judah under Artaxerxes. On the suggestion that the time of Ezra is meant, with a strong argument against
it, see Rudolph, pp. 44 f.

[The reply of Artaxerxes to Rehum, 17–22]: According to the
report, the warning of Rehum and his associates was taken seriously
by the king and given a formal reply. The letter confirmed the as-
sertions of the complainants, though it is couched in less extravagant
terms. Just what times or kings of Jerusalem are meant cannot be
determined. Batten, p. 179, thinks of Sennacherib's experience
with Hezekiah. Beneath the whole situation may lie more than appears on the surface, perhaps a clash between urban and rural centers of power—see *City Invincible,* eds. C. H. Kraeling and R. M.
Adams, 1960, pp. 79 f., and Lewis Mumford, *The City in History,*
1961, pp. 64–70. The letter included a peremptory order demand-
ing cessation of the building operations until a specific permit is
issued by the king. That Rehum and his associates were imperial
officials is clear from the king's command that they issue a decree
embodying his decision.

[Suspension of the work, 23–24]: Given royal authority, Rehum and his cohorts lost no time in confronting the Jews on the spot
and by force of arms compelled cessation of the work on the tem-

ple. I Esdras ii 30 says they came with horses and a mob of troops in battle array and hindered the work. Josephus supports that description, though he says they came during the time of Cambyses (*Antiquities* XI.ii). Whether they actually undid the work of the golah is not clear, though Rudolph, p. 44, has made a strong case for it, suggesting that the interference took place shortly before the time referred to by the report received by Nehemiah (i 3).

Verse 24 is the Chronicler's connecting observation; it marks, for him, the transition to the story carried forward in the next chapter. The introductory word (*b'dyn*) makes it appear as though Xerxes and Artaxerxes preceded Darius, which has been responsible for much misunderstanding on the part of commentators (e.g., Rudolph, pp. 35 ff.; Josephus *Antiquities* XI.ii.2.30 supports the statement in vs. 24). But what the writer suggests is simply that the difficulties attendant upon the construction of the temple were just like those that bedeviled Nehemiah and his immediate predecessors when they attempted to rebuild the walls of Jerusalem.

5. PERSIAN OFFICIALS INVESTIGATE
THE REBUILDING OF THE TEMPLE
(v 1–17)†

Rebuilding the temple

V ¹ When the prophets, Haggai the prophet and Zechariah the son of Iddo, prophesied to the Jews who were in Judah and Jerusalem, in the name of the God of Israel who was over them, ² then Zerubbabel the son of Shealtiel*a* and Jeshua the son of Jozadak began to reconstruct the house of God which is in Jerusalem; with them were the prophets of God, assisting them.

Investigation by provincial officials

³ At that time Tattenai the governor of [the province] Across the River, Shethar-bozenai, and their partners came to them and addressed them thus: "Who gave you an order to reconstruct this house and complete this *b*wooden structure*b*?" ⁴ Then *c*they said*c* to them as follows: "What are the names of the men who are reconstructing this house*d*?" ⁵ The eye of their God was upon the elders*e* of the Jews and they did not interrupt them until a report could reach Darius and they in turn received an official reply concerning this [matter].

† Ezra v 1–2 ‖ I Esdras vi 1–2; **3–5** ‖ I Esdras vi 3–6; **6–17** ‖ I Esdras vi 7–22.

a LXX "Salathiel."
b–b LXX reads *Choregia* "means," "wealth"; Vulg. reads *muros* "walls." See NOTE.
c–c With LXX. Aramaic has "we said."
d LXX "city."
e LXXᴬ "captivity." Both readings reflect the same original, consonantal text. MT *śby* vocalized *śābēy* means "elders"; LXXᴬ *śby* vocalized *śᵉbiy* means "captivity."

The governor's letter to the king

6 A copy of the letter which Tattenai the governor of [the province] Across the River, Shethar-bozenai, and his partners, the officials of [the province] Across the River sent to Darius the king. 7 In the message they sent to him the following was written: "To Darius the king, hearty greeting! 8 Let it be known to the king: we went to the province of Judah, to the house of the great God which is being reconstructed with ʰlarge stonesʰ; beams are being laid in the walls, and that work is being carried on energetically and is proceeding rapidly. 9 Then we asked these elders and said to them: 'Who has given you official permission to reconstruct this house and to complete this wooden structure?' 10 And also we asked them their names, to inform you, so that we could record the names of the men who were at their head. 11 In reply, they gave us the following message: 'We are the servants of the God of the heavens and the earth, and are reconstructing the house which was built earlier, many years ago; a great king of Israel built it and completed it. 12 But because our fathers irritated the God of the heavens he gave them into the hand of Nebuchadnezzar the king of Babylon, the Chaldean, who demolished this house and exiled the people to Babylon. 13 But in the first year of Cyrus the king of Babylon, Cyrus the king issued an official document [giving permission] to reconstruct this house of God. 14 And also the gold and silver vessels of the house of God which Nebuchadnezzar had taken from the temple of Jerusalem and brought to the temple of Babylon, Cyrus the king took from the temple of Babylon and they were given to one by the name of Sheshbazzar whom he had appointed governor. 15 He said to him, "Take these vessels, go, deposit them in the temple of Jerusalem and let the house of God be reconstructed in its place." 16 Then that Sheshbazzar came and laid the foundation of the house of God at Jerusalem and from then until now it has been under construc-

ʰ–ʰ LXX has *eklektos* "choice."

tion and is not yet complete. [17] And now, if it seem good to the king, let investigation be made in the royal treasuries there in Babylon whether it is true that an official document [granting permission] that that house of God in Jerusalem be reconstructed was issued by Cyrus the king and let the decision of the king concerning this [matter] be sent to us.'"

NOTES

v 1. *the son of Iddo.* Signifies grandson here (cf. Zech i 1).

2. *Shealtiel.* Shealtiel was the eldest son of Jehoiachin, the next to last king of Judah (I Chron iii 17). Jehoiachin was, in all probability, regarded as the last legitimate king of Judah. Although Zedekiah bore that title, it may have been from customary usage rather than a legally and technically correct one. Jehoiachin was regarded as king by the Babylonians even after his captivity, and the royal line is traced through him.

3. *Tattenai . . . Across the River.* See COMMENT below, on vs. 3.

wooden structure. The meaning of the Aramaic is obscure but the context demands something of the nature indicated in the translation. Bowman, p. 608, thinks it means "materials," "supplies," etc., referring to dressed stones, beams, or other building materials or to some kind of equipment for the finished building. Cf. also *'šrn* in Papyrus 3, line 23a, of the BMAP—Kraeling (p. 163) thinks it may mean "lumber." See further P. Joüon, *Biblica* 22 (1941), 38–40, and C. G. Tuland, *JNES* 17 (1958), 271–73; NOTE on vs. 16. Rosenthal (*A Grammar of Biblical Aramaic,* p. 59) thinks it may be of Persian origin (*āčār*).

6. *his partners, the officials.* Cf. Cowley, AP, 17:5, where the combination is paralleled, and Albright, JBL 40 (1921), 114. W. Eilers, *Iränische Beamtennamen in der keilinschriftlichen Überlieferung,* I, 1940, thinks it means something like "investigator."

7. *In the message . . . was written.* On certain occasions direct appeals were made to the king. See G. G. Cameron, *The Persepolis Treasury Tablets,* 1948, p. 13.

hearty greeting! On the *kl-kl'* emphatics see Joseph Fitzmeyer, *Biblica* 38 (1957), 170, and J. A. Montgomery, JAOS 43 (1923), 391–95.

8. The whole verse has undoubtedly been compressed, as may be seen from I Esdras vi 8, 9.

large stones. For another explanation of this phrase see Bowman, p. 610. The Chicago *Assyrian Dictionary,* V, p. 11, defines *gll* as "pebble," "chert," "stone."

beams are being laid in the walls. Just what is meant by this clause is debatable (cf. vi 4). It could refer to the paneling of the walls (Rudolph, p. 50; Gelin, p. 43); more likely it has something to do with the setting of the rafters.

energetically. Cf. Rudolph, p. 50.

proceeding rapidly. Literally "prospering in their hands."

9. *wooden structure.* 'šrn' "woodwork," "wooden beams," "planks."

14. *vessels.* Containers of some kind. Cf. Dan v 2, 23; AP, 20:5, 72:4; *Ahiqar,* 109.

the temple of Babylon. I Esdras vi 18 "his own sanctuary," i.e., Esagila, of which Nebuchadnezzar claimed to be a patron (Herodotus I.181–83).

Sheshbazzar. I Esdras vi 18 includes Zerubbabel, before Sheshbazzar.

15. *in its place.* On the use of *'tr* see ZAW 70 (1958), 209 ff., and Galling, in VuH, pp. 70 f.

16. *laid.* Literally "gave."

the foundation. A veiled reference to the failure of Sheshbazzar's attempt to consummate the building project. See K. Galling, "Königliche und nichtkönigliche Stifter beim Tempel von Jerusalem," *Beiträge zur biblischen Landes- und Altertumskunde* (ZDPV 68, Heft 2) (1950), 134–42. For meaning of term see Tuland, " 'Uššayya' and 'Uššarnâ'," JNES 17 (1958), 269–71.

17. *the royal treasuries.* On archives in the treasury see Bickerman, JBL 65 (1946), 251; also Cameron, *The Persepolis Treasury Tablets,* pp. 9–17, for a discussion on the Persian treasury idea and its significance.

COMMENT

It was well known that the temple was built early in the reign of Darius I, but why was there such a long interval between the initial activity under Sheshbazzar and that in the time of Zerubbabel, particularly in view of the enthusiasm that marked the setting up of the altar and the inauguration of cult services? For the Chronicler the answer was quite simple: the golah could not proceed because of the obstacles put in their way by the people of the land. Having illustrated the kind of interference that prevailed by transposing his Aramaic source, the writer now proceeds with the account of the reconstruction of the temple.

[Beginnings in the work of rebuilding the temple, v 1–2]: This represents virtually a new beginning in the process of reconstruction at Jerusalem (see also Schneider, p. 117). The initiative was taken

by the prophets Haggai and Zechariah (Hag i 1, 12, ii 1 f.; Zech iii
1, 6; the rebuilding is one of the Chronicler's favorite themes—see
my Introduction to *I Chronicles* [The Anchor Bible, vol. 12]), from
whose books the information in these two verses was taken. The
Jews of Judah and Jerusalem addressed by the prophets were those
who had returned from Babylon and the descendants of those who
remained in the land and had severed ties with the people of the
land. The religious zealots to whom Haggai and Zechariah belonged
were apparently disturbed by the slow progress of events at Jerusalem, which was due, doubtless, to the cautious attitude of Zerubbabel and Jeshua. The prophets apparently saw their way clear to
make a bold and determined public appeal to the leaders in the
wake of difficulties in the Persian empire following the death of
Cambyses and the accession of Darius (Olmstead, HPE, Ch. VIII).
Haggai was especially outspoken, predicting the downfall of Persia
(Hag ii 22) and pointing to Zerubbabel as the royal scion, the
signet ring (ii 23). While his visions were a bit blurred, he and his
compatriot did succeed in arousing the people and their leaders to
action.

[Investigation by the provincial officials, 3–5]: In the latter
part of November 521 B.C., the Babylonian revolt was finally quelled
(cf. K. Galling, "Von Naboned zur Darius," ZDPV 70 [1954], 18–
22) and with the beginning of the next year there was a new satrap
of Babylon and Across the River by the name of Ushtani. For
Across the River there was an assistant by the name of Tattenai who
was under the authority of Ushtani (see A. T. Olmstead, "Tattenai,
Governor of Across the River," JNES 3 [1944], 46, who quotes a
sentence from a Babylonian document dated June 5, 502 B.C.: "Ta-
at[-tan-ni] governor (*paḥat*) of Ebirnari." Cf. A. Ungnad, "Keilinschriftliche Beiträge zum Buch Esra und Ester," ZAW 58 [1940/
41], 240–43, and literature noted there).

Quite naturally the imperial authorities were concerned about the
apparent hesitation of the Jews to declare themselves openly for the
new Persian regime under Darius and took steps to clarify the situation. To that end, the local governor Tattenai, his secretary Shethar-
bozenai, and representatives of the hyparchy of Samaria came to
Jerusalem. There they found the Jews busily engaged in building the
house of God; they immediately demanded to see their credentials
and the names of those responsible, which may have been the
original reason for the list in chapter ii (Galling, ZDPV 70 [1954],

26). But there was no interruption of the work during the time the investigation was under way, which the writer interpreted as an act of God, probably because the work was undertaken at the instigation of the prophets who delivered the word of God. Apparently Tattenai was convinced by such proof as the Jews could muster but decided to refer the matter directly to the king for a decision after the original documents had been consulted.

[The governor's report to the king, 6–17]: Tattenai's report to the king consists of four main points: (a) he and his associates had carried out their mission, that is, had gone to Jerusalem; (b) they had observed the state of building operations which were being pursued energetically and which were nearing completion (vs. 9); (c) they had requested information on the authorization of the project and a list of the builders' names; (d) and the deposition they took from the Jewish authorities justifying their claims formed the conclusion of the report. Only the last point requires comment here. The Jews claimed to be servants of the God of the heavens and the earth—"the God of the heavens" may have been a studied attempt to appeal to the Persians, since that was the way they referred to their god. They were reconstructing his house, which had been built earlier by "a great king of Israel" (Solomon) but was destroyed by Nebuchadnezzar because that God had been angry with them. In no sense was that tragic event to be interpreted as marking the defeat of Yahweh, as may be seen from the writer's earlier notation (i 2) that Cyrus had been inspired by Yahweh and charged with the task of building his house. With that intention he issued an official decree; moreover, he returned the sacred vessels removed by the Babylonians when the first temple was leveled. The man to whom those cult objects were delivered and who was responsible for their delivery, and for carrying out the royal decree, was none other than Sheshbazzar (i 8, 11). He is here credited with laying the foundation for the temple whereas in iii 8, 10, Zerubbabel and Jeshua are regarded as the prime movers for its restoration. There can be no doubt as to the substantial historicity of both Sheshbazzar and Zerubbabel, though the Chronicler may attribute to the latter some of the achievements of the former. As was observed above (ch. i), Sheshbazzar (Sin-ab-usur), the fourth son of Jehoiachin, entered into negotiations with the Persians for the return of the sacred cult objects and arrangements for their transfer to Jerusalem. That involved the repatriation of at least a nucleus of

Jews charged with the responsibility for renewing the worship services and provision for the house of God, a place for those vessels.
It appears pretty certain that Sheshbazzar and his group did make a
beginning in discharging their obligations. In the course of the next
fifteen years others doubtless returned; one of the groups was led by
Zerubbabel (cf. P. R. Ackroyd, "Two Old Testament Historical
Problems of the Early Persian Period," JNES 17 [1958], 13–27),
who became the successor of Sheshbazzar, and Jeshua the priest.
It was this group that finally succeeded in bringing the protracted
work to completion. It may be that because of this the Chronicler
tended at times to attribute to Zerubbabel the work accomplished
by Sheshbazzar. On the other hand, it could be that by the time of
Zerubbabel the situation had deteriorated, for obvious reasons, to
the point where his work constituted a new beginning.

The communication to the Persian court concludes with the suggestion that the records at Babylon—the place where the Cyrus
records dealing with the Jews might naturally have been kept—be
searched out to determine whether the Jews were telling the truth.
Hormuzd Rassam found the Cyrus cylinder at Babylon, R. W.
Rogers, *History of Babylonia and Assyria,* 6th ed., 1915, I, pp.
286 f.

6. DARIUS I PERMITS
THE COMPLETION OF THE TEMPLE
(vi 1–22)†

The reply of Darius

VI 1 Then Darius the king issued an official document and they conducted an investigation in the archives of the treasuries deposited there at Babylon, 2 And a roll was found in the fortress of Ecbatana in the province of Media with the following written on it—"Memorandum:

3 In the first year of Cyrus the king, Cyrus the king issued an official document. About the house of God at Jerusalem: Let the house where sacrifices are offered be reconstructed and its foundations retained. Its height is to be sixty cubits, its width is to be sixty cubits, 4 with three layers of large stones and one layer of timber and the cost is to be met from the royal treasury. 5 Also let the gold and silver vessels of the house of God that Nebuchadnezzar took away from the temple at Jerusalem and brought to Babylon be returned and brought back to the temple at Jerusalem each one to its place and you must deposit [them] in the house of God. 6 Now, Tattenai governor of [the province] Across the River, Shethar-bozenai, and their partners, the officials of [the province] Across the River, keep away from there! 7 Let *the governor of the Jews* and *the elders of the Jews* alone for the work on that house of God; they may reconstruct that house of God at its place. 8 And herewith I issue an official document on how you are to assist these elders of the

† **Ezra vi 1–12** ‖ I Esdras vi 23–34; **13–18** ‖ I Esdras vii 1–9; **19–22** ‖ I Esdras vii 10–15.

a–a Omitted by LXX.
b–b LXX^A "the leaders of the Jews." Cf. I Esdras vi 26 "Zerubbabel the servant of the Lord and the governor of Judah." But the title may be secondary here (cf. Alt, KS, II, p. 333, n. 2).

Jews in the reconstruction of that house of God: the cost is to be paid fully to these men from the royal treasuries out of the tax from [the province] Across the River and without interruption. 9 And whatever is required—young bulls, rams, lambs for burnt offering to the God of the heavens, wheat, salt, wine, anointing oil, as the priests of Jerusalem request—let it be given to them day by day without ceasing, 10 that they may offer sacrifices to the God of the heavens and pray for the life of the king and his sons. 11 An official document has been issued by me that anyone who violates this order, let a beam be torn out of his house, let him be impaled upon it, and his house be made a dunghill on account of this; 12 and may the God who caused his name to dwell there overturn any king or people who dares to act contrary thereto so as to destroy that house of God at Jerusalem. I, Darius, have issued an official document; let it be carried out with precision!"

Progress and consummation of the work

13 Then Tattenai the governor of [the province] Across the River, Shethar-bozenai, and their partners carried out precisely the order that Darius the king had sent. 14 So the elders of the Jews built and progressed because of the prophecy of Haggai the prophet and of Zechariah the son of Iddo; they completed the reconstruction according to the order of the God of Israel and the official document of Cyrus, Darius, and Artaxerxes, the king of Persia. 15 This house was completed on the third day of the month Adar, in the sixth year of the reign of Darius the king. 16 And the Israelites, the priests, and the Levites, and the rest of the exiles celebrated the dedication of this house of God with joy. 17 They offered for the dedication of this house of God, a hundred bulls, two hundred rams, four hundred lambs, and twelve he-goats—corresponding to the number of the tribes of Israel—as a sin offering for all Israel. 18 And they put the priests in their divisions and the Levites in their positions for the service of [the house of] God at Jerusalem as prescribed in the book of Moses.

Celebration of Passover and feast of unleavened bread

19 The exiles also celebrated the Passover on the fourteenth day of the first month. 20 The priests and the Levites, without exception, had purified themselves, so that all of them were clean; then they slaughtered the passover for the exiles, for their brothers the priests, and for themselves. 21 So the Israelites who had returned from the Exile and all those who had separated themselves from the impurity of the nations of the land to join them and seek Yahweh God of Israel, ate [the passover]. 22 They joyfully celebrated the feast of unleavened bread for seven days, for Yahweh had caused them to rejoice in that he had turned the mind of the king of Assyria toward them to support them in the work of the house of God, the God of Israel.

NOTES

vi 2. *Memorandum. Dikrona*—a memorandum of an official oral decree or decision. Cf. AP, No. 32.

3. *the house where.* See NOTE on v 15 in Sec. 5.

foundations. The exact meaning here is uncertain but *'š* is now known to be an Akkadian architectural term (*uššu*) widely used in building inscriptions where it means "foundation."

retained. For this rendering of *mswblyn* see BMAP, p. 186, and Schneider, p. 121. Cf. Galling's discussion of *'tr* in VuH, pp. 70–72.

height . . . sixty cubits. About 90 feet, unless the royal cubit (20.57 in.) was used, in which case it would be about 103 feet.

width . . . sixty cubits. Twenty cubits with Syr. (cf. I Kings vi 2; II Chron iii 3; Ezek xli 2). See reconstruction by Rudolph, p. 54—he has 30 for height, 60 for length and 20 for width. So also Schneider, p. 121. Josephus (*Antiquities* XI.iv) and I Esdras vi 25 follow MT.

4. *layers. ndbk* is an Akkadian loanword (*nadbāku* "course or layer of a building"). Josephus (*Antiquities* XI.iv) has two courses of polished stone and one of native stone. Cf. photograph from Herod's palace at Masada in *Views of the Biblical World,* eds. M. Avi-Yonah and others, 1961, IV, p. 226. For a discussion of the technique see H. C. Thomson, "A Row of Cedar Beams," PEQ (January–June 1960), 57–63.

5. *to its place.* See NOTE on v 15.

you. On change of person see Bickerman, JBL 65 (1946), 251.

6. *their partners, the officials.* See NOTE on Ezra v 6.

keep away from there. An Aramaic legal formula. Cf. F. Rundgren, ZAW 70 (1958), 209 ff.

8. *without interruption.* Refers to payment of cost and not to work of reconstruction.

9. *anointing oil.* This phrase occurs only here and vii 22. Indicates Jewish scribal prompting (cf. Exod xxv 6, xxix 7, 21, and numerous times elsewhere but always with *šmn*).

11. *has been issued.* For this translation see Bauer and Leander, *Grammatik des Biblisch-Aramäischen,* p. 145k.

12. *any king.* On *kl mlk* see AJSL 57 (1940), 71, where H. L. Ginsberg suggests that *mlk* here means "kingdom."

who dares to act contrary thereto. Literally "send out his hand to alter [it]," i.e., the edict, not the temple.

with precision. Exactly, fully, at once.

14. *Cyrus, Darius, and Artaxerxes.* For Rabbinic interpretation that Darius was referred to also as Cyrus and Artaxerxes, see H. L. Ginsberg, *Studies in Daniel,* 1948, p. 72, n. 53. Cf. the argument in *Rosh Hashana* 3b.

15. February–March 515 B.C. I Esdras vii 5 "23d day." Cf. F. X. Kugler (*Von Moses bis Paulus,* 1922, p. 215), who calculates that the third day of Adar was a Sabbath while the twenty-third day fell on a Friday; hence I Esdras is probably right.

20. *The priests.* Many—e.g., Rudolph, Galling, Gelin—think "priests" was added later.

22. *They.* The Levites, as shown by the objective of their action—their brothers the priests.

the king of Assyria. A loose use of the term, for it certainly refers to the king of Persia (cf. Josephus *Antiquities* XI.iv.8); Assyria had long since passed from the scene of history. Cf. Herodotus (I.178) who refers to Babylon as the capital of Assyria, and Xenophon *Cyropaedia* II.i.5.

COMMENT

Chapter vi contains the Aramaic version of the edict of Cyrus, which is in substantial agreement with the Hebrew version recorded in chapter i (see COMMENT on Sec. 1 for the background of the edict, and cf. Bickerman, JBL 65 [1946], 250, 253, and De Vaux, RB 46 [1937], 56 f.). Darius' response to the request of his officials following their investigation of affairs at Jerusalem was not long in forthcoming.

[The reply of Darius, vi 1–12]: By order of the king, search for the decree of Cyrus was made in the royal archives, which were kept in the treasury. (No such documents have been found at Persepolis [cf. Cameron, *The Persepolis Treasury Tablets,* p. 9]. But R. T. Hallock [JNES 19 (1960), 90] points out that the treasury documents were of two types—letters directing payments to be made and memoranda indicating that such payments had been made. Though these documents are later than the period with which we are concerned, they reflect Persian practice. In Ezra i 8 Mithredath the treasurer is mentioned; the word for treasurer is exactly the same as that appearing in the Elamite texts. Inasmuch as the vessels from the temple were kept in the treasury, it is possible such a record as the one referred to here was kept there and that our "memorandum" may indeed point to an official statement to the effect that the directive was carried out. Cf. Bickerman, JBL 65 [1946], 251; and De Vaux, RB 46 [1937], 55. On the keeping of records at Babylon and Ecbatana, see BMAP, p. 35, n. 46.)

Whether there were such archives at Babylon as well as at Ecbatana is not clear, though it is possible. Babylon might refer simply to the general region (cf. also v 17); it could be that such records were kept in the royal residences the king occupied at different periods of the year (De Vaux, RB 46 [1937], 51 f.; see also Xenophon *Cyropaedia* VIII.vi.22) and that Cyrus issued his order from Ecbatana in 537. Its inscription on a roll is more difficult to explain in view of the Persepolis tablets, though such methods of recording were not unknown at the time (De Vaux, RB 46 [1937], p. 52). According to the memorandum, Cyrus had issued a decree, as the Jewish leaders claimed; it contained a directive to rebuild the house of God with the provision that it follow the pattern and dimensions of the one destroyed by the Babylonians and an order that the sacred cult objects be returned and deposited in the reconstructed building. The cult vessels doubtless took the place of the images involved in the repatriation of other cults.

Concern for rehabilitating the religious institutions of captive peoples was a matter of Persian policy and as such Darius felt himself obliged to honor the decisions of the past. Another reason may have been the Persians' veneration for royal decrees (cf. Esther i 19, viii 8). Not only were the Jews cleared of wrongdoing but the local imperial officials were enjoined against interfering with the progress of the work. In effect Darius confirmed the edict of his predecessor and once more spelled out its terms on the basis of which activities of the golah were to be dealt with. Instead of having obstacles put in their way, they were to be assisted in the project of reconstruction, expenses for which were to be defrayed from the tax income accruing to the royal treasury from the province. Moreover, provision was to be made for the daily religious observances (the festivals were not included) because in them oblations were offered and prayer was made for the welfare of the king. The knowledge of specifications for offering materials is due to the employment of a Jewish scribe (as Ezra had been; cf. Schaeder, EdS, pp. 39–59) and is based on the laws of the Pentateuch. As we know from other sources, the Persians were concerned about such matters (see references in Bowman, p. 617, and the discussion of De Vaux, RB 46 [1937], 39–43. See especially Kienitz, GÄJZ, pp. 61 ff.). Jeremiah had urged the first deporters to Babylon to pray for the welfare of the place to which they were sent (Jer xxix 7), and Cyrus requested prayer for his own and his son's welfare (ANET, p. 316, and cf. Cowley, AP, No. 30).

Finally, a threat of punishment is added as a warning to heed the royal decree. Assyrian and Aramaic documents frequently end with similar threats. Cf. E. F. Weidner, AfO 6 (1930), 14 f., and ANET, p. 500 (Azitawadda), p. 502 (Zakir), p. 504 (Ahiram), et al. Darius invokes the enmity of Ahura-mazda against anyone who might destroy his great inscription (Behistun, par. 67). The punishment meted out to the guilty is severe. Herodotus (III.159) says Darius crucified three thousand leading citizens of Babylon when he captured it.

The curse of Yahweh is invoked against king or people who in any way act contrary to the decree or impede its operation. The influence of the Jewish scribe in the composition of the order may be seen in his use of the Deuteronomic phrase "the God who caused his name to dwell there" (e.g., Deut xii 11, xiv 23, xvi 2, 6, 11, xxvi 2, and frequently the early chapters of I Kings and II Chronicles).

[Progress and consummation of the work, 13–18]: Tattenai and Shethar-bozenai dutifully carried out the order of Darius. The provincial officials delivered a copy of the edict of Darius to the Jews at Jerusalem, which was placed in the temple archives where it was preserved. It then became the source for the present document. Josephus (*Antiquities* XI.iv) records a counterclaim of the Jews, carried to the king by an embassy, informing him of the Samaritan interference in their religious enterprise. Work on the temple advanced rapidly, thanks to the exhortations of the prophets Haggai and Zechariah. This is another illustration of the Chronicler's high regard for the prophets. Note that Zerubbabel is not mentioned; the elders of the Jews directed the work. Whether Haggai and Zechariah remained active after the dates given in their prophecies is not known definitely (Haggai's activity is confined to the second year of Darius; Zechariah's continued to the fourth year of Darius, Zech vii 1), though it seems probable. In any case, the completion of the work on the temple is attributed to the "order of the God of Israel" and "the official document" of Cyrus and Darius. Artaxerxes may be a later addition, possibly because he was king at the time of the Chronicler or because of the tradition that in his time the wall around the city, including the temple, was constructed (Neh iii 29–31) or the finishing touches put upon it (II Maccabees i 18). The work was completed in 515 B.C. A service of dedication marking the event took place. Much of the order follows closely the dedication of Solomon's temple (cf. I Kings viii; II Chron vii 3 ff.), though it reflects the situation of an impoverished community as compared to the affluence marking the elaborate ceremonies with which the first temple was dedicated. Naturally the offerings were consonant with the resources of the people but the essentials were present. Of particular importance is the emphasis upon the legitimacy of the community as illustrated by the shift from "Jews" to "Israelites" composed of priests, Levites, and laity, and the sin offering of twelve he-goats corresponding to the twelve tribes of Israel. Even the priestly and Levitical orders of service were reinstituted—in accordance not with command of David but with the law of Moses (cf. Exod xxix; Lev viii; Num iii 5 ff., viii 5 ff.). I Esdras vii 9 adds gatekeepers to the list. Galling, p. 201, following Torrey (ES, p. 204), thinks the Chronicler himself was responsible for vss. 15–18. But would the writer then have attributed the priestly and Levitical orders to prescriptions in the "book of Moses"? Would he not have referred the order to David (I Chron xxiii–xxvi)?

[Passover and unleavened bread, 19–22]: The concluding verses of the chapter represent the Chronicler's addition, perhaps emphasizing the people's gratitude for the consummation of the reconstruction of the temple through a celebration of the Passover and feast of unleavened bread. Frequently the building pattern followed by Solomon became the model for the second temple. At the

time of the dedication there were similar services (I Kings viii 62 ff.;
II Chron vii 8–10), though no Passover took place then because
of the time the temple was finished. But in connection with the
rededication in the periods of Hezekiah (II Chron xxx 13 ff.) and
later Josiah (II Chron xxxv 1 ff.), there was a Passover. The hand
of the Chronicler may be seen in the comment that the Levites slew
the paschal lambs, as they are said to have done in the instances
just noted (II Chron xxx 17, xxxv 11). The participants were members of the golah, priests, Levites, and those who had absolved
themselves of the impurities of the people of the land in order to
join Israel, that is, proselytes (cf. ix 1 ff.; Neh ix 2, x 29). Outsiders
were permitted to celebrate the Passover with Israelites if they observed the regulations imposed on the latter (Num ix 14).

As in the time of Hezekiah (II Chron xxx 21), the feast of unleavened bread followed the celebration of the Passover and lasted
seven days. It was always connected with the Passover and an expression of joy because of the goodness of Yahweh. In this case, the
specific cause for rejoicing was Yahweh's inspiring the king of Persia
to help them in the work of building God's house.

7. EZRA AND HIS MISSION
(vii 1–28)†

Ezra

VII 1 After these things, during the reign of Artaxerxes the king of Persia, [came] Ezra, the son of Seraiah, the son of Azariah, the son of Hilkiah, 2 the son of Shallum, the son of Zadok, the son of Ahitub, 3 the son of Amariah, the son of Azariah, the son of Meraioth, 4 the son of Zerahiah, the son of Uzzi, the son of Bukki, 5 the son of Abishua, the son of Phinehas, the son of Eleazar, the son of Aaron the high priest. 6 That was the Ezra who came from Babylon; he was a scribe skilled in the law of Moses which Yahweh God of Israel had given. The king gave him everything he requested because the hand of Yahweh his God was upon him. 7 Some of the Israelites, of the priests, the Levites, the singers, the gatekeepers, and the temple slaves went up to Jerusalem in the seventh year of Artaxerxes the king. 8 ᵃHe arrivedᵃ at Jerusalem in the fifth month which was in the seventh year of the king—9 for he had ordered the departure from Babylon on the first day of the first month and arrived at Jerusalem on the first day of the fifth month because the kind hand of his God was upon him. 10 For Ezra had set his mind on investigating the law of Yahweh in order to teach effectively [its] statutes and judgments.

The rescript of Artaxerxes

11 This is a copy of the official document that King Artaxerxes gave to Ezra, the priest, the scribe, a student of matters pertain-

† Ezra vii 1–10 ‖ I Esdras viii 1–7; 11–26 ‖ I Esdras viii 8–24; 27–28 ‖
I Esdras viii 25–27.

ᵃ⁻ᵃ LXX "they arrived."

ing to the commandments and statutes of Yahweh concerning Israel. 12 "Artaxerxes, king of kings, to Ezra the priest, student of the law of the God of the heavens [. . . .]ᵇ And now 13 a formal document has been issued by me that any one of the people of Israel in my kingdom, as well as their priests and Levites, who is willing to go to Jerusalem, may go with you, 14 because you have been sent by the king and his seven advisers to conduct an investigation about Judah and Jerusalem in harmony with the law of your God which is in your hand, 15 and to transport the silver and gold which the king and his advisers have contributed voluntarily for the God of Israel whose dwelling place is at Jerusalem, 16 together with all the silver and gold which you get from the entire province of Babylon and the voluntary offerings of the people and the priests, freely contributed for the house of their God at Jerusalem. 17 Therefore, you must apply this money scrupulously to purchase bulls, rams, lambs, and [materials for] their meal offerings and drink offerings, and offer them upon the altar of the house of your God at Jerusalem, 18 and whatever appears desirable to you and your brothers to do with the rest of the silver and the gold you may do in accordance with the will of your God. 19 Deliver to the God of Jerusalem the vessels which were given to you for the [cultic] service of the house of your God. 20 The rest of the requirements for the house of your God for which it is incumbent upon you to provide, you may provide from royal treasuries. 21 By me, Artaxerxes the king, a formal order has been issued to all the treasurers of [the province] Across the River that whatever Ezra the priest, the student of the law of the God of the heavens, shall request of you is to be complied with precisely, 22 up to a hundred talents of silver, a hundred kors of wheat, a hundred baths of wine, a hundred baths of anointing oil, and salt without prescribed [limit]. 23 Everything demanded by the God of the heavens for the house of the God of the heavens must be provided for diligently. Why should wrath fall upon the realm of the king and his sons? 24 Also let it be known to you that it is not permissible to impose

ᵇ See NOTE.

tribute, tax, or duty upon any of the priests, Levites, singers, gatekeepers, temple slaves, or [other] servants of this house of God. 25 And you, Ezra, appoint magistrates and judges, in accordance with the wisdom of your God which you possess, who shall judge all the people of Across the River, all who know the laws of your God; and you must communicate [them] to whoever does not know [them]. 26 But anyone who does not comply with the law of your God and the law of the king, let sentence be pronounced [upon him] speedily, whether for death, or for exclusion, or for fine, or for imprisonment."

Doxology

27 Praised be Yahweh God of our fathers who has put [such a thing] as this in the mind of the king to adorn the house of Yahweh which is at Jerusalem, 28 and has extended to me the devotion of the king, his advisers, and all the powerful officials of the king; and I have been encouraged because the hand of Yahweh my God was upon me and I have assembled [family] heads of Israel to go up with me.

NOTES

vii 1. *Ezra*. '*zr*', a late form of '*zrh*. A hypocoristicon originally composed of '*zr* plus some other element such as *yhw*, '*l* or *qm*. Cf. M. Noth, *Die israelitischen Personennamen im Rahmen der gemeinsemitischen Namengebung* (abbr. IPN) (Beiträge zur Wissenschaft vom Alten und Neuen Testament), 1928, p. 154. It means "help, assistance, support." The full name with the above-noted elements is fairly common.

2. *Zadok*. On the enigmatic Zadok see further I Chron v 34, 38 (vi 8, 12E), ix 11; Neh xi 11. For a discussion of his origin see H. H. Rowley in *Festschrift für Alfred Bertholet*, 1950, pp. 461–72, and JBL 58 (1939), 113–32; C. F. Hauer, JBL 82 (1963), 89–94.

3. *Amariah . . . Azariah*. These names occur on inscribed jar handles from Gibeon. See *Hebrew Inscriptions and Stamps from Gibeon*, ed. J. B. Pritchard, 1959, pp. 10 f.

6. *a scribe skilled*. *spr mhyr* as in Ps xlv 2. Cf. AP, *Ahiqar* 1:1, *spr ḥkym w-mhry* "a wise and skilled scribe." On *šapiru-sipiru* as "secretary" or "bureau official" in Neo-Babylonian period see *Reallexikon der*

Assyriologie, I, 1932, p. 456. Possibly also at Mari—*Archives royales de Mari, I: Correspondance de Samsi-Addu*, 1950, 28:20. On meaning of *mhr* in Ugaritic, see J. Aistleitner, *Untersuchungen zur Grammatik des Ugaritischen*, 1945, p. 45. On the function of the scribe, see J. Begrich, "Sofer und Mazkir," ZAW 58 (1940), 1–29; and for portrait of the Egyptian scribe see H. Schäfer and W. Andrae, *Die Kunst des Alten Orients*, 1925, Pls. 233, 237, 341.

the hand of Yahweh his God was upon him. Expression may indicate dependence on Nehemiah memoirs (Neh ii 8, 18). Cf. also Ezra vii 28, viii 18, 22, 31. See Noth, ÜS, p. 147.

8. *the fifth month . . . in the seventh year of the king.* For discussion with references see Bowman, pp. 624 f.

9. *first day of the first month.* I.e., Nisan 1 (March–April).

first day of the fifth month. Ab 1 (July–August).

the kind hand of his God. Phrase occurs in an Akkadian prayer to Marduk (A. Falkenstein and W. von Soden, *Sumerische und akkädische Hymnen und Gebete*, p. 300).

10. *to teach effectively.* Literally "to do and to teach," probably hendiadys.

11. *official document.* Cf. iv 18, 23.

12. *Artaxerxes, king of kings.* See AJSL 57 (1940), 71.

the law. dt "law," is used; equivalent of Heb. *torah* (see Schaeder, EdS, p. 44).

student of the law of the God of the heavens. Schaeder (EdS, pp. 48 f.) thinks the phrase ought to be reordered: Sekretar (oder Minister) vom Gesetz des Himmelsgottes "secretary (or minister) of the law of the God of heaven." It is an official title.

[. . . .] The Aramaic word here is "finished," which does not fit the context. It may be a corruption. Syr. and I Esdras viii 9 have "greeting"; LXX "the matter is concluded and the answer." Perhaps some such meaning as "so be it" or "done" is involved, the idea being that the decree is hereby set forth and is unalterable.

14. *his seven advisers.* Cf. Esther i 14. Cyrus the Younger had seven of the best Persians serve as his advisers (Xenophon *Anabasis* I.vi.4 f.); Histiaeus was a counselor of Darius (Herodotus v.24) and Artabantus of Xerxes (Herodotus VII.46 ff.).

17. *scrupulously.* Literally "exactly." The money was to be used precisely for the purpose for which it was allotted and for no other.

offer. Theological use of *qrb* in Aramaic inscription from Tell el-Mask-huta (JNES 15 [1956], 2).

20. *royal treasuries.* See NOTES on v 17 and vi 1. Cf. the Elamite *ka₄-ap-nu-iš-ki*="treasury" in Cameron, *The Persepolis Treasury Tablets*.

21. *all the treasurers.* Such treasuries were located at various centers of the Persian empire. See Cameron, *op. cit.*, pp. 10 f.

Nehemiah and Hanani is not clear, though the position of Nehemiah and Hanani may have led to some misunderstanding at times. If Ezra was originally a Persian court officer he must have been skilled in the scribal art, that is, in the knowledge of Jewish affairs. The Chronicler considered him well versed in the law of Moses, which he had investigated thoroughly and intended to teach so that it might be carried out among his people. Both the introductory verses and the edict of Artaxerxes emphasize that point, which the memoirs of Ezra support. The whole portion reflects a combination of religion and government characteristic of the postexilic period and, indeed, of the Chronicler. Ezra's mission appears to have been to assist in improving the situation at Jerusalem. He was, like Sheshbazzar, Zerubbabel, and Nehemiah, charged with a task he carried out with zeal. He was accompanied by a contingent of Israelites (ordinary folk) and religious personnel, which indicates his primary interests —to promote the religious aspects of the Jerusalem community.

[The rescript of Artaxerxes, 11–26]: The Aramaic document quoted here contains two orders. The main thrust of it is, of course, the specific permission given to Ezra to proceed to Jerusalem and carry out the purpose of his mission. But included in it is the order that went out to the treasurers involved in the execution of the king's plan (vss. 21–24). With certain exceptions, this reads almost like some of the Persepolis Treasury Tablets, notably Nos. 4–8, which were orders issued by the king directly or at his command. However, it must be observed that the Persepolis Tablets are orders for the payment of various types of workmen; none of them have to do with anything like the situation described in Ezra. Probably a part of the record deposited in the temple archives, it is of the same general type of material as the Aramaic document quoted in Chapters iv–vi.

The rescript is introduced with the notice in vs. 11, in Hebrew. It was doubtless Ezra's copy of the official order issued to him by the king, permitting those Israelites residing in the kingdom, presumably in the eastern regions, who were minded to do so to accompany the royal agent to Jerusalem. This is another indication of the successive waves of returnees making their way back to the ancestral home, obviously a long, drawn-out, and painful process, extending over a century or more. The document was written for the king by someone familiar with Jewish affairs, as is evident from the reference to priests and Levites (vs. 13) and other temple per-

sonnel (vs. 24) and to types of offerings (vs. 17). The dual purpose of Ezra's visit to Jerusalem was to investigate the (religious)
situation at Jerusalem and bear the contributions offered for the
improvement of conditions there by the government and the Jews
still residing at Babylon. Josephus (*Antiquities* XI.vii) has suggested
that Ezra was sent to look into the matter of Johanan the high priest
and Bagoas in the reign of Artaxerxes II (404–359 B.C.). But as
Schneider, pp. 132 f., points out, the terms of the firman provide for
an investigation of the conduct of cultic services at Jerusalem in order to bring them into line with the requirements of the law of the
God of the heavens, "the law of your God" (i.e., the law of Moses,
vs. 6). Then there is the matter of the uncertainty of Ezra's date.
If, as assumed in this treatment, Ezra followed Nehemiah's second
visit and was a contemporary of his, he could hardly have come for
the purpose suggested by Josephus.

Special emphasis is laid on cultic services, though building repairs
are not excluded (vss. 18, 20). In view of the Passover papyrus
issued by Darius II in 419 B.C. (a letter sent by Darius II to the
Jews at Elephantine regarding the date and method for celebrating
the Passover; see Letter 21 in AP, pp. 60–65), the concern of
Artaxerxes for the temple cultus is quite understandable (cf.
ANET, p. 491, and De Vaux, RB 46 [1937], 29–57). Cyrus, too,
had requested that those he had resettled say prayers for him and
his son in their sacred cities (ANET, p. 316). Antiochus Soter
(280–262/1) reconstructed the great shrines of Esagila and Ezida
at Babylon and offered prayers for the welfare of his kingdom (see
also Olmstead, HPE, pp. 91 f.). Cultic practices were to be brought
into harmony with "the law of your God which is in your hand"
(vs. 14). This can only refer to a well defined document, perhaps
the priestly edition of the Pentateuch (see Nehemiah, COMMENT
on Sec. 11, viii 1–12), since Ezra is said to have been skilled in the
law of Moses (vs. 6). Ezra was invested with authority to appoint
magistrates and judges to carry out the provisions of the law of
Moses in the province Across the River, that is, in the district of
Judah (for the duty of such officials as appointed by David, according to the Chronicler, see I Chron xxvi 29 ff.). Moreover that law
was to be communicated to those who were unaware of its demands.
The reference may be to those persons who remained in the land
during the Exile and those who intermarried with the people of the
land (ch. x). Significantly, Ezra had the power of imposing the

death penalty upon those guilty of capital crimes (e.g., idolatry [Exod xxii 20; Lev xx 2 ff.; Deut xiii 6–10] or adultery [Lev xx 10; Deut xxii 22]), whether against the law of God or the law of the king. This simply means that Ezra had behind him the authority of the Persian government.

To supplement the financial assistance supplied through offerings from Babylon, a directive was issued by the king to the treasury officials of Across the River to contribute from their funds as may be demanded by Ezra. Each category of contribution except for that of salt was limited, however. The temple personnel were granted immunity from taxes, a Persian practice attested elsewhere. Gadatas was censured by Darius because he imposed tribute on the servants of Apollo at Magnesia (Olmstead, HPE, p. 156). For the act of Antiochus Epiphanes, see Josephus *Antiquities* XII.iii. For the Persian attitude toward other religions, see Meyer, *Geschichte des Altertums,* IV, Pt. I, pp. 87–89. Herodotus (III.91) writes of exemptions from tribute granted to the district of Arabia by Darius Hystaspis. In view of these attestations, the magnanimity of Artaxerxes is altogether possible and the codicil may be regarded as authentic (but cf. Ahlemann, ZAW 58 [1942/43], 84 f., who would eliminate the whole edict on grounds of incongruity between it and the Ezra source; see also Pfeiffer, *Introduction to the Old Testament,* p. 826).

[Doxology, 27–28]: Ezra expresses his gratitude to Yahweh for having inspired the king to beautify the temple. He is equally grateful that he has been chosen to carry out the king's directive and that God has led the king and his advisers to entrust the task to him. Armed with the royal edict and convinced that Yahweh has chosen him to go to Jerusalem to execute its provisions, he invites the family heads and summons those of their families who so desire to accompany him.

8. EZRA'S DEPARTURE FROM BABYLON.
HIS ENLISTMENT AND SELECTION OF PERSONNEL
(viii 1–36)†

The list of returning exiles

VIII 1 These are the family heads [with their official geneal-ogy], who went up with me from Babylon in the reign of Artaxerxes the king: 2 of the sons of Phinehas, Gershom; of the sons of Ithamar, Daniel; of the sons of David, Hattush, 3 of the sons of Shecaniah; of the sons of Parosh, Zechariah, and with him a hundred and fifty males officially registered; 4 of the sons of Pahath-moab, Eliehoenai the son of Zerahiah and two hun-dred males with him; 5 of the sons of Zattu, Shecaniah the son of Jahaziel and three hundred males with him; 6 of the sons of Adin, Ebed the son of Jonathan and fifty males with him; 7 of the sons of Elam, Jeshaiah the son of Athaliah and seventy males with him; 8 of the sons of Shephatiah, Zebadiah the son of Michael and eighty males with him; 9 of the sons of Joab, Obadiah the son of Jehiel and two hundred and eighteen males with him; 10 of the sons of Bani*ᵃ*, Shelomith, the son of Josiphiah and a hundred and sixty males with him; 11 of the sons of Bebai, Zechariah the son of Bebai and twenty-eight males with him; 12 of the sons of Azgad, Johanan the son of Hakkatan and *ᵇ*a hundred and ten*ᵇ* males with him; 13 of the sons of Adonikam, the last ones, whose names were Eliphelet, Jeiel, and Shemaiah and sixty males with them; 14 and of the sons of Bigvai, Uthai and Zabbud*ᶜ* and seventy males with him*ᵈ*.

† **Ezra viii 1–14** ‖ I Esdras viii 28–40; **15–20** ‖ I Esdras viii 41–49; **21–23** ‖ I Esdras viii 50–53; **24–30** ‖ I Esdras viii 54–60; **31–36** ‖ I Esdras viii 61–64.

ᵃ So with I Esdras viii 36 and LXXᴬ.
ᵇ–ᵇ Some manuscripts and Syr. have "120."
ᶜ I Esdras viii 40 "Istalkouros." Omitted by LXXᴮ.
ᵈ Many manuscripts read "with them." See NOTE.

Enlistment of temple personnel

15 I assembled them at the canal that runs to Ahava where we encamped for three days. I saw laymen and priests but found no Levites there. 16 Then I sent for Eliezer, Ariel, Shemaiah, Elnathan, Jarib, Elnathan, Nathan, Zechariah, Meshullam, leaders, and for Joiarib and Elnathan, teachers, 17 whom I sent to Iddo the head of the place Casiphia*e* and I told them what to say to Iddo [and] his brothers who were located at the place Casiphia*e*, that is, to send us ministers for the house of our God. 18 Because the good hand of our God was upon us they brought to us a wise man, of the sons of Mahli, the son of Levi, the son of Israel, by the name of Sherebiah with his sons and brothers, eighteen men; 19 and Hashabiah and Jeshaiah, of the sons of Merari with his brothers and their sons, twenty men; 20 also two hundred and twenty temple slaves—[descendants] of the temple slaves David and the princes had appointed for the service of the Levites—all of them designated by name.

Farewell services

21 Then I proclaimed a fast there by the canal Ahava that we might humble ourselves before our God and inquire of him the right way for ourselves, our retinue and all our possessions, 22 for I was ashamed to request a contingent of cavalry from the king to protect us from the enemy en route because we had told the king as follows: "The hand of our God deals favorably with all those who seek him, but his mighty wrath comes upon all those who forsake him." 23 So we fasted and prayed to our God about it; and he listened to us.

Selection of treasure bearers

24 Then I selected twelve of the leading priests, namely Sherebiah and Hashabiah with ten*f* of their brothers, 25 to whom

e LXX "in silver."
f LXX*B* "twelve"; under influence of number given for the priests.

I weighed out the silver, the gold, and the vessels, the contributions for the house of our God which the king, his advisers, and all Israel there present had made. 26 I weighed out into their hand six hundred and fifty talents of silver, a hundred vessels of silver valued at . . .^g talents, a hundred talents of gold, 27 twenty golden bowls valued at a thousand darics and two vessels of shining red copper as precious as gold. 28 I said to them, "You are holy to Yahweh and the vessels too are holy; the silver and the gold are a voluntary offering to Yahweh God of your^h fathers. 29 Guard them carefully until you weigh them out to the officials of the priests, the Levites, and the family chiefs of Israel at Jerusalem in the rooms of the house of Yahweh." 30 Then the priests and the Levites received the consignment of silver, gold, and vessels, to bring [them] to Jerusalem to the house of our God.

Journey to and arrival at Jerusalem

31 Then we departed from the canal of Ahava on the twelfth day of the first month to journey to Jerusalem and the hand of our God was upon us and en route delivered us from the hand of the enemy and waylayer. 32 When we arrived at Jerusalem, we waited there for three days. 33 On the fourth day, the silver, gold, and vessels were weighed out in the house of our God into the hand of Meremoth, the son of Uriah, the priest with whom was Elazar the son of Phinehas; with them were also Jozabad the son of Jeshua and Noadiah the son of Binnui, the Levites. 34 Everything was checked by number and weight and the total weight recorded ⁱat the same timeⁱ. 35 When the exiles of the captivity arrived, they offered burnt offerings to the God of Israel —twelve bulls on behalf of all Israel, ninety-six rams, seventy-seven lambs, and twelve he-goats as a sin offering, all of it as a burnt offering to Yahweh. 36 They also delivered the orders of

^g See NOTE.
^h LXX^B "our," which may be corrected in view of vs. 30. LXX^A "your."
ⁱ⁻ⁱ LXX^{AB} take the phrase with the following verse. See NOTE.

the king to the king's satraps and governors of [the province] Across the River who then supported the people and the house of God.

NOTES

viii 2. *Daniel.* I Esdras viii 29 "Gamel."

3. *of the sons of Shecaniah.* LXX does not help here. Perhaps text ought to be corrected with LXX[A] of I Esdras viii 29 "Hattush the son of Shecaniah." Cf. I Chron iii 21, 22.

4. *Pahath-moab.* See NOTE on ii 6.

5. *Zattu.* So with I Esdras viii 32.

7. *Athaliah.* I Esdras viii 33 "Gotholiah."

8. *Zebadiah.* I Esdras viii 34 "Zeraiah." But "Zebadiah" is a name now found on a fifth-century ostracon from Ashdod.

10. *Shelomith.* On form of name see Noth, IPN, p. 165, n. 6.

14. *Zabbud.* The Massora parva has Zakkur (Zaccur).

with him. See textual note *c*. As the text now stands, the preposition requires the reading, "Uthai, the son of Zabbud"; that means that only one family head was involved. Cf. I Esdras viii 40.

16. It has been suggested that some of the names may be duplications —Elnathan ‖ Nathan, Jarib ‖ Joiarib.

17. *Casiphia.* For form and possible meaning of name see BMAP, No. 12, and W. Eilers, AfO, 17, 2, (1956), p. 334.

I told them what to say. Literally "I put in their mouth words to say."

18. *the son of Levi.* Actually the grandson of Levi (cf. Exod vi 19; Num iii 20; I Chron vi 19 [vi 29E]). Cf. K. Möhlenbrink, "Die levitischen Überlieferungen des Alten Testaments," ZAW 52 (1934), 209.

21. *a fast there by the canal Ahava.* Cf. A. Parrot, *Babylon and the Old Testament*, 1958, pp. 125 f.

our retinue. Literally "children" or "little ones," but here used in the sense of "adherents" or those who had joined Ezra and his group.

22. *his mighty wrath.* Literally "his strength and his wrath."

"The hand of our God . . . those who forsake him." Latter part of verse sharply curtailed in I Esdras viii 52. On the possible historical reason for Ezra's motive in not seeking an armed escort see Pavlovsky, *Biblica* 38 (1957), 286 f.

24. *I selected.* Literally "I set apart."

in addition to. Reading conjunction before "Sherebiah" as in I Esdras viii 54.

26. *six hundred and fifty talents.* Slightly over 24½ tons.

[. . .] The number has fallen out of the text; some read "dual" ("two talents," i.e., about 151.1 lbs.). I Esdras viii 56 and LXX have "100 talents."

a hundred talents. About 3¾ tons. On the value of these contributions, cf. Pavlovsky, *Biblica* 38 (1957), 297–301.

27. *a thousand darics.* If the Persian gold daric is meant the value would be roughly 18½ lbs.; if the silver daric is meant it would amount to slightly over 12⅕ lbs.

30. *consignment.* Literally "weight."

32. Cf. Neh ii 11. See F. Nötscher, *Biblica* 35 (1954), 316, n. 3.

33. *Uriah.* A *yhwd 'wryw* seal was found by Miss Kathleen Kenyon at Jericho in 1955 (cf. P. C. Hammond, PEQ 89 [January–June 1957], 68 f., Pl. xvi, and Avigad, IEJ 7 [1957], 146 ff.) which Avigad thinks bears the name of Uriah (Urio), the father of the Meremoth who was active in the second quarter of the fifth century B.C.

34. *at the same time.* See textual note ᵗ⁻ᵗ. Galling, p. 208, n. 2, thinks this phrase introduced the story of the reading of the law described in Neh viii 2 ff., which was originally found here. The recording was necessary for the report to the king.

35. *seventy-seven.* I Esdras viii 63 (LXXᴬ) has seventy-two, probably under the influence of the number 12 and multiples thereof. Josephus (*Antiquities* XI.v.2) also has seventy-two but differs on the number of rams.

36. *the orders.* See NOTE on vi 12.

who then. Cf. Josephus *Antiquities* XI.v.2.138, "As they [i.e., the king's officials] were under the necessity of doing what was enjoined by him [the king], they honored our nation and were assistant to them in all their necessities."

COMMENT

Verse 27 of chapter vii marked the beginning of the Ezra memoirs. They are composed in the first person, the "I" and "me" referring to Ezra, who compiled the materials after his arrival at Jerusalem. The memoirs open with an expression of praise and thanksgiving to Yahweh for inspiring the king to permit the mission and selecting Ezra to undertake it.

Chapter viii starts with a list of those who accompanied him. It is followed by the story of the enlistment of temple servants, the farewell service by the canal Ahava, the selection of priestly officials as custodians of the contributions for the temple, and the departure from Babylon and arrival at Jerusalem, with the presentation of the contributions and the thanksgiving service.

[The list of those who accompanied Ezra, viii 1–14]: The list
in Ezra ii began with the laymen and was followed by priests,
Levites, temple slaves, and the sons of Solomon's servants. This
one begins with the priests and is followed by Hattush and the
volunteers from twelve families of laymen. That this is not a list
copied from that in chapter ii is evident from two important facts.
First, the priests here are reckoned after the Aaronite line, whereas
in Ezra ii they follow the Zadokite line. There was apparently a
shift in the priority of priestly authority in Babylon between the
time of Zerubbabel and Ezra. For a thorough discussion of the
problem see Kittel, GVI, III, pp. 402 ff., and Meyer, EJ, p. 175,
n. 2. Perhaps not too much should be made of this shift as the
Zadokites were attached to the line of Eleazar-Phinehas in I Chron
v 30–34 (vi 4–8E). Second, the Pahath-moab family here represents only the Jeshua line, the Joab line now having independent
status; in Ezra ii both are reckoned to Pahath-moab. Although all
the family names occur in both lists, they follow a different order in
each. The numbers indicate order in the respective lists with reference
to Ezra viii.

Ezra ii	Neh vii	Ezra viii	Neh x	Ezra x
(1) Parosh	(1) Parosh	(1) Parosh	(1) Parosh	(1) Parosh
(6) Shepha-tiah	(6) Shepha-tiah	(2) Pahath-moab	(2) Pahath-moab	(5) Elam
(2) Pahath-moab	(2) Pahath-moab	(3) Zattu	(5) Elam	(3) Zattu
(5) Elam	(5) Elam	(4) Adin	(3) Zattu	(9) Bebai
(3) Zattu	(3) Zattu	(5) Elam	(8) Bani	(2) Pahath-
(8) Bani	(8) Binnui*	(6) Shepha-tiah	(10) Azgad	(8) Bani† moab
(9) Bebai	(9) Bebai	(7) Joab	(9) Bebai	(8) Bani
(10) Azgad	(10) Azgad	(8) Bani	(10) Bigvai	
(11) Adoni-kam	(11) Adoni-kam	(9) Bebai	(4) Adin	
(12) Bigvai	(12) Bigvai	(10) Azgad		
(4) Adin	(4) Adin	(11) Adoni-kam		
		(12) Bigvai		

* This may be Bani.
† This may be Bigvai, as (12).

Not all the members of each of these families returned with
Zerubbabel, as may be seen from the qualification appearing in the
case of Adonikam (vs. 13); that is, the last ones of that family

returned with Ezra. But that is not said about any of the others, here or in the earlier list. The number of families named is doubtless influenced by the Chronicler's feeling for all Israel, which ideally consisted of the twelve tribes, though of course only descendants of Judah and Benjamin were involved in the return (Ezra i 5, iv 1, x 9; Neh xi 4–8, 25, 31, 36, and frequently in Chronicles). Interestingly enough, a member of the Davidic family is included—Hattush, of the family of Shecaniah (according to I Chron iii 22, the grandson of Shecaniah; I Esdras viii 29 says "the son of Shecaniah." I Chron iii 17 ff. has Jehoiachin-Pedaiah-Zerubbabel-Hananiah-Shecaniah-Shemaiah-Hattush). The number of males returning with Ezra, including the scribe himself, and Gershom, Daniel, and Hattush, is exactly fifteen hundred. (LXX has 1510 and I Esdras viii, 1794—including the four leaders in each case.) But Gershom and Daniel were no doubt family heads (cf. vs. 24), in which case the actual number of returnees would be increased, but how much cannot be determined. In addition there were thirty-eight Levites and 220 temple slaves. Since these figures do not include wives and children, there must have been a relatively large contingent that went to Jerusalem with Ezra.

[Enlistment of temple personnel, 15–20]: Ezra assembled his compatriots at the canal Ahava, apparently named after a town, otherwise unknown. After three days' inspection, it was discovered that no Levites were in the group. (For reasons for the paucity of Levites, see COMMENT on Sec. 2, ii 40. Cf. Meyer, EJ, pp. 176 f.; Kittel, GVI, p. 394; De Vaux, IAT, II, pp. 254 ff.). To supply this deficiency Ezra appointed nine leaders and two teachers to confer with Iddo, the head of the community at Casiphia where the Levitical families lived or were concentrated for other purposes (IAT, II, p. 187; Casiphia is otherwise unknown). By the grace of God, a Levitical chief by the name of Sherebiah, of the family of Mahli, and two others, also of the Merari line, consented to go with thirty-eight of their brothers. Whether the temple slaves came from Casiphia, or whether the verse is to be interpreted independently, is not clear. Ezra does not give the names of the members of this group or their leaders though he had them in his files. It may be that the decision of such a large number of temple slaves to accompany Ezra was a factor in persuading the Levites to go.

[The farewell services, 21–23]: The farewell services took the form of a fast to invoke Yahweh's protection for the caravan on the dangerous way to Jerusalem. Because of a declaration of trust in

Yahweh before the king, Ezra felt it inappropriate to request the customary escort (cf. I Esdras v 2; Neh ii 9). They carried much treasure and feared for their helpless wives and children, so there may have been other motives for the decision not to ask for a guard. It has been suggested that there is here a subtle hint of the superiority of Ezra's method over that of Nehemiah. Others think it was to avoid unduly attracting the attention of their future neighbors whose enmity might be further aroused thereby.

[The selection of treasure bearers, 24–30]: According to the Torah, the priests were to have charge of the sacred objects connected with the tabernacle while the Levites were to carry them (Num iii 8, 31, iv 7–15). That provision doubtless underlies the selection of priests and Levites to have charge of transporting the dedicated contributions from Babylon to Jerusalem. The number chosen may have some connection with the Chronicler's love for the number twelve (cf. I Chron xxv 9–21) and may somehow be related to the twelve tribe idea. Ezra's address to these select priests and Levites, reminding them of their holiness as well as that of the contributions delivered into their care, must not be interpreted as casting suspicion on their honesty; it was rather a warning to possible robbers on the way that these valuables were under Yahweh's protection. Molestation of the bearers or theft of the sacred objects would bring tragic consequences to the guilty.

The special gifts brought to Jerusalem by Ezra and attested by witnesses (vs. 33) were contributed by the king of Persia, members of his court, and the Jewish exiles. This practice parallels that recorded in I Chron xxvi 26, where contributions are said to have been made to the old temple by the king, the family heads, and royal officials. The contributions offered by the Persian officials were a way of recognizing the Jerusalem temple as a legitimate sanctuary; see Galling, *Beiträge zur biblischen Landes- und Altertumskunde* (ZDPV 68, Heft 2) (1950), 139.

[Journey to and arrival at Jerusalem, 31–36]: The sequence of events was approximately as follows (cf. vii 8–9): (a) Summons sent out to all who wanted to go to Jerusalem on the first day of the first month; (b) three days required for assembling (vs. 15); (c) search for Levites and further preparations required still more time; (d) departure from Ahava on the twelfth day of the first month (vs. 31); (e) arrival at Jerusalem on the first day of the fifth month (vii 9b); (f) three days' wait upon arrival (vs. 32); (g) delivery of sacred contributions on the fourth day after arrival (vs. 33). According to the Jubilees calendar (A. Jaubert, "Le calendrier des Jubilés," VT 3 [1953], 261), the actual departure took place on a Sunday (first day of the week) and the arrival at Jerusalem on a Friday. The proximity of the Sabbath necessitated the three days' delay before the delivery of the sacred contributions (cf. Neh ii 11; on the matter of the three days' wait, see H. Schmidt, *Sellin Festschrift*, 1927, p. 122, and F. Nötscher, "Zur Auferstehung nach drei Tagen," *Biblica* 35 [1954], 313–19). Josh iv 19 has the Israelites entering Canaan on the tenth day of the first month, which was also a Friday (Jaubert, VT 3 [1953], 259). Liturgical arrangements could have been involved. The distance between Ahava and Jerusalem is difficult to calculate exactly; it has been reckoned as near nine hundred miles. Such a large company would naturally proceed slowly, no more than an average of about nine miles per day.

On the fourth day after the arrival, the sacred treasures brought along by Ezra's group were officially presented to Meremoth, in the presence of other priests and Levites. It should be noted that Meremoth had by this time proven his priestly status. He was of the family of Hakkoz, which earlier was unable to document its claims (ii 61f.); in Neh iii 4, 21, Meremoth appears without title, though his building lot was next to the priests. See Rudolph, p. 17, n. 2, and references given there. Upon the successful completion of this portion of their mission, they offered sacrifices to Yahweh. Verses 35–36 are from the Chronicler, as shown by the style and the religious emphasis. The twelve bulls were offered as a whole burnt offering (Lev i 1–9) for all Israel (cf. II Chron xxix 24); the twelve he-goats were for the twelve tribes (cf. Ezra vi 17; on the matter of the same number of animals for burnt offering and sin offering, see II Chron xxix 21)—another instance of the writer's interest in the ideal Israel. Ezra doubtless delivered to the local authorities copies of the royal edict. "Satraps" (a Persian term) is explained by "governors" (a Babylonian term); both terms occur together also in Esther iii 12, viii 9; Dan iii 2, 3, 27, vi 7). The use of the plural for satraps is extraordinary, unless the local provincial officials are intended. For the character and distribution of satraps, see O. Leuze, *Die Satrapieneinteilung in Syrien und im Zweistromlande von 520 bis 320*, 1935, especially pp. 19 ff., and Abel, AGP, II, pp. 108–20; Abel deals with the Palestinian organization in particular.

9. EZRA REPRIMANDS
THE JERUSALEM JEWS FOR THEIR SINS
(ix 1–15)†

The sin of the returned exiles

IX ¹ After the conclusion of these events, the officials approached me, saying, "The people of Israel, the priests, and the Levites have not held themselves aloof from the peoples of the lands despite their abominations—from the Canaanites, the Hittites, the Perizzites, the Jebusites, the Ammonites, the Moabites, the Egyptians, and the Amorites—² inasmuch as they and their sons have married some of their daughters, so that the holy race has become contaminated by the peoples of the lands; indeed the officials and chiefs were the worst offenders in this breach of loyalty." ³ When I heard about this matter, I tore my clothes and my mantle, I pulled hair off my head and out of my beard, and sat down horrified. ⁴ Then all those who were terror-stricken because of the words of the God of Israel on account of the disloyalty of the exiles congregated around me, while I remained sitting horrified until the evening sacrifice. ⁵ At the evening sacrifice I arose from my self-abasement and in my torn clothes and mantle I fell upon my knees, spread out my hands to Yahweh my God,

The prayer of Ezra

⁶ and said, "O my God, I am profoundly ashamed to lift up my face to you, O my God, for our iniquities have multiplied [until they are] higher than our heads and our guilt has risen as high as the heavens. ⁷ We have remained in great guilt from the days of our fathers until this very day and we, our kings, and our priests have been delivered into the hand of the kings of

† Ezra ix 1–5 ‖ I Esdras viii 68–73; 6–15 ‖ I Esdras viii 74–90.

the lands, to the sword, to captivity, to plunder, and to open shame by our iniquities, just as this day. 8 Now, for a short time, the favor of Yahweh our God has left us a remnant and provided us with a firm hold in his holy place that our God may make our eyes shine and revive us for a little while in our servitude. 9 For we are servants, but our God has not abandoned us in our servitude; he has extended his devotion to us [even] before the kings of Persia and has revived us so that we might erect the house of our God, restore its ruins, and provide for ourselves a wall [of protection] in Judah and Jerusalem. 10 And now, O our God, what shall we say after this, for we have abandoned your commandments 11 which you gave through your servants the prophets, saying, 'The land you are going to possess is a polluted land, polluted by the peoples of the lands and their abominations which have filled it with their uncleanness from one end to the other. 12 So, now, do not give your daughters in marriage to their sons, nor marry their daughters to your sons and do not ever seek for their peace and good relations, that you may be strong, eat the good things of the land, and bequeath it to your sons forever.' 13 After all that has befallen us because of our evil deeds and our great guilt—for you, O our God, have requited us far less than our iniquities deserved and have given us such an escape as this—14 shall we again break your commandments by entering into marriage relationships with the people who commit these abominations? Would you not be angry with us [to the point] of destroying us utterly, without remnant or escape? 15 O Yahweh God of Israel, you are the Righteous One. Now [indeed] we are this very day an escaped remnant. Behold, we [stand] in your presence in our guilt; yet no one can abide in your presence under [such circumstances] as this."

NOTES

ix 1. *the peoples of the lands.* For phrase see also 1QM 10:9; 1QH 4:26.

2. *race.* Literally "seed."

contaminated. I.e., mixed.

chiefs. sgn—a Babylonian word meaning "official," "governor"; similar
to Heb. "elder." See BMAP, p. 243, discussion of line 19 of Papyrus
No. 9, and index in AP.

were the worst offenders in this breach of loyalty. Literally "the hand
of . . . was foremost in this unfaithfulness."

3. *pulled hair off my head and out of my beard.* A sign of sorrow and
mourning. Cf. Neh xiii 25.

4. *terror-stricken.* Cf. Isa lxvi 2, 5.

words. I Esdras viii 72 has the singular and has in view specifically
Deut vii 2 ff.

5. *self-abasement.* Occurs only here in the Bible. The root means "to
be humble," "abased," and here refers to Ezra's self-abasement because
of his overwhelming sense of disappointment with the intermarriage situation, especially the involvement of the leaders.

6. *and said.* G. von Rad (*Theologie des Alten Testaments,* I, 1957,
p. 355) thinks this is a *Gerichtsdoxologie* (doxology of judgment).

higher than our heads. The possibility of parallelism need not be overlooked—"[summit] of the mountains." Cf. *hr'š* in II Sam xv 32.

7. *in great guilt from the days of our fathers.* Cf. Ps cvi 6; 1QS
1:23 f.

the kings of the lands. Refers in the Murashu documents to Persian
kings. Cf. A. T. Clay, *Business Documents of Murashu's Sons,* 1904,
p. 28, No. 6 (of Darius II); Schneider, p. 149.

8. *a remnant.* See NOTE on vs. 15.

a firm hold. Literally "a tent peg," which indicates a firm hold, a fixed
place of abode (cf. Isa liv 2).

make our eyes shine. Means "to revive the spirit" (cf. I Sam xiv 29;
Ps xiii 3; Prov xxix 13).

9. On this verse see 1QH 5:8.

a wall [of protection]. See Pritchard, *Hebrew Inscriptions and Stamps
from Gibeon,* pp. 9 f. Because of the use of the term *gdr* in the stamps,
this passage ought to be interpreted in the light of Isa v 5 f.; cf. Ezek
xiii 5. Revived Israel is the vineyard of Yahweh with its enclosure. For
the earlier interpretations see Bowman, pp. 649 f., and the observation of
Schaeder, EdS, p. 68, n. 1. Cf., however, Snaith, ZAW 63 (1951), 53–66.

11. *your servants the prophets.* Cf. Dan ix 6, 10.

polluted. ndh occurs frequently in the Qumran documents where it refers to the impurity of the individuals within the community.

13. *for you, O our God . . . iniquities deserved.* Literally "You, O
our God, have kept from the rod some of our iniquities." Cf. also M. Da-
hood, *Proverbs and Northwest Semitic Philology,* 1963, p. 51, n. 2.

14. *destroying us utterly.* Cf. 1QH 6:32; 1QM 14:5.

15. *an escaped remnant.* The monks at Qumran spoke of those who
follow the way of rebellion ending without remnant or escape (1QS
4:14; cf. Zadokite Document 2:7). 1QM 1:6 hopes for the destruction

of wickedness without survival and the Zadokite Document 2:11 says that God has always provided men for himself that there might be survival for the earth.

can abide. Probably a legal term meaning "win acquittal."

COMMENT

[The sin of the returned exiles, ix 1–5]: The story of mixed marriages begins innocently enough since its introductory words appear to connect it directly with the events related in the preceding chapter. However, x 9 states unequivocally that the affair took place after the middle of the ninth month—that is, the ninth month in the year of Ezra's arrival. What went on during the four month interval? It has been suggested that the time was occupied with the reading of the Torah and instruction as related in Neh vii 73–viii 18— that was the purpose of Ezra's coming to Jerusalem (vii 10, 25, 26). In that case "these events" would refer to the ceremonies of the Feast of Tabernacles (see Torrey, ES, pp. 255 ff., and CHI, pp. 114–16). But it is unlikely that Ezra was informed about the problem so late. There is more than a hint in x 2 f. that the issue was under consideration for some time and that there were earlier attempts to cope with it. What appears here seems to be the final, successful resolution of the difficulty.

The prohibition of mixed marriages is reiterated in later literature, for example, Jubilees xx 4, xxii 20, xxv 1–10, xxx 17; Testament of Levi ix 10. Earlier, marriages with foreigners were not frowned upon—for example, Joseph married an Egyptian (Gen xli 45), Moses a Cushite woman (Num xii 1 ff.), Mahlon and Chilion Moabite wives (Ruth i). Deut xxi 10 ff. permitted the marriage of women taken captive in war. However, that was not the normal custom (cf. Gen xxiv 3, xxviii 1, 6; Judg xiv 3). Legal restraints were early placed on marriages with certain groups in Canaan (Exod xxxiv 16 J), probably because of the observation that they led to illicit religious practices (cf. Judg iii 5–6; I Kings xi 1, xvi 31). Deut vii 1–4 prohibits outright connubium with those groups. The inclusion here of Ammonites and Moabites may be due to Deut xxiii 4 ff.; so far as we now know, Egyptians and Edomites were never placed under such interdiction, again possibly on the basis of the injunction of Deut xxiii 7.

Such a serious threat to the community could not be ignored by the local leaders and had been dealt with by Nehemiah (xiii 23 ff.; on the problem of time, see COMMENT on Sec. 14 of Nehemiah xiii). Indeed, it may have been one of the chief reasons for Ezra's mission (x 4). Intermarriage with "the peoples of the lands" was fraught with dire consequences for the struggling community, especially since it involved the ruling families of the Jews. "The peoples of the lands" were not merely the mixed population—Edomites, Moabites, Ammonites, etc.—that filled the vacuum created by the Exile of 586 B.C. As Würthwein has shown (Der 'amm ha'arez im Alten Testament, pp. 51–71), they were outside landholders who took over after the Exile. In postexilic times the term "people of the land" never refers to Judeans, though it still means the landed class of the various districts and includes some of the groups mentioned in vs. 1; however, others may have been added under the influence of the Deuteronomic list (cf. Deut vii 1; Josh iii 10, xxiv 11).

Undoubtedly they were in fairly good circumstances economically. On the other hand, the returnees were poor and, because of drought and crop failure (Hag i), were, in some instances at least, reduced to want. Under such conditions, many no doubt took the easy way out when offered the opportunity. Others, seeing the affluence of their neighbors, and a bit envious, did the same. Mal ii 10 ff. is an excellent commentary on the situation perhaps somewhat earlier. The Jews divorced their wives to take the daughters of foreigners. But the orthodox religious leaders clearly saw the danger of contaminating the pure religion of Yahweh, for intermarriage led to compromise and idolatry. That was why the returnees felt compelled to refuse commerce with the Samaritans, who were syncretists at best (cf. iv 10 and Albright, Archaeology and the Religion of Israel, p. 173). The efforts of Nehemiah and Ezra were successful, as may be seen from the failure of the Jews of Jerusalem to reply to the overture for help from the Elephantine colony in 408 B.C. See Cowley, AP, No. 30.

Part of Ezra's concern arose from his feeling for the "holy race," that is, the purity of Israel as the people of Yahweh. The maintenance of the true relationship between Yahweh and his people could be achieved only through purity of race. Israel was a holy people, chosen by a holy God (Lev xi 44; Isa vi 13), the seed of Abraham (II Chron xx 7). Israel had been set apart for Yahweh

(Deut vii 6) as his servant (Isa xlii 1) to be a light to the nations
(Isa xlii 6), which could not be done by watering down its faith
through compromise, as was apparent from the experience not only
of those who had remained in the land during the Exile but also of
many who chose to remain in Babylon. But the worst offenders
were those who should have been examples. "Officials" (vs. 2) is
the same term used in vs. 1 to categorize those who reported to
Ezra. In vs. 2 it refers to those who had succumbed to the tempta-
tion of compromise, possibly confined in large part to those who had
remained in the land or who had returned in the early stages of
repatriation.

Generally known though this state of affairs was, its full implication became apparent only when recognized by the officials and the
scribe. This may point to a period of preoccupation with the Torah
and instruction. The words of the God of Israel concerning the disloyalty of the exiles seems to indicate as much, since no specific
texts appear to be involved (cf. Deut vii 2 ff.). Ezra's chagrin is
reflected in the outward signs of pulling out hair from his head and
beard, the tearing of clothes, and the public self-abasement—all of
which took place in the plaza before the temple. This act represented
more than personal disappointment; Ezra was, in a sense, an em-
bodiment of the word of God to the people. Around him congregated
a group of the disloyal exiles whom he led into a service of confession at the time of the evening sacrifice.

[Ezra's prayer, 6–15]: Ezra's prayer of confession naturally follows his act of self-abasement, the congregating of the people, and
the evening oblation. One of the remarkable characteristics of this
prayer sermon is the shift from the first person singular, "I," in vs. 6
to the first person plural, "We," in vs. 7. Ezra not only intercedes for
the guilty community—a priestly function—but identifies himself with
that community. Nehemiah (i 5–11) had expressed the same attitude, though he was a layman. A shift from Ezek xviii is clearly
evident. The influence of Isaiah (vi 5, liii 4 ff.) is marked. This
principle of identification with the community is present in later
writings—cf. Tobit iii 5; Additions to the Book of Esther xiii 9–17,
xiv 6; Prayer of Azariah 6 f. Verse 7 also veers away from Ezekiel
since the cumulative guilt of the fathers, together with that of the
more recent officials and people, was responsible for their exile.
That was essentially what the Deuteronomist believed (cf. Judg ii
11 ff.). God had not permitted his people to be utterly destroyed; a

remnant survived (i.e., those returning from exile) and anchored itself in his holy place (Jerusalem). Hope for survival was once more raised during and after the return of 538. Though the Jews were still in servitude—as they had been since the days of the captivity—God did not abandon them. He moved the Persian kings to grant them permission to return and restore his house at Jerusalem. However, they are threatened once again by guilt as great as that of the fathers. The commandments of God given through the prophets had been violated. Verses 11–12 represent a patchwork of Mosaic and prophetic ideas brought together by the writer, possibly under the influence of the Deuteronomist, who regarded Moses as a prophet (Deut xviii 15, xxxiv 10). Later prophets repeated his injunctions, though there is only one reference (Mal ii 11 ff.) to marriage with outsiders. These verses, 11 and 12, are built up of many pieces, as may be seen from the following parallels in words or thought: (a) "the land you are going to possess" (cf. Deut iv 5 ff.); (b) "a polluted land," "polluted by the peoples of the lands" (cf. Lam i 17; Lev xviii 25 ff., xx 22 ff.); (c) "their abominations" (cf. Deut xviii 9; II Kings xvi 3, xxi 2; II Chron xxviii 3, xxxiii 2; Ezekiel, often); (d) "[they] have filled . . . it from one end to the other" (cf. II Kings xxi 16); (e) "do not give your daughters . . ." (cf. Deut vii 3); (f) "do not ever seek their peace or welfare" (cf. Deut xxiii 7 [6E]); (g) "that you may be strong" (cf. Deut xi 8); (h) "eat the good things of the land . . ." (cf. Isa i 19; Gen xlv 18); (i) "bequeath it to your sons forever" (cf. Ezek xxxvii 25b).

How can they in good conscience again ask for forgiveness in view of what has taken place in the past? The rhetorical question of Ezra is to the point! Yahweh did not then requite them to the extent their sins deserved. If their abominations continue, can they expect anything less than utter destruction? Can they hope for the good fortune of a remnant, such as they are now, who escaped the first destruction? Such conduct cannot be condoned; the guilty ones cannot abide in his presence. Thus, the whole prayer was directed toward the assembled members of the community in the hope that the guilty ones might take the necessary steps to rid themselves of contamination.

10. REPENTANCE OF THE JEWS
(x 1–44)†

Response to Ezra's prayer sermon

X 1 While Ezra, weeping and prostrating himself before the house of God, was praying and confessing, a very large congregation of men, women and children of Israel assembled themselves around him—for all the people wept profusely. 2 Then Shecaniah the son of Jehiel, of the sons of Elam replied to Ezra: "We have wronged our God in that we married foreign wives from the peoples of the land, but now there is, despite this, still hope for Israel. 3 Let us now make a covenant with our God to eject all the [foreign] wives and their children in accordance with the advice of *my lord* and those who fear the commandment of our God and let it be done according to the law. 4 Arise! for it is your duty; we are with you. Act with determination!" 5 Then Ezra arose and made the officials of the priests, the Levites, and all Israel swear to act in accordance with this proposition, and they swore. 6 Ezra then left the place before the house of God and went to the room of Jehohanan the son of Eliashib where he lodged*b* without eating food or drinking water because he continued mourning over the unfaithfulness of the exiles.

The assembly and its decision

7 So they circulated a proclamation in Judah and Jerusalem directing all the exiles to assemble themselves at Jerusalem;

† Ezra x 1–6 ‖ I Esdras viii 91–ix 2; 7–17 ‖ I Esdras ix 3–17; 18–44 ‖ I Esdras ix 18–36.

a–a MT "the Lord"; but cf. I Esdras viii 90 "as you and those . . . decide."
b MT has "he went," which is probably a scribal error. Cf. I Esdras ix 2, and Syr.

8 anyone who fails to appear within three days in accordance with the demand of the officials and elders will have all his possessions forfeited and he himself will be excluded from the congregation of the exiles. 9 Then all the men of Judah and Benjamin assembled themselves at Jerusalem within three days —it was the twentieth day of the ninth month. All the people sat down in the plaza before the house of God, trembling because of the matter and the torrents of rain. 10 Ezra the priest arose and said to them: "You have been unfaithful and have married foreign wives, thus adding to the guilt of Israel. 11 Therefore make confession to Yahweh God of your fathers, do his pleasure and separate yourselves from the peoples of the land and from the foreign wives." 12 The whole congregation responded and cried with a loud voice, "Just so; we must act as you have commanded us. 13 But the people are numerous and it is the season of rain; it is impossible to stand in the open and the job cannot be done in a day or two, for many of us have transgressed in this thing. 14 Let now our officials have charge of the whole congregation and let all those in our cities who have married foreign wives come at appointed times, together with the elders and judges of each city, until the hot anger of our God on account of this thing is turned away from us." 15 Only Jonathan the son of Asahel and Jahzeiah the son of Tikvah were ᶜopposed to thisᶜ and Meshullam and Shabbethai the Levite supported them. 16 But the exiles did so. Ezra the priest selectedᵈ men who were family heads for their families, all of them by name; they sat down on the first day of the tenth month to look into the matter. 17 By the first day of the first month they had finished [considering] every one of the men who had married foreign wives.

The list of those who had married foreign wives

18 Among the sons of the priests who had married foreign wives were found the following: of the sons of Jeshua the son of

---

ᶜ⁻ᶜ LXX "with me"; i.e., with Ezra. See COMMENT on vss. 18–44.
ᵈ Singular for MT plural, because Ezra evidently made the selection himself. Cf. I Esdras ix 16; some MSS have singular.

Jozadak and his brothers: Maaseiah, Eliezer, Jarib, and Gedaliah.
19 They agreed to put away their wives; *their guilt offering* was
a ram from the flock for their guilt. 20 Of the sons of Immer:
Hanani and Zebadiah. 21 Of the sons of Harim: Maaseiah, Elijah,
Shemaiah, Jehiel, and Uzziah. 22 Of the sons of Pashhur:
Elioenai, Maaseiah, Ishmael, Nethanel, Jozabad, and Eleasah.
23 Of the sons of the Levites: Jozabad, Shimei, Kelaiah—that is,
Kelita—Pethahiah, Judah, and Eliezer. 24 Of the singers: Eliashib; of the gatekeepers: Shallum, Telem, and Uri. 25 Of the
Israelites, the following: of the sons of Parosh: Ramiah, Izziah,
Malchijah, Mijamin, Eleazar, Malchijah, and Benaiah. 26 Of the
sons of Elam: Mattaniah, Zechariah, Jehiel, Abdi, Jeremoth,
and Elijah. 27 Of the sons of Zattu: Elioenai, Eliashib, Mattaniah, Jeremoth, Zabad, and Aziza. 28 Of the sons of Bebai:
Jehohanan, Hananiah, Zabbai, and Athlai 29 Of the sons of
Bani[f]: Meshullam, Malluch, Adaiah, Jashub, Sheal, and Jer-
amoth. 30 Of the sons of Pahath-moab: Adna, Chelal, Benaiah,
Maaseiah, Mattaniah, Bezalel, Binnui, and Manasseh. 31 Of the
sons of Harim: Eliezer, Isshiah, Malchijah, Shemaiah, Shimeon,
32 Benjamin, Malluch, and Shemariah. 33 Of the sons of
Hashum: Mattenai, Mattattah, Zabad, Eliphelet, Jeremai,
Manasseh, and Shimei. 34 Of the sons of Bani: Maadai, Amram,
Uel, 35 Benaiah, Bedeiah, Cheluhi, 36 Vaniah[g], Meremoth,
Eliashib, 37 Mattaniah, Mattenai and Jaasu. 38 [h]Of the sons[h]
of Binnui: Shimei, 39 Shelemiah, Nathan, Adaiah, 40 Machnadbai, Shashai, Sharai, 41 Azarel, Shelemiah, Shemariah, 42 Shallum, Amariah and Joseph. 43 Of the sons of Nebo: Jeiel, Mattithiah, Zabad, Zebina, Jaddai, Joel, and Benaiah. 44 All these
had married foreign wives, but [i]they sent away the wives and
children.[i]

e-e So for MT "they gave their hand." Cf. I Esdras ix 20.
f LXX[B] "Banoui," but "Binnui" appears in vs. 38. Rudolph thinks Bigvai
ought to be read here since Bani occurs in vs. 34.
g Probably corrupt, but cf. LXX[A] and I Esdras ix 34.
h-h MT "and Bani." Cf. LXX "the sons of Bani and sons of Semei."
i-i MT "and there were from them wives and they put sons," which makes no
sense. I Esdras ix 36, "they sent them away with [their] children," is the
basis for our translation. See also J. Prignaud, RB 71 (1964), 377.

Notes

x 2. *Shecaniah.* For form of name cf. *Sa-kan-da-da,* Tallquist, APN, p. 190b; and *Sa-ak-nu* in *Archives royales de Mari,* II, 1950, 135, line 3.

hope for Israel. For use of the phrase see Jer xxxi 17; Job xi 18, xiv 7; Ruth i 12; Lam iii 29; 1QH 3:20; 6:6; 9:14.

3. *make a covenant with.* This is a typical suzerainty covenant in which the terms are binding only on the vassal or inferior party, as is confirmed by the oath sworn in vs. 5.

the [foreign] wives. I Esdras viii 90 "our wives," a stronger term. That foreign wives are meant is clear from vs. 2.

the law. Here doubtless refers to the regulation issued by Ezra (cf. Neh viii), since there is no prohibition against marrying foreigners in the Pentateuchal legislation, though there are strong hints elsewhere about its undesirability.

7. *circulated a proclamation.* "To make a proclamation" (*h'byr qwl*) is a late expression found first in *P* (Exod xxxvi 6). It was used by the Chronicler in connection with Hezekiah's Passover invitation (II Chron xxx 5), with Cyrus' decree granting release of the Jews (II Chron xxxvi 22; Ezra i 1), and with the celebration of the Feast of Tabernacles in Neh viii 15.

8. *within three days.* See also 1QSa 1:25–27—three days' sanctification required before assembly on certain occasions.

will have all his possessions forfeited. yhrm—earlier the word was used in connection with the ban, i.e., the devotion of something to Yahweh, hence rendering the object tabu for ordinary use.

9. *the ninth month.* The month of Chislev, i.e., December of the year of Ezra's arrival.

trembling. mr'ydym, used only here and Dan x 11; it is a poetic word and signifies visible agitation.

10. *unfaithful. m'l,* a late word meaning "failure to measure up to expectations."

11. *make confession.* For this meaning of *twdh* see F. Horst, ZAW 47 (1929), 50 ff., and H. Grimme, ZAW 58 (1940/41), 234–40.

19. *They agreed.* Literally "they gave their hand." Cf. Ezek xvii 18; II Kings x 15.

20. *Zebadiah.* See NOTE on viii 8.

25. I Esdras ix 26 has "Asebeias" for the second "Malchijah."

28. *Zabbai.* See Nehemiah, Sec. 4, NOTE on iii 20.

34. *Bani.* Schneider reads "Bigvai" here. See textual note *f*.

39. *Shelemiah.* Cf. vs. 41; Neh iii 30, xiii 13. *Lšlmy* occurs on a tomb-

stone at Azor dating from the sixth century B.C. (*The Israel Digest,*
January 6, 1961, p. 7).

41. *Shelemiah.* Cf. NOTE on vs. 39.

COMMENT

[Response of the leaders to Ezra's prayer sermon, x 1–6]:
Chapter x continues the story begun in the preceding chapter though
it switches from the first to the third person, perhaps reflecting the
author's use of a source other than the memoirs of Ezra (Eissfeldt,
EAT, p. 738). Noth thinks the switch was made by the Chronicler
(ÜS, p. 147), Rudolph, p. 93 (following K. Budde) thinks this part
is based on another segment of the Ezra memoirs where first person
replaced the third. See also Kittel, GVI, III, pp. 570–75. This
part was modified in some points by the editor. In any case, the
present story reflects profound psychological perception in showing
that Ezra's prayer and personal conduct produced the hoped-for
effect. His actions drew the attention of a large group of men,
women, and children who caught his spirit and joined in his self-
abasement. Shecaniah the layman came forward as spokesman for
his brethren; though he is not listed as one of the guilty, he identifies
himself with them as Ezra had done (ix 6 ff.). Despite the gravity
of the situation and the persistence of the intermarriage problem
(see COMMENT on Sec. 19 of Nehemiah, xiii 23 ff.), he voices
hope for the community. His proposal for dealing with the matter
was obviously in harmony with the sentiment of Ezra. What appears
ruthless to us may have been regarded as unjustified by the author
of Ruth. The Book of Ruth is regarded by most scholars as a reaction against the demands of Ezra-Nehemiah, though not as its
original purpose. It should be observed that the question of intermarriage does not exist in Ruth, because she had already become
a convert, that is, first she turns to the faith of Naomi and becomes
an Israelite, and then she marries. Ezra-Nehemiah grapples with
the marriage of Jews with unconverted people; conversion is not
remotely hinted at. The only possible point of contact would be that
a maiden like Ruth was allowed to convert and become an Israelite,
or that Judahite males married Moabite girls to begin with, contrary, presumably, to law (cf. Deut xxiii 3). But actually, these
practices are not specifically prohibited by the law of Moses, though

in Ezra ix 1 the Moabites are brought in through the combination
of laws concerning intermarriage with the Canaanites and the prohibition against the Moabites and Ammonites having a place in the
congregation of the Lord. Cf. J. M. Myers, *The Linguistic and
Literary Form of the Book of Ruth,* 1955.

But the situation faced by Ezra required stern measures if the
community of Yahweh was to survive. One need only recall that
one of the political expedients employed by the Hebrews in the
process of the conquest of Canaan was absorption (see Albright,
Archaeology and the Religion of Israel, p. 102; BASOR 89 [Febru-
ary 1943], 16). The little community was in grave danger of being
absorbed in the syncretism of its stronger and more powerful neighbors. The recommendation of Shecaniah amounted to a concession
to Ezra, whose decision was accepted as authoritative. His exhortation in vs. 4 reminds us of that of the Deuteronomist in Josh i 6, 9
(cf. I Chron xxii 16). Ezra accepted the challenge and put the
congregation under oath to carry out the provisions suggested by
Shecaniah for the purpose of guarding against repudiation of the
agreement. Nehemiah also bound the people with an oath (xiii 25)
not to intermarry, but his efforts apparently proved ineffectual. The
difference may have been the method employed by Ezra and the
legal (religious) sanction imposed by him ("the commandment of
our God"). The seriousness of the infraction in Ezra's view is shown
by his further fasting in Jehohanan's room.

Verse 6 is exceedingly important for the dating of Ezra. The
crucial point is the identity of this Jehohanan—whether he was the
high priest Jehohanan, simply an otherwise unknown priest by the
name of Jehohanan, or an entirely different person. Eliashib was
high priest in the time of Nehemiah (iii 1, xiii 28). Jehohanan was
high priest in the reign of Darius II (424–405), as we know from one
of the Elephantine papyri dated in the seventeenth year of his reign
(AP, Nos. 30, 31). Three years earlier—i.e., in the fourteenth year
of Darius II—Jedoniah and his associates had sent a letter to the
same officials, that is, Bagoas and Jehohanan, without response,
which means that the latter occupied the office in ca. 411 B.C.
He seems to have come into disfavor soon after 408 B.C. because of
the slaying of his brother Jeshua in the temple. Just when he assumed
office is uncertain; but nothing is said about him in the memoirs
of Nehemiah. One point appears certain—Ezra came after Nehemiah since Jehohanan would hardly have had separate quarters,

even as a priest, as early as 458 B.C., the traditional date of Ezra. Cf. Albright, JBL 40 (1921), 121 ff. I Esdras ix 1 says Ezra went to "the priestly dwelling" of Jehohanan; hence this Jehohanan was a priest. It is quite probable that he was more than an ordinary priest since Ezra, an important official with Persian credentials, would hardly have been quartered in an ordinary priest's apartment. More-over, the Book of Ezra mentions the high priest only once (vii 5, in connection with Ezra's relationship, referring to Aaron).

[Summoning the assembly and its decision, 7–17]: Following through on Shecaniah's suggestion, Ezra issued a summons to all the returnees requiring them to appear at Jerusalem within three days. This was an oral proclamation carried by delegates from Ezra throughout Judah and Jerusalem. His authority as representative of the Persian government and the attachment of a heavy penalty as-sessed against those failing to comply lent it force. Enforcement, and perhaps also the circulation, of the proclamation was placed in the hands of the local officials. The result was that "all the men of Judah and Benjamin"—which may be a geographical reference, though the expression "Judah and Benjamin" is a favorite one of the Chronicler (cf. I Chron ix 3; II Chron xi 1, 12, 23, xv 2, 8, 9, xxv 5, xxxi 1, xxxiv 9; Neh xi 36, xii 34, 1QM 1:2)—appeared within the specified time, though the season was anything but fa-vorable. It was the time of the winter rain (*gšm*). Those who gath-ered there were shaken by the gravity of the matter concerning which they had been summoned. The bad weather added to the emotional reaction of the people.

Ezra's address to the people makes the following points: (a) they had been unfaithful, as shown by the marrying of foreign wives; (b) they thus added to the guilt of Israel; (c) to avert disaster they should have confessed their share in the guilt by acting reso-lutely to do Yahweh's will and to sever all ties with the peoples of the land. Despite the favorable reaction of the congregation to Ezra's demand, compliance was not a simple matter. This in itself indicates how widespread the practice of intermarriage had been and why such drastic measures were essential. The plan proposed by the majority was opposed by a few (vs. 15), who may have pressed for more immediate action; they do not seem to have resisted the demand itself (but see Ryle, pp. 136 f., and Galling, p. 215). The family chiefs selected by Ezra took three months to investigate the matter; at the end of that period they presented their report and, apparently, the list of those who had erred and were ready to make amends.

[The list of those who had married foreign wives, 18–44]: The order of the list follows that of chapter viii—clergy first, then laymen—rather than that of Ezra ii (‖ Neh vii), which reverses the sequence. On the basis of the unemended text, 27 names of clergy occur and 84 names of laymen, or a total of 111 persons in a group of around 30,000. The totals vary somewhat in the lists: LXX has 27 clergy and 82 (+2 or 3) laymen, which comes to 109 (+2 or 3, due to the uncertainty in the reading at the end of vs. 37 and the beginning of vs. 38); I Esdras ix has 26 clergy and 75 (or 76) laymen, which comes to 101 (+1, if Simon Chosamaeus is to be read as two names). The number of offenders is extraordinarily small considering the furor and the census figures in chapter ii. Three explanations suggest themselves: (a) the problem was not as serious as appears on the surface, (b) this is only a partial list, (c) the reform was not as successful as the Chronicler would have us believe.

The first possibility can be dismissed at once, since the difficulty was noted more than once (Mal ii 10 ff.; Neh xiii 23 ff.) and was a threat to the community, as evidenced by the machinations of Sanballat, Tobiah, and Geshem. The third suggestion is given some credence by Batten, p. 346, who thinks the Greek of vs. 15 may reflect a portion of the Ezra memoirs that escaped the Chronicler's revision. It reads as follows: "Only Jonathan the son of Asael and Jaziah the son of Thekone were with me in this, and Mesoulam and Sabathai the Levite helped them." (Cf. also I Esdras ix 14–15.) This might mean that there was relatively little real support for Ezra's drastic move and could account for the meager list. But vs. 15 may have to do with the method of procedure, which would put an entirely different construction on the matter. That brings up the second, and most likely, of the suggestions noted above—that only a fragment of the original list has survived. Some scholars (e.g., Schneider, pp. 158 f.) see a schematic arrangement in the list of laymen corresponding to the Chronicler's favorite theme of twelve, which could indicate the presence in the list of only representative names, pointing to the extension of guilt throughout the whole community. Galling, p. 215, thinks that while a few lesser groups may be represented, the list includes, for the most part, members of the upper classes. The absence of temple slaves and

Solomon's servants seems to support that conclusion. It has also been suggested (Rudolph, p. 97) that the full list would have proved embarrassing to the Chronicler in view of his conception of the religious community. But would not the appearance of prominent names have been equally disconcerting? The writer was not attempting to minimize the seriousness of the intermarriage problem; as a matter of fact he clearly shows how widespread it really was by implicating so many prominent families—if the list originally included representatives from the twelve groups. It was not the Chronicler's habit to play down what he considered to be evils in Yahweh's community.

NEHEMIAH

1. NEHEMIAH DISTRESSED BY
NEWS OF THE CONDITIONS IN JERUSALEM
(i 1–11)

Report on Jerusalem

I ¹ The history of Nehemiah the son of Hacaliah. Now it happened in the month of Chislev of the twentieth year while I was in the citadel of Susa, ² that Hanani, one of my brothers, with some of the Judeans, arrived. I inquired of them about the Jews, those who had escaped and those who survived from the captivity, and about Jerusalem. ³ They informed me, "The survivors who remained there in the province after the captivity are in dire straits and in disgrace, the wall of Jerusalem is broken down and its gates ruined by fire." ⁴ Now when I heard these things, I sat down, wept and mourned for days while I fasted and prayed before the God of the heavens.

Prayer of Nehemiah

⁵ I said, "O Yahweh God of the heavens, you great and awe-inspiring God, who maintains the covenant and devotion with those who love him and keep his commands; ⁶ Let your ear be attentive and your eyes open so that you may listen to the prayer of your servant which I am praying before you now day and night on behalf of your servants, the Israelites, confessing the sins of the Israelites which we have committed against you—both I and my father's house have sinned. ⁷ We have acted very malevolently toward you in that we have not observed the commands, the statutes, and the judgments which you enjoined upon Moses your servant. ⁸ Remember the warning you directed to Moses your servant, saying, 'If you are unfaithful, I will disperse you among the nations, ⁹ but if you return to me, keep my

commands and act accordingly, though your scattered ones be
as far as the end of the heavens; thence will I gather them and
bring them to the place where I chose to establish my name.'
10 They are your servants and your people whom you redeemed
by your great might and your strong hand. 11 O Yahweh, let
now your ear be attentive to the prayer of your servant and the
prayer of your servants who desire to reverence your name and
grant success to your servant today and accord him mercy in
the sight of this man." I was then the king's cupbearer*.

a See NOTE.

NOTES

i 1. *Hacaliah.* Meaning uncertain; name occurs only here and x 2 in
the Bible. One of Cleopatra III's generals bore the name (Josephus *Antiquities* XIII.X, xiii). It is also found in Alexandrian Jewish papyri—
borne by a Jewish landholder of the Bousirite district (13 B.C.); a son of
Damion (A.D. 106); and a son of Petros, a descendant of the Persian
Jews who resided in the Heliopolitan nome (cf. V. A. Tcherikover and
A. Fuks, *Corpus Papyrorum Judicarum*, 1957, I, p. 17, n. 45; II, Nos.
145, line 16, 337, line 1, 417, line 4). Nehemiah, the name of a slave,
occurs in one of the Samaria papyri dating from the fourth century B.C.
(See Cross, BA 26 [1963], 111 f.).

of the twentieth year. Rudolph, p. 102, thinks the text following
Chislev ought to read "in the nineteenth year of Artaxerxes the king,"
since the month Chislev is later than the month Nisan in ii 1 (but cf.
E. R. Thiele, *The Mysterious Numbers of the Hebrew Kings*, 1951, p. 35,
n.). There were two systems of time reckoning in Israel, one beginning
in the spring, the other in the autumn. Two possibilities present themselves here: one suggested by Rudolph—that the phrase "the nineteenth
year of Artaxerxes the king" dropped out after Chislev because of the
similarity of the last consonants of *kslw* (Chislev) and *hmlk* (the king),
the lacuna being filled in mechanically from ii 1; the other that the
twentieth year of Artaxerxes was regarded as beginning in the autumn
of the year. In the latter case, Chislev would be the third month of the
year and Nisan (ii 1) the seventh month. It is generally assumed that
Artaxerxes I is intended here. Josephus (*Antiquities* XI.v) says Nehemiah
came to Jerusalem in the twenty-fifth year of Xerxes, which is impossible
because Xerxes reigned for only twenty years (485–465). Perhaps
Josephus gives that name and date because he reserved Artaxerxes for
the time of Esther.

2. *Hanani.* Apparently the blood brother of Nehemiah; if so, the one in charge of Jewish affairs at Jerusalem during Nehemiah's absence (vii 2). For name see AP, Nos. 21, 38, and W. F. Albright, BA 9, (February 1946), 14.

those who . . . the captivity. Probably those Jews who escaped the captivity of Nebuchadnezzar.

5. *God of the heavens.* See Ezra, Sec. 1, NOTE on i 2.

8. *the warning.* Heb. *hdbr;* the word which here includes both threat and promise.

11. *this man.* I.e., the king, Artaxerxes.

cupbearer. LXX[B] has *eunouchos* "eunuch"; LXX[A] has *oinochoos* "cupbearer." Origen *To Africanus* refers to *Neemias oinochoos Tou Basileos kai eunouchos autou* "Nehemiah cupbearer of the king and his eunuch" (*Library of Greek Fathers and Ecclesiastical Historians,* XVI, p. 360).

COMMENT

At the beginning of the Nehemiah section of the Ezra-Nehemiah-Chronicles complex stands a simple statement informing the reader that what follows is the history of Nehemiah. Whether this was the heading of the source used by the compiler or whether he inserted it himself is not known. Two other persons of the same name are mentioned elsewhere (Ezra ii 2; Neh iii 16, vii 7). The name Nehemiah is composed of two elements—*nhm,* "comfort," "console," and *yh,* a shortened form of Yahweh—and is closely related to such names as *nhwm, nhmi, mnhm. nhm* is found on seals from Lachish (Tufnell, *Lachish III: The Iron Age,* p. 341) and *nhmyhw* appears on a seal of unknown origin (cf. Diringer, *Le iscrizioni antico-ebraiche Palestinesi,* p. 190), but of pre-exilic date. Our Nehemiah was apparently highly esteemed in later times. Sirach praises him (xlix 13) but makes no reference to Ezra. II Macabees i 18–36 connects Nehemiah with the kindling of the fire ceremony at the Feast of Tabernacles and credits him with memoirs and the foundation of a library (ii 13).

[Report on conditions at Jerusalem, i 1–4]: Nehemiah was present at the citadel of Susa when a detachment of Jews arrived from the west. Susa was the winter residence of the kings of Persia (cf. Xenophon *Cyropaedia* VIII.vi.22). It was the place where Ahasuerus held his great feast (Esther i) and Daniel had his vision (Dan viii). The citadel (*byrh*) was the fortress of the city (see

Encyclopaedia Biblica (Hebrew), II, col. 51). The time of the Jews' arrival there is specified exactly (see NOTE on vs. 1 above) and, as it now stands, would place the event in December 445 B.C. if the reign is that of Artaxerxes I, as appears virtually certain since Eliashib the grandfather of Jonathan (Neh xii 10 f.) was high priest. In 408, when the sons of Sanballat (Nehemiah's opponent) were in charge of affairs at Samaria, Jonathan was high priest (see Cowley, AP, No. 30). This communication from the Jews of Elephantine to Bigvai the governor of Judea is dated in the seventeenth year of Darius II (408 B.C.). But there is mention of a letter to the high priest Johanan when the trouble began three years earlier (line 19). On the identity of Johanan see Pavlovsky, *Biblica* 38 (1957), 291 ff. Who Hanani was is uncertain. See NOTE to i 2. W. R. Arnold (JBL 31 (1912), 30 f.) thinks he was the Hanani mentioned in Cowley (AP, Nos. 21 and 38) who delivered the Passover decree to the Jews at Elephantine in 419 B.C. Schneider, p. 163, thinks he was the brother of Nehemiah (vii 2).

The reason why the group of Jews came with him to Susa is also uncertain, but see Olmstead, HPE, p. 314. He thinks it was a private delegation sent by the leaders of Jerusalem directly to the king. Diplomatic channels could not be used since Judah was still under Samaritan control, and correspondence would thus have had to pass through hostile hands. To judge from the report to Nehemiah, it seems that their mission had something to do with the state of affairs in Judah; perhaps the Jewish leaders were attempting to purge themselves of false accusations which resulted from troubles in the west subsequent to Artaxerxes' accession. In any event, it is doubtful that Jerusalem had been directly involved. There is not the slightest hint that any misfortune had befallen the temple. Had the Jews been implicated in that unrest, the temple surely would not have been left untouched. Moreover, the city had been in conditions like those described in vs. 3 ever since the days of the captivity. Compare what happened to Babylon after the revolt under Zopyrus: Xerxes destroyed the city, leveled the temple of Esagila, and removed the great symbol of Bel Marduk (Olmstead, HPE, p. 237). Some scholars think the devastation of Jerusalem was the result of more recent events. Cf. Morgenstern, HUCA 27 (1956), 101–179; 28 (1957), 15–48; 31 (1960), 1–29; Olmstead, HPE, pp. 313 f.; S. A. Cook in *Cambridge Ancient History*, III, 1925, pp. 413, 488. Gelin, p. 65, n. f., thinks several attempts were made to get Persian permission to rebuild the walls (Ezra iv 6—in the time of Xerxes; Ezra iv 12–13, 16—in the time of Artaxerxes, clearly,) but favorable action came only after the Egyptian revolt after 448 B.C.

The walls of Jerusalem could hardly have been effectively repaired so long as Jerusalem and Judah were under the direct control of Samaria. That consideration alone is responsible for the great care taken by the Jewish authorities not to overstep their bounds. It is altogether possible, however, that the new events in the west, particularly in Egypt, had some bearing on the Jewish mission to the great king. The Jews had always been friendly to Persia but if that friendship was to be maintained they would have to have a free hand in Judah, untrammeled by hostile powers working for their destruction or at least for the maintenance of the debilitating status quo. Then too a relatively strong Judah friendly to Persia could be of great service to the king by way of discouraging dissidents in the western provinces of the empire from hostile activity.

The effect of the report on Nehemiah (cf. Josephus *Antiquities* XI.v.6) points to the sensitive nature of the man as well as to the quality of his faith. Though his reaction may be typically oriental and one expected of religious leaders, it reveals much about the character of this Jewish layman so highly esteemed by the Persian court. Amid the pagan surroundings he held firm in his religious practices.

[The prayer, 5–11]: Most commentators regard Nehemiah's prayer as a construction of the Chronicler—or at least greatly expanded by him (e.g. Mowinckel [in *Studien zu dem Buche Ezra-Nehemia, II,* p. 18.], Hölscher, Schneider, Galling, Bowman. Rudolph argues for its authenticity). To be sure, it is stylistically similar to the other prayers recorded in his work and is particularly rich in Deuteronomic phraseology. It is characterized by the attitude of self-involvement of the supplicant (the pronouns *we* and *our* are prominent—cf. I Chron xvii 20, xxix 13, 14–16; II Chron xx 7, 11, 12; Ezra ix 6 ff.; Neh ix 32 ff.). But all of these qualities are present also in Dan ix; and Nehemiah's prayer, like most of our prayers today, was certainly in conformity with contemporary usage. The Deuteronomist had a powerful influence in postexilic times and his language and ideas are written all over the literature of the period. The present prayer is no exception. Compare the following: vs. 5 with Deut vii 9, 21; vs. 6 with I Kings

viii 29, II Chron vi 20, 40, vii 15, Ps cxxx 2; vss. 8 f. with Deut xxx
1–4; vs. 10 with Deut ix 29. The strongest argument for expansion
by the Chronicler is Josephus (*Antiquities* XI.v.6), who records a
much shorter prayer: "How long, O Lord, wilt thou overlook our
nation, while it suffers so great miseries, and while we are made
prey and the scorn of all men?" Some think the last words of the
prayer here in Neh i—"this man"—indicate it is out of place and
ought to follow ii 4. But Nehemiah undoubtedly prayed on this
occasion, particularly the kind of prayer given here, as well as later
before the king in ii 4.

[THE ROYAL CUPBEARER, 11d]: The cupbearer was an important
official in the royal household; he was also a eunuch since he
served in the queen's presence (ii 6). See NOTE on vs. 11 above
on "cupbearer" as rendered by LXX^B. Herodotus (III.34) says the
office of cupbearer was an honored one among the Persians. Tobit
i 22 says Esarhaddon made his cupbearer (Ahikar) second to
himself in the administration of the kingdom. E. Weidner's recent
study, "Hof- und Harems-Erlasse assyrischer Könige," AfO 17
(1956), 264 f., confirms the cupbearer's importance. Regulations
were set for cupbearers, courtiers, eunuchs, gatekeepers of the
palace, singers, and bakers, thus pointing to their significance in the
economy of royal affairs. For the situation in Egypt see Gardiner,
Ancient Egyptian Onomastica, I, p. 43*, No. 122. In the middle
Assyrian period the eunuch was a highly trained and important
personage, a tradition apparently adopted by the Persians.

2. NEHEMIAH GOES TO JERUSALEM
BY PERMISSION OF ARTAXERXES
(ii 1–10)

II ¹Now in the month of Nisan in the twentieth year of Artaxerxes the king, when *ªI had charge of the wineª*, I took the wine and gave it to the king. Verily I was depressed *ᵇin his presence.ᵇ* ²So the king said to me, "Why are you so depressed? You are not sick! This is nothing else than heart sickness." Then I was exceedingly alarmed ³and replied to the king, "May the king live forever! Why should I not be depressed when the city, the site of the graves of my fathers, is in ruins and its gates destroyed by fire?" ⁴The king then said to me, "What is it that you want?" I prayed to the God of the heavens ⁵as I answered the king, "If it please the king and if your servant has found favor in your sight, then send me to Judah, to the city of the graves of my fathers, that I may rebuild it." ⁶The king asked me [while the queenᶜ was sitting beside him], "How long will your mission take and when will you return?" So the king approved and sent me after I had given him a definite time. ⁷Then I said to the king, "If the king approves, let them give me orders to the governors of [the province] Across the River that they may permit me to pass through until I reach Judah; ⁸also an order for Asaph, the keeper of the king's forest, that he may furnish me with timber for the beams of the gates *ᵈof the citadel guarding the houseᵈ* and for the wall of the city and for the house which I am to occupy." The king gave [them] to me because the good hand of my God was with me. ⁹When I came to the

a–a So with LXX. MT "wine [was] before him [the king]."
b–b LXX "no one else was present" (literally, "before him"); LXXᴬ adds, "and I was gloomy."
c LXX "pallake," "concubine." The Hebrew word (*šgl*) occurs only here and Ps xlv 10, where LXX has *basilissa*, "queen." Vulg. has *regina* "queen."
d–d Omitted by LXX.

governors of [the province] Across the River, I gave them the orders of the king. The king had sent along with me a cavalry escort. 10 When Sanballat the Horonite and Tobiah the Ammonite official heard about it, it displeased them very greatly that someone had come to seek the welfare of the Israelites.

NOTES

ii 1. *I was*. Reading the *l'* "not" as asseverative. Cf. LXX[L] "I was before him," thus omitting the negative.

6. *the queen*. The queen of Artaxerxes was Damaspia. She may have had something to do with the king's decision, for the influence of women was strong during Artaxerxes' reign (W. W. Tarn, *Cambridge Ancient History*, VI, 1927, pp. 2–3). Cf. also the case of Esther. The scene was apparently private since queens were not ordinarily present at public banquets. But see Dan v 2, where wives and concubines are mentioned.

8. *Asaph*. Nothing more is known about this man. Josephus (*Antiquities* XI.v.6) says Addaios was governor of Syria, Phoenicia, and Samaria. J. A. Bewer (JBL 43 [1924], 225 f.) thinks the name was corrupted from LXX ACAΦOC to ADDAIOS. There were local parks under the care of officials of the Persian government. See Xenophon *Oeconomicus* IV.13, Diodorus XVI.41; for further references see E. Meyer, *Geschichte des Altertums*, IV, Pt. I, p. 55, notes 2, 4.

the gates of the citadel guarding the house. I.e., the temple. The word for citadel is *byrh*, an Akkadian loanword meaning fortress. Cf. L. H. Vincent and A. M. Steve, *Jerusalem de l'Ancien Testament*, I, 1954, p. 242—it was located north of the temple area; A. Parrot, *Golgotha*, 1957, p. 32, n. 5; and IEJ 7 (1957), 140.

the house which I am to occupy. Literally "the house I shall enter." Does it refer to a special house (the governor's residence)?

9. *the governors*. Refers to the local authorities mentioned in vss. 10, 19.

a cavalry escort. Literally "captains of the army and horsemen." For translation see Kapelrud, QAEN, p. 52.

10. *Sanballat*. A Babylonian name. [d]Sin-uballit "Sin has called into life." See Tallquist, *Neubabylonisches Namenbuch*, 1905, p. 276, item 168.

Tobiah the Ammonite official. Literally "the servant of the king," which in this instance means an official of the king. *ṭbyh h'bd h'mmwni* "Tobiah, the slave, the Ammonite." For the meaning of the title see C. C. McCown, BA 20 (1957), 71 ff. Tobiah was a Yahwist, though a syncretist. The term Ammonite does not mean foreigner as such, i.e., one from Ammon, but rather the governor of Ammon. Cf. W. F. Albright, "Geschichte und Altes Testament," in *Festschrift A. Alt* (Tübingen, 1953), p. 4, n. 5.

COMMENT

For some reason Nehemiah had no opportunity to present his case to the king for several months after his conference with Hanani and his group, which had occurred in the winter (the month of Chislev). The time here is spring (Nisan, i.e., April, 445 B.C.). The interval must have had an increasingly debilitating effect on Nehemiah: he was doubtless engaged much in fasting and prayer, all of which took their toll. Consequently, he could not hide his gloom from the king. In view of Nehemiah's serious nature and the gravity of the situation, his physical appearance can hardly be regarded as a device to attract the king's attention. In any event, the king observed the contrast between Nehemiah's expression and, presumably, that of his guests at the banquet (such banquets were common; cf. I Esdras iii 1 ff. and Herodotus IX.110–11). Nehemiah had never appeared so depressed before. The king's question alarmed him because his dejection was a consequence of the investigation into the activities of the Jerusalem Jews that the king himself had been persuaded to order (Ezra iv 7, 8–23). The report on conditions in Jerusalem was ample evidence that the Samaritan authorities had succeeded by attrition in preventing the Jews from undertaking any effective measures to protect their city and its temple. It remained pretty much in the state it had been since the time of Zerubbabel unless there was a later destruction. See COMMENT on Sec. 1, i 1–4. Observe the personal basis of Nehemiah's appeal, a master stroke of diplomacy in view of the manifestly high standing of the cupbearer. It is in all probability no accident that nowhere in the conversation between Nehemiah and the king is Jerusalem mentioned by name; it is referred to as the city or the "site of the graves of my fathers." This evasion was probably the result of the suspicion of subversion aroused by the Samaritans, which had led to the temporary ban on all building.

The king's reponse to his cupbearer's complaint encouraged Nehemiah to ask for what would ease the burden of his heart—a

royal commission to go to Judah to carry out a program for rebuilding the defenses of Jerusalem. Cf. I Esdras iv 42 ff. for a
similar story about Darius. For Josephus' version see *Antiquities*
XI.v. Some details of Nehemiah's story are spelled out in vs. 8—
the citadel guarding the temple, the wall of the city, and a residence
for himself. The last could refer to the construction of an official
residence for the governor of the new province of Judah, which
had up till now been a portion of the province of Samaria; or it
could mean simply the repair of a house for his occupancy.

The assent of the king to Nehemiah's request apparently marked
only the initial step in protracted negotiations and preparations for
the mission. The first conversation took place early in 445 B.C.,
but according to Josephus (*Antiquities* XI.v) Nehemiah did not arrive in Jerusalem until five years later (his chronology is probably
correct, though the name of the king [Xerxes] is wrong. See NOTE
on i 1). What went on during the interval is clear from vss. 7–9.
Nehemiah requested orders for safe conduct by military escort
through the provinces of the western satrapies; these required careful preparation. His appeal for material assistance must have en-
tailed further consideration too. (The royal forests were doubtless
in the mountains of Lebanon, the source of timber for the construction of Solomon's temple [I Kings v; II Chron ii 8 f., 16] and for
the rebuilding of the temple in the reign of Darius [Ezra iii 7].
Darius I brought cedar wood from Lebanon for his palace at
Susa [Olmstead, HPE, p. 168; Meyer, *Geschichte des Altertums,*
IV, Pt. I, pp. 55 f., 82 f.]. Cf. also the assistance rendered by the
managers of the pharaoh's fields, W. Helck, *Zur Verwaltung des
Mittleren und Neuen Reichs,* 1958, pp. 103, 107, 108 ff., 111 ff.,
235. Cf. AGP, II, p. 118.) In all this good fortune, Nehemiah was
conscious of "the good hand of my God." He himself was the bearer
of the royal orders to be delivered to the imperial authorities in
Across the River. They did not look upon Nehemiah's venture with
favor but his preparations stood him in good stead because the
authorities were duly impressed by the royal escort and the official
documents.

Three of the local governors are named in vss. 10, 19. Sanballat,
who is called the Horonite, was a native of one of the Beth-horons,
though the epithet may signify more than a place of origin; it may
be partly a term expressing contempt, referring to his syncretism
as a devotee of the god Horon (cf. J. Gray, "The Canaanite God

Horon," JNES 8 [1949], 27–34. C. C. McCown thinks Sanballat
came from Horonaim in Moab [Isa xv 5] and was therefore of
doubtful ancestry [*Man, Morals and History,* 1958, pp. 121 f.]). He
was a descendant of the mixed group that settled in Samaria after the
Assyrian conquest (II Kings xvii 24, 29–31). His sons were apparently acting for their father in 408 because he was too old
(cf. Cowley, AP, No. 30, line 29). That accords well with his
activities around 440 B.C. when he was in his prime and had just
succeeded Rehum as governor (Ezra iv). He was undoubtedly a
Yahwist since his two sons had Yahweh names, but certainly not a
pure Yahwist as his rejection by the Jerusalem leaders demonstrates.
Tobiah too regarded himself as a Yahwist, as may be seen from
his association with Eliashib (Neh xiii). He was not an Ammonite;
he was governor of the Transjordan province of Ammon. (On
Tobiah, see B. Mazar, "The Tobiads," IEJ 7 [1957], 137–45,
229–38, and C. C. McCown, "The 'Araq el-Emir and the Tobiads,"
in BA 20 [September 1957], 63–76.) To judge from the literary
and archaeological sources, the Tobiads were an old and famous
family. Geshem (vs. 19) was also involved in the local conspiracy
against Nehemiah and his co-workers. As has been shown, he was
the father of Kain, the king of Kedar, who had united the north
Arabian tribes into a vast confederation covering the entire area
around the eastern and southern regions of the Dead Sea as far
as the Nile delta (see I. Rabinowitz, "Aramaic Inscriptions of the
Fifth Century B.C.E. from a North Arab Shrine in Egypt," JNES
15 [1956], 1–9; and F. M. Cross, Jr., BA 18 [1955], 46 f.). These
opponents of Nehemiah were not petty local princes; they were
Persian officials, at least nominally, and used their official status
to harass him. (Alt [KS, II, pp. 338–45] has correctly evaluated
the situation without the benefit of the Rabinowitz, McCown, and
Mazar articles. Cf. also Abel, AGP, II, pp. 119–23.) A man with
lesser courage might easily have succumbed to their wiles.

3. NEHEMIAH'S SECRET INSPECTION
OF JERUSALEM ANGERS THE OFFICIALS
(ii 11–20)

Tour of inspection

II   11 So I came to Jerusalem. After I had been there three days,
12 I arose in the night, I, together with a few men—I had not
told anyone what my God had inspired me to do *for Jerusalem*. Not even a beast was with me except the one upon
which I was riding. 13 I went out at night *by the Valley
Gate* toward* the Dragon's* Fountain to the Dung Gate and
examined* the walls* of Jerusalem which had been breached and
whose gates had been destroyed by fire. 14 Then I crossed over
to the Fountain Gate and to the Pool of the King but there was
not room enough for the beast I was riding to pass through.
15 So I went up by night through the valley and examined* the
wall; then I entered again through the Valley Gate and returned
16 without the local officials* knowing where I had gone or what
I was doing; nor had I as yet informed the Jews, the priests, the
nobles, *the local officials* and the other participants in the
task.

Report to the officials

17 So I said to them, "You see what straits we are in, that
Jerusalem is in ruins and its gates are destroyed by fire. Come

a–a LXX "for Israel."
b–b LXX "by the gate of the *golela*" (a transliteration of Heb. *gy' lylh*).
c LXX *pros*, "in the direction of." Note the Heb. *'l-pny* . . . *w'l* "in the
direction of . . . and to."
d LXX "figs."
e LXX reads *šbr* "smash" for *sbr* "examine." Cf. Alt, KS, III, p. 342, n. 1.
f LXX "wall."
g LXX "watchmen," "guards."
h–h Omitted by LXXᴮ.

now, let us restore the wall of Jerusalem that we may be held in derision no longer." [18] I told them how favorable the hand of my God had been to me and also the words of the king which he had spoken to me. *They replied,* "We will set to work building." And they supported the good work.

Reaction of the authorities

[19] When Sanballat the Horonite, Tobiah the Ammonite official, and Geshem the Arabian heard about it, they laughed at us and *derided us*. They said, "What is this thing you are doing? Are you going to rebel against the king?" [20] Then I gave them the following reply: "The God of the heavens will give us success and we, his servants, will *set to work building*; but you have no share or right or memorial in Jerusalem."

ⁱ⁻ⁱ LXX "I said."
ʲ⁻ʲ LXX "they came to us."
ᵏ⁻ᵏ Literally "rise and build." LXX reads *katharoi*, "pure," "right," "in the clear," for "rise." Both MT and LXX reflect the same text: MT reads *nqwm*, LXX reads *nqy(y)m*.

NOTES

ii 15. *the valley.* The Kidron Valley, since it alone appears to be referred to as *nhl*.

16. *the other participants in the task.* Not the laborers but those who were to participate in carrying out the plan of Nehemiah. Cf. H. Kaupel, *Biblica* 21 (1940), 40–44.

18. *set to work building.* Literally "rise and build."

19. *Tobiah the Ammonite.* See second NOTE on ii 10.

COMMENT

[Tour of inspection, ii 11–16]: Nehemiah's plan for the rehabilitation of Jerusalem had been in the process of formulation since the time he received the bad news from Hanani and his companions. So much is clear from the negotiations with the king and the whole tenor of the story here related. Now he had to devise a method of procedure, which required an on-the-spot evaluation of the situation. Hence he made his nocturnal inspection tour a short time after his arrival. On the three-day interval see Ezra viii 15, 32, x 8, 9; Esther iv 16. It may signify nothing more than a little while (John xvi 16). (Josephus does not mention an interval between the time of Nehemiah's arrival and inspection; indeed he makes no reference whatever to an inspection tour. According to him, Nehemiah immediately called a public assembly and made a speech to the people [*Antiquities* XI.v].)

The time and method chosen by Nehemiah are significant. With a small group of carefully selected men and only one donkey, he quietly set out on his mission. His plan of attack was kept secret so as not to arouse the people or to tip his hand prematurely to the enemies within or without (vss. 12, 16). With that first-hand information he confronted the officials and people of Jerusalem, who responded enthusiastically to his plan (vss. 17–18).

Verses 13–15 with iii 1–32 and xii 31–39 offer the best topographical description of Jerusalem in the Bible. To be sure not everything is clear to us, nor are the authorities agreed on the precise locations. The Valley Gate (II Chron xxvi 9) has been placed at various points around the city. See J. Simons, *Jerusalem in the Old Testament,* 1952, pp. 124 f., and also sketches and maps in M. Avi-Yonah, SY, I, Map 9, opposite p. 160 (presents sketches of locations by K. Galling and G. Dalman), as well as A. Alt, "Das Taltor von Jerusalem," PJB 24 [1928], 74–98; M. Burrows, BASOR 64 [December 1936], 11–21; K. Galling, *Biblisches Reallexikon,* 1937, cols. 301–2; Parrot, *Golgotha,* p. 30. It is most often located near the northwestern corner of the City of David. According to iii 13, the Dung Gate (apparently the same as the Potsherd Gate of Jer xix 2) was some five hundred yards away to the south (on the distance between the two gates see M. Burrows, AASOR 14 [1934], 131); hence it must have been at the extreme southern end of the city. The direction of Nehemiah's night ride was out through the Valley Gate, thence toward the Dragon's Fountain as far as the Dung Gate. The Dragon's Fountain, not mentioned elsewhere in the Bible, is generally identified with En-rogel, Job's well, at the juncture of the Valley of Hinnom and the Kidron Valley. The Fountain Gate was some 150 yards north of the Dung Gate, on the east side of the city, at the edge of the Kidron Valley. The pool of the king is uncertain but was certainly beyond the Fountain Gate (vs. 14). Just what is meant by 14b is obscure. Miss Kenyon's excavations now show that Nehemiah could not continue his course of inspection because of the massive ruins left by the overthrow of the city by the Babylonians. (See *Illustrated London News,* April 21, 1962, p. 619, and Fig. 8, p. 621, and PEQ [January–June 1963], p. 15; BA 27 [May 1964] 34–52.) Perhaps there was not room for the beast to pass inside the wall, so that Nehemiah rode up the valley, that is, the Kidron. Or, perhaps, when it was impossible to proceed farther he returned by the valley of the Kidron, which he had entered at the Dung Gate, and then continued back, the way he had come, to the Valley Gate. All this seems to indicate that he inspected the walls of the City of David only and not those of the temple area.

[Report to the officials, 17–18]: After his tour of inspection, Nehemiah revealed his plan to "them," that is, to those mentioned in vs. 16. It was based on his assessment of the situation and for the first time disclosed to the local people of standing the purpose of his mission, which was to rebuild the walls of Jerusalem. The wall itself was more than a protection for Jerusalem and its citizens. Its condition at the time was symbolic of the low esteem in which the Jews were held by their neighbors. Moreover, it was a reflection on the status of their religion in the eyes of surrounding peoples, and perhaps in the sight of the Persian officials of Across the River. Nehemiah saw clearly that the reproach could not be removed until the devoted Jews acted. Verse 18 makes it clear that he justified his mission religiously: Yahweh had shown his favor by granting him success in negotiations with the king. At any rate, his hearers were impressed and resolved to support the work to which he summoned them.

[The reaction of the authorities, 19–20]: Whether the king's firman (vss. 7–9) included specifics, such as authority to rebuild the walls, is not stated, but the local governors could not be kept in the dark for long. Hitherto they had succeeded fairly well in keeping the Jews demoralized but now they were forced to reckon with a man of vigor, armed with royal authority. At first they ridiculed the work. They knew full well what was involved in the rebuilding of the walls of Jerusalem. To them the work spelled rebellion, not against the Persian king as they intimated but rather against their authority, which they endeavored to maintain, in part at least, by intermarriage and casual participation in the religious

affairs of the Jews. Sanballat and Tobiah regarded themselves as
Yahwists and as such claimed certain rights, the granting of which
would have compromised the faith of the Jews. Nehemiah did not
confront them with his royal authority; he responded to their jests
by a declaration of faith in the power of God to bless the work
with success. Sanballat, Tobiah, and Geshem had no real religious
interest in Jerusalem. Their concern, as will appear later, lay elsewhere.

4. RECONSTRUCTION OF THE CITY WALLS
(iii 1–32)

III 1 Then Eliashib the high priest with his brothers, the priests, set to work and rebuilt the Sheep Gate; they repaired^a it and hung its doors and they repaired^a as far as the Tower of the Hundred [and] the Tower of Hananel. 2 Next to him the men of Jericho rebuilt and next to them^b Zaccur the son of Imri rebuilt. 3 The sons of Hassenaah rebuilt the Fish Gate; they repaired it and hung its doors [and fixed] its bolts and bars. 4 Next to them Meremoth the son of Uriah the son of Hakkoz reconstructed; next to him^c Meshullam the son of Berechiah the son of Meshezabel reconstructed and next to him^c Zadok the son of Baana reconstructed. 5 Next to him^c the Tekoites reconstructed, though their nobles^d did not support the work of their master. 6 Joiada the son of Paseah and Meshullam the son of Besodeiah reconstructed the Jeshanah Gate; they repaired it and hung its doors [and fixed] its bolts and bars. 7 ^eNext to them Melatiah the Gibeonite, Jadon the Meronothite, [and] the men of Gibeon and Mizpah, which belonged to the jurisdiction of the governor of Across the River, reconstructed.^e 8 ^fNext to them Uzziel the son of Harhaiah, of the goldsmiths' guild, reconstructed and next to him Hananiah, one of the ointment mixers, reconstructed; and so they renovated [the wall of] Jerusalem as far as the Broad Wall.^f 9 Next to them Rephaiah ^gthe son of Hur^g, the chief of half of the district of Jerusalem,

---

^a So for MT *qdš* "consecrate." Cf. *qrwhw* "they repaired it," in vs. 6.
^b MT "him."
^c MT has plural suffix, "them."
^d LXX transliterates: *adoreem*.
^{e-e} Omitted by LXX.
^{f-f} LXX has "Next to them worked Ananias the son of Rokeeim (or Ioakeim), and they abandoned Jerusalem as far as the broad wall."
^{g-g} Omitted by LXX by homoioarkton with "Harumaph" in next verse. See Note.

reconstructed. 10 Next to him Jedaiah the son of Harumaph reconstructed in front of his house; and next to him Hattush the son of Hashabneiah reconstructed. 11 Malchijah the son of Harim and Hasshub the son of Pahath-moab reconstructed a second section *as far as* the Furnace* Tower. 12 Next to him Shallum the son of Hallohesh, the chief of [the other] half of the district of Jerusalem reconstructed, he and his daughters. 13 Hanun and the inhabitants of Zanoah reconstructed the Valley Gate; they rebuilt it, hung its doors, [and set] its bolts and its bars, and [rebuilt] a thousand cubits of the wall as far as the Dung Gate. 14 Malchijah the son of Rechab, the chief of the Beth-haccherem district reconstructed the Dung Gate; *he rebuilt it,* hung its doors, and [set] its bolts and its bars. 15 *Shallun the son of Colhozeh, the chief of the Mizpah district, reconstructed the Fountain Gate; he rebuilt it, roofed it, hung its doors, and [set] its bolts and its bars;* and [he rebuilt] the wall of the Pool of Shelah at the King's Garden as far as the steps going down from the City of David. 16 After him Nehemiah the son of Azbuk, the chief of half of the Beth-zur district, reconstructed from a point in front of the Graves of David as far as the Artificial Pool and *the House of the Mighty Men*. 17 After him the Levites reconstructed: Rehum the son of Bani and next to him Hashabiah, the chief of half of the Keilah district, reconstructed for his district. 18 After him their brothers reconstructed: Bavvai the son of Henadad, the chief of the [other] half of Keilah. 19 Next to him Ezer the son of Jeshua, the chief of Mizpah, reconstructed *another section from in front of the Ascent to the Armory at the Angle.* 20 After him* Baruch the son of Zabbai reconstructed another section

h-h So with LXX for MT w't.
    LXXᴬ thannoureim, a simple transcription of the Hebrew. LXXᴮ has nathoureim.
i-j So with Vulg.; Hebrew reads hw' ybnnu "he will build it"; LXX reads hw' wbnyw "he and his sons" and adds skepadzo "cover."
k-k LXXᴮ reads Bethabareim; LXXᴬ reads Beththagaareim, apparently a transliteration of the Hebrew.
l-l LXX "another section of the tower of ascent of the connecting corner."
m Hebrew adds hḥrh "zealously," but probably dittography after 'ḥryw, since it is omitted by LXX; Vulg. reads "in the mountain."

from the Angle to the door of the house of Eliashib, the high priest. 21 After him Meremoth, the son of Uriah the son of Hakkoz reconstructed another section from the door of Eliashib's house as far as the end of Eliashib's house. 22 After him the priests, the men of "the district", reconstructed. 23 After them Benjamin and Hasshub reconstructed in front of their house; after him Azariah the son of Maaseiah the son of Ananiah reconstructed beside his house. 24 After him Binnui the son of Henadad reconstructed another section from the house of Azariah as far as the Angle at the Corner. 25 Palal the son of Uzai [reconstructed] from in front of the Angle and the Tower that Projects from the Upper Palace of the King at the Court of the Guard. After him Pedaiah the son of Parosh [reconstructed] —26 now the °temple slaves° lived^p on the Ophel—^qas far as the point opposite the Water Gate^q to the East and the Projecting Tower. 27 After him the Tekoites reconstructed another section from in front of the Great Projecting Tower as far as the wall of the Ophel. 28 The priests reconstructed above the Horse Gate, each one in front of his own house. 29 After them Zadok the son of Immer reconstructed in front of his house, and after him Shemaiah the son of Shecaniah, the keeper of the East Gate, reconstructed. 30 After him Hananiah the son of Shelemiah and Hanun the sixth son of Zalaph reconstructed another section; after him Meshullam the son of Berechiah reconstructed in front of ^rhis cell^r. 31 After him Malchijah ^sof the goldsmiths' guild^s reconstructed as far as the House of the Temple Slaves and of the Merchants, in front of ^tthe Muster Gate^t as far as the Upper Room at the Corner. 32 And the goldsmiths' guild and the Merchants reconstructed ^ubetween the Upper Room at the Corner and^u the Sheep Gate.

ⁿ⁻ⁿ LXX *Achechar*, a transliteration of Heb. *hkkr*.
°⁻° LXX^A *nathinim*, a transliteration. LXX^B *Katheineim*.
ᵖ See NOTE.
ᑫ⁻ᑫ LXX "as far as the garden of the Water Gate" (reads '*d gn* for '*d ngd*).
ʳ⁻ʳ LXX *godzophulakion autou* "his treasury"; Vulg. transliterates the Greek.
ˢ⁻ˢ LXX "son of Saraphei."
ᵗ⁻ᵗ LXX has *Maphekad*, a transliteration of the Hebrew. See NOTE.
ᵘ⁻ᵘ LXX "up to the middle of the ascent of. . . ."

NOTES

iii 1. *its doors.* The *dltt* "doors" were the wings of double doors. See Galling, *Biblisches Reallexikon,* cols. 525 f.

Hananel. The name occurs on an Aramaic ostracon from Nimrud (*Iraq* 19 [1957], 139 ff.) and on a seal (from Jericho?). See Avigad, PEQ 78 (1946), 125–32.

3. *Hassenaah.* Cf. Ezra ii 35, where "Senaah" may be a place name. But in I Chron ix 7 and Neh xi 9 it is a personal name (spelled Hassenuah).

the Fish Gate. Parrot (*Golgotha,* p. 33) locates it in the dip of the Tyropaean Valley.

4. *Uriah.* For names see Avigad, IEJ 7 (1957), 146–53, and Hammond, PEQ 89 (January–June 1957), 68 f. If the identification is correct, here is the first evidence that fiscal matters were in the hands of religious (temple) officials before the time of Nehemiah-Ezra, since Uriah antedated them.

Meshezabel. A Babylonian name "the god delivers." See Tallquist, APN, p. 141; the name, but of a different person, occurs also in x 21, xi 24.

Baana. See NOTE on x 28, in Sec. 14.

5. *did not support the work of their master.* Literally "they did not bring their neck to the work."

6. *Besodiah.* Besodiah=*b*+*sod*+*iah*=preposition+noun (assembly, council)+divine name.

Jeshanah gate. Jeshanah, a town in II Chron xiii 19 and Josephus *Antiquities* xiv.xv.12. Cf. A. Alt, PJB 22 (1926), 43 f.; Abel, AGP, II, p. 364; Galling, *Biblisches Reallexikon,* col. 304; Parrot, *Golgotha,* p. 31, n. 3.

7. *Melatiah.* Not otherwise known.

Mizpah. Mizpah may have had special status at the time (H. L. Ginsberg, BASOR 109 [February 1948], 21 f.).

8. *Harhaiah.* Only here.

renovated. For this meaning cf. Ugaritic *'db* "make," "prepare," "set" for Heb. *'zb;* see also Burrows, AASOR 14 (1934), 123. Cf. Vulg.

9. *Rephaiah.* The name occurs also in I Chron iii 21, iv 42, vii 2, ix 43.

the son of Hur. Hur occurs also among Midianite names and at Elephantine (Noth, IPN, p. 221).

10. *Harumaph.* Means "split nose" (Noth, IPN, p. 227).

Hattush. Also the name of a descendant of David in Ezra viii 2, one of those who set his seal on the covenant in Neh x 5, of a priest who returned with Zerubbabel in Neh xii 2.

Hashabneiah. Name of a Levite in Neh ix 5.

11. *Harim.* A relatively common name in Chronicles, Ezra, Nehemiah. Occurs in Arabia (Jaussen and Savignac, *Mission archéologique en Arabie,* II, pp. 322, 337, 498 f.). A tribal name *bn ḥrm* found in Ras Shamra, 400, line 9.

12. *Hallohesh.* On this name see Meyer, EJ, p.143.

13. *a thousand cubits.* Fifteen hundred feet.

Dung Gate. Cf. ii 13, iii 14.

14. *Rechab.* This was also the name of Jonadab's father (II Kings x 15, 23), but whether this Rechab was a descendant of that family is uncertain.

Beth-haccherem. For possible connection with Ramat Rahel, see Y. Aharoni, IEJ 6 (1956), 152–55. The name occurs only in 3Q 10:5 and *Genesis Apocryphon,* eds. N. Avigad and Y. Yadin, 1956, 22:14.

15. *Shallun.* For name cf. *bn ṭlln* in Ras Shamra 321:16.

Colhozeh. Only here and xi 5.

roofed it. Heb. *ṭll* occurs only here in the Bible.

16. *Azbuk.* Name means "Buk is strong." Cf. such name formations as Azgad (Ezra ii 12), Azmaveth (II Sam xxiii 31), and Uzziah.

18. *Bavvai.* Many emend to "Binnui" (cf. vs. 24).

Henadad. Means "Grace of Adad"; cf. Akk. ^{m}*hinni-* ^{d}*ilanu.* Only here and iii 24, x 10 and Ezra iii 9.

20. *Zabbai.* Only here and Ezra x 28. Cf. APN, p. 241, col. 2; "Zabe" occurs in Alalakh Texts (D. J. Wiseman, *The Alalakh Tablets,* 1953, 192:21).

21. *Uriah.* See NOTE on vs. 4.

25. *Palal.* Only here; cf. formation of Palaliah in Neh xi 12.

Uzai. On this name see APN, p. 235, col. 1.

26. *lived.* Burrows, AASOR 14 (1934), 125, suggests *hywšbym* "those living" for *hyw yšbym* "they were living," thus doing away with the parenthesis. But LXX supports MT.

31. *the house.* Probably does not mean residence in view of its association with the merchants' place. Cf. Gelin, p. 76, "the house of the gifts and the merchants."

the Muster Gate. Vincent and Steve, *Jerusalem de l'Ancien Testament,* I, refer to it as the Inspection Gate.

COMMENT

The Book of Nehemiah is rich in topographical material about Jerusalem (see CHART I at end of this section). Not all the place names can be identified positively; scholars differ on many points. Archaeology has been of some assistance (the site is covered with residential and religious structures), though its contributions have been limited because of the lack of extensive excavations. This section is of special importance because, as the position of the high priest indicates, it was taken from the temple archives. It does not mention Ezra, which has a bearing on the date of Nehemiah (see CHART II). Another significant point is the reference to outlying areas controlled by Jews at the time, or at least resettled by them (see CHART III). Finally, there are the guilds (vss. 8, 31; see CHART IV). Verses 1-32 interrupt the memoirs of Nehemiah and are composed of materials taken directly from the temple archives.

[Reconstruction of the walls, iii 1-32]: The work of repairing the walls and rebuilding the gates was no haphazard matter. The various sections were allotted according to a well-worked-out plan. The presence of some forty sections, of unequal proportions, alone points to a considerable amount of planning by Nehemiah and to careful negotiation with those assigned them. (Burrows, "Nehemiah 3:1-32 as a Source for the Topography of Ancient Jerusalem," AASOR 14 [1934], 115-40, thinks there were forty-one sections. He has an excellent analysis of the text and deals judiciously with the topographical situation; cf. also Vincent and Steve, Jé-rusalem de l'Ancien Testament, I, pp. 239-50 [Pl. LXI]; Simons, Jerusalem in the Old Testament, Ch. 7, and Fig. 56, p. 443. On the Nehemiah wall see PEQ [January–June 1963], p. 15, and Pls. VII B, VIII B; and Kathleen Kenyon, BA 27 [1964], 45.) How long it took before the work actually began is not mentioned, but despite the delicacy of the matter, it could not have been too long because it apparently surprised Sanballat.

The list is not a complete copy taken verbatim from the files of the temple archives, as may be seen from vss. 11, 16, 19, 20, where first or second sections are mentioned without any reference to the corresponding sections. Moreover, some of the important places and families apparently did not participate or have been omitted, for some reason—for example, Bethlehem. Not all the people of Judah were sympathetic to Nehemiah's plan: witness the lack of support from authorities of Tekoa (vs. 5), though those who did take part displayed notable enthusiasm (vs. 27). It is possible that the writer was most interested in the over-all work, that is, the reconstruction of the entire wall, and the participation by representatives of all classes: priests—even the high priest, though he was not the prime mover—Levites, doorkeepers, laymen, and representatives of guilds (cf. Meyer, EJ, pp. 139 f.). The widespread cooperation may, in part, account for the incompleteness of the list at several points. Perhaps it was not necessary to spell out every detail of the gigantic operation because the writer was sufficiently close to the time, and his readers were still familiar with every aspect of the work.

The chapter is organized around the high priest, as its point of departure shows. Description of the work begins with reference to Eliashib's rebuilding the Sheep Gate and a stretch of the wall extending as far as the Tower of Hananel. The Sheep Gate was located on the north side of the city complex, which was the most important part of the wall both because of the terrain and proximity to the enemy. But it was also nearest the temple and the most logical place for the high priest and his associates to build. It may have gotten its name from the fact that sheep for sacrificial purposes were brought in through this gate. The Tower of the Hundred and the Tower of Hananel must also have been along the north wall, though their exact locations are uncertain (cf. Burrows, AASOR 14 [1934], 137, and Avi-Yonah, SY, I, Pl. 9, p. 160; The substance of the Avi-Yonah article is presented as "The Walls of Nehemiah," in IEJ 4 [1954], 239–48).

Counterclockwise, the next point is the Fish Gate, which seems to have been near the northwest corner of the wall. The emphasis on gates is significant since, for the most part, they would have been most in need of repair and at the same time marked the main points of reference in any description of the city wall. Between the Sheep Gate and the Fish Gate three groups operated—Eliashib, the men of Jericho, and Zaccur. The Fish Gate was repaired by the sons of Hassenaah. The Jeshanah Gate is uncertain. It has been identified with the First Gate (Zech xiv 10), the Middle Gate (Jer xxxix 3), the Ephraim Gate (Neh viii 16, xii 39; II Kings xiv 13 ‖ II Chron xxv 23), and the Gennath Gate of Josephus (*Wars*

V.iv [Burrows, AASOR 14 (1934)], 134). The work between the
Fish Gate and the Jeshanah Gate was carried on by four groups
—Meremoth, Meshullam, Zadok, and the Tekoites—while the gate
itself was handled by two groups led by Joiada and Meshullam.
The next major point of reference, the Broad Wall, cannot be ex-
actly determined, nor can the jurisdiction of the governor of Across
the River, the House of Jedaiah, and the Furnace Tower. The
Valley Gate has been discussed in the preceding chapter. Between
the Jeshanah Gate and the Valley Gate eight groups worked—
Melatiah, Jadon, the men of Gibeon and Mizpah; Uzziel; Hananiah;
Rephaiah; Jedaiah; Hattush; Malchijah and Hasshub; Shallum. The
Valley Gate and a thousand cubits (1800 feet; on this point cf.
AASOR 14 [1934], 131—Burrows thinks the figure is unreliable)
of the wall between it and the Dung Gate were worked by Hanun
and the people of Zanoah. The Dung Gate marked the south-
western extremity of the wall and was rebuilt by Malchijah. Who
did the work on the wall between the Dung Gate and the Fountain
Gate is not said, though it may have been Malchijah. Shallun reconstructed the Fountain Gate and the wall of the Pool of Shelah
at the King's Garden as far as the steps going down from the City
of David. None of these points can be identified at present; they
were doubtless at the southern end of the city, in the valley. The
Pool of Shelah may have been inside the wall, the King's Garden
outside in the Kidron Valley (Avi-Yonah, SY, Pl. 9; M. Dalman,
Jerusalem und sein Gelände, 1930, p. 168). The steps going down
(or up) to the City of David were possibly located near the entrance of the Fountain Gate. The Graves of David were located
somewhere in the vicinity of the King's Garden. It is impossible to
pinpoint the House of the Mighty Men, the Ascent to the Armory,
the Angle, Eliashib's house, the Corner, the Projecting Tower, and
the Court of the Guard, though, if the order of listing is correct,
they were somewhere on the east side of the City of David and
the Ophel, which was between the City of David and the temple
area. Between the Fountain Gate and the point opposite the Water
Gate fourteen groups operated—Shallun, Nehemiah; the Levites:
Rehum, Hashabiah, Bavvai, Ezer, Baruch, Meremoth; the Priests:
Benjamin and Hasshub, Azariah, Binnui, Palal, and Pedaiah. There
is no mention of a reconstruction of the Water Gate which has
caused some scholars (Rudolph, p. 119; Schneider, p. 181) to
affirm that it was not a gate of the city wall. But, as Burrows

(AASOR 14 [1934], 120) remarks, "Where would a water gate be if not in the main wall of the city?" (See also Batten, p. 219. Gelin, p. 75, renders vs. 26: "He repaired [i.e., Pedaiah] as far as the Water Gate, toward the east and as far as the front of the Projecting Tower.") The omission points to the incompleteness of the list and not to lack of need for repair. The Water Gate has been placed at the northeastern corner of the City of David or a point farther north toward the Ophel. The Horse Gate is problematical because in II Kings xi 16 ‖ II Chron xxiii 15 it appears to be between the temple area and that of the palace. Yet Jer xxxi 40 and the passage here point to a city gate so designated. See K. Galling, "Die Halle des Schreibers," PJB (1931), p. 52 and diagram on p. 53; but also Burrows, AASOR 14 (1934), 119 f., who thinks it refers to an inner gate. Dalman and Avi-Yonah, *opere citato,* regard it as a city gate. The East Gate was, in all probability, an inner gate; it does not figure in the construction of the wall. The cell of Meshullam is otherwise unknown. The House of the Temple Slaves and of the Merchants is said to have been directly in front of the Muster Gate. These houses were apparently points where the temple slaves' and merchants' functions were carried on or where their supplies were kept; they were not residences. The temple slaves lived in the Ophel (iii 26, xi 21) or in their cities (Ezra ii 70 ‖ Neh vii 73; I Chron ix 2). Since they were to assist the Levites (Ezra viii 20) they had to be on hand when the services of the temple were conducted. The Merchants doubtless maintained supplies nearby for sacrifices to be sold to the offerers as required. All indications, therefore, point to an area near the entrance to the temple. It was directly in front of the Muster Gate which was probably an entrance to the temple area rather than a city gate (cf. Burrows, AASOR 14 [1934], 120 f.; Avi-Yonah, SY, Pl. 9). The Upper Room (Ascent) at the Corner could have been the northeastern corner of the wall. The sections between the Water Gate and the Sheep Gate—the starting place in our list—were worked by eight groups—the Tekoites, Priests, Zadok, Shemaiah, Hananiah and Hanun, Meshullam, Malchijah, and the goldsmiths' guild and the Merchants.

As the list now stands, at least two groups worked two sections each; it is possible that six others did the same, though we cannot be sure that the names refer to the same persons. The task was not easy or the operation simple but required ingenuity and decision on Nehemiah's part.

CHART I. TOPOGRAPHY OF JERUSALEM AS REFLECTED IN NEHEMIAH

A. Gates referred to*:

Ch. ii	*Ch. iii*	*Ch. xii*
1. VALLEY GATE (13, 15)	1. SHEEP GATE (1, 32)	1. DUNG GATE (31)
2. DUNG GATE (13)	2. FISH GATE (3)	2. FOUNTAIN GATE (37)
3. FOUNTAIN GATE (14)	3. JESHANAH GATE (6)	3. WATER GATE (37)
	4. VALLEY GATE (13)	4. Ephraim Gate (39)
	5. DUNG GATE (13, 14)	5. JESHANAH GATE (39)
	6. FOUNTAIN GATE (15)	6. FISH GATE (39)
	7. WATER GATE (26)	7. SHEEP GATE (39)
	8. Horse Gate (28)	8. Prison Gate (39)
	9. East Gate (29)	
	10. Muster Gate (31)	

B. Other locations:

Ch. ii	*Ch. xii*	*Ch. iii*
1. Dragon's Fountain (13)	1. STEPS OF CITY OF DAVID (37)	1. TOWER OF THE HUNDRED (1)
2. King's Pool (14)	2. Stairway to the Wall (37)	2. TOWER OF HANANEL (1)
3. Valley (15)	3. House of David (37)	3. BROAD WALL (8)
	4. TOWER OF FURNACES (38)	4. House of Jedaiah (10)
	5. BROAD WALL (38)	5. FURNACE TOWER (11)
	6. TOWER OF HANANEL (39)	6. Pool of Shelah (15)
	7. TOWER OF THE HUNDRED (39)	7. King's Garden (15)

* Normal type indicates that the name occurs only in the given chapter; small caps indicate that the name occurs in two chapters; large caps indicate three chapters. The verses are given in parentheses.

Ch. ii   *Ch. xii*   *Ch. iii*

8. STEPS FROM CITY
   OF DAVID (15)
9. Graves of David
   (16)
10. Artificial Pool
    (16)
11. House of the
    Mighty Men
    (16)
12. Ascent to the
    Armory at the
    Angle (19)
13. Angle to Eliashib's
    House (20)
14. Eliashib's House
    (21)
15. House of Benjamin
    and Hashshub
    (23)
16. Azariah's House
    (23)
17. Angle at Corner
    (24)
18. Angle and Tower
    that projects from
    Upper Palace of
    the King at
    the Court of the
    Guard (25)
19. Ophel (26)
20. The Projecting
    Tower (26)
21. The Great Pro-
    jecting Tower
    (27)
22. Wall of Ophel
    (27)
23. Priests' Row (28)
24. House of Zadok
    (29)
25. Cell of Meshullam
    (30)

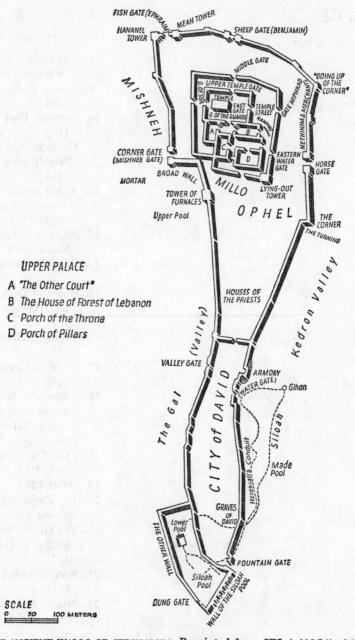

FISH GATE (EPHRAIM)
MEAH TOWER
HANANEL TOWER
SHEEP GATE (BENJAMIN)
MISHNEH
MIDDLE GATE
"GOING UP OF THE CORNER"
UPPER TEMPLE GATE
G. OF SIR
TEMPLE
EAST GATE
TEMPLE STREET
G. OF THE GUARDS
RAMPART
GATE MIPHKAD
NETHINIM & MERCHANTS
A
B
CORNER GATE (MISHNEH GATE)
C
D
EASTERN WATER GATE
HORSE GATE
MORTAR
BROAD WALL
MILLO
LYING-OUT TOWER
TOWER OF FURNACES
Upper Pool
OPHEL
THE CORNER
THE TURNING

UPPER PALACE
A "The Other Court"
B The House of Forest of Lebanon
C Porch of the Throne
D Porch of Pillars

HOUSES OF THE PRIESTS

Kedron Valley

The Gai (Valley)

VALLEY GATE

CITY of DAVID

ARMORY
WATER GATE)
Gihon

Siloah

Hezekiah's Conduit

Made Pool

GRAVES OF DAVID

THE OTHER WALL
Lower Pool

FOUNTAIN GATE

Siloah Pool
WALL OF THE SILOAH POOL

DUNG GATE

SCALE
0   50   100 METERS

THE ANCIENT WALLS OF JERUSALEM. Reprinted from IEJ 4 (1954), 240, by permission of *The Israel Exploration Journal*. Redrawn by Stefen Kraft.

Ch. ii   *Ch. xii*   *Ch. iii*

26. House of the
Temple Slaves
(31)
27. Upper Room at
the Corner (31,
32)

CHART II. PARTICIPANTS IN THE WORK†

Eliashib
Men of Jericho
Zaccur son of Imri
Sons of Hassenaah
MEREMOTH SON OF URIAH SON OF
HAKKOZ
Meshullam son of Berechiah son
of Meshezabel
Zadok son of Baana
TEKOITES
Joiada son of Paseah
Meshullam son of Besodeiah
Melatiah
Jadon
Uzziel son of Harhaiah
Hananiah
Rephaiah son of Hur
Jedaiah son of Harumaph
Hattush son of Hashabneiah
Malchijah son of Harim
Hasshub son of Pahath-moab
Shallum son of Hallohesh
Hanun
Inhabitants of Zanoah
Malchijah son of Rechab
Shallun son of Colhozeh

Nehemiah son of Azbuk
Levites
Rehum son of Bani
Hashabiah
Bavvai son of Henadad
Ezer son of Jeshua
Baruch son of Zabbai
MEREMOTH SON OF URIAH SON
OF HAKKOZ
Priests
Benjamin
Hasshub
Azariah son of Maaseiah son of
Ananiah
Binnui son of Henadad
Palal son of Uzai
Pedaiah son of Parosh
TEKOITES
Zadok son of Immer
Shemaiah son of Shecaniah
Hananiah son of Shelemiah
Hanun son of Zalaph
Meshullam son of Berechiah
Malchijah
Goldsmiths' guild
Merchants

† Normal type signifies that the name occurs only once; names in small
caps are those of the same persons or groups; names in italics *may* be those
of the same persons or groups.

Chart III. Cities Occupied and Controlled by Jews at the Time*

Jericho
Tekoa
Gibeon
Mizpah (district)
Jerusalem (two districts)
Zanoah
Beth-haccherem (district)
Beth-zur (district)
Keilah (two districts)

Chart IV. The Guilds Mentioned

Goldsmiths' guild
Ointment mixers
Merchants

* On the matter of borders of Judah at this time see Alt, KS, II, p. 328, n. 1; p. 335, n. 2.

5. SAMARITAN OPPOSITION AND HARASSMENT NECESSITATE PROTECTIVE MEASURES
(iii 33–38, iv 1–17)

Reaction of the neighbors

III   33 Now when Sanballat heard that we were rebuilding the wall, he became furiously angry and derided the Jews. 34 *a*He said in the presence of his brothers and the host of Samaria, "What are those wretched Jews doing? Can they renovate them, offer sacrifices and complete them in a day? Can they revive the stones from the dust heaps, even when they have been burned?" 35 Tobiah the Ammonite stood by him and added, "Yes, what are they building! If a fox should jump upon [it] he would demolish their stone wall."

Nehemiah's prayer

36 "Listen, O our God, for we are despised! Return their reproach upon their own head and make them booty in a land of captivity. 37 Do not forgive their iniquity *b*and may their sin not be blotted out before you, for they have insulted the builders." 38 But we continued to repair the wall and the whole wall was [soon] joined together half of its [intended] height because the people wanted to work.*a,b*

Threats against the workers

IV   1 When Sanballat, Tobiah, the Arabians, the Ammonites, *c*and the Ashdodites*c* heard that the repair of the walls of Jerusalem was progressing—that the breaches were beginning to

a–a LXX varies considerably from MT in these verses.
b–b Omitted by LXX.
c–c Omitted by LXX.

fill up—*they became very angry* 2 and all of them conspired to come and fight against Jerusalem*ᵉ* *ᶠand ᵍcreate disturbanceᵍ* for us.*ᶠ* 3 But we prayed to our God and set up a guard as a protection *ʰagainst themʰ* day and night. 4 And in Judah it was said,

> *ⁱThe strength of the burden bearer is drooping,
>> The rubbish heap so vast;
> And we are unable by ourselves
>> To rebuild the wall.ⁱ*

5 Our opponents said, "They will not find out until we arrive in their midst to slay them and put a stop to the work."

Protective measures

6 When the Jews who lived near them came and told us ten times *ʲabout all the evil designs they planned against us,ʲ* 7 I stationed spearmen *ᵏat the place behind the wall at the open placesᵏ* and arranged the people according to families with their swords, their lances, and their bows. 8 Observing [their anxiety], I rose and addressed the nobles, the officials, and the rest of the people: "Do not be afraid of them; remember the great and awe-inspiring Lord and fight for your brothers, your sons, your daughters, your wives, and your houses." 9 When our enemies heard that it was known to us and that God had frustrated their plan, we all returned to the wall, each one to his work. 10 From that day on half of my servants continued at the work while the other half held the lances, the shields, the bows and the coats of mail, and the captains were *ˡbehind the*

ᵈ⁻ᵈ LXX "it appeared very evil to them."
ᵉ See NOTE.
ᶠ⁻ᶠ Omitted by LXX.
ᵍ⁻ᵍ Vulg. *molirentur insidias* "plotted a secret attack(s)."
ʰ⁻ʰ See NOTE.
ⁱ⁻ⁱ LXX reads: "The strength of our enemies is crushed,
    The mound [Codices ᴮᴺⱽ *ochlos* "crowd, then disturbance"] great
    And we are not able to build for ourselves the wall."
ʲ⁻ʲ See NOTE.
ᵏ⁻ᵏ See NOTE.
ˡ⁻ˡ Not clear in MT and Vrs. May mean "behind the wall [?]" or "behind the people working."

whole house of Judah[l] 11 [m]who were rebuilding the wall.[m] The burden bearers [n]carried on,[n] working with one hand and holding the spear in the other. 12 As for the builders each had his sword girded at his side as he was building. But the trumpeter was at my side. 13 Then I said to the nobles, the officials, and the rest of the people, "The work is spread out in all directions and we are widely separated on the wall, one from another; 14 assemble yourselves to us at whatever place you hear the sound of the trumpet; our God will fight for us." 15 And so we carried on the work—[o]half of them holding lances[o]—from the beginning of the dawn until the stars appeared. 16 At that time I also said to the people, "Let each one with his helper lodge in Jerusalem that they may be our guard by night and work during the day." 17 Neither did I, my brothers, my servants, or the guards behind me[p] remove our clothes; [q]each one had his spear in his right hand.[q]

[m-m] Following division of LXX and Vulg.
[n-n] LXX "those holding the equipment in arms." Hebrew reads '*mśym* (?), taken here for a variant of '*msym* "carry a load." So also Vulg. Some read *ḥmśym* "armed," "prepared," which is supported by LXX *en oplois* or by LXX[L] *enoploi*. Cf. xiii 15.
[o-o] May have come in from vs. 10, though LXX follows MT.
[p] MT adds collective subject: "we did not."
[q-q] Omitted by LXX.

NOTES

iii 33. Marks beginning of ch. iv in EVV.

34. *the host.* Samaria was not a military colony. Alt (KS, II, p. 323) thinks it refers to the *'am ha'arets*, the officials and important citizens around him.

them . . . them. Meaning obscure. Perhaps *lhm* is an ethical dative "on their own" or "for themselves."

37. *Do not forgive . . . before you.* Cf. Jer xviii 23 and expressions similar to those used in this prayer in the confessions of Jeremiah.

38. *the whole wall was . . .* Literally "the whole wall was joined together as far as the middle of it." Does that mean that half the wall was built? or that all of it was built, but only halfway, meaning half of its height? It could also mean half its width or thickness.

iv 2. *Jerusalem*. Jerusalem is feminine and thus MT *lō* "for him" is incongruous. The writer thought of Nehemiah.

3. *against them day and night*. Omitting "from before them." Perhaps *'lyhm* "against them" was originally another word, though LXX supports MT. It could be a case of conflation or it may indicate how the guard was placed, i.e., facing them.

4. *And in Judah it was said*. So for "and Judah said," because this was a popular song.

5. *find out*. Literally "know and see."

6. *about all the evil designs they planned against us*. Following Rudolph, p. 124, for the impossible "from all the places whence they will return against us." LXX reads "they are coming against us from all sides (places)."

7. *at the place . . . open places*. So with Rudolph, reading *mty ḥnyt* for "at the deep places." LXX reads "I set at the lowest parts of the place behind the walls in the sheltered places. . . ."

8. *[their anxiety]*. So with Bertholet, as required by the context. Rudolph makes it into a *ky* clause, *ky yr'w* "that they were afraid." It may have been omitted by haplography. For Josephus' comment on situation, see *Antiquities* XI.v.8.

9. *frustrated their plan*. Rudolph adds *wyšwbw mmnh* "they desisted from it." So also Gelin, who thinks the phrase dropped out by haplography.

13. *spread out in all directions*. Literally "very great and expansive." Another instance of hendiadys.

17. *each one had his spear in his right hand*. So for "each his spear the water" or "each one threw it [into] the water."

COMMENT

The chapter division in the English translations (iii 33–38H [iv 1–6E], iv 1–17H [iv 7–23E]), following the older versions (LXX and Vulg.) is based on the opposition aroused and heightened by Nehemiah's plans, rapidly being carried out. But the division followed in the Hebrew Bible is perhaps more subtle, since it appears to distinguish two phases in the progress of the hostility between the surrounding peoples and the Jews: iii 33 ff. describes the emotions displayed by Sanballat and his associates when they were informed about the beginning of the work of rebuilding the walls; iv 1 ff. represents a later period when the opponents saw that Nehemiah's plans were succeeding and steadily moving toward consummation.

[Reaction of the neighbors, iii 33–35]: The news of the Jews' enterprise surprised and angered Sanballat, who was by now aware of the true import of Nehemiah's mission. The address of the Samaritan official was delivered to the people around him and was for home consumption. However, it reflects the determination of Nehemiah and his co-workers, as well as the rapidity with which they pursued their task and the condition of the wall before they began their work. Tobiah resorted to ridicule. Both of Nehemiah's opponents must by now have had a healthy respect for him, for their words and actions manifest increasing alarm over the progress of his work.

[Nehemiah's prayer, 36–38]: The reaction of Nehemiah to the conspiracy of Sanballat and Tobiah was like Jeremiah's against his enemies. He looked upon his work as that of Yahweh so that opposition thereto was tantamount to opposition to Yahweh himself. Hence he prayed for vindication. The answer to his prayer may be seen in vs. 38.

[Threats against the workers, iv 1–5]: Judah was surrounded by the four Persian provinces here named explicitly or inferentially, as in the case of Samaria, which was represented by Sanballat. Alt (KS, II, pp. 338–45) points out that the eastern border of Judah was contiguous with Ammon, which extended to the west side of the Jordan. Ashdod represents the Philistines, whose territory became an Assyrian province in 711 B.C., and the seat of its governor. This arrangement was continued into Persian times and it is not difficult to see why the Philistines were referred to as Ashdodites. The Arabians were apparently the immediate southern neighbors at the time. The Chronicler mentions them as being earlier domiciled in regions between Beer-sheba and Gerar. Since Nehemiah does not mention Edom or Edomites, it is pretty clear that he reckons what was later Idumea with the Persian province of Arabia.

The reason for including only two personal names may be due to the close collaboration of Sanballat and Tobiah (cf. ii 10, iii 35, vi 12); Geshem, not mentioned here, was often a willing third party. In one way or another all four Persian provinces participated in attempts to thwart the reconstruction of Jerusalem, as is made evident in vs. 2 and is reflected elsewhere in the book (e.g., xiii 23). However, it appears that their bark was worse than their bite: they resorted to threats rather than overt action since that would have involved them in difficulties with the imperial authorities. Still Nehemiah and his people could afford to take no chances; they relied on prayer and such other measures as were deemed appropriate and necessary.

The little poem in vs. 4, in qinah meter (i.e., a 3+2, the meter of lamentation), is certainly authentic, though it may be out of place. It reflects the popular attitude and spirit prevalent at the time. Its popular character may be seen also from the rhyme:

> kašál koáh has-sabbál   w he'apár harbéh
> wa'anáhnu ló' nukál   libnóth bahomáh

It looks like a kind of theme song that resounded everywhere as the workers busied themselves at their tasks and, as such, conveys feelings of inadequacy and despair *and* of hope. The job was too much for them, the carping and menacing opposition was overwhelmingly discouraging; yet the assistance of Yahweh and the resourcefulness of Nehemiah were ample cause for confidence.

[Protective measures, 6–17]: Those who kept Nehemiah and his workmen informed of the plans and movements of their enemies rendered both service and disservice. They "told us ten times" shows that they often relayed information to the Jews at Jerusalem. Perhaps that was just what Sanballat wanted them to do—it was a kind of psychological warfare intended to keep them off balance and so to delay progress as much as possible. Nehemiah, however, could take no chances. He provided a guard for the workmen, allayed their fears by speaking to them, and even encouraged his servants to wear their arms. The n'rym "servants" were men of some wealth, as the equipment they possessed indicates. They were armed retainers. See W. F. Albright, AfO 6 (1930), 221, and JPOS 11 (1931), 124 f. The masons and their helpers carried swords. A trumpeter was provided, ready to sound the alarm wherever and whenever necessary. Moreover, Nehemiah, his brothers, his retainers, and the guards (possibly the bodyguard) slept in their work clothes.

Strict orders were issued to the workers to remain in the city, partly for self-protection and partly to assist in guarding the city. It may also have been a subtle attempt to guard against possible subversion. Perhaps Nehemiah sought in this way to keep the workmen on the job and thus complete the task more quickly so that the wall itself would soon afford protection against the enemy.

6. ECONOMIC PROBLEMS. NEHEMIAH'S SOLUTION
(v 1–13)

A grave internal problem

V ¹ There was a great outcry from the people, especially from their wives, against their Jewish brothers. ² Some said, "ᵃOur sons and our daughters are numerousᵃ and we must get grain to eat so that we may stay alive." ³ Others said, "We have to mortgage our fields, our vineyards, and our houses to obtain grain ᵇto prevent starvation.ᵇ" ⁴ Still others said, "We must borrow money to pay the royal tax [levied] against our fields and our vineyardsᶜ." ⁵ "Now we belong to the same race as our brothers, and our sons are just as good as theirs; and yet we have to subject our sons and our daughters to bondage—some of our daughters have already been brought into bondage—and we are helpless because our fields and our vineyards belong to others."

Nehemiah's reaction

⁶ I was very angry when I heard their complaint and these words. ⁷ So I considered [the matter] very carefully and reprimanded the nobles and the officials. I said to them, "Each one of you is ᵈimposing a burdenᵈ upon his brother." Then I assembled a great convocation to deal with them, ⁸ and said to them, "So far as we were able, we have redeemed our Jewish brothers who had to sell themselves to the nations; but you too are selling your brothers, ᵉso that [I suppose] they will have to be bought back by us!ᵉ" They remained silent because they

ᵃ⁻ᵃ See NOTE.
ᵇ⁻ᵇ Literally "because of the famine." LXX reads "that we may get grain and eat."
ᶜ LXX adds "our houses."
ᵈ⁻ᵈ See NOTE.
ᵉ⁻ᵉ Omitted by LXX. Vulg. reads "shall we redeem them?" See NOTE.

could find no reply. 9 "The thing you are doing is not good,"
I continued. "Ought you not to walk in the fear of our God
because of the reproach of the nations, our enemies? 10 I, too, as
well as my brothers and my retainers have lent them money
and grain. Let us now desist from this claim. 11 Return their
fields, their vineyards, their olive groves, and their houses to
them immediately and [rescind] the claim for the money, the
grain, the new wine, and the olive oil which you laid upon
them."

12 Then they agreed, "We will return [it] and demand nothing further of them; we will do just as you say". But I summoned the priests and made them swear to fulfill this promise.

13 Then I shook out my girdle and said, "So may God shake
out from his house and possessions every one who does not fulfill this promise; so may he be shaken out and empty!" The
whole assembly responded, "Amen" and praised Yahweh. And
the people kept this promise.

NOTES

v 2. *Our sons and daughters are numerous.* Cf. Vulg. "Our sons and
our daughters are too numerous: let us have grain in exchange for them."
Note that text here reads *'nḥnw rbym* "we are numerous," whereas in
the next verse the phrase is *'nḥnw 'rbym* "we have to mortgage." Perhaps
Rudolph, p. 128, and Galling, p. 225, following the suggestion in Kittel,
Biblia Hebraica, 3d ed., are right in reading, "We must give our sons and
daughters in pledge . . .". So also *The Bible, an American Translation,*
1931, and Monsignor Knox (1949).

4. *the royal tax.* Only here in OT. From Akk. *mandattu>maddatu*
"tribute."

5. *we are helpless.* Heb. *w'yn l'l ydnw* "and it is not to the power of
our hands," i.e., it is not within our power.

because our fields . . . belong to others. Eichrodt (*Theology of the
Old Testament,* p. 97) thinks an emergency law is involved here. Cf. II
Chron xxviii 10.

7. *I considered. mlk* in the Aramaic sense; cf. Akk. *malâku,* I_2 "to
take counsel with oneself."

imposing a burden. MT reads *mš'* "interest." So also Vulg. LXX has
"[what] the man demands of his brother you demand." But in view of

the context (requirement of pledges), it is better to read "imposing a burden," with Rudolph and Gelin.

8. *so that . . . back by us.* Present rendering follows Rudolph's suggestion *in loco* that MT *wnmkrw-lnw* "and they will sell themselves to us" was influenced by the preceding *tmkrw* "you are selling" and should be emended to *wnkrw-lnw* "they must be bought back by us," after Vulg. The wealthy Jews were compelling their brethren to sell themselves into slavery and give up their property in order to pay their taxes and keep from starvation. Nehemiah reprimands the exploiters severely for their dastardly practices and asks scornfully whether he and his supporters will now have to redeem the victimized Jews from their own brothers as they once redeemed Jews from the heathen.

10. *this claim.* I.e., the matter of taking pledges.

11. *immediately.* Literally "this very day."

the claim. Reading *mš't* for *m't* "hundredth part." But see E. Neufeld, "The Rate of Interest and the Text of Neh. 5:11," JQR 44 (1953/54), 194–204.

13. *girdle.* Related to Akk. *ḫuṣannu* "sash," "girdle," one in which personal belongings were carried, as in pockets.

And the people kept this promise. Rudolph suggests rather that the people did as Nehemiah had just done, since only the rich were involved in guilt.

COMMENT

No sooner had the external difficulties been resolved than internal ones reared their ugly heads. They may have been brought on, or at least accentuated, by outside circumstances. Increased responsibilities, particularly Nehemiah's order for the workers to remain in Jerusalem (iv 16), evidently had much to do with aggravating the situation.

[The problem, v 1–5]: The gravity of the problem may be seen in the women's joining the populace in clamoring for redress. The complaints centered around difficulties that afflict every age, namely social and economic inequity. The specific points mentioned are also familiar ones—hunger, debts, and taxes. Conditions reflected here recall those detailed in Malachi (iii 5–15). The basic problem was a scarcity of food. To meet elemental needs, the poor were required to pledge their possessions, even to sell their sons and daughters into slavery; those with property were required to pledge it. Such pledges were sometimes claimed at the most inopportune times (Isa v 8; Amos ii 8, iv 1, v 11; Mic ii 2; Hab ii 6–7). Moreover, the people had to pay the taxes, levied by the imperial authorities upon the small property holders, for the treasury from which local projects were financed (cf. Ezra vi 8, vii 20).

Who were these moneylenders? They were members of the community who, in one way or another, had become affluent by taking advantage of every opportunity to further their own selfish interests at the expense of their fellow Jews. So much is evident from the question of consanguinity raised in vs. 5. Almost the same idea is voiced in Mal ii 10. The covenant of brothers no longer meant what it said. The manner in which many of the Jews of the golah obtained their wealth and standing is hinted at in Würthwein, *Der 'amm ha'arez im Alten Testament*, pp. 64 ff. They conspired with the people of the land (the upper classes of those who had taken over the land after the Exile) through intermarriage. Indeed the outcry of the Jews at the time indicated here may have marked the beginning of the struggle that ended in the stern measures taken later to dissolve those marriages of convenience. If the problem was one of long standing, the law which permitted pledging (Exod xxii 25–27; Deut xxiv 10–13) and even selling oneself or members of one's family (Exod xxi 7; Lev xxv 39–40), required release after seven years. The native born could not be treated like other slaves (Lev xxv 42–46). Not only did the law regard all Jews as brothers, presumably to be treated as such, but the common interest, participation, and requirements of Nehemiah's project of reconstruction demonstrated their fundamental equality in his time. The seriousness of the matter became apparent only when double duty was laid upon the members of the community. These poverty-stricken Jews simply could not make ends meet, and the fact that their more prosperous though not overscrupulous brothers seemed to get along well, even to the point of becoming creditors, was beyond their comprehension. The rupture of families brought on by dire need of food compelled the victims to cry out against a condition that was far from brotherly.

[Nehemiah's reaction, 6–13]: Nehemiah's reaction, when he was apprised of existent conditions, was altogether characteristic of the man. His ire was aroused against those guilty of violating the covenant of brotherhood; and he was led to a thorough consideration of the whole social problem involved because his program was in jeopardy. He appealed to the officials. When that appeal failed he called an assembly of the people. In his address he spoke of the redemption of the brethren from enslavement to foreigners only to enslave their own brothers (whether this refers to the redemption of exiles from Persian authorities or from surrounding peoples is not clear). Note that Nehemiah implicates himself as well as his brothers. He and his retainers too had lent money and grain to those in need. Hence he demanded cessation of the practice by all concerned (vs. 10). He further proposed the *immediate* return of property taken in pledge as well as the rescission of claims for tax money and produce originally advanced to meet the barest needs of the borrowers. The pressure of events rendered action imperative. There could be no delay until the year of release (Deut xv). Of course the assembly supported Nehemiah, and the lenders were forced to agree. Since there was still some question in his mind about the genuineness of their agreement to comply with the assembly's decision, Nehemiah had them take an oath before the priests. He may have recalled the reprehensible action of the slaveholders in the time of Jeremiah (xxxiv 8 ff.). To the oath sworn before the priest, he added a double symbol. He took his sash or girdle in the folds of which he carried personal belongings and shook it out; at the same time he pronounced the penalty for failure to comply with the oath, which was, in effect, a curse. When he had shaken his girdle out, he held it up empty, signifying the fate of the man who failed to carry out his promise. Throughout this section emphasis is laid on the brotherhood of the Jews and the ridicule to which they were subject for failing to act like brothers (vs. 9). But the prime motive for consideration was the fear of God.

7. NEHEMIAH'S ADMINISTRATION
(v 14–19)

V 14 Accordingly from the time he appointed me to be their governor*a* in the land of Judah—from the twentieth to the thirty-second years of King Artaxerxes, for twelve years—neither I nor my brothers consumed the governor's food allowance. 15 The former governors who preceded me laid a heavy burden upon the people; they collected from them forty shekels of silver per day for food and wine, while their retainers tyrannized the people. I did not act thus from fear of God. 16 I also*b* applied myself to the work on this wall although *cI acquiredc* no land and all my retainers were assembled there for the work. 17 Though there were at my table Jews *dand officialsd* to the number of one hundred and fifty men, in addition to those who came to us from the surrounding nations 18 and though one ox and six select sheep were prepared daily, beside fowl*e* for myself, and every ten days skins of wine in abundance, despite this I did not lay claim to the governor's food allotment because the service was heavy upon the people. 19 "Remember to my credit, O my God, all that I did on behalf of this people."

a Vulg. *dux* "governor"; without suffix.
b LXX adds *l'* "not."
c–c So with some MSS for MT *qnynw* "we bought."
d–d Omitted by LXX.
e LXX "he-goat."

[1933], 150–56.) The reason for Nehemiah's refusal of a subsistence allowance was precisely the heavy burden already being borne by the people. The little prayer that concludes this episode should be interpreted in the spirit of the times (cf. the Wadi-Brisa Inscription of Nebuchadnezzar II in ANET, p. 307, col. 2; also the requests of Cyrus, *ibid.*, p. 316, col. 2, and Xerxes, *ibid.*, p. 317, col. 1).

NOTES

v 15. *shekels of silver*. *bksp šqln* "silver shekels," occurs on an A
contract tablet found in Syria dating from the reign of Nebucha
II (*Syria* 37 [1960], 99–115).

per day. Reading *lywm 'ḥd* with Vulg. for *wyyn 'ḥr* "ar
besides." So also Rudolph, Gelin, Schneider, and Batten.

18. *skins*. So for *bkl yyn* "with all the wine."

COMMENT

Nehemiah's conduct as chief administrator of Jewish
Judah was exemplary. He was unquestionably the govern
such, had replaced the authority of Sanballat, whose res
at Samaria. The governing officials were granted certain
that came out of the local tax levy for carrying out the
bilities. The amount was forty shekels, which has been
about one dollar. There is some uncertainty about wha
the Median shekel (valued at 5.60 grams each) or w
In either case, the value cannot be accurately determin
terms as the biblical purchasing power was much
hemiah's incumbency lasted for twelve years, from 44
The "former governors" (vs. 15) could refer to Sh
Zerubbabel or to the officials at Samaria immediat
hemiah; more likely the latter are meant. The term (
to Sheshbazzar (Ezra v 15), Zerubbabel (Hag i 1
and the Persian officials (Ezra v 3, 6, vi 6, 7, 13,
9, iii 7). See Alt, KS, II, p. 333, n. 2. Galling (Vu
Judah before the time of Nehemiah was still part o
Samaria. Nehemiah refused the allowance though h
ligations laid upon him by the imperial edict, despi
official family was large. The cost was considerable
the number of people who sat at his table and the
stuffs required. The fowl for himself were doubt
though wild birds could also have been includ
fowl were known in Palestine at the time is sho
the rooster found by W. F. Bade at Tell N

8. PLOTS AGAINST NEHEMIAH
(vi 1–14, 17–19)

Attempt to ensnare Nehemiah

VI ¹ Now when Sanballat, Tobiah, Geshem the Arabian, and the rest of our enemies were informed that I had rebuilt the wall, that no breach remained in it—though at that time I had not yet hung the doors of the gates—² Sanballat and Geshem sent the following communication to me: "Come, let us meet together at Hakkephirim*a* in the valley of Ono." But they were plotting to harm me. ³ So I sent messengers to them with the reply, "I am doing a great work and I cannot come down; why should the work stop while I leave it to come down to you?" ⁴ They communicated with me in this manner *bfour times*b and I responded to them in the same way.

Attempt to frame Nehemiah

⁵ Sanballat sent his servant to me in the same manner *ca fifth time*c with an open letter in his hand ⁶ in which was written: "It is reported among the nations—*dand Gashmu confirms it*d—that you and the Jews are planning to rebel; for that reason you are rebuilding the wall and, according to these reports, you want to be king over them. ⁷ You have even appointed prophets to acclaim you in Jerusalem as follows: 'There is a king in Judah.' Now the king will be informed of these matters; so come, let us have a conference." ⁸ I sent back to him the following reply: "Such things as you mention are not done; you have

a LXX and Vulg. read "villages." Since meaning is uncertain, it is better to take "Hakkephirim" simply as a place name. M. Noth, ZDPV 77 (1961), 156, reads *ihre Vorratshäuseranlagen,* "their storehouses."
b–b Omitted by LXX.
c–c Omitted by LXX.
d–d Omitted by LXX^AB.

fabricated them out of your own imagination." 9 For all of them wanted to terrorize us, thinking, "They will desist from the work and it will not be accomplished." *e*And now strengthen my hand.*e*

Plot of false prophets

10 Then, when I came to the house of Shemaiah the son of Delaiah the son of Mehetabel who was *f*shut up*f*, he said,

> Let us assemble at the house of God,
> Inside the temple itself,
> And shut the doors of the temple;
> For they are coming to kill you,
> By night they are coming to kill you.

11 I replied, "Should a man *g*like me take flight*g*? And who like me would enter the temple to save his life? *h*I will not go in*h*." 12 *i*Besides, I recognized that God had not sent him, for the prophecy he uttered concerning me was instigated by Tobiah and Sanballat who had hired him;*i* 13 *j*for he had been hired to terrorize me, to make me act accordingly and commit sin, that I might get a bad name among them so that they could reproach me.*j* 14 "Remember, O my God, Tobiah and Sanballat *k*for these deeds of theirs*k*, and also Noadiah the prophetess*l* and the rest of the prophets*m* who tried to terrorize me."

e–e LXX and Vulg. read "and now I strengthened my hands." MT makes it a prayer.

f–f LXX *suneXomenos* "to be confined"; Vulg. *secreto* "in private."

g–g Omitted by LXX^AB.

h–h Omitted by LXX^AB.

i–i LXX "And I knew, and behold God had not sent him because the prophecy [was] a word against me; and Tobiah and Sanballat had hired a crowd against me."

j–j LXX "In order that I might be afraid and do so and sin and become [through] a bad name [get a bad name through them] so that they could reproach me."

k–k MT and LXX "his deeds," which has led some scholars to believe that "Sanballat" was a later insertion. But both names occur also in LXX and Vulg.

l LXX has *masculine*. Cf. Ezra viii 33.

m LXX^Bℵ "priests"; LXX^A "prophets."

Tobiah correspondence

17 Also in those days numerous letters from the nobles of Judah went to Tobiah and Tobiah's came to them, 18 for many in Judah were bound to him by oath, because he was a son-in-law of Shecaniah the son of Arah and his son Jehohanan had married the daughter of Meshullam the son of Berechiah. 19 Moreover, *his good deeds* were mentioned before me and they relayed my utterances to him. And Tobiah sent letters to terrorize me.

n–n LXX "his words." See NOTE.

NOTES

vi 1. *Geshem the Arabian.* See NOTE on ii 10.

7. *let us have a conference.* Literally "let us take counsel together."

10. *Mehetabel.* The name occurs only here and Gen xxxvi 39 (I Chron i 50), where it is the name of an Edomite princess.

Let us assemble . . . coming to kill you. The poetic structure is 3+2, 3+2, 3.

17. *numerous letters from the nobles of Judah.* Literally "the nobles of Judah multiplied their letters."

18. *bound to him by oath.* Literally "lords of oath." Only here. Cf. Akk. *bēl adê* "one sworn or bound by oath"; see W. von Soden, *Akkädisches Handwörterbuch*, 1959, p. 119, col. 2.

19. *good deeds.* Another pointing of Hebrew (*ṭibbothaw* for *ṭobothaw*) makes it possible to render "rumors" for "good deeds." See I. Löw, ZAW 33 (1913), 154.

COMMENT

After dealing with internal difficulties arising from economic inequities, Nehemiah returns to the personal problems brought on by the persistent attempts of his enemies to halt the work of rehabilitation of Jerusalem. After power politics had failed, they tried treachery, which proved equally ineffective.

[Attempt to entrap Nehemiah, vi 1–4]: The three conspirators (some commentators rule out Tobiah as a later addition because

Tobiah lacks the preposition [*l*] prefixed to the other two names in
the Hebrew text and he is not mentioned in vss. 2, 6—hardly a
conclusive argument, since Sanballat and Tobiah frequently appear
together elsewhere [e.g., ii 10, 19, iv 7, vi 12, 14]) refused to admit failure before every avenue to thwart Nehemiah had been ex-
plored. Final repairs to the wall had been completed but the doors
had not yet been hung. In the meantime Sanballat and Geshem sent
a message to Nehemiah requesting a meeting at an unknown village
in the valley of Ono some eight miles east of Joppa, a neutral zone
between Ashdod and Samaria and outside the borders of Judah.
(Cf. A. Alt, PJB 27 [1931], 72, n. 5; G. Beyer, ZDPV 56 [1933],
236–38. But Jews whose home was at Ono are mentioned in the
list of Ezra ii 33 and Neh vii 37.)

As Nehemiah knew, they had no other purpose than to do him
harm. So he replied in no uncertain terms that he had to remain at
his task to carry to completion the work he had come to perform.
The desperation to which Sanballat and his associates had been
driven is shown by the repeated messages sent to Nehemiah.

[A scheme to incriminate Nehemiah, 5–9]: The second of
their schemes was to raise a false report contained in an open letter
sent by courier affirming that after the wall was completed, Nehemiah planned to have himself proclaimed king. He was doubtless aware of the danger of such a rumor in view of what may have
happened in the case of Zerubbabel. The whole thing appears to
have been an attempt to pin messianic pretensions on Nehemiah.
Such is, in all probability, the significance of the reference to the
reputed acclamation of the prophets (vs. 7). Shades of Haggai and
Zechariah! But Nehemiah had no such ideas in mind; he was doing
just what his commission called for (ii 5 ff.). The report was pure
fabrication.

[Plot of false prophets, 10–14]: The attempt to involve Nehemiah in violation of religious tabu, though more subtle than the
previous scheme, still underestimated Nehemiah's character and
purposefulness. Under pretense of having an important message for
him, Shemaiah requested and received a call from the governor. Just
why he was confined is uncertain; it could have been part of the
plot—pretending to be the hunted man Nehemiah appeared to be.
Various reasons have been given, though none are fully convincing.
For one thing the meaning of '*ṣwr* is far from clear in this context.
The following conjectures on Shemaiah's confinement have been ad-

vanced: (a) it was a hint to Nehemiah that he too must confine himself to the temple to escape assassination; (b) he was ceremonially unclean; (c) he was having an ecstatic experience just at the time Nehemiah arrived. The prophecy of Shemaiah seemed fantastic to Nehemiah. Being a courageous man, as he demonstrated on more than one occasion, he refused to jeopardize himself and his work by paying attention to idle threats. Besides, it was forbidden for a layman to enter the temple itself, though he could seek asylum at the altar (Exod xxi 13–14; I Kings i 50–53, ii 28 ff.), outside the temple proper. Since Nehemiah was also a eunuch (see NOTE on i 11), it would have been doubly offensive for him to enter the house of God (Lev xxi 17–23; Deut xxiii 1). Thus one who occupied the position of governor and was a layman could not violate that which to him was sacred. Little acumen was required to see through the plot that Tobiah and Sanballat hatched to trap him into committing an act with dangerous consequences. This was one more attempt to terrorize him. As such it was just one of the numerous efforts by unscrupulous prophets and Noadiah to pressure him into a precipitate act that might undermine his work.

[Tobiah correspondence, 17–19]: While this pericope is Nehemian, it does seem out of place. It was doubtless placed in its present position because of the mention earlier (vs. 14) of Tobiah; perhaps there was also a tendency to group together the stories of personal opposition to Nehemiah, as vs. 19c appears to indicate. The exulting announcement of the completion of the wall ought to be followed by an account of its dedication, though this does not come until xii 27.

Tobiah had married the daughter of Shecaniah (cf. iii 29), a member of the family of Arah (Ezra ii 5). His son Jehohanan in turn married a daughter of Meshullam son of Berechiah, the leader of one of the repair groups (iii 4, 30). These intermarital relationships put him in close contact with the prominent families of Judah, to whom he was thus bound and with whom he had made friends. That there was constant contact between them is to be expected, particularly in view of Tobiah's purpose of subverting Nehemiah's work through the intervention of mutual friends. They sang Tobiah's praises to Nehemiah and Nehemiah's utterances were relayed to Tobiah: a perfect circumstance for misunderstanding and hostility. Apparently Nehemiah also received letters from Tobiah.

9. COMPLETION OF THE WALL
(vi 15–16, vii 1–3)

VI 15 But the wall was finished on the twenty-fifth of Elul, in a period of fifty-two days. 16 When all our enemies heard about it and all the nations round about us *saw it*, *their self-esteem was decidedly diminished* because they knew that this work had been achieved by [the assistance] of our God.

Appointment of security guards and service officials

VII 1 Now when the wall was rebuilt and I had hung the doors, the gatekeepers, the singers, and the Levites *were appointed.* 2 Then I placed Hanani my brother and Hananiah the chief of the citadel in charge of Jerusalem, because he was a more loyal and God-fearing man than many others, 3 and gave them the following order: "The gates of Jerusalem must not be opened until the sun gets hot and the doors must be shut and barred while they are still standing [guard]. Appoint guards from the residents of Jerusalem, each to his position and each in front of his own house."

a–a Taking verb from *r'h* "he saw," against MT and LXX (which read *yr'* "to be afraid, fear"), but contextually better; Vulg. follows MT.
b–b See NOTE.
c–c Vulg. "I appointed."

NOTES

vi 16. *their self-esteem was decidely diminished.* Rudolph, following Klostermann, reads *kl'* "be wonderful," "marvelous," for *npl* "to fall." LXX "great fear fell in their eyes." MT "they fell very much in their eyes," which could mean either the enemies of Nehemiah fell greatly in the estimation of the Jews or as indicated in the translation here given.

vii 1. *the singers, and the Levites.* This phrase may be an intrusion into the text resulting from a confusion of the city-gate guards with the doorkeepers of the temple (cf. vss. 43–45). So also Rudolph, Gelin, Schneider, Galling, Noordtzij and others.

2. *Hanani my brother.* Kittel, *Biblia Hebraica,* 3d ed., suggests the omission of this phrase, making the verse read: "Then I put Hananiah [or Hanani my brother, i.e., Hananiah], the chief of the citadel, in charge of Jerusalem because he was a more loyal and God-fearing man than many." Vs. 3 would then connect with vs. 1 rather than with vs. 2, the latter being a reference to the chief of the Jerusalem functionaries.

the citadel. See NOTE on ii 8.

COMMENT

In view of Josephus' (*Antiquities* XI.v.8) statement that it took two years and four months to rebuild the walls, the fifty-two days here have been regarded as too short a time for such a gigantic task. He places the consummation of the rebuilding of the wall in the twenty-eighth year of the reign of Xerxes (i.e., Artaxerxes) (438–37 B.C.), the completion day falling in the ninth month (Kislew). On the Josephus account see J. A. Bewer, JBL 43 (1924), 224–26. Bright (*A History of Israel,* p. 365) and Albright (*The Biblical Period,* pp. 53, 63, notes 126, 127) think Josephus is probably right in stating the time required to mend the wall. But see Kittel, GVI, III, pp. 633 ff. If the wall was finished on Elul 25 (August–September) and the work took fifty-two days, it must have begun about the fourth of Ab (July–August). The year, though generally assumed to have been 445 B.C., the year of Nehemiah's arrival, is not given. But see COMMENT on Sec. 1 and the Introduction. It is to be noted that in all probability the wall had not been so completely destroyed that the builders had to begin *de novo* (see ZAW 74 [1962], 191). Possibly, for considerable stretches only breaches had to be filled in or a top replaced. Elul, the sixth month, is mentioned only here in the Bible. While the interpretation of vs. 16 is not quite certain, the verse suggests that Nehemiah's opponents were reduced in stature and influence. Moreover, the consummation of the project of rebuilding the walls was achieved only through the help of Yahweh.

[Appointment of security guards and service officials, vii 1–3]: The erection of the wall and the placement of the doors were no guarantee by themselves against the enemies of Jerusalem. Special precaution had to be taken against possible treachery, particularly because numerous Jews were related in one way or another to Tobiah and Sanballat, and the former was constantly trying to enlarge his circle of friends. To guard against the possibility of betrayal, Nehemiah selected his sentries with great care. The city was placed in charge of his brother Hanani, who was loyal to both Nehemiah and the Persian government, and Hananiah, the commander of the citadel. The extraordinary order to close the gates before the guards went off duty and to open them only when the sun was high reflects both the times and Nehemiah's alertness. In addition to the security police, there was a citizen patrol whose duty it was to keep watch around their own houses—a deft move since they might be more circumspect where their own homes were directly involved.

10. POPULATION RECORDS
(vii 4–72a)

VII 4 Now the city was extensive and spacious, the people in it few, and the houses not yet built.

5 Then my God inspired me to assemble the nobles, the officials, and the people to be officially registered, and I discovered the book of the official genealogy of those who came up first in which I found the following record: 6 These are the citizens of the province who came up from the captivity of the Exile whom Nebuchadnezzar king of Babylon had exiled; they returned to Jerusalem and Judah—each going to his own town—7 coming along with Zerubbabel, Jeshua, Nehemiah, Azariah, Raamiah, Nahamani, Mordecai, Bilshan, Mispereth, Bigvai, Nehum, Baanah. ᵃThe numberᵃ of the men of the people of Israel: 8 of the sons of Parosh, 2172; 9 of the sons of Shephatiah, 372; 10 of the sons of Arah, 652; 11 of the sons of Pahath-moab, that is, of the sons of Jeshua and Joab, 2818; 12 of the sons of Elam, 1254; 13 of the sons of Zattu, 845; 14 of the sons of Zaccai, 760; 15 of the sons of Binnui, 648; 16 of the sons of Bebai, 628; 17 of the sons of Azgad, 2322; 18 of the sons of Adonikam, 667; 19 of the sons of Bigvai, 2067; 20 of the sons of Adin, 655; 21 of the sons of Ater, that is, of Hezekiah, 98; 22 of the sons of Hashum, 328; 23 of the sons of Bezai, 324; 24 of the sons of Hariph, 112; 25 of the sons of Gibeon, 95; 26 of the men of Bethlehem and Netophah, 188; 27 of the men of Anathoth, 128; 28 of the men of Beth-azmaveth, 42; 29 of the men of Kiriath-jearim, Chephirah, and Beeroth, 743; 30 of the men of Ramah and Geba, 621; 31 of the men of Michmas, 122; 32 of the men of Bethel and Ai, 123; 33 of the men of the other Nebo, 52; 34 of the sons of the other

ᵃ⁻ᵃ LXX reads Heb. *mspr* "number" as a proper name. But see its version of Ezra ii 2.

Elam, 1254; 35 of the sons of Harim, 320; 36 of the sons of
Jericho, 345; 37 of the sons of Lod, Hadid, and Ono, 721; 38 of
the sons of Senaah, 3930. 39 Of the priests of the sons of Jedaiah
of the house of Jeshua, 973; 40 of the sons of Immer, 1052; 41 of
the sons of Pashhur, 1247; 42 of the sons of Harim, 1017. 43 Of
the Levites, of the sons of Jeshua belonging to Kadmiel of the
sons of Hodevah, 74. 44 Of the singers, of the sons of Asaph,
148. 45 Of the gatekeepers, of the sons of Shallum, the sons
of Ater, the sons of Talmon, the sons of Akkub, the sons
of Hatita, the sons of Shobai, 138. 46 Of the temple slaves there
were the sons of Ziha, the sons of Hasupha, the sons of Tabbaoth, 47 the sons of Keros, the sons of Sia, the sons of Padon,
48 the sons of Lebanah, the sons of Hagabah, the sons of Shalmai,
49 the sons of Hanan, the sons of Giddel, the sons of Gahar,
50 the sons of Reaiah, the sons of Rezin, the sons of Nekoda,
51 the sons of Gazzam, the sons of Uzza, the sons of Paseah,
52 the sons of Besai, the sons of Meunim, the sons of Nephu-
shesim, 53 the sons of Bakbuk, the sons of Hakupha, the sons of
Harhur, 54 the sons of Bazlith, the sons of Mehida, the sons of
Harsha, 55 the sons of Barkos, the sons of Sisera, the sons of
Temah, 56 the sons of Neziah, the sons of Hatipha. 57 Of the
sons of Solomon's servants there were the sons of Sotai, the sons
of Sophereth, the sons of Perida, 58 the sons of Jaala, the sons of
Darkon, the sons of Giddel, 59 the sons of Shephatiah, the sons
of Hattil, the sons of Pochereth-hazzebaim, the sons of Amon.
60 All the temple slaves and the sons of Solomon's servants numbered 392. 61 These are the ones who came up from Tel-melah,
Tel-harsha, Cherub, Addon and Immer, though they were not
able to prove that their family or their descendants came from
Israel: 62 the sons of Delaiah, the sons of Tobiah, the sons of
Nekoda, numbering 642. 63 And of the priests there were the
sons of Hobaiah, the sons of Hakkoz, the sons of Barzillai—who
had married one of the daughters of Barzillai the Gileadite and
was named after them. 64 These sought their record in the official genealogy but it could not be found; so they were disqualified from serving in the priesthood, 65 and the Tirshata ordered

them to abstain from eating the consecrated food until a priest with Urim and Thummim should appear.

66 The whole assembly together numbered 42,360, 67 apart from their men servants and maid servants to the number of 7337. They also had 245 male and female singers. 68 There were 435 camels and 6720 asses.

69 Some of the heads of families contributed to the work; the governor put into the treasury a thousand drachmas of gold, fifty bowls, and *b*five hundred and thirty priestly vestments.*b* 70 Others of the heads of families contributed to the work treasury twenty thousand drachmas of gold and twenty-two hundred minas of silver. 71 What the rest of the people gave amounted to twenty thousand drachmas of gold, two thousand minas of silver, and sixty-seven priestly vestments. 72 The priests, the Levites, the gatekeepers, the singers, some of the people, the temple slaves, and all Israel lived in their own towns.

b–b See NOTE.

NOTES

vii 11. *Pahath-moab.* See NOTE on Ezra ii 6.

12. *1254.* Same number as that for second Elam in vs. 34. Suggests some contamination due to identity of name.

26. *Netophah.* B. Mazar originally identified Netophah with Ramat Rahel (IEJ 5 [1955], 127), but later thought it to be Beth-haccherem (IEJ 6 [1956], 151 f.).

63. *was named after them.* See NOTE on Ezra ii 61.

65. See NOTE on Ezra ii 63.

69. *Some. Mqṣt* "part," "some," an Aramaic loanword.

five hundred and thirty priestly vestments. LXX "30"; Vulg. follows MT. Virtually all recent commentators (Rudolph, Galling, Gelin, Schneider, Batten) think *ksp mnym* "minas of silver" dropped out before *ḥmš m'wt* "500," thus making it read: "30 priestly garments and 500 minas of silver."

70. *twenty-two hundred minas.* Value uncertain. See NOTE on Ezra ii 69.

COMMENT

The first three verses of chapter vii form the conclusion to the first part of the memoirs of Nehemiah (see Sec. 9), and the last line of vs. 72 (72b) is an introduction to the ceremony of reading the law (see Sec. 11), but the bulk of the chapter is the list of returnees. These verses, 4–72a, are a duplicate of Ezra ii (q.v. for detailed discussion with references). The list here is employed for a purpose different from that in Ezra ii where it becomes a part of the sequence of historical events related by the Chronicler, though brought up to date. Here it seems to be used as the starting point for a campaign to induce some of those who had settled elsewhere to move to Jerusalem, which was now a safe place to live and offered space and other advantages. Moreover, if the province was to flourish its capital would have to be populated (see Pavlovsky, *Biblica* 38 [1957], 304; the story is, however, postponed until ch. xi). Albright has pointed out (BP, pp. 52 f.) that the list is composed of two groups: (a) those who returned after the Exile and (b) those who returned soon after the Babylonian invasion or who had never gone into exile. Albright thinks it is a revised census list dating from the time of Nehemiah. The settlement around Jerusalem was already fairly dense in 538 B.C., whereas farther south there was more room. That is why such place names as Beth-zur, Tekoa, and Keilah do not appear in this list but do appear in Nehemiah's builder list. (On the original position of the list see Noth, ÜS, pp. 128 ff., and Schaeder, EdS, p. 29.) A comparison of the towns mentioned in this list with those referred to in the building list presents an interesting picture of pressures of the politico-social situation and the popular response thereto.

Neh vii	*Neh iii*
Gibeon	Jericho
Bethlehem	Tekoa
Netophah	Gibeon
Anathoth	Mizpah
Beth-azmaveth	Zanoah
Kiriath-jearim	Beth-haccherem
Chephirah	Beth-zur
Beeroth	Keilah

Neh vii	*Neh iii*
Ramah	
Geba	
Michmas	
Bethel	
Ai	
Jericho	
Lod	
Hadid	
Ono	
Senaah (?)	

Only Gibeon and Jericho appear in both lists. Settlement in the southern part of Judah had taken place between the time of the return under Zerubbabel and the coming of Nehemiah, and it was perhaps these latecomers who exhibited greater enthusiasm than their brethren, who, because they were subjected to more social and economic pressure, failed to participate wholeheartedly in the work of rebuilding. But there can hardly be doubt that Nehemiah used this old list to exert pressure of his own—both to people his new city and to strengthen the entire province of Judah (cf. Kittel, GVI, III, pp. 639 ff.). The success of his venture will be discussed below in Sec. 15.

As may be seen from a comparison of the lists in Appendix I, there is substantial variation only in the matter of contributions (Neh vii 69–71 ‖ Ezra ii 68–69; on the variation in numbers in the census lists see Allrik, BASOR 136 [1954], 21–27). Ezra ii 68–69 contains a summary of the contributions, which are listed in detail here in Nehemiah, and presented in more or less round numbers, as pointed out by Rudolph, pp. 26 f. He presents the following picture:

a. Priestly garments
 (1) Those contributed by the people, 67
 (2) Those contributed by the governor, 30 (see NOTE on vs. 69) A total of 97, or 100 in round numbers
b. Contributions of silver
 (1) By heads of familes, 2200 minas
 (2) By rest of the people, 2200 minas
 (3) By the governor, 500 minas (see NOTE on vs. 69) A total of 4900, or 5000 in round numbers

c. Contributions of gold
  (1) By governor, 1000 drachmas
  (2) By heads of families, 20,000 drachmas
  (3) By rest of the people, 20,000 drachmas

This is a total of 41,000 drachmas, against the 61,000 of Ezra ii 69. But the 50 bowls must then have been valued at 20,000 drachmas and have been included in the total. On the calculation see Rudolph, p. 26.

It would appear, therefore, that Neh vii is closer to the original document. Another telling argument in favor of this view is that the contributions here are said to have been made for "the work" (vs. 69), whereas in Ezra ii they were made for "the house of Yahweh" (vs. 68), under the influence of Cyrus' declared directive permitting the return of the Jews for the purpose of reconstructing the temple. On the other hand, Neh vii records the contribution of priestly garments and (temple) bowls which had nothing to do with rebuilding the wall. In effect the Chronicler may have fitted his source into the context of both situations, at least in part.

Verse 72a is a rewriting of Ezra ii 70, which marks the concluding reference to Ezra's activity ending with his arrival at Jerusalem. There it stands between the list and the worship service that follows; here between the list and the ceremony of the reading of the law. It fits in better with the former than the latter, as may be seen from the context. There it shows that Jerusalem was already well settled and those who returned with Ezra went to live in their respective ancestral cities, though some remained because they were needed in the service of the temple. Here Nehemiah was trying to persuade people to take up residence in the capital.

11. THE READING OF THE LAW
(vii 72b, viii 1–12)†

VII 72b When the seventh month arrived the Israelites were in their cities.

VIII 1 When all the people assembled themselves as one man at the plaza in front of the Water Gate, they requested Ezra the scribe to bring the book of the law of Moses which Yahweh had prescribed for Israel.

2 So on the first day of the seventh month Ezra the priest brought the law before the congregation consisting of men and women, and of all who could listen intelligently, 3 and he read from it in front of the plaza before the Water Gate from dawn until midday before the men and women and [the others] who could understand [it]; all the people listened attentively to the book of the law. 4 Now Ezra the scribe stood upon a wooden podium which they had constructed for the purpose; beside him, to his right, stood Mattithiah, Shema, Anaiah, Uriah, Hilkiah, and Maaseiah; to his left stood Pedaiah, Mishael, Malchijah, Hashum*a*, Hashbaddanah*a*, Zechariah, and Meshullam*a*. 5 Then Ezra opened the book in the sight of all the people—for he stood higher than all the people—and when he opened it all the people stood. 6 When Ezra praised Yahweh, the great God, all the people responded, "Amen, Amen," *b*with their hands uplifted*b*, knelt down and worshiped Yahweh with their faces to the ground. 7 And Jeshua, Bani, Sherebiah, *c*Jamin, Akkub, Shabbethai, Hodiah, Maaseiah, Kelita, Azariah, Jozabad, Hanan,

† Neh viii 1–12 ‖ I Esdras ix 37–55.

a Omitted by LXX^B. See NOTE on vs. 4.
b–b Omitted by LXX^B. See NOTE.
c–c LXX omits all these names. Vulg. has the names and then reads: "They quieted the people to hear the law."

Pelaiah, and the Levites*c* instructed the people in the law while all the people remained in their place. 8 They read from the book of the law of God in translation to make it intelligible and so helped them to understand the reading.

9 Then Nehemiah *d*the governor*d*, and Ezra the priest and the scribe, and the Levites who instructed the people said*e* to all the people, "This day is sacred to Yahweh your*f* God. You must neither mourn nor weep"; for all the people wept when they heard the words of the law. 10 He further said to them, "Go, eat of the fat, drink of the sweet*g* and send portions to *h*him who has nothing prepared*h*, for the day is sacred to Yahweh. So do not be dejected, *i*for the joy of Yahweh is your strength*i*."

11 The Levites too urged the people to be calm, saying, "Be still, for the day is sacred, and do not be dejected."

12 Then all the people went away to eat, to drink, to send portions, and to celebrate a great festival, for they comprehended the things which they brought to their attention.

d–d Omitted by LXX. See NOTE.
e Verb is singular as it stands in MT.
f LXX "our."
g Vulg. reads *mulsum* "wine mixed with honey."
h–h See NOTE.
i–i LXX reads "for he is your [our] strength" or "for it is your [our] strength." Cf. I Chron xvi 27; Ezra ix 8–9.

NOTES

vii 72b. This belongs with ch. viii. For interpretation see Ezra, COMMENTS on Secs. 2 and 3, ii 70 and iii 1.

viii 1. For an artistic conception of the story related in ch. viii, see C. H. Kraeling, *The Synagogue*, 1956, pp. 232–35, and Pl. LXXVII. *Water Gate*. See NOTE on iii 26.

4. The lists vary in the number of those present to the right and left of Ezra as he read the law. In view of the constant emphasis on the number 12, he probably had six men on each side. The present text is impaired.

I Esdras ix 43–44	*Neh viii 4* (LXX)	*Neh viii 4* (MT)
Those on right	Those on right	Those on right
Mattathias	Mattathias	Mattithiah
Sammou(s)	Samaias	Shema
Ananias	Anania(s)	Anaiah
Azarias	Ouria	Uriah
Ourias	Elkia; LXXᴬ Chelkeia	Hilkiah
Ezekias	Maasaia	Maaseiah
Baalsamos		
Those on left	Those on left	Those on left
Phadaios; LXXᴮ Phaladaios	Phadaias	Pedaiah
Misael; LXXᴮ Meisael	Misael; LXXᴮ Meisael	Mishael
Melchias; LXXᴮ Melcheias	Melchias	Malchijah
Lothasoubos	Osam (LXXᴮ omits)	Hashum
Nabarias	Asabaama (LXXᴮ omits)	Hashbaddanah
Zacharias	Zacharias	Zechariah
	Mosollam (LXXᴮ omits)	Meshullam

5. *all the people stood.* 'md can also mean "rise" (synonym of qwm) but here signifies more than that. It means to stand in respect for the law. Possibly the origin of the practice of standing up during the reading of Scripture. In Catholic and many Protestant churches people stand while the Gospel lesson is read.

6. *the great God.* Cf. Deut x 17; Jer xxxii 18; Dan ix 4; Neh i 5, ix 32; and Akk. *ilu rabu* "the great god."

with their hands uplifted. Cf. Ps xxviii 2 and commentaries on that passage for the significance of the uplifted hands.

8. *in translation.* Cf. Ezra iv 18 with different pointing. On the basis for this rendering, see Schaeder, *Iranische Beiträge*, I, pp. 204 f. But G. von Rad (*Studies in Deuteronomy*, 1953, pp. 13 f.) raises a question about it.

the reading. Later on the word meant "Scripture"; the transitional stage may be reflected here.

9. *Nehemiah the governor . . . the Levites.* "Nehemiah the governor" and "the Levites" are regarded as secondary additions because the verb is singular, as is the continuation in the following verse. See Rudolph, p. 148. Nehemiah is also omitted in I Esdras ix 49, but the exhortation is put in the mouth of the governor.

10. *him who has nothing prepared.* On this characteristic phrase of the Chronicler, see A. Kropat, *Die Syntax des Autors der Chronik,* 1909, p. 66, and Kapelrud, QAEN, p. 86. LXX and I Esdras ix 51 interpret it to mean "those who have nothing." Vulg. follows MT.

12. *they brought.* "They" here refers to Nehemiah and Ezra and also to the Levites, who urged the people to be calm.

COMMENT

In I Esdras ix, this portion of chapter viii follows immediately upon the agreement of those who had married foreign wives to divorce them and represents a ceremony confirming the law and disseminating its teaching among the people. That Neh viii–ix is composed of Ezra material seems fairly clear, though scholars differ as to its character and its relationship within the Ezra-Nehemiah narrative. Eissfeldt (EAT, p. 744) regards as quite possible that the Chronicler composed Neh vii–viii himself from Ezra memoirs and is responsible for its present position. Cf. also Noth (ÜS, p. 128), who thinks the passage not only consonant with the work of the Chronicler but that only he could have been responsible for it. Schaeder (EdS, pp. 17 f., 30) places the transitional verses between Neh vii and viii (vii 72 and viii 1) after Ezra viii 36; he (p. 20) thinks Neh viii follows Ezra vii. So does De Vaux (IAT, II, p. 419). Mowinckel's opinion (VuH, p. 212) is that chapter viii belongs after Ezra x and forms the conclusion to the Ezra story. As such it does not contain an account of the promulgation of a new law coming from Ezra but relates the story of a New Year's celebration rendered regular and significant by the events with which it was connected. Pavlovsky, on the other hand, places it after Neh xiii 4–31 in time (*Biblica* 38 [1957], 436–39). As they now stand, chapters viii and ix, with chapter x, interrupt the story of Nehemiah, which is resumed in chapter ix.

[Ceremony of law reading, vii 72b, viii 1–12]: The preceding chapter concludes with the notice that after the rebuilding of the wall the people went to live in their respective cities; the priests, Levites, and some of the people, perhaps the most important ones, dwelt in Jerusalem (cf. Ezra ii 70, where the comment refers to those who came with Ezra). The last part of vii 72 belongs to chapter viii as indicated by the Vrs. and modern translators. As such it introduces the law-reading ceremony which took place in the seventh month. Whether the time is schematic or represents an actual time after Ezra's return is not altogether clear. If Schaeder is correct in placing the story after Ezra viii 36, the latter could well be the case. However, since the seventh month was a feast month par excellence, it is possible that that tradition had something to do

with the specified time, although it must be observed that this was
not a worship service—which follows with the celebration of the
Feast of Tabernacles (vss. 13–18). It was not a regularly constituted service, as may be seen from the place (the Water Gate—
regular services were held in the temple courts) and character of
the participants (men, women, and anyone who could understand
what was read).

The seventh month was the time for celebration of the Atonement (Lev xvi 29, xxiii 27, xxv 9) and the Feast of Tabernacles
(Lev xxiii 34, 39, 41). Other solemn occasions fell in that month
(Lev xxiii 24; Num xxix 1, 7, 12). It should not be overlooked
that the ark was moved from Zion to the temple at the feast of
the seventh month (II Chron v 3), that tithes were brought in
between the third and seventh months (II Chron xxxi 7), that the
people assembled at Jerusalem and began offerings before the foundations of the temple were laid (Ezra iii 1, 6), that the fifth and
seventh months were times for mourning in the captivity (Zech vii
5), and that the fast of the seventh month was a period of rejoicing (Zech viii 19). See Kittel, GVI, III, pp. 589 f.; and
Schneider, p. 105.

The object of the assembly was instruction in the torah ("law")
which Ezra had carried with him from Babylon (Ezra vii 14). In
fact, the chief purpose of his coming to Jerusalem was to apply the
law of God to the situation as he found it—as the rescript of the
king specified. It was "the book of the law of Moses which Yahweh
had prescribed for Israel" and was doubtless the latest recension of
the Pentateuch. That Ezra did not read the whole corpus of material
may be inferred from the statement that he read "from it" (*bō*), and
that he read only from dawn until midday, which was far too short
a time to read the whole of it. He stood upon a platform or podium
so that both the book and the reader were in clear view of the entire
assembly. The presence of those who stood on his right and on his
left lent weight to the occasion. Who these supporters were is not
said; they may have been the heads of the families, later the elders.
The sight of the book and Ezra in the act of opening it was the
signal for the people to rise in adoration; they remained standing
quietly and reverently while the reading was in progress (vs. 3).
The ceremony began with the blessing (invocation) of Ezra and
the vocal symbolic response of the people. The Chronicler again
shows his hand by the position he accords to the Levites, who share

with Ezra knowledge of the law and its interpretation. (See Von Rad, *Studies in Deuteronomy*, pp. 14 f.; G. E. Wright, "The Levites in Deuteronomy" in VT 4 [1954], 325–30. For the Messiah of Aaron as the interpreter of the law at Qumran see J. T. Milik, *Dix ans de découvertes dans le désert de Juda*, 1957, p. 84; for the whole problem of the Messiah complex at Qumran see Cross, *The Ancient Library of Qumran*, pp. 219 ff.) Elsewhere the Chronicler refers to the Levites as "the instructors of all Israel" (II Chron xxxv 3)—and their function as teachers seems to have been a matter of course with him. Earlier Ezra alone (vss. 3–4) seems to have been the reader; but in vs. 8 they too read "in [from] the book of the law," but "in translation." Apparently Ezra read from the Hebrew while the Levites gave what he read in Aramaic and so assisted in making the law intelligible to the people, though the whole matter is far from clear (cf. P. Kahle, *The Cairo Geniza*, 1st ed., 1947, p. 124, who thinks the Targum goes back to Ezra. The rabbis thought this was the first mention of the Targum [*Megillah* 3a].).

The reading and interpretation of the law struck a responsive chord in the hearts of the people. They had either never heard it expounded so forcefully or had forgotten its demands. Perhaps Ezra had selected relevant passages whose application was almost automatic. In any case, the people were made aware of their failure to keep the law; and the threats contained therein indicated their jeopardy (cf. Lev xxvi; Deut xxvii, xxviii). Their history was full of illustrations of what happened to those who neglected the commandments of God. Hence their reaction was a sign of sorrow and repentance (Josephus *Antiquities* XI.v.5). But the people were cautioned not to weep on "this day" because it was a festival day to Yahweh. "This day" refers to vs. 2; the first day of the seventh month was the festival of trumpets (Lev xxiii 23–25) and the holy convocation (Num xxix 1–6). (On the New Year's festival see De Vaux, IAT, II, pp. 407–9. He thinks it does not appear in the OT.) The reference to festival joy reflects Deuteronomy (xii 7, 12, 18, xiv 26, xvi 11, 14; cf. G. E. Wright, IB, II, pp. 412 f.), which the Chronicler followed (II Chron xxix 36, xxx 25). Such eating and drinking and sharing—a sign of hospitality—was associated with certain offerings (cf. Deut xvi 11, 14, xxvi 12; I Sam ix 13; II Sam vi 19). For Ezra and his people, the festival of the reading of the law was thus a joyous one.

12. CELEBRATION OF THE FEAST OF BOOTHS
(viii 13–18)

VIII 13 On the second day the heads of the families of all the people together with the priests and Levites assembled themselves to Ezra the scribe to gain further insight into the words of the law. 14 And they discovered written in the law Yahweh commanded through Moses that the Israelites are to dwell in booths during the festival of the seventh month. 15 So they issued the following proclamation and had it passed along to all their cities and in Jerusalemᵃ: "Go out to the mountain and bring in olive branches, pine branches, myrtle branches, palm branches, and [branches of] other leafy trees to make booths, as it is written."

16 Then the people went out and brought them and made booths for themselves, each upon his roof, and in their courtyards, and in the courtyards of the house of God, and in the plaza of the Water Gate, and in the plaza of the Ephraim Gate. 17 The whole congregation who had returned from the captivity made booths and occupied the booths—for the Israelites had not done so from the days of Jeshua the son of Nun until that day—and there was very great joy. 18 And he read from the book of the law of God day by day, from the first day until the last day [of the celebration]. They celebrated the feast for seven days and on the eighth day they held a solemn assembly in accordance with the decree.

ᵃ LXX adds "and Esdras said."

NOTES

viii 16. *the plaza.* See Parrot, *Golgotha,* p. 32, n. 2.
the Water Gate. Cf. COMMENT on Sec. 4, iii 1–32.
the Ephraim Gate. Some scholars equate it with the Fish Gate located
at the northwest corner of the city (Galling, and Avi-Yonah, SY, p. 160).
Vincent and Steve (*Jérusalem de l'Ancien Testament,* I, Pl. LXI) and
Dalman place it on the south side of the palace of the governor to the
south of the northwest corner of the city. Burrows, AASOR 14 (1934),
137, favors a location between the Jeshanah and Valley Gates.

COMMENT

The law-reading ceremony that took place on the first day of the
seventh month (New Year's day) was only the starting point for
Ezra in carrying out his chief mission to the returnees. After that
ceremony, the people returned to their homes and towns. But the
heads of families, the priests, and Levites continued their reading
and study of the law on the following day. In the course of their
study, they discovered more about the traditional religious activities
set for the seventh month. The association of the study (reading)
of the law with the seasonal religious observances is striking, since
it appears to follow a pattern (cf. ix 3, xiii 1). On this occasion
they found the prescription for celebrating the Festival of Booths
in connection with the season of ingathering, which was one of rejoicing and happiness. On the development of this festival see De
Vaux, IAT, II, pp. 397–407. It was an agricultural festival connected with the ingathering first noted in Exod xxiii 16 (cf. Deut
xvi 13) and was one of the three annual festivals. The first ritual
prescriptions are given in Deut xvi 13–15 and more precisely in
Lev xxiii 34–43 (on the latter passage see IAT, II, p. 369).
Josephus (*Antiquities* XI.v) also has the story of the Celebration
of Booths and the reading of the law.

The Festival of Booths was originally a local festival which the
Deuteronomist transferred to "the place which Yahweh will choose."
The Leviticus passage (xxiii 40) speaks of rejoicing before Yahweh,
which doubtless means at the sanctuary. In Leviticus it is associated

with the Exodus and desert period of Israel. The specific date (Lev xxiii 33, 39) for the Celebration of Booths was the fifteenth day of the seventh month. It was to continue for seven days (cf. De Vaux, IAT, II, pp. 401–4, who shows that there is no conflict between our passage here and the prescription of Deuteronomy; see especially p. 404). Deut xxxi 10–13 adds the injunction that the law is to be read in conjunction with this festival, which therefore had a double significance: it marked the ingathering and also the time for the reading of "this law" (Deut xxxi 11). The Chronicler's respect for Deuteronomy is indicated by both his comment that the celebration take place in Jerusalem (vs. 16) and his having Ezra follow its dictum with respect to reading the law. Whether this was a year of release (Deut xxxi 10) or not is unclear from the text; but the association with the festival of the reading of the law seems to suggest as much (see ALT, KS, I, pp. 325–28).

The observation that such a celebration of the Festival of Booths had not taken place since the days of Joshua recalls similar statements on other occasions (II Kings xxiii 22; II Chron xxx 26, xxxv 18). But there may be more to it than appears on the surface. To recall the time of Joshua is to associate the Festival of Booths with the wilderness period when Yahweh dwelt in a tabernacle and the people in booths (Lev xxiii 43; Hos xii 9), and to dissociate it from the vintage customs related to the agricultural festivals that proved to be so attractive to Israel. (De Vaux [IAT, II, p. 405] thinks it was originally associated with agricultural pursuits; on the writer's shift, see also Schneider, p. 211.) The celebration with all its implications went back to the law of Moses.

13. PENANCE
(ix 1–37)

A day of penance

IX 1 On the twenty-fourth day of this month the Israelites assembled themselves with fasting, with sackcloth, *and with dirt upon them*. 2 Then those of Israelite stock who had severed relations with all foreigners stood up and confessed their sins and the iniquities of their fathers. 3 While they remained standing in their place they read from the book of the law of Yahweh their God *for the fourth part of the day* and confessed and worshiped Yahweh their God *for another fourth part.* 4 Now there stood upon the podium of the Levites, Jeshua, Bani, Kadmiel, Shebaniah, Bunni, Sherebiah, Bani, and Chenani who cried unto Yahweh their God with a loud voice. 5 The Levites, Jeshua, Kadmiel, Bani, Hashabneiah, Sherebiah, Hodiah, Shebaniah, and Pethahiah said, "Rise and praise Yahweh your God for ever and ever! May your glorious name, exalted above all blessing and praise, be praised!"

The penitential prayer

Creater and preserver

6 *You alone are Yahweh,
You have created the heavens,
The heaven of heavens and all their host,
The earth and everything upon it,
The waters and everything in them.

---

a–a Omitted by LXX. Vulg. follows MT. Syr. interprets: "ground upon their heads."
b–b Omitted by LXX. Vulg. follows MT.
c LXX introduces the prayer with: "And Ezra said." Vulg. follows MT.

You preserve all of them,
And the heavenly host worships you.

Choice of Abraham and covenant with him

7 You are Yahweh God,
Who chose Abram,
And brought him up from Ur^d of the Chaldees;
You changed his name to Abraham.

8 When you discovered his heart was faithful before you,
You made a covenant with him,
To give [him] the land of the Canaanites
The Hittites, the Amorites,
The Perizzites, the Jebusites, and the Girgashites—
To give [it] to his descendants.
And you have kept your promises,
For you are righteous.

Deliverance from Egypt

9 You saw the affliction of our fathers in Egypt
And you heard their cry at the Reed^e Sea.

10 You offered signs and tokens^f against Pharaoh,
Against all his servants and against all the people of his
   land.
Because you knew that they acted haughtily toward them
You made a name for yourself that has persisted to this day.

11 You split open the sea before them,
So they went through the midst of the sea on dry ground;
Their pursuers you hurled into the depths,
Like a stone into the raging waters.

12 With a cloud pillar you led them by day,
With a fire pillar by night,
To illumine for them the way
In which they were to go.

13 You came down upon the mountain of Sinai,

---

^d LXX *Chora* "country, place," as in Genesis. Vulg. "fire."
^e LXX "Red or Erythrean Sea." Vulg. *mare rubrum.*
^f LXX adds: "in Egypt."

And spoke with them from heaven;
You gave to them
    right judgments
    and reliable laws,
    good statutes and commands.
14 Your holy Sabbath
You made known to them;
You decreed commands, statutes, and law for them
Through Moses your servant.
15 You provided bread from heaven
    for them for their hunger;
You brought forth water from a rock
    for them for their thirst;
You told them to go in
    to possess the land
    which you swore
    to give to them.

God's continued support despite the stubbornness of Israel

16 But they and our fathers acted haughtily;
They became stubborn
And would not obey your commands.
17 They refused to listen,
They failed to remember your miracles
Which you did among them;
They became stubborn
And determined to return
To their servitude *in Egypt*.
But because you are a forgiving God,
    gracious and compassionate,
Patient and of unstinted devotion,
You did not abandon them
18 Even when they made for themselves
A molten calf,
    and said, "This is your god*,

g-g So with LXX for MT "in their rebellion."
h LXX and Vulg. have plural, indicating that an idol was meant. Wherever
the plural form *elohim* refers to Yahweh they used the singular.

Who brought you[i] up from Egypt,"
And committed colossal [j]impieties[j],

19 You, in your great compassion,
        did not abandon them in the desert.
The cloud pillar did not depart from them
        by day to guide them on the way,
Nor the fire pillar by night
        to illumine for them the way
        in which they were to go.

20 Your good spirit
        you gave to instruct them,
Your manna you did not withhold from their mouth,
        you gave them water for their thirst.

21 Forty years you supported them
        in the desert so that they were not in want;
        their garments did not wear out,
        nor did their feet swell.

22 You gave them
        kingdoms and peoples,
        and allotted [them] to them as a boundary.
They took possession of the land of Sihon,[k] the king of
                Heshbon,
        and the land of Og, the king of Bashan.

23 You made their children as numerous as the stars of the
                heavens,
And brought them into the land
        which you promised to their fathers
        they would enter and possess.

Promise fulfilled through Israel's possession of Canaan

24 [l]The children entered
        and took possession of the land[l],
You subdued before them
        the inhabitants of the land, the Canaanites,

[i] LXX "us."
[j–j] LXX "provocations [to anger]."
[k] Omitting "and the land," with LXX and Vulg.
[l–l] Omitted by LXX.

and gave them into their hand,
together with their kings and the peoples of the land,
to do with them as they pleased.

25 They captured fortified cities
and 'the productive land';
they took possession of houses
full of all kinds of good things,
hewn cisterns, vineyards, and olive groves,
and fruit trees in abundance.
So they ate, were filled, grew fat
and reveled in your great goodness.

Israel's disobedience

26 But they became disobedient, rebelled against you
and cast your law behind their back;
they slew your prophets
who had accused them
so as to cause them to return to you,
and they committed colossal ʲimpieties.ʲ

27 Then you gave them over to their adversaries
who oppressed them;
but when they called to you in the time of their
affliction,
you heard them from heaven
and in accordance with your great compassion
you gave them saviors
who delivered them from the hand of their oppressors.

28 But as soon as they were relieved,
they did evil again in your sight;
then you abandoned them into the hand of their enemies
who ruled over them.
When they cried to you again
you heard them from heaven
And, in accordance with your compassion, delivered them
many times.

29 You warned them to bring them back to your law,
but they 'became haughty',

did not obey your commands
and sinned against your judgments,
by which if he observes them a man lives;
they turned a stubborn shoulder,
stiffened their neck and disobeyed.

30 You bore with them many years
and warned them by your spirit
through your prophets,
but they did not listen;
so you turned them over into the hand of the peoples of
the land.

31 Because of your great compassion
you did not destroy them utterly
nor forsake them;
for you are ᵐa Godᵐ
of grace and compassion.

Confession of guilt and prayer for redress

32 Now, our God, the great God,
the mighty and awe-inspiring one,
Who maintains the covenant loyally:
let not appear insignificant to you the hardship
that has befallen us, our kings, our princes,
our priests, our prophets, our fathers, and all your people,
from the days of the Assyrian kings
until this very day.

33 You are in the right with respect
to everything that has come upon us;
for you acted faithfully,
while we did wrong.

34 Our kings, our princes, our priests
and our fathers did not fulfill your law,
nor pay attention to your commands
and stipulations about which you warned them.

35 Even in theirⁿ own kingdom—

m–m LXX "strong."
n LXX "your."

despite your manifold goodness
which you bestowed upon them,
despite the expansive and productive land
which you marked out before them—
they did not serve you
nor turn away from their evil deeds.

36 Behold, we are
servants today—
and the land you gave to our fathers
to eat its produce °and its good,
behold we are
servants on it.

37 Its abundant produce goes° to the kings
Whom you set over us because of our sins;
they rule over our persons,
and over our cattle as they please.
We are in great distress.

°–° Omitted by LXX.

NOTES

ix 2. *their sins . . . fathers.* Cf. *'t 'wwnnw w't 'wwn 'bwtynw* "our
iniquity and the iniquity of our fathers" in 4Q Dib Ham, col. 6:5 f. (M.
Baillet, "Un Recueil liturgique de Qumran, Grotte 4: 'Les paroles des
luminaires,'" RB 68 [1961], 195–250).

5. *be praised. wyborak* for *wybār^ekū.*

6. *everything in them.* Cf. 4Q Dib Ham, col. 7:8.

10. *toward them.* I.e., the fathers.

14. *Through Moses.* Literally "by the hand of Moses." The exact
phrase occurs in 4Q Dib Ham, col. 5:14.

15. *you swore.* Literally "lifted up your hand."

16. *became stubborn.* Literally "stiffened or hardened their neck."

17. *your miracles.* Cf. 4Q Dib Ham, col. 2:11–12.

stubborn. See NOTE on vs. 16.

25. *reveled. 'dn* "reveled" occurs only here in the Bible. Cf. 4Q Dib
Ham, col. 4:14, *wyw'klw wyśb'w wydšnw* "and they ate and gorged
themselves and grew fat."

26. *accused.* I.e., they bore witness in court against Israel, before God.

32, 34. *our kings*. Cf. Ezra ix 7; 4Q Dib Ham, col. 3:15, reads
wmlkynw "our kings," in a series.

34. *stipulations*. Cf. Aram. *'d, 'dn* (plural) in A. Dupont-Sommer,
Les Inscriptions araméennes de Sfiré (Paris, 1958), p. 147, where references to textual occurrences are given.

COMMENT

[A day of penance, ix 1–5]: In the present sequence of chapters in Ezra-Nehemiah, the day of penance falls in the seventh
month (vii 73b). The whole series of events of that month began
with a reading of the law in which was found an exhortation to
celebrate the Feast of Booths (viii 14). It began forthwith on the
fifteenth day of the month and lasted for seven days (Lev xxiii 33).
Then, "on the twenty-fourth day of this month," a day of penance
was celebrated. This appears to have been a special day of penance
and is not to be connected with the Day of Atonement, since the
latter fell on a different day. (For a discussion of the Day of Atonement in general see De Vaux, IAT, II, pp. 415 f.) However, it does
not follow that the Day of Atonement was not yet instituted simply
because there is no specific mention of it in Ezra-Nehemiah. It is
difficult to imagine how such a significant celebration could have
been introduced with Mosaic authority after the Exile.

Something is wrong with the order of events here since it would
be strange to have a day of penance following a festival of joy
(Lev xxiii 40). Most commentators believe that (see COMMENT
on Sec. 11) chapters viii–x have been displaced. Rudolph, p. 154,
is probably right in placing chapter ix after the proceedings described in Ezra x, which were concerned with the thorny problem
of marriages between the Jews and the people of the land. The
sequence of events would then be as follows: (a) a Jerusalem
assembly on the twentieth day of the ninth month (Ezra x 9); (b)
examination of cases begun on the first day of the tenth month
(x 16); (c) examination completed by the first day of the first
month (x 17); (d) reconvening of the assembly for confession on
twenty-fourth day of "this month" (Neh ix 1). (Ahlemann has the
same order, except that he places vss. 1–5 between Ezra x 15 and
x 16 [ZAW 59 (1942/43), 88–90]. So also Torrey, CHI, *in loco*.
On the possible reasons for the shift see Torrey, ES, pp. 257 f.

Mowinckel says chapters ix–x have nothing to do literarily with the Ezra history or the memoirs of Nehemiah [VuH, p. 212].) Certainly vs. 2a connects this penitential service with the putting away of foreign wives. The service itself seems to have been held for the benefit of those who were guilty and not the whole assembly of Israel, as vs. 1 appears to indicate. The influence of the ceremonies of the preceding chapter is apparent here. The service consisted of the reading of the law and the confession, each occupying a fourth part of the day. As in the law-reading ceremony, the Levites occupied a prominent place; their duty was to lead the congregation in worship (cf. II Chron xx 21), as well as to help the people understand the law (viii 7 f.). Why there are two lists is uncertain. It may be that the Levites led the people first in confession and then in exhortation and praise. But that is by no means certain since the names are not all the same—only five are alike.

[The penitential prayer psalm, 6–37]: One of the Chronicler's favorite methods of exhortation and instruction—partly taken over from the Deuteronomist—was prayer; cf. David's prayer before the congregation of Israel (I Chron xxix 10–19), Jehoshaphat's prayer when faced by invasion (II Chron xx 6–12), and Ezra's prayer when informed of the mixed marriages (Ezra ix 6–15). (See discussion by O. Plöger, "Reden und Gebete im deuteronomischen und chronistischen Geschichtswerk," in *Festschrift für Günther Dehn* [1957], especially pp. 44–49. Cf. Baillet, RB 68 [1961], 195–250, which contains an excellent illustration of a later liturgical prayer of penitence.)

Doubtless some prayer of confession and petition formed a part of the original penitential service carried out by Ezra for those who had been guilty of contamination through intermarriage. Whether it was this prayer—especially that part of it applying to the situation at hand (vss. 32–37)—may be questioned. As it stands, the prayer is a composition drawn from many areas and, like Pss lxxviii, cv–cvi, reflects a deep feeling for the nation's historical experiences, as illustrated by the conceptions of the Deuteronomist. As such it centers around the manifestation of Yahweh's covenant of grace and love always evident in his dealings with his chosen people (for the character of the prayer, cf. D. N. Freedman, CBQ 23 [1961], 440). Their sorry plight now was the result of their defection from him and through their stubbornness and rebellion—as was the case at other points in their history (vss. 16 ff., 26 ff.). This prayer psalm is a marvelous expression of God's continued faithfulness to his covenant despite the nation's equally continued apostasy.

The language and thought relationships—sources and influences —of this prayer psalm may be seen from the following parallels, which are illustrative though they may not be direct quotations. The parallels follow the versification of Kittel, *Biblia Hebraica,* 3d ed. Each line is identified by the number of the verse with a letter indicating the sequential order of the line; for example, 6a means the first line of vs. 6, 6b the second line of vs. 6, etc.

Verse 6a: II Kings xix 15; Isa xxxvii 16, 20; Ps lxxxvi 10 (all with *'lhym*); II Kings xix 19 (adds *'lhym*).

    6b: II Kings xix 15; Isa xxxvii 16; Jer xxxii 17.

    6c: Deut x 14; I Kings viii 27; Ps cxlviii 4; II Chron ii 5, vi 18.

    7a: Cf. 6a.

    7c: Gen xv 7.

    7d: Gen xvii 5.

    8:    Cf. Gen xv (*J*).

    8h: Jer xii 1; Ps cxix 137; Lam i 18; Ezra ix 15. See 1QH 14:15.

    9a: Cf. Exod iii 7, iv 31.

    10a: Cf. Deut iv 34, vii 19, xiii 2, 3, xxvi 8, xxviii 46, xxix 2, xxxiv 11; Isa xx 3; Jer xxxii 20, 21; Ps cxxxv 9.

    10d: Isa lxiii 12, 14; Jer xxxii 20; Dan ix 15.

    11a: Cf. Isa lxiii 12; Ps lxxviii 13.

11c, d: Exod xv 5.

    11d: Cf. Isa xliii 16.

12a, b: Exod xiii 21; Num xiv 14.

    12c: Exod xiii 21; Neh ix 19.

    12d: Cf. II Chron vi 27; Neh ix 19.

13a, b: Exod xix 11, 20; cf. Exod xx 22.

    13e: Cf. Mal ii 6.

    15a: Exod xvi 4; Ps cv 40.

    15c: Num xx 8.

15e, f: Cf. vs. 23; Deut xi 31; Josh i 11, xviii 3; Judg xviii 9.

15g, h: Exod vi 8; Num xiv 30; Ezek xx 6, 15, 28, 42, xlvii 14.

    16b: Deut x 16; II Kings xvii 14; Jer vii 26, xvii 23, xix 15; II Chron xxxvi 13; 1QS 4:11, 5:5, 6:26; 1QH f. 12:4.

16c: Deut xi 28 (positive commands—Deut xi 13, 27, xxviii 13).

17a: Cf. I Sam viii 19; Jer xi 10.

17b: Cf. Ps cv 5 ‖ I Chron xvi 12.

17d: Cf. 16b.

17e, f: Cf. Num xiv 4.

17g: Cf. Ps cxxx 4; Dan ix 9.

17h: Joel ii 13; Jon iv 2; Pss cxi 4, cxii 4, cxlv 8; II Chron xxx 9; Neh ix 31; Exod xxxiv 6; Pss lxxxvi 15, ciii 8.

17i: Exod xxxiv 6; Num xiv 18; Joel ii 13; Jon iv 2; Pss lxxxvi 15, ciii 8; 1QS 4:4, 5; 1QH 12:14, 16:16; 1QH f. 2:5.

17j: Cf. vss. 19, 28, 31; Ezra ix 9.

18a: Exod xxxii 4, 8; Deut ix 16.

18c, d: Exod xxxii 4, 8.

18e: Cf. vs. 26; Ezek xxxv 12; 4QT 28.

19a: Cf. vs. 31; Dan ix 18; Isa liv 7; Pss li 3, lxix 17, cxix 156.

19c–g: Cf. vs. 12.

20a: Ps cxliii 10.

20c, d: Cf. vs. 15.

21a, b: Deut ii 7.

21c, d: Deut viii 4, xxix 4.

22d, e: Num xxi, xxxii 33; Deut ii, iii; Pss cxxxv 11, cxxxvi 19–20.

23a: Cf. Gen xxii 17, xxvi 4; Exod xxxii 13; Deut i 10, x 22, xxviii 62; I Chron xxvii 23.

23b: Judg ii 1; cf. Jer ii 7.

23c, d: Cf. Deut x 11, xxxi 7; Josh i 6, v 6, xxi 43–44.

24a, b: Cf. Deut iv 1, viii 1, x 11, xi 8.

24c, d: Cf. Deut ix 3; Judg iv 23; I Chron xvii 10.

24e: Cf. vs. 30; Judg i 4.

24f: Cf. vs. 30; Deut vii 24; Josh xi 12, 17.

25a: Cf. Deut iii 5, ix 1 ff.; Josh xiv 12.

25b: Cf. vs. 35; Num xiii 20.

25c–f: Deut vi 11; cf. Deut viii 7 ff.

25g, h: Deut xxxii 15 (cf. LXX); 1QH 10:16.

26a, b: I Kings xiv 9; Ezek xxiii 35; Ps l 17.

26c: I Kings xviii 4, xix 10, 14.

26d, e: Cf. vs. 34; II Kings xvii 15; Amos iii 13; II Chron xxiv 19.

26f: See 18e.

27a: Ezek xxxix 23; Ps lxxviii 61.

27b: Judg ii 15 (vs. 27 refers to the period of Judges); cf.
       I Kings viii 37 || II Chron vi 28; Jer x 18.

27c: Exod xiv 10 f.; Josh xxiv 7; Judg iv 3, etc.; Ps cvii 6, 28;
       cf. Ps xxxiv 18.

27d: Cf. II Chron vi 21, 23, 25, 30, 33.

27e: Cf. vss. 19, 28, 31; Ps cxix 156; Dan ix 18; II Sam
       xxiv 14; I Chron xxi 13.

27f: Cf. Judg iii 9, 15; II Kings xiii 5.

27g: Cf. Judg ii 18, vi 14, viii 22, x 12; I Sam ix 16; Zech
       ix 16; Pss xxxiv 7, xliv 8.

28:    Cf. vs. 27 (period of Judges).

29a: Cf. vs. 26d.

30b: Cf. Zech vii 12; I Sam viii 19; Jer xi 7, xlii 19; Amos
       iii 13.

30c: II Kings xvii 13; II Chron xxiv 19.

30e: Cf. Judg vi 1, xiii 1; II Kings xiii 3; Jer xx 4, 5, xxi 7,
       xxii 25; Ezek vii 21, xxi 36 (31E); Ps cvi 41.

31a: Cf. vs. 19.

31b: Cf. Jer iv 27, v 18, xxx 11, xlvi 28.

31d, e: Cf. vs. 17i.

32a, b: Deut x 17; cf. Jer xxxii 18; Pss lxxvii 14, xcvi 3; Dan
         ix 4; Neh i 5.

32c: Deut vii 9; I Kings viii 23; Dan ix 4; Neh i 5; II Chron
       vi 14.

32d: Cf. Exod xviii 8; Num xx 14.

33a: Cf. Jer xii 1; Ps cxix 137; Dan ix 14; Ezra ix 15, cf. vs. 8.

33d: Ps cvi 6; Dan ix 5; 1QS 1:25.

34:    Cf. vs. 32; note omission of the prophets.

34d: Cf. II Kings xvii 15; Ps cxxxii 12.

35b: Cf. vs. 25; Ps cxlv 7.

35g: Cf. Deut xxviii 20; Jer iv 4, xxi 12, xxiii 2, xliv 22;
       Zech i 4.

36c: Cf. Deut vi 23, xix 8, xxvi 9; Josh ii 9; II Chron vi 31.

36d: Jer ii 7; cf. Isa i 19b.

37:    Cf. I Sam viii 11–17.

The author of our prayer psalm drew upon a wide knowledge of
the theology and traditions of his people, skillfully weaving into it

elements of instruction, exhortation, and confession. As such it is prophetic rather than priestly. Galling, p. 239, thinks it was taken from an extracanonical collection of hymns. The last verse may reflect a period different from that of the time of Ezra, when the Persian king endeavored to assist the Jews. For a similar view see v 15; for that of a later period see the Greek of Dan iii 32. See Rudolph, pp. 156 f., who thinks the prayer was not composed by Ezra; he could hardly have harbored such hostility toward the Persian authorities as are expressed in the last verse. J. Morgenstern (HUCA 20 [1947], 21, n. 34) thinks it was originally "part of the synagogue liturgy" of the period before Ezra. On its influence on the synagogue liturgy, see L. J. Liebreich, HUCA 32 (1961), 227–37.

The whole prayer ends with an acknowledgment of the wrongs committed by the people and emphasizes the consequent hardships being endured by them. Through it all runs the implied hope that Yahweh has taken note and will grant them relief. Inasmuch as there is no direct connection between the prayer and the surrounding events—it is not ascribed to any person or persons by MT—it may have been added later.

14. THE WRITTEN PLEDGE OF REFORM: SIGNERS AND PROVISIONS
(x 1–40)

The sealed document with its signatories

X ¹ In view of all this we are executing a written agreement whose sealed document bears [the name of] our princes, our Levites, and our priests. ² Upon the sealed document were the names of Nehemiah, *the governor*, the son of Hacaliah and Zedekiah, ³ Seraiah, Azariah, Jeremiah, ⁴ Pashhur, Amariah, Malchijah, ⁵ Hattush, Shebaniah, Malluch, ⁶ Harim, Meremoth, Obadiah, ⁷ Daniel, Ginnethon, Baruch, ⁸ Meshullam, Abijah, Mijamin, ⁹ Maaziah*ᵇ*, Bilgai, Shemaiah—these were the priests.

¹⁰ The Levites were Jeshua the son of Azaniah, Binnui of the sons of Henadad, Kadmiel ¹¹ and *their brothers* Shebaniah*ᵈ*, Hodiah, Kelita, Pelaiah*ᵉ*, Hanan*ᵉ*, ¹² *Mica, Rehob, Hashabiah*, ¹³ Zaccur, Sherebiah, Shebaniah, ¹⁴ Hodiah, Bani*ᵍ*, Beninu.

¹⁵ The heads of the people were Parosh, Pahath-moab, Elam, Zattu, Bani*ʰ*, ¹⁶ Bunni*ʰ*, Azgad, Bebai, ¹⁷ Adonijah, Bigvai, Adin, ¹⁸ Ater, Hezekiah, Azzur, ¹⁹ Hodiah, Hashum, Bezai, ²⁰ Hariph, Anathoth, Nobai*ⁱ*, ²¹ Magpiash*ʲ*, Meshullam, Hezir, ²² Meshezabel, Zadok, Jaddua*ᵏ*, ²³ Pelatiah, Hanan, Anaiah, ²⁴ Hoshea, Hananiah, Hasshub, ²⁵ Hallohesh, Pilha, Shobek, ²⁶ Rehum, Hashabnah, Maaseiah, ²⁷ Ahijah*ˡ*, Hanan, Anan, ²⁸ Malluch, Harim, Baanah.

ᵃ⁻ᵃ Omitted by LXX. See NOTE.
ᵇ LXXᴮ "Nadeia." LXXᴬ follows MT.
ᶜ⁻ᶜ LXX "his brothers."
ᵈ Some MSS, LXXᴸ "Shekaniah."
ᵉ Omitted by LXXᴮ.
ᶠ⁻ᶠ Omitted by LXX.
ᵍ MT, LXX "sons."
ʰ MT, LXX "sons of Bani."
ⁱ LXXᴮ "Bonai." LXXᴬ follows MT.
ʲ LXX "Bagaphes." LXXᴬ "Maiaphos."
ᵏ Omitted by LXX.
ˡ LXXᴮ "Ara."

Introduction to code

29 The rest of the people, the priests, the Levites, the gate-keepers, the singers, the temple slaves, and all those who had separated themselves from the peoples of the land to the law of God, together with their wives, their sons, their daughters, and all those who had [reached the age of] discretion 30 joined their worthy brethren in a solemn oath to follow the law of God which had been transmitted through Moses the servant of God, and to observe and act in accordance with all the commands of Yahweh, our Lord, with his judgments and his statutes.

The code of Nehemiah

31 We will not give our daughters in marriage to the peoples of the land nor allow our sons to take their daughters in marriage; 32 we will not buy from them on the Sabbath or holy day the wares or any grain which the peoples of the land might bring on the Sabbath day to sell, and we will forego [the produce] of the seventh year and the exaction of any debt therein. 33 Moreover we obligated ourselves to contribute one third shekel yearly for the service of the house of our God—34 for the layer bread, for the continual meal offering, for the continual burnt offering, the Sabbaths, the new moons, festivals, and consecrated [gift] offerings and the sin offerings to atone for Israel, and for all the work of the house of our God. 35 We determined by lot the supply of wood which the priests, the Levites, and the people by families, at the appointed times year by year, were to bring to the house of our God to burn upon the altar of Yahweh our God, as prescribed in the law^m. 36 We further obligated ourselves to bring in yearly the first fruits of our land and the first fruits of all our orchards to the house of Yahweh, 37 and in addition thereto bring in the first-born of our sons and our cattle, as prescribed in the law, and the first-born of our herds and our

^{m} LXX^B *biblio* "book." LXX^A has *tō nomō* "the law."

flocks to the house of our God for the priests who minister in the house of our God. 38 We will bring also the choicest of our dough[n], our contributions, and of the fruit of every tree, of wine and of oil to the priests in the chambers of the house of our God and the tithe of our land to the Levites—the Levites being the ones who collect the tithes in all our cult cities: 39 the Aaronite priest must accompany the Levites when they collect the tithes and the Levites must take up a tithe of the tithes to the house of our God, to the chambers of the treasury, 40 for the Israelites and the Levites must bring the produce of grain, wine, and oil to those chambers where the vessels of the sanctuary, the ministering priests, the gatekeepers, and the singers are. We will not neglect the house of our God.

[n] LXX *sitos* "grain."

NOTES

x 1. *In view of all this* . . . *[the name of]*. Literally "and because of all this we are making an agreement and writing [it], and upon the sealed [document are the names of] . . .". For an excellent study of seals and sealing in OT see S. Moscati, "I sigilli nell' Antico Testamento," *Biblica* 30 (1949), 314–38; on Neh x 1–2, p. 320.

A written agreement. krtym 'mnh is a surrogate for *krt bryt* "to cut a covenant."

2. *the names of*. Reading *'l hḥtwm* (as in vs. 1) for *w'l hḥtwmym* "and upon those sealed." Cf. Vulg. *signatores autem fuerunt,* which means "but the signers were."

the governor. May have been added from viii 9. But the office of high officials is sometimes specified before their family connection—cf. C. C. Torrey (AASOR 2/3 [1921–22], 107 f.), who describes a seal inscribed: "Judah, overseer, son of Abba." Also in Persian documents of the same period as Nehemiah-Ezra; see Clay, *Business Documents of Murashu Sons,* pp. 27, 31; F. E. Peiser, *Texte juristischen und geschäftlichen Inhalts,* (Berlin, 1896), pp. 217, 237.

7. *Ginnethon*. May appear on a spindle whorl from Beth-shean Valley dating possibly from sixth–fifth centuries (IEJ 9 [1959], 191 f.).

21. *Hezir*. The name occurs in I Chron xxiv 15 and on the architrave of the hypogeum of St. James. Cf. Parrot, *Golgotha,* pp. 90–92, and

references there. On the meaning of the name, see Noth, IPN, p. 230, and R. de Vaux in *Von Ugarit nach Qumran*, 1958, p. 257, n. 46.

22. *Meshezabel*. See NOTE on iii 4, Sec. 4.

24. *Hasshub*. See NOTE on I Chron ix 14 in *I Chronicles* (The Anchor Bible, vol. 12).

28. *Baanah*. May appear on a seal impression from Ramat Rahel (IEJ 7 [1957], 153).

29. *All those who had [reached . . .] discretion*. Literally "everyone knowing understanding." Cf. I Sam xvi 16.

30. *a solemn oath*. Literally "a curse and an oath," i.e., an oath with penalty or sanction.

transmitted through Moses. Literally "given by the hand of Moses."

31. *W'šr*, meaning "and that," which opens the verse, is omitted in translation. It appears to connect with vs. 1. If translated it might read "namely," "to wit."

32. *exaction of any debt therein*. Literally "loan [debt] of every hand." Adding *bh* "therein," i.e., in the seventh year. For meaning of *mš'* see De Vaux, IAT, I, p. 263.

33. *we obligated ourselves to contribute*. Literally "we placed ourselves under obligation to contribute."

one third shekel. Approximately 58.76 grains.

38. *the ones who collect*. So with Gesenius-Buhl, *Hebraisches und Aramäisches Handwörterbuch*, 14th ed. Cf. also Rudolph and Schneider, *in loco*.

COMMENT

Chapter x seems to be out of place, though its original position and date are uncertain. (Cf. A. Jepsen ["Nehemia 10," ZAW 66 (1954), 87–106], who thinks it belongs to the period of Ezra, whom he places before Nehemiah.) The editor's association of the legal document with the immediately preceding Ezra material is clearly responsible for its present position. There is some doubt as to whether the connecting phrase "In view of all this" stood in the original document or whether it is the editor's (see Schneider, p. 219). Rudolph, pp. 172 f., thinks that chapter x is speech and not narrative and that the Chronicler views it as the conclusion of the Ezra story, with the pledge of the people to keep the law of Ezra. The stipulations of the document, however, favor connection with Ezra at only one point—the vow against mixed marriages. But they do, on the other hand, fit in with the community situation reflected in Neh xiii as may be seen from the following table.

Chapter x	Chapter xiii
a. Agree to follow the law of God (vs. 30) which forbids	a. Desecration of temple by Tobiah (vss. 1–9).
(1) intermarriage with foreigners (31)	b. Neglect of tithe (10–13).
(2) trading on the Sabbath (32).	c. Problem of Sabbath trade (15–22).
b. Agree to contribute ⅓ shekel per year for the service of the house of God (33–34).	d. Mixed marriages (23–28).
	e. Provision for the services of priests and Levites (30).
c. Agree to supply wood for the altar (35).	f. Provision of wood for altar and presentation of first fruits (31).
d. Agree to bring yearly first fruits	
(1) of land and orchards (36)	
(2) of sons and cattle (37).	
e. Agree to contribute other choice products and tithes of the land (38).	

[Introduction, x 1]: The introductory verse points up clearly the nature of the document reproduced here. Its legal character is illustrated in two ways: it bore the names of the religious and lay leaders, and it was officially sealed. The order—princes, Levites, priests —is not the same as the list that follows, indicating that it is the work of the compiler.

[The signatories, 2–28]: The list is composed of four groups: (a) the leaders, (b) priests, (c) Levites, (d) laymen. It looks like an official list taken from the temple archives. The order of the groups is interesting. Verse 1 has princes, Levites, priests. The editorial verses in II Chron xix 8 and xxx 21 also place the Levites before the priests, though the laymen are last. The lists in Ezra-Nehemiah, which appear to be archival, always have the priests before the Levites.

Ezra ii & Neh vii	Ezra viii	Ezra x	Neh x 3 ff.	Neh xi	Neh xii
Laymen	Priests	Priests	Priests	Laymen	Priests
Priests	Laymen	Levites	Levites	Priests	Levites
Levites		Laymen	Laymen	Levites	
Temple slaves				Gatekeepers	
Solomon's slaves					

The names themselves and the order are just what might be expected. At the head of the present list stands the name of Nehemiah, the governor, followed by that of Zedekiah, who may have been his secretary. Neh xiii 13 records a Zadok as secretary. Legal documents generally were attested by the scribe and witnesses (ANET, pp. 219–23). The name of the scribe stands before that of the other witnesses.

Apparently the priestly attestations were by families, at least in part. The high-priestly family signed under the name of Seraiah, who held office at the time of the Exile (cf. II Kings xxv 18; Jer lii 24; for the genealogy of the high priests see I Chron vi 1–15). Pashhur and Harim are old family names, as may also be true of Amariah (Immer?). The family of Daniel, of the Ithamar line, is mentioned also in Ezra viii 2. The list in Ezra ii 36–39 and Neh vii 39–42 records only four families; that in Ezra viii has two, one of which is the Ithamar line represented by Daniel, whose name appears in this chapter also. The Nehemiah lists are earlier than the arrangement of the twenty-four courses of I Chron xxiv 7–18, since x 2–8 and xii 12–21 have only twenty-one names; xii 1–7 has twenty-three. The parallels in Appendix I illustrate the situation as it exists. Clearly some of the families continued to maintain their identity. Others were added, perhaps from those remaining in the land or as soon as they were able to prove their genealogy (Ezra ii 59–63; Neh vii 61–65). For example, the family of Hakkoz, whose identity could not be proven earlier, was included among the courses of I Chron xxiv. As they stand, Neh x seems to be the earliest of the expanded lists (see Jepsen, ZAW 66 [1954]).

The Levites are listed, for the most part, as individuals and not by families (cf. Meyer, EJ, pp. 178–79). This may be seen from I Chron vi, xxiii, where the genealogy of Levi is given. That there were additions to the Levites is evident from a comparison of the lists in Nehemiah (see Appendix I). Ezra ii 40 ‖ Neh vii 43 has only three families, as does Ezra viii 18–19 (here the names are different but they represent only those whom Ezra was able to persuade to return with him). The list here in Neh x contains seventeen names. Those in Neh ix 4–5 contain eight each; six of the names in vs. 4 are identical with those found in chapter x, though not in the same order, while the other two (Bunni and Hanani) are probably so. Verse 5 also has six, also found in chapter x one (Hashabneiah) probably so; one new name appears there (Pethahiah). The first list in Neh xii (8–9) also has eight names, four of which occur in chapter x, one probably so, and in Neh xii there are three new names. The second list in Neh xii (24–25) has only three names, with the family of Kadmiel represented by Jeshua. From this list we learn that Mattaniah and Bakbukiah of the earlier Neh xii list (in vss. 8–9) were gatekeepers.

The list of laymen is expanded far beyond that of Ezra ii and Neh vii, but fourteen of the first twenty-one names occur there. Whether the Harim of our list is the Harim of the others is not certain, though probably so because he appears near the end in all three lists. This expanded list represents the growth of the community by the addition of those who had not gone into exile or who had returned to the land from hideouts during the Babylonian invasion. Also included are families that were probably new but developed as separate branches from older ones (e.g., Hezekiah from Ater, vs. 18; cf. Ezra ii 16; Neh vii 21) or took the names of the towns in which they settled (e.g., Anathoth and Nobai, vs. 20; Meyer, EJ, p. 156). Several of the family names occur in the builders list of Neh iii—Parosh, Pahath-moab, Meshezabel, Hallohesh, Ananiah, Baana(h), Harim, Hananiah, Hashabanah. The omission of such prominent family names as Shephatiah, Arah, and Zaccai may be accidental (EJ, p. 154; Rudolph, p. 175) or they could have been replaced by descendants who may have adopted other names. Two of the names are missing from Ezra viii and all three from Ezra x, where other names occur. The family of Joab in Ezra viii 9 is apparently a new independent branch of the Pahath-moab family (cf. Ezra ii 6; Neh vii 11). The people at Nob (Nebo, in Ezra x 43) adopted the town name. See Schneider, p. 221.

[Summary statement of oath, 29–30]: With the possible exception of "The rest of the people," these two verses offer a summary statement of the oath-taking ceremony. The groups are listed in more detail—the gatekeepers, the singers, the temple slaves. Special emphasis is laid upon those who had cut all ties with "the peoples of the land," that is, those who were regarded as unclean through intermarriage and other relationships. The whole community of Israel bound itself by a solemn oath to observe the law of God, which was doubtless that brought along by Ezra. Verse 30b is simply an explanatory clause in the language of the Deuteronomist.

[The code of Nehemiah, 31–40]: The obligations the community laid upon itself were sealed by a covenant. They centered around strategic needs and problems. The problem of community obligations was a community enterprise involving every segment of the population; though inspired by the leadership, it had the whole-hearted co-operation of all the component groups.

[AGAINST INTERMARRIAGE WITH THE PEOPLES OF THE LAND, 31]: This was one of the most persistent problems that plagued the new community. Ezra (ix–x) had to deal with it; so did Nehemiah (xiii). The basis for the injunction is mostly D (Deut vii 3), though the undergirding legal principle is undoubtedly J's prohibition against having covenantal relationships with foreigners (Exod xxxiv 12–16). Observe the sweeping nature of the self-imposed regulation that has to do only with prospective marriages. It says nothing about those who had already entered upon such marriages; presumably they were dealt with earlier. It was really the incidents noted above that precipitated the present rule.

[AGAINST SABBATH TRADE, 32ab]: This regulation resulted from the practices noted in xiii 15–22 and rested on the well-known commandment to hallow the Sabbath day (Exod xx 8–11; Deut v 12–15). However, this precept goes beyond the Sabbath regulation; it includes holy days—the new moon and festivals. It takes for granted that the people would not trade among themselves on the holy days and hence specifies only transactions with the peoples of the land who had no such prohibition.

[ON THE SEVENTH YEAR, 32c]: The command for the seventh-year rest for the land and fruit trees appears in the Covenant Code (Exod xxiii 10–11; cf. Lev xxv 2–7). The specification that the natural produce was for the poor of the land probably is responsible for the addition here of the Deuteronomic law of release (Deut xv 1–3), which enjoined the collection of debts during the Sabbath year. This precept doubtless grew out of the complaint of the poor dealt with in Neh v and was meant to prevent the recurrence of such a situation.

[PROVISION FOR THE TEMPLE SERVICE, 33–34]: The temple services required considerable expenditure of funds that were earlier provided by the Persian court. Here there is recognition of Israel's responsibility, hence a reversion to Pentateuchal principles. The P code (Exod xxx 13) specified that every male Israelite twenty years and over must contribute a half shekel yearly for the sanctuary. The Chronicler (II Chron xxiv 6) refers to the Mosaic tax levied for the sanctuary. The shift from a half to a third shekel may be explained by the fact that the Persian monetary system was based on ten silver shekels for one gold shekel, whereas the sacred shekel was in the proportion of fifteen to one.

(a) The layer bread. The four names by which it was known were (1) *lhm hm'rkt* "the layer bread" (Lev xxiv 6); (2) *lhm hpnym* "presence bread" (I Sam xxi 7; I Kings vii 48); (3) *lhm htmyd* "the continual bread" (Num iv 7); (4) *m'rkt tmyd* "continual layer [bread]" II Chron ii 3). The layer bread is mentioned first because it was connected directly with the temple itself. The *P* code alone provides for it (Exod xxv 30; Lev xxiv 5–9) but the references in I Sam xxi 6 and I Kings vii 48 indicate that it was an old custom. (b) The continual meal offering and continual burnt offering (cf. Exod xxix 38–42; Num xxviii 3–8). The continual burnt offering specified one lamb each for morning and evening. The continual meal offering was really an adjunct thereto. Both were provided for earlier by the Persian authorities (Ezra vi 9, vii 17). (c) Offerings for Sabbath, new moon, and festivals (cf. Num xxviii 9–xxix 39). To care for all such offerings would probably require more than could be provided by the head tax, which may thus have been supplementary to governmental subsidy. (d) Consecrated gift offerings, which were apparently the materials for the public offerings since they were provided for out of the one third shekel tax (cf. II Chron xxix 33, xxxv 13b). (e) The sin offering (cf. Lev iv 1–v 13; Num xv 22–29), which assumed a prominent place in Ezekiel and in the rituals of the *P* code. De Vaux, IAT, II, pp. 296–99). (f) The work of the house of God refers to the care of the property itself, as may be seen from the different terms for work employed here and in vs. 33 (*'bdt* "service").

This passage once again reflects the strong cultic interests of the Chronicler. As has been noted elsewhere, those interests were not just idiosyncrasies; they were born of necessity, as attested in almost every postexilic document. The survival of the Jewish community depended on the maintenance of cultic identity and the rejection of compromise with the peoples of the land.

[WOOD SUPPLY FOR SACRIFICES, 35]: So far as we know there was no law dealing with supplying wood for the altar. It is probable that the last clause of the verse refers to Lev vi 12 f. (vi 5 f.H), which prescribes continual fire upon the altar and the burning of wood every morning (i.e., in connection with the sacrifice). The regulation here simply lays down the principle by which the various groups were to operate in the fulfillment of their obligation to supply the wood to be burned upon the altar. Cambyses withdrew the wood

income of the Egyptian temples (cf. Kienitz, GÄJZ, p. 59). Josephus *Wars* II.xvii.6 mentions a festival of Xylophory. See also
Mishna *Taanit* 4:5.

[OTHER CONTRIBUTIONS, 36–40]: The regular support for the religious institutions is one of the most insistent injunctions of the law.
The offering of the first fruits (*bkwrym*) of the land is an old and
fundamental practice, as may be seen from Exod xxiii 19, xxxiv 26;
Deut xxvi 1–11; it is emphasized in Ezek xliv 30 and in *P*. On
the first-born and tithes, see Eissfeldt, *Erstlinge und Zehnten im
Alten Testament*. The offerings of first fruits are to be brought directly to the house of Yahweh; nothing is said here (vs. 36) of the
specific use to which they were put, though they probably went to
support the clergy (cf. Num xviii 13; Ezek xliv 30, etc.). Designation of Yahweh's house rather than the priests' may have been to
avoid contributions to individuals or families directly or to encour-
age the movement of the clergy to Jerusalem. The law upon which
these regulations rests (Num xviii 8–20) also includes the gift of
the first-born of man and cattle. Probably the latter were used in
sacrifices whose meat went to the priests. Further support for the
priests came from the choicest products (*r'šyt*) of home and farm.
This too was an application of older practices. The dough here appears in the Torah as coarse meal in Num xv 20–21 (*P*) and
Ezek xliv 30. The legal basis for the best of the products of orchard
and vineyard is Num xviii 12 (*P*); Deut xviii 4, xxvi 1–4. This was
in effect a double portion of the products of the land set aside for
the services of God's house. The law of the tithe for the Levites is
clearly stated in Num xviii 21–32. Originally the tithe may have
been brought to them directly for consumption in their cities. But
support for the Levites was apparently unsatisfactory (Ezra viii 15)
and in the new community a new method of collecting the tithe had
to be instituted or renewed. The Levites thus were to collect the
tithes in their cult cities. The presence of a priest with the collectors
is mentioned only here. The tithing of the tithe itself is simply the
reassertion of the law of Num xviii 26.

The chief purpose of this little code (the code of Nehemiah, vss.
31–40) was to guarantee provision for the house of God through
support for the personnel and supplies for the offerings. For Nehemiah as for Ezra, the temple was all important, for without a strong
religious institution the nation could not survive.

15. DISTRIBUTION OF THE JEWS
IN AND OUTSIDE JERUSALEM
(xi 1–36)

Campaign for more residents

XI ¹ But the heads of the people lived in Jerusalem; so the rest of the people drew lots to bring one out of ten to live in Jerusalem, the holy city, while nine tenths*ᵃ* remained in the [outlying] towns. ² The people praised all the men who volunteered to take up residence in Jerusalem.

Lay leaders

³ These are the heads of the province who lived in Jerusalem— those in the towns of Judah lived, each one, on his own property in their towns:—the Israelites, the priests, the Levites, the temple slaves, and the descendants of Solomon's servants. ⁴ Some of the Judeans and some of the Benjaminites lived in Jerusalem—of the Judeans there was Athaiah the son of Uzziah, the son of Zechariah, the son of Amariah, the son of Shephatiah, the son of Mahalalel of the descendants of Perez; ⁵ and Maaseiah the son of Baruch, the son of Colhozeh, the son of Hazaiah, the son of Adaiah, the son of Joiarib, the son of Zechariah of the descendants of the Shilonites. ⁶ All the descendants of Perez who lived in Jerusalem numbered 468 outstanding men. ⁷ These are the descendants of Benjamin: Sallu the son of Meshullam, the son of Joed, the son of Pedaiah, the son of Kolaiah, the son of Masseiah, the son of Ithiel, the son of Jeshaiah, ⁸ and *ᵇhis brothersᵇ* Gabbai and Sallai, 928. ⁹ Joel the son of Zichri was

ᵃ LXX "parts."
ᵇ–ᵇ So with LXXᴸ. MT, Vulg., and LXX "after him."

their chief and Judah the son of Hassenuah was second in command over the city.

The priestly leaders

10 Of the priests there were Jedaiah the son of Joiarib, Jachin, 11 Seraiah the son of Hilkiah, the son of Meshullam, the son of Zadok, the son of Meraioth, the son of Ahitub, the chief of the house of God 12 and their brothers who conducted the service of the house, *822; and Adaiah the son of Jeroham, the son of Pelaliah, the son of* Amzi, the son of Zechariah, the son of Pashhur, the son of Malchijah, 13 *and his brothers*, family heads, 242; and Amashsai the son of Azarel, *the son of Ahzai, the son of Meshillemoth, the son of Immer*, 14 and *his brothers,* outstanding men, 128. Their chief was Zabdiel[d] the son of Haggedolim.[e]

The Levites

15 Of the Levites there were Shemaiah the son of Hasshub, the son of Azrikam, *the son of Hashabiah, the son of Bunni— 16 Shabbethai and Jozabad, Levitical chiefs, were in charge of the work outside the house of God*, 17 Mattaniah the son of Micah, *the son of Zabdi, the son of Asaph, who was the praise leader who intoned the thanksgiving in connection with the prayer while Bakbukiah was second among his brothers; and* Abda the son of Shammua, *the son of Galal, the son of Jeduthun.* 18 All the Levites in the holy city numbered* 284.

Other groups

19 The gatekeepers who kept watch at the gates were Akkub, Talmon, and their brothers; there were 172 of them. 20 *The rest of Israel, including the priests and the Levites, [remained]

c-c Omitted by LXX.
d LXX "Badiel." See NOTE.
e See NOTE.
f-f Omitted by LXX.

in all the towns of Judah, each on his own inheritance. 21 The temple slaves lived on Ophel, and Ziha and Gishpa were in charge of the temple slaves.ᶠ 22 The official in charge of the Levites ᶠin Jerusalemᶠ was Uzzi the son of Bani, the son of Hashabiah, the son of Mattaniah, the son of Mica, of the sons of Asaph who were the song leaders for the [worship] service of the house of God; 23 they were under royal orders ᶠand there was an ordinance for the singers setting forth the daily requirementsᶠ. 24 Pethahiah the son of Meshezabel, ᶠof the sons of Zerah the son of Judahᶠ, represented the interests of the people at the royal court.

List of towns in Judah and Benjamin

25 ᵍSome of the Judeans lived in the villages near their farms: in Kiriath-arbaᵍ ʰand its dependencies, Dibon and its dependencies, Jekabzeel and its villagesʰ, 26 ⁱJeshua, Moladah, Beth-pelet, 27 Hazar-shual, Beer-sheba and its dependencies, 28 Ziklag, Meconah and its dependencies, 29 En-rimmon, Zorah, Jarmuth,ⁱ 30 Zanoah, Adullam, ʲand their villages, Lachish and its farms and Azekah and its dependencies. They settled from Beer-shebaʲ ᵏas far as the Valley of Hinnom.ᵏ 31 The Benjaminites [lived] ˡin Gebaˡ, Michmas, Aijah, ᵏBethel and its dependencies, 32 Anathoth, Nob, Ananiah, 33 Hazor, Ramah, Gittaim, 34 Ha-did, Zeboim, Neballat, 35 Lod and Ono, the Valley of Craftsmen.ᵏ 36 Some of the Levitical groups of Judah were assigned to Benjamin.

ᵍ–ᵍ LXX "and at the dwellings in their territory [field]; some of the sons of Judah lived in Qirjath-arbok."
ʰ–ʰ Omitted by LXX.
ⁱ–ⁱ LXX omits all but Jeshua and Beer-sheba.
ʲ–ʲ LXX has only "and their villages, Lakish and its farms" and "they settled in Beer-sheba."
ᵏ–ᵏ Omitted by LXX.
ˡ–ˡ MT "from Geba."

NOTES

xi 1. *the holy city.* The expression occurs in Isa xlviii 2, lii 1 and in Dan ix 24; also in Tobit xiii 9; Matt iv 5, xxvii 53; Rev xi 2. Cf. Arabic name for Jerusalem: *el quds* "the holy." The holy city idea was rather widespread, as the term "hierapolis," the name of a number of cities, indicates. As far as its designation of Jerusalem is concerned, it probably grew out of the "holy of holies," so called because of the presence of Yahweh, this, in turn, made the temple holy and then, by extension, the city where the temple stood was referred to as the holy city.

nine tenths. Literally "nine of the hands or parts."

2. Permission to have their names considered was probably regarded as volunteering. That the ones who were thus chosen were praised for consenting to move to Jerusalem indicates that they were considered relatively unlucky; most of them would doubtless have preferred to remain where they were.

4. *Amariah.* For an Arabic tradition concerning this family, see *Anatolian Studies* 8 (1958), 82; and Dozy, *Die Israeliten zu Mekka von Davids Zeit bis in's fünfte Jahrhundert unsrer Zeitrechnung,* 1864, pp. 136 ff.

5. *Hazaiah.* The name *ḥz'l* occurs on an Aramaic ostracon from Nimrud, probably from seventh century B.C. See *Iraq* 19 (1957), 139 ff. "Hazaiah" is found only here in the Bible.

Shilonites. Cf. Num xxvi 20.

8. *Gabbai and Sallai.* Since these names do not occur elsewhere, the text has been emended by several commentators to read *gbwry ḥyl* "outstanding men" (cf. vs. 14). But the name "Sallai" occurs also in xii 20. Cf. *slw'* in Cowley, AP, 18:2; and the feminine name *slw'h,* AP, 67:3.

9. *chief.* On *pqyd* "chief," see references cited by Bowman, p. 774. In Cowley, AP, 37:6, it refers to the chief official of a province. E. Ebeling (*Neubabylonische Briefe aus Uruk* [Berlin, 1930–34], p. 44) thinks it means "chief of the city police."

second. On connection of "second" with Judah rather than with "city," cf. vs. 17. *Amel šanu* in Akkadian means "second in command in a series of officers"; see Peiser, *Texte juristischen und geschäftlichen Inhalts,* p. 189, XII, 15–18.

10. There is apparently some confusion here since the two following lines of priestly descent are given in regular form. It has been suggested that the verse read: "Jedaiah the son of Joiakim, the son of Seraiah," etc.

For details see Rudolph, *in loco,* and Bowman, p. 774; cf. Albright, JPOS 6 (1926), 96 f.

12. *their brothers.* If Rudolph is correct in reasoning that vss. 10, 11, give the Jedaiah line, i.e., the high priest's line, then we would have to read "his" brothers.

13. *Amashsai.* '*mšsy* is a combinatory spelling for '*mšy* and '*msy;* it stands for Amasiah (cf. II Chron xvii 16). For '*msy* cf. I Chron vi 25, 35, xii 18, xv 24; II Chron xxix 12. See Noth, IPN, p. 253, No. 1089.

14. *Zabdiel.* Zabdiel, as a name, occurs in I Chron xxvii 2 and in the papyri (Cowley, AP, 81:2) as Zabdiah.

Haggedolim. Missing in LXX; Vulg. *filius potentium* "son of the mighty." Meaning in context obscure; "the great ones" is hardly a personal name. It may refer to high-priestly descent (see Galling, p. 243, n. 8, and Rudolph, *in loco*).

15. *Hasshub.* See *I Chronicles,* NOTE on ix 14.

17. *praise.* Reading *hthlh* for *hthlh* "beginning"; cf. Vulg.

Bakbukiah was second among his brothers. Bakbukiah's position is not clear; he may have been the other leader or Mattaniah's substitute.

22. *service.* For this meaning of *ml'kh* "work," "service" see xiii 10; cf. I Chron ix 13.

24. *Meshezabel.* See NOTE on iii 4 in Sec. 4.

at the royal court. Literally "to the hand of the king, at the king's side" (cf. I Chron xviii 17). Thus he must have been a kind of Jewish ambassador handling their affairs at the court; but cf. Meyer, EJ, p. 190.

25. *Kiriath-arba.* On Kirjath-(ha)arba in this verse see Albright's remark in *Alexander Marx Jubilee Volume,* English Section, p. 364, n. 47a.

30. *Adullam.* There is some archaeological evidence for occupation of the area around Adullam in the Persian period (cf. RB, 67 [1960], 403–4). Lachish was also occupied. (Tufnell, *Lachish III: The Iron Age,* pp. 131 ff., and A. Dupont-Sommer in *Mélanges Isadore Levy* [Bruxelles], 1955, pp. 135 ff.)

COMMENT

For a detailed comparison between this chapter and I Chron ix, see my *I Chronicles,* COMMENT on Sec. 9. It is fairly clear that neither list was copied from the other; there are too many differences. Schneider may be right in surmising that both were copied from archival material (pp. 42 f., 231). I Chron ix attributes the list to the time of the return; Neh xi to that following the completion of the rebuilding of the wall. The work of Nehemiah centers about the construction of the walls of Jerusalem and the fortunes of the city thereafter. The story was interrupted by chapters viii–x. Chapter xi connects directly with vii 72, which speaks of "all Israel" dwelling in their towns. The security offered by the walls made the city a safer place and made additional space available for occupation. Both Sirach (xlix 13) and Josephus (*Antiquities* XI.v.8) credit Nehemiah with either rebuilding the ruined houses or constructing new ones. More emphasis upon the proper functions of the cultus demanded the services of more people and officials.

[Campaign for more residents, xi 1–2]: The leaders of Israel already resided in Jerusalem. Some of the builders doubtless remained after their task was finished. But there was need for others to fill the vacant places. Consequently an appeal was made to those who lived in the province and outside Jerusalem to take up residence in the city. As a result, some of the people residing elsewhere voluntarily agreed to move to Jerusalem. The selection was made by lot. Whether the "tenth" applies to those from the outlying areas who were chosen to dwell in the city or the proportion that was to be maintained between city and country is not quite clear. The willingness of the people to change their residence received praise from the nation.

[List of lay leaders in Jerusalem, 3–9]: The class order follows that of Ezra ii ‖ Neh vii and I Chron ix (see COMMENT on Sec. 14, ch. x). The list of heads of the province (i.e., Judah) who resided in Jerusalem represents a considerable expansion from the one in I Chron ix. This is only to be expected in view of the orientation of the two recensions. Verse 3 is an editorial introduction accommodating the statement of I Chron ix 2 to the new situation; Batten, p. 267, suggests that the parenthetical clause fits in better after vs. 20. Only two family heads are named: (a) Athaiah of the Perez line and (b) Maaseiah of the Shiloh line. The total given for Perez (vs. 6) is lacking in I Chron ix, though a larger number, which may refer to all the descendants of Judah, is noted. The tabular lists given in connection with I Chron ix show the variations and extensions. For an analysis and evaluation see Meyer, EJ, pp. 184–90.

The Benjaminite line is represented by only one certain family, that of Sallu. I Chron ix has four representatives with a total of thirteen names; here there is a total of only ten, including the names of Gabbai and Sallai. The list is somewhat smaller, therefore, than in the parallel list. The total is twenty-eight less than in I Chron ix —928 and 956 respectively.

The chief and second in command were "over the city" and not Benjaminite chiefs. Who these men were, or what their family identity was, is not known. It has been conjectured that since the name of Joel's father, Zichri, occurs three times in the Benjaminite list of I Chron viii (vss. 19, 23, 27), he was a Benjaminite (Schneider, p. 232). The same is true of Judah, who may have belonged to the Hassenaah family, which played an important role in the postexilic community (cf. Neh iii 3; Ezra ii 35 ‖ Neh vii 38).

[List of priests, 10–14]: Five family heads are listed definitely; if, as seems probable, "the son" before Joiarib is an intrusion, then there are six, exactly as in I Chron ix, which this list parallels very closely. The only difference is the addition here of the names of Pelaliah, Amzi, and Zechariah to the genealogy of Adaiah, and the specification of Zabdiel as the chief. Amashsai is certainly meant to be the same as Maasai in I Chron ix; so also Azarel for Adiel and Meshillemoth for Meshullam. Zabdiel is otherwise unknown and Haggedolim is difficult. Rudolph, p. 185, and Schneider, p. 234, suggest that Zabdiel was a scion of the high-priestly family. The total number of priests is 1192 as opposed to 1760 in I Chron ix.

[List of Levites, 15–18]: The MT lists six families of Levites. They are not connected with the traditional ancestral families. The Shemaiah family is the same as that listed in I Chron ix, except for the addition of Bunni; "Bunni" could be an error for "sons of," Merari having fallen out of the text by accident. The families of Mattaniah and Abda (Obadiah) also are the same as those in I Chron ix, though there are spelling variants. Bakbukiah might be in place of Bakbakkar in I Chron ix. The Elkanah family represented by Berechiah is missing here; so are Heresh and Galal. However, Shabbethai and Jozabad are added and may represent replacements; both were active in the time of Ezra (Ezra viii 33, x 15; Neh viii 7). Perhaps the Chronicles list had a different purpose or represents another time. These men (or families) were in charge of "the work outside the house of God," which probably indicates cultic duties beyond those assigned to the priests. Such duties might include the gathering and storing of provisions for the temple, care for the structure itself (Cf. Ezra viii 33; I Chron xxvi 29 has the Levites perform "outside" tasks, which are described as those of officials and judges, but such is hardly the meaning here). Mattaniah was the song leader or worship leader (cf. xii 8)—being of the Asaph line (cf. Ezra ii 41). In this list the singers are placed with the Levites. Bakbukiah, whose family was among the returnees ("among the temple slaves," Ezra ii 51), was apparently the substitute for Mattaniah, although "the second" could equally well refer to his rank among the Levites. I Chron ix has omitted the total number of Levites. Here it is 284, but still proportionately very small, though our list may not include all the Levites.

[Other groups and services, 19–24]: The list of gatekeepers has only two names, q.v., the third column below:

Ezra ii 42 ‖ Neh vii 45   I Chron ix 17   Neh xi 19

Shallum	Shallum	Akkub
Ater	Akkub	Talmon
Talmon	Talmon	
Akkub	Ahiman	
Hatita		
Shobai		

Even the Chronicles list is larger; the two names on the Nehemiah list are in the same order in the Chronicles list. Note that in Ezra ii ‖ Neh vii, Shallum and Ahiman (of Chron ix 17) might have resided outside the capital (cf. vs. 20) and for that reason are not mentioned in Neh xi 19. Verse 20 seems to be out of place here (cf. Ezra ii 70; Neh vii 73); it may have served originally as an introduction to the town list beginning with vs. 25. In that case, vss. 21–24 must have been a later addition to the chapter. The *ntynym,* "temple slaves", appear outside of Ezra-Nehemiah only in I Chron ix 2, where they stand last in the series of classes of people in the land. According to Ezra ii 43–54, there were thirty-five families; Neh vii 46–56 has thirty-two. Ziha occurs in all three lists. Gishpa is otherwise unknown; some regard it as a corruption of Hasupha of Ezra ii 43 ‖ Neh vii 46, but that is doubtful. Only those in charge are named here but whether they are persons or families is uncertain. The reference to Uzzi as the Levitical official in Jerusalem looks very much like a later addition, since the line of descent is carried further. In the writer's time, Uzzi was the chief of the Levites in Jerusalem. The royal orders may refer to the ordinances of David (cf. xii 24; I Chron xxv) but the Persian kings also were concerned about cultic matters and could have been responsible for such provisions, as may be seen from the decree of Darius (Ezra vi 8–10) and the official order of Artaxerxes (Ezra vii 21–24). See COMMENT on Ezra vii 11–26. Rudolph, p. 187, is emphatic in denying any reference to I Chron xxv here. The matter of provisions for singers is mentioned in xii 47. But the order here may also refer to service requirements laid upon them. Verse 24 is interesting because of the hint it offers about certain governmental procedures. Pethahiah, of the Perez line of Judah, was apparently a kind of ambassador who represented Jewish interests at the court. Since the Zerah family is not mentioned elsewhere in Ezra-Nehemiah, Pethahiah probably still resided in the east, as the text implies (see NOTE).

[List of towns occupied by Jews, 25–36]: Evidently the writer was concerned primarily with relating how, after the reconstruction of the wall and the consequent multiplication of space, the authorities put on a campaign to repopulate the capital. That move emphasized the other side of the matter, namely, that many of the people were content to live in the outlying areas of Judah. Some of these places are mentioned elsewhere in the Ezra-Nehemiah material (Ezra ii [|| Neh vii], Neh iii, xii).

[IN THE TERRITORY OF JUDAH, 25–30]: All the names of Judahite cities, with the exception of Dibon, Jeshua, and Meconah, appear also in Josh xv. Dibon may be Debir (Josh xv 49) or Dimonah (Josh xv 22); Jeshua could possibly be the Shema of Josh xv 26. Meconah occurs only here. Since the Levites figure prominently in vss. 15–22, this list may have been influenced somewhat by the Levitical city lists in Josh xxi 8 ff. and I Chron vi 54 ff. The order of the tribes—Judah and Benjamin—is the same, though that could be due to other factors. Moreover, Kirjath-(ha)arba (Hebron) stands first in all three lists of towns given to or occupied by Levites (cf. Alt, KS, II, p. 303). On the Hebron situation with reference to Levitical occupation, see W. F. Albright, *Louis Ginzberg Jubilee Volume*, 1945, p. 59, and Möhlenbrink, ZAW 52 (1934), 184 ff. Cf. also B. Mazar, "The Cities of the Priests and Levites," SVT 7 (1959), 193–205, for a discussion of their location.

The omissions and the different order of towns in the latter part of the list suggests that it was not copied directly from any other list. Albright has dealt with the problem of the five lists in JPOS 4 (1924), 149 ff., as follows: *a*. Josh xix 2–7 is a Simeonite list before the Simeonite absorption into Judah; *b*. Josh xv 26–32, 42 comes

from the time of "Greater Judah"; *c*. I Chron iv 28–33 represents
a fourth century list based on earlier tradition; *d*. Neh xi 26 ff. is
a partial list of Simeonite towns reoccupied by Jews in the fifth
century B.C.; *e*. I Sam xxx 27 ff. is based on a tradition going back
to the tenth century.

Alt (KS, III, p. 418) thinks there were two independent lists.
The Samuel list comes from the time of David or a little later. The
Vorlage of the four other lists comes from a later period—the time
of Josiah. F. M. Cross, Jr., and G. E. Wright (JBL 75 [1956],
224–26) regard Josh xv 21–62 as a revision of the Judahite
province list dating from the ninth century B.C.—in the reign of
Jehoshaphat. Y. Aharoni ("The Negeb of Judah," IEJ 8 [1958],
26–38), thinks the first three lists come from the same source
(p. 31). He thinks there is no reason to doubt the statement of
I Chron iv 31, which says the cities of Simeon listed were those
before David.

That the compiler followed the traditional order in a general way
is to be expected, since that was the established one, the original
orientation of which may well have been geographical (see W. F.
Albright, JPOS 4 [1924], 150 ff.). As the list now stands, the towns
appear to center around five areas: (a) Hebron, (b) Beer-sheba
(Jekabzeel, Jeshua, Moladah, Beth-pelet, Hazar-shual), (c) Ziklag
(En-rimmon), (d) Zorah (Jarmuth, Zanoah, Adullam), (e) Lachish (Azekah). For locations, see Abel, AGP, II, Map 2. Identifica-
tions are Kirjath-(ha)arba=Hebron=el-Khalil, Dibon=?; Kabzeel
=? (Aharoni [IEJ 8 (1958), 36 f.] suggests Khirbet al-Gharra
some twelve to fifteen miles east of Beer-sheba); Jeshua=Tell
es-Sa'wi (?); Moladah=Tell el-Milḥ (?) (Albright [JPOS 4
(1924), 152] suggests Khirbet Quseifeh; Beth-pelet=? (Albright
[JPOS 4 (1924), 153] thinks of Tell el-Milḥ); Beer-sheba=Tell
es-Seba'; Ziklag=Tell el-Khuweilfeh; En-rimmon=Khirbet Umm
er-Ramamin; Zorah=Ṣar'ah; Jarmuth=Khirbet yarmuq; Zanoah=
Zanuḥ; Adullam=Tell esh-Sheikh Madhkur; Lachish=Tell-ed-
Duweir; Azekah=Tell ez-Zakariyah. There was a governor's residence at Lachish in the Persian period, Tufnell, *Lachish III: The
Iron Age,* Ch. VI.

Several major questions come to mind. How did the Jews get so
far south in the time of Nehemiah? Is the list fictitious? (Cf. E.
Meyer, EJ, p. 106; Kittel, GVI, III, pp. 47–49.) Does it contain
an element of fact but is otherwise greatly exaggerated? At present

these questions cannot be answered with finality, but several observations may bring them into sharper focus: the list could reflect
an earlier situation, in which case it must have been copied from
Josh xv by the compiler; it could reflect the situation in the Maccabean period (cf. I Maccabees v 65, xi 34) and therefore must
have been inserted here by a later hand; or it is a revised list,
based on Josh xv, but substantially from the period from which it
purports to come. While LXX does omit most of the place names,
it retains the Negeb area covered in MT. However, it suggests that
there may have been some tampering with the list.

If the list comes from the hand of the Chronicler, it might be one
cessors, when religious officials were present in their cities (cf. II
more instance of his feeling for the kingdom of David and his suc-
Chron xi 13–14, xxiii 2, xxxi 19; See Albright, in *Alexander
Marx Jubilee Volume,* English Section, pp. 74–82; and cf. Mazar,
SVT 7 (1959), especially pp. 200–5). It is specifically stated that
the returning Jews went to their own towns (Ezra ii 1, 70, iii 1;
Neh vii 6, 73), and, as the early Canaanites dwelt among the Israelites (Judg i), so the Jews dwelt among the people of the land
after the return (Ezra ix 1–2). So far as we can judge from our
sources, the Jews returning from Babylonian exile could move about
in the land, at least in small groups. There is no indication of serious
conflict with the people of the land until the movement of the returnees acquired some momentum and they began to organize.
Moreover, central and southern Palestine under the fifth satrapy of
the Persian empire consisted of four provinces—Samaria, Judah,
Ashdod, and Edom—governed by a local prefect under the satrap.
The Jews were citizens of the empire and as such were doubtless
granted normal citizenship rights, which included permission to come
and go in the empire. Some of those who temporarily left their
homes during the Babylonian invasion probably returned when the
invaders left; they undoubtedly took up village life in their several
communities despite the penetration of the territory by outsiders
(such as Geshem and his people). Even though their towns and
villages were outside the provincial limits of Nehemiah's Judah (cf.
Albright, BP, p. 48, and *Alexander Marx Jubilee Volume,* English
Section, p. 364, n. 47a), there is no reason to assume that they
did not attempt to establish contact with their brethren at Jerusalem,
who would certainly have welcomed them if they conformed to the
strict religious regulations that prevailed there. It is interesting to

note that only one of the towns mentioned here—Zanoah—is referred to in the builder's list of Neh iii. Could the list refer, for the
most part, to those who were not too eager to move to Jerusalem
or who had no representatives there as yet and whom the authorities
were eager to bring in?

[IN THE TERRITORY OF BENJAMIN, 31–36]: This list includes some
towns that originally belonged to Dan and Ephraim. When Dan
was squeezed out, in the period of the Judges (Judg xviii), its
territory fell to Judah and Ephraim. After the fall of the Northern
Kingdom, portions of southern Ephraim became the possessions of
Benjamin (see Cross and Wright, JBL 75 [1956], 224–26).

Comparison with other Benjaminite lists is instructive. Only
Bethel and Geba occur in Josh xviii 21–27; Geba, Ono, and Lod
appear in I Chron viii 1–40. None of the towns of the list here is
found in Neh iii; but all of them are mentioned in Neh vii ‖ Ezra
ii, which seems to indicate that we have here an expanded list of
settlements of perhaps a slightly later period. The towns are located
to the north and west of Jerusalem—at least in so far as they have
been definitely identified: Geba=modern Jeba; Michmas=Mukh-
mas; Aijah=? Khirbet Haiyan; Bethel=Beitun; Anathoth=Ras el-
Kharrubeh; Nob=et-Tor; Ananiah=el-'Azariyeh (Bethany); Hazor
=Khirbet Hazzur; Ramah=er-Ram; Hadid=el-Haditheh; Lod=
Ludd; Ono=Kefr 'Ana; Neballat=Beit Nabala. Zeboim is unknown, and Gittaim has recently been identified with Tell Ras Abu
Hamid, near Ramleh (cf. B. Mazar, IEJ 4 [1954], 227–35). The
little notice on the distribution of Levites from Judah to Benjamin
again accentuates the writer's interest.

16. POSTEXILIC CLERICAL GENEALOGIES
(xii 1–26)

List of priests

XII [1] These are the priests and Levites who came up with Zerubbabel the son of Shealtiel and Jeshua: Seraiah, Jeremiah, Ezra, [2] Amariah, Malluch, Hattush[a], [3] Shecaniah, [b]Rehum, Meremoth, [4] Iddo, Ginnethoi, Abijah, [5] Mijamin, Maadiah, Bilgah, [6] Shemaiah, and Joiarib, Jedaiah, [7] Sallu, Amok, Hilkiah, Jedaiah[b]—these were the heads of the priests and their brothers in the days of Jeshua.

List of Levites

[8] The Levites were Jeshua, Binnui, Kadmiel, Sherebiah, Judah, Mattaniah[c] who, with his brothers, was [d]in charge of the songs of praise[d]; [9] and Bakbukiah and Unni[e], their brothers, were directly opposite them in the service divisions.

Genealogy of high priests

[10] Jeshua fathered Joiakim, Joiakim fathered Eliashib, Eliashib fathered Joiada, [11] Joiada fathered Jonathan and Jonathan fathered Jaddua.

[a] Omitted by LXX[B].
[b–b] Omitted by LXX.
[c] LXX[B] "Machania."
[d–d] LXX "upon their hands"; so also Kethib. LXX[L] *epi ton exomologeseon* "upon the praises." Cf. *hwdwt bywm hšbt* "praises on the Sabbath day" in 4Q Dib Ham, col. 7:4 (RB 68 [1961], 212).
[e] Kethib reads "Unno."

Priestly heads in time of Joiakim

12 In the days of Joiakim[f] there were the following heads of priestly families: of Seraiah, Meraiah; of Jeremiah, Hananiah; 13 of Ezra, Meshullam; of Amariah, Jehohanan; 14 [g]of Malluch[g], [h]Jonathan; of Shebaniah, Joseph; 15 of Harim, Adna; of Meraioth, Helkai; 16 of Iddo, Zechariah; of Ginnethon, Meshullam; 17 of Abijah, Zichri; of Miniamin [. . .]; of Moadiah, Piltai; 18 of Bilgah, Shammua; of Shemaiah, Jehonathan; 19 and of Joiarib, Mattenai; of Jedaiah, Uzzi; 20 of Sallai, Kallai; of Amok, Eber; 21 of Hilkiah, Hashabiah; of Jedaiah, Nethanel[h].

Levites

22 The Levites, in the time of Eliashib, Joiada, and Johanan and Jaddua were registered as heads of families; so also were the priests from the reign of Darius the Persian. 23 The Levites who were heads of families were registered in the book of the Chronicles up until the time of Johanan the son of Eliashib. 24 The Levitical heads were Hashabiah, Sherebiah, and Jeshua [i]the son of[i] Kadmiel and their brothers, who stood directly opposite them during the rendering of praise and thanksgiving as David [j]the man of God[j] had prescribed, division corresponding to division. 25 [k]Mattaniah and Bakbukiah [and] Obadiah were the singers. Meshullam, Talmon, and Akkub[k] were the gatekeepers guarding the stores at the gates. 26 These lived in the time of Joiakim the son of Jeshua the son of Jozadak and in the time of Nehemiah the governor and Ezra the priest and scribe.

[f] LXX adds "his brothers."
[g-g] Cf. vs. 2; Heb. *lmlwky* "to Malluchi."
[h-h] Omitted by LXX[B].
[i-i] See NOTE.
[j-j] Syr. "the prophet of the Lord."
[k-k] Omitted by LXX[B].

NOTES

xii 4. *Ginnethoi*. See NOTE on x 7 in Sec. 14.

8. *Judah*. Only place in OT where name is used to designate a Levite.

11. *Jonathan*. Doubtless to be read Johanan, as in vs. 22.

16. *Ginnethon*. See NOTE on x 7 in Sec. 14.

17. *Miniamin* [. . .]. Name is apparently missing.

21. *Hashabiah*. Name occurs in Yavneh-Yam letter of seventh century B.C. (cf. IEJ 10 [1960], 129 ff.).

22. *from*. Albright (JBL 40 [1921], 113) reads *m'l* for *'l*, the *m* having been lost by haplography. The statement here then is the antecedent to *w'd ymy ywḥnn* "and until the time of Johanan" in the following verse. Cf. Rudolph, p. 194, for another suggestion, and Bowman, p. 789. *'l* "from," sometimes has this meaning elsewhere and perhaps no emendation is necessary.

Darius the Persian. Contrast with Darius the Mede in Dan v 31, ix 1, xi 1. Cf. Aram. *prsy'* "the Persian" in Dan vi 29, referring to Cyrus.

24. *the son of*. Perhaps "Binnui," as suggested by LXX "sons"; cf. x 10, xii 8.

25a. Inserting *hmsrrym*, "the singers," which may have fallen out by virtue of its similarity to Meshullam. So also Rudolph; Galling reads "singers" for "doorkeepers" and omits Meshullam.

26. Note the order of names; only here does Nehemiah precede Ezra.

COMMENT

Chapter xii is introduced by a series of clerical lists purporting to come from various periods in the postexilic age; they illustrate the writer's fondness for names and genealogies and reflect his interest in the maintenance of authentic traditions. There was much tampering with these lists, as is indicated by the omissions of LXX and the apparent additions marked by the "and" before Joiarib (vs. 6) and before Bakbukiah (vs. 9), and elsewhere.

[Priests in time of Zerubbabel and Jeshua, xii 1–7]: The fondness of the compiler of Chronicles-Ezra-Nehemiah for lists of names is demonstrated once again. The slightest opportunity is seized upon to give a list of one kind or another. The lists in this section may be due to the preceding town list, the reference to the place occupied by Levites and priests at the dedication of the wall as set forth in the introductory statement (vss. 27–30 [Sec. 17]), and the description of the processions and the ceremonies taking place thereafter in the temple (31–43).

This list purports to give the names of the priestly families who returned from exile with Zerubbabel and Jeshua. No fewer than twenty-two names are in the list. It appears to be later than those in x 2–8 because some of the family names are absent and there has been an addition of names not in evidence there. It may be earlier than I Chron xxiv 7–18, which contains the full complement of twenty-four orders and has Joiarib and Jedaiah at the top, whereas here they come near the bottom. Moreover, the list from Joiarib on seems to be an addition introduced by "and." The conjunction also appears before Joiarib in vs. 19—the only occurrence in the list of Neh xii 12–21. For suggestions as to dates of lists, see Meyer, EJ, p. 173; Kittel, GVI, III, p. 685; Albright, JPOS 6 (1926), 98 ff. Only eleven of the names are in certain correspondence with those in chapter x; four others are probably so. Six (possibly seven) names in this list occur also in that of I Chron xxiv. See Appendixes for lists of priests. Apparently the same names as found in I Chron xxiv occur in the Mišmarot MSS of 4Q from Qumran, though not in the same order. Milik's quotation for the order of service for the first year contains the names of Meoziah (Maaziah), Jedaiah, Seorim, Jeshua, and Joiarib (*Volume du Congrès, Strasbourg, 1956,* VTS, IV [Leiden, 1957], p. 25). Rudolph, p. 191, following Hölscher, may be right in observing that the compiler had lists of priests for the time of Joiachim (vss. 12–21) and Eliashib (vs. 22) but lacking a similar list for the period of Jeshua, simply copied the family heads from the Joiakim list.

[Levites of the same time, 8–9]: At the head of the Levite list stand the four family names given in vii 43 (∥ Ezra ii 40), if Judah here stands for Hodeviah. Between Kadmiel and Judah is inserted the name of Sherebiah, a contemporary of Ezra (viii 18) and Nehemiah (x 13). Mattaniah and Bakbukiah were important persons, especially the former, as may be seen from xi 17. Unni (Unno) occurs elsewhere only among the Levitical singers in I Chron xv 18, 20. Bakbukiah and Unni were additions to the list, as is apparent from the insertion of the conjunction (for an evaluation of the list, see Meyer, EJ, p. 179, and Möhlenbrink, ZAW 52 [1934], 209). The system of divisions (*mišmarot*) is referred to without further specification. The participants were apparently regarded as members of the Levitical choir, whose praises were rendered antiphonally.

[The high-priestly line, 10]: The six high priests named here functioned from the time of Zerubbabel (somewhere between 538 and 522 B.C.) to sometime in the fourth century; the extreme limits are 538 to 323 B.C., or a period of over two hundred years. The matter is further complicated by the declaration of Josephus (*Antiquities* XI.viii) that Jaddua and Alexander died at about the same time, the former as an old man. For a discussion of the whole problem, see: Kraeling, BMAP, pp. 100–110; Albright, BP, p. 54; Rowley, "Sanballat and the Samaritan Temple" BJRL 38 (1955/56), 166–98, and "The Chronological Order of Ezra and Nehemiah," in *Ignace Goldziher Memorial Volume*, Pt. I, pp. 117–149.

Jeshua, the son of Jehozadak, held office in the time of Haggai (i 1, 12, 14, ii 2, 4) and Zechariah (iii 1, 3, 6, 9, vi 11). How long he served is not known. He was succeeded by Joiakim. Baruch i 7 mentions a Joakim, son of Hilkiah, son of Shallum, as high priest in Jerusalem five years after the captivity. So does the author of Judith (iv 6, 8, 14, xv 8). (Cf. also Josephus *Antiquities* XI.v.1). But these apocryphal writings cannot be taken seriously.

Joiakim was succeeded by Eliashib, who was high priest in the time of Nehemiah (iii 1, 20, 21, xiii 4, 7; Ezra x 6 || I Esdras ix 1). Josephus (*Antiquities* XI.v) says that Joiakim died at the celebration of the Feast of Tabernacles and was succeeded by his son Eliashib. Eliashib directed the priests in the reconstruction of the Sheep Gate in the early period of Nehemiah (iii 1) but later succumbed to outside influence when he provided room in the temple for Tobiah the Ammonite (Neh xiii 4, 7). He thus appears to have been high priest during the governorship of Nehemiah. The whole family of Eliashib was deeply interrelated with outsiders, since the grandson (Josephus *Antiquities* XI.vii.2 says the brother of Jaddua was Manasseh) was a son-in-law of Sanballat (Neh xiii 28). Of Joiada we know nothing except the point just mentioned. Josephus calls him Judas (*Antiquities* XI.vii). Jonathan (Johanan) must have been in office in the time of Ezra since the latter went into his room in the temple after his confession (Ezra x 6). Josephus (*loc. cit.*) tells us something of this high priest, whose brother Jesus was supported for the high priesthood by the governor Bagoas. Jesus precipitated a quarrel with Johanan, by whom he was slain in the temple. This is the same Johanan referred to in Jedoniah's letter to the officials at Jerusalem and Samaria in the fourteenth year of Darius (ca. 410 B.C.). See Cowley, AP, Nos. 30–32. Nothing is known about Jaddua except what Josephus reports (*Antiquities* XI.viii). His name here and in vs. 22 may be a later addition.

[Heads of the priestly families in the days of Joiakim, 12–21]: Joiakim was high priest between Jeshua and Eliashib, but the exact dates escapes us at present. Whether or not there was only one high priest during that long period is uncertain. This list is said to be that of heads of the priestly families in time of Joiakim. As noted above, the families are substantially the same as those mentioned in vss. 1–7. The family of Hattush is missing, which reduces the number of families from twenty-two to twenty-one. Also the name of the representative of the Miniamin family has dropped out, and there are some spelling variants:

Verses 1–7	Verses 12–21
Shecaniah	Shebaniah
Rehum	Harim
Meremoth	Meraioth
Ginnethoi	Ginnethon
Mijamin	Miniamin
Maadiah	Moadiah
Sallu	Sallai

[The roll of Levites in time of Joiakim, 22–26]: Verses 22–23 appear to be an explanatory insertion dealing with matters of registration of Levites and priests. It looks as if the original list of high priests ended with Johanan, since the names of both Johanan and Jaddua are preceded by the conjunction "and" in MT (so also LXX; Vulg. has the conjunction between all the names. For a suggestion as to the chronology of the priestly succession, see Albright, JBL 40 [1921], 122).

Verse 22, if the above translation is correct, becomes important evidence for dating the passage and the book. Darius the Persian would be Darius I (Hystaspis; see references in NOTE) and the time of Johanan would fall in the reign of Darius II (Nothus). Because "the Persian" suggests a period long past and because Josephus (*Antiquities* XI.viii) associates Jaddua with Alexander, Darius III (Codomanus) has been thought to be the Persian king referred to. But the phrase "until the time of Johanan" in vs. 23 appears to preclude that identification. (Bowman, p. 789, thinks the reference is to what took place *in* the reign of Darius.) The meaning seems to be that the register of priests and Levites covered the period from Darius I to Johanan; or possibly, the roster *in* the time of Darius II. Verse 23 says quite definitely that the register of Levites was recorded until the time of Johanan. The "book of the Chronicles" is the official record kept by the temple authorities.

If the above translation is correct, the Levite list is given in three parts—family heads, singers, and gatekeepers, as in vii 43–45 (|| Ezra ii 40–42), chapter xi, and I Chron xxiv–xxvi (MT gives the family heads and lists the others together without distinction). The old list (Ezra ii 40 || Neh vii 43) has three family heads. So does Ezra viii 18–19, which has the same three names, with Sherebiah at the head of the list. The list purports to represent the situation at the time of Joiakim and Nehemiah and Ezra. This is hardly possible since Eliashib was the high priest in the time of Nehemiah. The compiler does transmit an authentic tradition: that the period of Nehemiah-Ezra included the interval between the high priesthood of Joiakim and Johanan—and perhaps of Jaddua. Interestingly enough, vs. 26 names the three outstanding personalities of postexilic Jewish history in order (Joiakim, Nehemiah, Ezra).

17. DEDICATION OF THE WALL
(xii 27–43)

XII 27 At the dedication of the wall of Jerusalem they sought out and brought the Levites from all their dwelling places to Jerusalem to perform the dedicatory rites with gladness, with hymns of thanksgiving and with songs to the accompaniment of cymbals, harps, and zithers. 28 So Levitical*a* singers gathered in from the district around Jerusalem, from the villages *b*of the Netophathites*b*, 29 *c*from Beth-haggilgal*c* and from their farms *c*at Geba and Azmaveth*c*—for the singers had built villages for themselves in the region around Jerusalem. 30 When the priests and Levites had performed the ceremony of cleansing themselves, they did the same for the people, the gates, and the wall.

Those going around to the right

31 Then I had the chiefs of Judah come up upon the wall *d*and appointed two large choirs: *e*One went [around]*e* on the wall toward the right in the direction of the Dung Gate*d*. 32 Hoshaiah and half the chiefs of Judah followed them; 33 so did Azariah, Ezra, Meshullam, 34 Judah, Benjamin, Shemaiah, Jeremiah, 35 *f*of the priests,*f* with trumpets; [and] Zechariah the son of Jonathan, the son of Shemaiah, the son of Mattaniah*g*, the son of Micaiah, the son of Zaccur, the son of Asaph, 36 and his brothers, Shemaiah, Azarel, *h*Milalai, Gilalai, Maai, Nethanel, Judah, and Hanani*h*, with the musical instruments of David, the man of God. Ezra the scribe went ahead of

---

a So with LXX*L*, *lwy* "Levi" having fallen out after *bny* "sons of."
b-b Omitted by LXX*AB*.
c-c Omitted by LXX*AB*.
d-d Omitted by LXX*B*.
e-e See NOTE.
f-f MT and Vulg. "and of the sons of the priests."
g LXX*B* "Nathaniah." LXX*A* follows MT.
h-h Omitted by LXX.

them. 37 At the Fountain Gate they proceeded directly up the steps of the City of David, on the stairway of the wall, above the House of David to the Water Gate ʻtoward the east.

Those going around to the left

38 The other choir ʲproceeded toward the leftʲ. I and half of the people followed them on the wall [as they went] from the Tower of Furnaces to the Broad Wall,ⁱ 39 from the Ephraim Gate to the ᵏJeshanah Gate,ᵏ the Fish Gate, the Tower of Hananel, and the Tower of the Hundred as far as the Sheep Gate ˡand came to a halt at the Prison Gate. 40 Then the two choirs took their place in the house of God—but I and half of the officials with me [. . .]—41 [as did] the priests, Eliakim, Maaseiah, Miniamin, Micaiah, Elioenai, Zechariah, Hananiah with the trumpets, 42 and Maaseiah, Shemaiah, Eleazar, Uzzi, Jehohanan, Malchijah, Elam, and Ezer.ˡ The singers ᵐunder the direction of Jizrahiahᵐ sang vociferously. 43 That day they offered great sacrifices and rejoiced because God had given them great joy; the women and children rejoiced too, so that the [sound] of Jerusalem's jubilation could be heard from afar.

ⁱ⁻ⁱ Omitted by LXXᴮ.
ʲ⁻ʲ So with many MSS and to correspond with the movement of "the procession to the right." MT "to the fore."
ᵏ⁻ᵏ Omitted by LXXᴮ; Vulg. antiquam "old."
ˡ⁻ˡ Omitted by LXXᴮ.
ᵐ⁻ᵐ Omitted by LXX.

NOTES

xii 31. *choirs.* twdt "thanksgiving choirs."
One went [around]. Reading wh'aḥt hlkt for MT wthlkt (only here) "and the procession." Vulg. "they proceeded." Cf. vs. 38.
36. *Ezra . . . them.* Inserted by the same agent who added the name of Nehemiah in viii 9. Cf. Rudolph, p. 198, and Pavlovsky's explanation in *Biblica* 38 (1957), 447, n. 4.
38. *choir.* See first NOTE on vs. 31.
40. *choirs.* So with vss. 31, 38.
me [. . .]. What they did is not stated; they may have stood guard during the service of dedication. See Galling, p. 248, for a suggestion.

42. *The singers . . . sang vociferously.* Literally "the singers made heard." The meaning is that the vocal and instrumental music resounded throughout the area.

43. *rejoiced . . . great joy.* Literally "God made them rejoice with great joy."

COMMENT

As the text now stands, this portion of chapter xii connects with xi 36. Gelin, p. 111, n. a., is probably right in pointing out that its original position is following vi 15. Portions of it are from the Chronicler's hand, others from the memoirs of Nehemiah. Verses 27–30 appear to come from the former since they have to do with the Levites, who were summoned to participate in the service of dedication. The Levites always had a prominent place in such rites (cf. I Chron xv 4; II Chron v 4 ff.). Just how long after the completion of the wall the service took place is not known, though it probably was not long afterward. The view of the compiler is clear: such matters as the festivals of the seventh month (vii 72), the services of confession, purification, and rededication to the law (ix–x), and the relocation of people from the outlying districts in Jerusalem (xi) had to be taken care of first. Then the Levites had to be summoned from their homes to fulfill their function in the dedicatory services (cf. II Chron xxix 25–27; Ezra iii 10, vi 16). The Levites were scattered throughout the land (cf. vii 73 ‖ Ezra ii 70) and had to be summoned, on occasion, to come to Jerusalem for important functions (II Chron xi 14, xxiii 2). According to I Chron ix 16, they dwelt at Netophah. Josh xxi 17 and I Chron vi 60 reckon Geba a Levitical (priestly) city. The former was southeast of Bethlehem (cf. K. Kob, "Netopha," PJB 28 [1932], 47–54); Geba and Azmaveth were Benjaminite cities some five or six miles northeast of Jerusalem. Beth-haggilgal was doubtless the Gilgal of Joshua (but cf. De Vaux, IAT, II, p. 95); for the location and Levitical residences see Alt, PJB 28 (1932), 9–13. But before the Levites could officiate they had to purify themselves (cf. Gen xxxv 2 f.; Num viii 21 f.; I Chron xv 14; II Chron xxix 15, xxxv 6; Ezra vi 20; Neh xiii 22; Mal iii 3). Just what was involved is not specified; perhaps the clergy fasted, abstained from marital intercourse, and offered a sin offering. The laity doubtless washed their garments (Exod xix 10, 14), bathed, or underwent aspersion (Num viii 5 ff., xix 12, 19; Ezek xxxvi 25). The gates and walls too had to be purified to avoid any possible misfortune because of contamination during construction. So too the temple had first been cleansed and purified before it was formally dedicated in the time of Hezekiah (II Chron xxix 15 ff.); Ezekiel's altar was to be ritually purified (xliii 26). For the ritual cleansing of private houses, hyssop was used (Lev xiv 48 ff.) and that may have been the case here also.

The actual ceremony of dedication consisted of a consecrating procession and a great sacrifice. Certain of the Psalms reflect such processional celebrations (cf. H. Gunkel and J. Begrich, *Einleitung in die Psalmen,* 1933, pp. 17 f.). Gunkel points to Ps xlviii (*ibid.,* p. 64); M. Buttenwieser thinks Ps cxlvii may have been composed for the dedication of the walls (*The Psalms Chronologically Treated with a New Translation,* 1938, p. 395). Processions with musicians must be quite old, as witness Ps lxviii 25. Josephus mentions the sacrifices but says nothing of the processions (*Antiquities* XI.v). This was hardly a circumambulation in the ordinary sense of the rite. The procession was organized into two groups—one going around toward the right, the other toward the left, but just what that means is not certain (cf. M. Burrows, "The Topography of Nehemiah 12:31–43," JBL 54 [1935], 29–39); it all depends on where they started and how they proceeded. The formation and character of the processions are clear. Each one apparently consisted of half of the participants in the ceremony and was made up of a choir, an official of high rank, half of the family heads, priests, and Levites (see List of Participants below. On vss. 38–39, cf. Parrot, *Golgotha,* pp. 30, 33. See COMMENT on Sec. 4, ch. iii). More was involved than an ordinary dedication, as may be surmised from the ritual purification of the participants (vs. 30); this was a ritual performed to assure the removal of any possible impurity and perhaps to invest the wall itself with a kind of sanctity or power to be what it was supposed to be. The processions went on the battlements wherever possible (cf. Burrows, JBL 54 [1935], 33). The locations of all the points touched are not certain (see the sketch of Jerusalem in Sec. 4. Cf. Vincent and Steve, *Jerusalem de l'Ancien Testament,* I, pp. 250–54, for an excellent treatment of the topography of Jerusalem reflected in this chapter of Nehemiah). They apparently entered the temple area from different points. Ceremonies consisting of further ritual and sacrifices followed in the temple court around the altar. Verse 43 has captured something of the enthusiasm of the people on that occasion by using the root śmḥ "joy," "rejoice" no less than five times.

List of Participants in the Dedication Ceremony

Group led by Ezra the scribe that went toward the right was:
  Choir
  Hoshaiah
  Chiefs
  Priests with trumpets:
    Azariah
    Ezra
    Meshullam
    Judah
    Benjamin
    Shemaiah
    Jeremiah
  Levites with musical instruments:
    Zechariah
    Shemaiah
    Azarel
    Milalai
    Gilalai
    Maai
    Nethanel
    Judah
    Hanani
Places mentioned:
  Dung Gate (vs. 31)
  Fountain Gate
  Steps of the City of David
  Stairway of the wall
  House of David
  Water Gate

The group that went toward the left was:
  Choir
  Nehemiah
  Chiefs
  Priests with trumpets:
    Eliakim
    Maaseiah
    Miniamin
    Micaiah
    Elioenai
    Zechariah
    Hananiah
  Levites:
    Maaseiah
    Shemaiah
    Eleazar
    Uzzi
    Jehohanan
    Malchijah
    Elam
    Ezer
    (Jizrahiah)
Places mentioned:
  Tower of Furnaces
  Broad Wall
  Ephraim Gate
  Jeshanah Gate
  Fish Gate
  Tower of Hananel
  Tower of the Hundred
  Sheep Gate
  Prison Gate (Muster Gate?)

18. TEMPLE PROVISIONS.
EXPULSION OF FOREIGNERS
(xii 44–47, xiii 1–3)

Provision for the temple services

XII 44 At that time men were appointed to take charge of the rooms for the treasures, the contributions, the offerings of first fruits and the tithes, and to gather in to them, from the farms*a* belonging to the towns, the portion *b*prescribed by the law*b* for the priests and the Levites; for Judah was elated over the officiating priests and Levites—45 because they, as well as the singers and gatekeepers conducted the service of their God and the service of purification in accordance with the order of David and Solomon his son—46 for in the days of David and Asaph of old they were the song leaders in rendering hymns of praise and thanksgiving to God. 47 In the days of Zerubbabel *c*and Nehemiah*c* all Israel supplied regular daily portions for the singers and gatekeepers and gave the dedicated contributions to the Levites, and the Levites gave the dedicated contributions to the Aaronites.

Expulsion of foreigners

XIII 1 At that time they read aloud to the people from the book of Moses and found written in it that no Ammonite or Moabite should ever enter into the congregation of God 2 because they did not come to welcome the Israelites with food and drink and even hired Balaam to oppose them by cursing them; but our God turned the curse into a blessing. 3 When they heard the law they excluded all foreigners*d* from Israel.

a LXX "princes, chiefs," reading *śry* for *śdy*.
b–b Vul. *twdh* "thanksgiving," i.e., portions for thanksgiving of the priests.
c–c Omitted by LXXᴮ.
d See Note.

NOTES

xii 44. *officiating.* Literally "those standing"; cf. Deut x 8 and II Chron xxix 11, where standing before Yahweh means to officiate.

46. The verse is not very clear as it stands. Literally "for in the days of David and Asaph of old, the chief of the singers and song of praise and thanksgiving to God." The context demands some such rendering as given. The writer refers to the Levites, who were placed in charge of music by David.

xiii 1. *they read aloud.* Literally "it was read."

congregation of God. qhl h'lhym "congregation of God" only here; *qhl yhwh* "congregation of Yahweh" is found eight times in the Bible; *'dt yhwh* "assembly of Yahweh" four times; *'dt 'l* "assembly of God," i.e., the council of the gods, or the divine council in Ps lxxxii 1.

2. *they.* I.e., the Ammonite and Moabite.

but our God . . . a blessing. Cf. Deut xxiii 3 ff.; Neh ix 2.

3. *excluded. bdl* is found only in the late documents of the Pentateuch and other late documents; it is generally, though not always, in a cultic context. It is distributed as follows: twenty-two times in the Pentateuch, thirteen times in Chronicles, Ezra, and Nehemiah, once in I Kings, and three times in Isa (lvi, lix).

foreigners. Meyer, EJ, p. 130, reads "Bedouin" (vocalizing *'arab*). MT *'ereb* "mixed group"; so also LXX. See J. A. Montgomery, *Arabia and the Bible,* 1934, p. 29. The context seems to require "foreigners" here; "those of foreign descent" (RSV), is a bit broad. Cf. Vulg.

COMMENT

[Provision for temple services, xii 44–47]: This highly laudatory description of provision for the temple services reflects the views of the Chronicler, who is doubtless responsible for its composition. Most commentators think it has been placed here in anticipation of the unfavorable impressions made by the episodes related in the following chapter. Certainly it presents an idealistic picture expressing the hope and aim of the writer.

Two matters are stressed: (a) the provision for and care of the storage chambers in the temple, which assumes liberal and regular contributions in accordance with the prescriptions already laid down (x 35–39); (b) the praiseworthy conduct of the Levites in the performance of their responsibilities in the cult. Indeed, this looks like the main point of the section, growing out of the joyous observation in vss. 42b–43 (Sec. 17). No opportunity was ever lost by the Chronicler to magnify the Levites and to commend their services. He appears to follow protocol too, since he gives proper, though scant, credit to the priests. They served well and did everything just as prescribed by David (I Chron xxiii–xxvi) and Solomon (II Chron viii 14). Special emphasis is placed on the singers— whose ancestor was Asaph, himself appointed by David (cf. I Chron xv 16 ff., xvi 5, 37)—and the gatekeepers. Verse 47 seems to confirm what has been said above, that this passage was written to give a favorable impression to counteract the comparatively few deviations noted later. Things were not always so ideal, as can be seen from the grave difficulties encountered by both Nehemiah and Ezra, and the situation in the time of Malachi (first half of fifth century B.C.). Zerubbabel and Nehemiah are mentioned because they were the only known official governors of Judah up to the time covered by our book. The smooth functioning of the ecclesiastical system visualized by the writer is further illustrated by the Levites' meticulous observance of the law of tithes (Num xviii 28; Neh x 38b).

[Expulsion of foreigners, xiii 1–3]: Reading from the Torah of Moses must have taken place regularly at community festivals and certainly at assemblies called for one purpose or another (viii 1 ff.). While these verses are apparently the Chronicler's, it can scarcely be doubted that they reflect the situation of Nehemiah and not that of Ezra already mentioned in ix 2. It may be that the law is recalled here as the basis for and prelude to the action taken against Tobiah (cf. Jahn, p. 167). The law of Moses referred to is Deut xxiii 3–6. (For a discussion and date of the regulation on foreigners see K. Galling, "Das Gemeindegesetz in Deuteronomium 23," in *Festschrift für Alfred Bertholet,* 1950, pp. 176–91, especially pp. 186–89.) Only in this chapter in Deuteronomy is the phrase *qhl yhwh* "the congregation of Yahweh" used. Hence it is argued that the legal exclusion of those named pertained to the cultus and not to other relationships. Inasmuch as this law pertains to the cult, the reason for its being invoked here is clear. The writer was first of all concerned with purity of worship—of paramount importance to the whole scheme of the Chronicler. Since his view of the postexilic community is religious, the law of exclusion would probably go beyond the temple and city of Jerusalem. Its use as a basis for the exclusion of all foreigners points to both broad application of the principles involved and the cultic zeal of the author.

19. NEHEMIAH'S REFORMS
(xiii 4–31)

Exclusion of Tobiah

XIII 4 Earlier Eliashib the priest, who was in charge of the chambers of the house of our God, and who was close to Tobiah, 5 had provided for him a large chamber where they customarily stored the meal offerings, the frankincense, the vessels, the tithes of the grain, wine, and oil prescribed for the Levites, the singers, and the gatekeepers, and the contributions for the priests. 6 While all this was going on I was not [present] in Jerusalem, for in the thirty-second year of Artaxerxes, king of Babylon, I had gone to the king. Some time later, however, I requested leave of absence from the king 7 and came to Jerusalem where I learned about the wrong Eliashib had done in the case of Tobiah when he provided a room for him in the courts of the house of God. 8 I was very greatly displeased and threw out of the room [and] into the street all the household furnishings of Tobiah. 9 Then I ordered them to purify the room, after which I put back there the vessels of the house of God with the meal offerings and the frankincense.

Renewal of Levitical support

10 I learned further that the Levites had not been given their allotments so that the Levites and singers who conducted the [worship] service had retired each to his own farm. 11 I also reprimanded the officials, saying, "Why has the house of God been abandoned?" So I brought them together again and reinstated them, 12 and all Judah brought in the tithe of grain, wine, and oil to the treasuries. 13 I put Shelemiah the priest, Zadok the scribe, and Pedaiah of the Levites in charge of the trea-

suries, with Hanan the son of Zaccur, the son of Mattaniah[a], as their assistant, because they were regarded as reliable persons; it was their duty to distribute the allotments to their brothers. 14 Remember me, O my God, for this and do not blot out my good deeds which I have done for the house of my God [b]and its observances.[b]

Sabbath regulations

15 In those days I observed in Judah some who treaded wine presses, brought in sacks of grain, and loaded asses on the Sabbath; they also brought into Jerusalem on the Sabbath day wine, grapes, figs, and all sorts of merchandise. So I admonished[c] [them] on the day they sold food. 16 Tyrians[d] living there brought in fish and all sorts of merchandise which they sold to the Judeans and in Jerusalem on the Sabbath. 17 So I also reprimanded the chiefs of Judah, saying to them, "What is this wicked thing you are doing by profaning the Sabbath day? 18 Did not your fathers do this very thing for which our God brought upon us and upon this city all this misfortune? Yet you are adding to the wrath upon Israel by profaning the Sabbath." 19 As soon as the gates of Jerusalem were emptied at the approach of the Sabbath, I ordered the doors to be shut and directed that they should not open them until after the Sabbath. I stationed some of my servants at the gates [to see that] no merchandise might enter on the Sabbath day. 20 So the traders and dealers in all sorts of merchandise spent the night outside Jerusalem once or twice, 21 until I reprimanded them. I said to them, "Why do you spend the night in front of the wall? If you do it again, I will use force against you." From that time on they did not come on the Sabbath. 22 Then I ordered the Levites to purify themselves and function as guards at the

---

[a] LXX[B] "Nethaniah." LXX[A] follows MT.
[b-b] Omitted by LXX. The suffix, which is the third person masculine singular "his, its," could have as its antecedent either "the house" or "my God."
[c] See NOTE.
[d] Omitted by LXX. See NOTE.

gates to preserve the sanctity of the Sabbath day. Remember this also to my credit, O my God, and have compassion upon me in accordance with your great goodness.

The problem of mixed marriages

23 Moreover, in those days I observed Jews who had married Ashdodite, Ammonite and Moabite wives; 24 half of [their] children spoke Ashdodite or ᵉthe language of one of the other people [mentioned]ᵉ and could no longer speak the language of Judah. 25 So I argued with them, cursed them, struck some of them and plucked out their hair, and made them swear by God: "You must not marry your daughters to their sons or permit their daughters to marry your sons or take them yourselves. 26 Did not Solomon, the king of Israel, sin because of [such women as] these? Though, among many nations there was no king like him, and he was loved by his God and God made him king over all Israel, foreign women misled him to sin. 27 ᶠWere you obedientᶠ when you committed all this great evil by acting faithlessly toward our God, by marrying foreign wives?" 28 One of the sons of Joiada the son of Eliashib the high priest was a son-in-law of Sanballat the Horonite; I chased him away from me. 29 Remember them, O my God, for their defilement of the priesthood and of the covenant of the priests and Levites.

Summary of Nehemiah's cult reforms

30 Then I cleansed them of all foreign elements and set up orders of service for the priests and the Levites, so that each knew his work, 31 as well as for the supply of wood [for the altar] at the proper times and for the first fruits. Remember it to my credit, O my God.

ᵉ⁻ᵉ Heb. "and according to the tongue [language] of people and people."
ᶠ⁻ᶠ See NOTE.

NOTES

xiii 4. *Earlier.* Literally "before this," i.e., during Nehemiah's absence. *close to. qrwb* in Ruth ii 20 means "close relative." But if the high priest is meant, that can hardly be the case here. There is no indication elsewhere of a consanguineous or marital relationship between Eliashib and Tobiah.

5. *for him.* I.e., for Tobiah.

6. *the thirty-second year of Artaxerxes.* Artaxerxes I (Longimanus) ruled from 465 to 425 B.C. His thirty-second year would be 433/2 B.C. Neh v 14 says he began his first term as governor in the twentieth year of Artaxerxes (cf. ii 1); it ran until the thirty-second of Artaxerxes or for a period of twelve years. The "some time later" is very indefinite. It might require as many as six months of travel, both ways, between Jerusalem and the royal court, even if it was only at Babylon. How much time was occupied with reports and other matters is not known (see Rudolph, p. 203). Arsames was away from his post around three years (cf. Cowley, AP, 27:2; 30:4; 32:2–7). He left in the fourteenth year of Darius (410 B.C.) and was still absent in the seventeenth year (30:30), though he appears to have been back shortly afterward, to judge from the directive sent to him by Bigvai in reply to Jedoniah's letter. Incidentally, this correspondence points to anti-Jewish activity in Elephantine as soon as Arsames nad departed; and the Jews were in dire straits until his return (AP, 30:17–22).

king of Babylon. Cyrus assumed this title as we know from his cylinder (ANET, p. 316). See S. A Pallis, "The History of Babylon 538–93 B.C." in *Studia Orientalia Ioanni Pedersen,* 1953, pp. 276–79.

10. *who conducted the [worship] service.* See COMMENT on Sec. 15, xi 22.

11. *them.* I.e., the Levites.

13. *I put.* Cf. LXX[NL], Vulg., Syr. Gesenius-Kautzsch, 53g, thinks it is *hiphil* denominative of *'wṣr* "treasury."

Shelemiah. Name probably occurs on seal found at Azor (*The Israel Digest,* January 6, 1961, p. 7), on a seal from sixth century B.C.(?) (Reifenberg, *Ancient Hebrew Seals,* p. 37) and in the Elephantine papyri.

Pedaiah. Occurs on Ophel seal from sixth century(?) (Diringer, *Le iscrizioni antico-ebraiche Palestinesi,* pp. 203 f.) and in Elephantine documents (Cowley, AP, 43:12).

Zaccur. Common in Elephantine materials and Brooklyn Museum Aramaic Papyri.

15. *sacks.* So with Rudolph, *in loco,* for "heaps" or "bundles."

I admonished. Heb. "I bore witness," which signifies here "to admonish or warn." Underlying the statement is the Deuteronomic expression *h'yd b . . . hywm* (Deut iv 26, viii 19, xxx 19; Jer xlii 19, etc.).

the day they sold food. For other emended readings, see Rudolph and Galling.

16. *Tyrians.* Cf. Ezra iii 7 *lṣrym* "to the Tyrians." The absence of the word in LXX^AB and Syr. has given rise to attempts to emend the text, but none are convincing. The chief offenders were merchants, and since foreigners are involved, as shown by the reference to the Judeans, Tyrians seems correct. For the mercantile fame of Tyre, see Ezek xxvii 12–36, xxviii 16. It is probable that Phoenician commercial agents and missions were present in Jerusalem, as in the great population centers elsewhere. Cf. J. M. Myers, ZAW 74 (1962), 178–90; *Reallexikon der Vorgeschichte,* 5, pp. 67–71. For a description of such trade colonies in Arabia see W. Caskel, *Lihyan und Lihyanisch,* pp. 51 f., and *Das altarabische Königreich Lihjan,* pp. 6 ff.

living there. I.e., in Jerusalem, where their trade mission operated.

17. *chiefs.* See NOTE on Ezra ix 2.

profaning the Sabbath day. Phrase occurs elsewhere only in Ezek xx 16, 21, 24, xxii 8, xxiii 38; the idea, in Isa lvi 2, 6; Exod xxxi 14 (*P*).

18. *you are adding to the wrath.* Cf. Ezra ix 14, x 10.

19. *emptied.* Syriac cognate has this meaning. Hebrew means "to become shadowy or dark"—the Sabbath began at sunset. See Rudolph for other suggestions.

21. *I will use force against you.* Literally "a hand I will send against [or upon] you."

24. *the language of Judah.* Literally "Jewish"; only here and II Kings xviii 26, 28 ‖ Isa xxxvi 11, 13; II Chron xxxii 18.

25. *argued with them.* Some render "reproach."

cursed. Bowman, p. 816, suggests "treat with contempt," since Hebrew root signifies "to be light" and the Akkadian cognate means "to be trifling or despised."

26. *he was loved by his God.* Cf. personal name of Solomon: Jedidiah "beloved of Yahweh" in II Sam xii 24–25.

God made him king over all Israel. Cf. I Kings iv 1, xi 42.

27. *Were you obedient.* *hnšm'* could be either niphal perfect third masculine or qal imperfect first plural. The translation takes it as former. Literally "and to/for you was it heard. . . ." LXX renders MT literally; Vulg. "shall we disobediently do all this great evil that we should act faithlessly toward our God and marry foreign wives?" It could possibly be read: "Were you informed when you did . . ."; the implication being that they did it deliberately and not blindly (cf. Neh vi 1, 7).

COMMENT

With the possible exception of vss. 1–3 [Sec. 18] chapter xiii
originated in the memoirs of Nehemiah and deals exclusively with
cultic reforms. While Nehemiah does not appear officially to have
taken the lead in cultic matters—because he was both layman and
eunuch—he did maintain a vital interest in the religious activities
of the people in Jerusalem and Judah, as may be seen from his
co-operation with the religious authorities, his observance of cult
regulations (vi 11), and his arrangement of and participation in
the ritual of dedication of the wall (xii 31 ff.). The perils of subversion had already been demonstrated by the governor's experience
with neighboring peoples in connection with the reconstruction of
the city wall. It must have been quite evident to Nehemiah that
they would bore from within if allowed religious privileges (cf. the
attempt of Shemaiah to deceive him, vi 10 ff.) and thus he took
resolute measures to strengthen the only organization that could save
the community from compromise and collapse. The reforms noticed
here apparently took place during the second period of Nehemiah's
activity at Jerusalem.

[Exclusion of Tobiah, xiii 4–9]: When Nehemiah's leave of
absence from the Persian court had expired, he returned to resume
his duties. Some time later he came back to Jerusalem, where he
found the old troubles besetting the community again. Tobiah had
moved into spacious quarters in the temple precincts with the express permission of Eliashib, the priest in charge of the storage
chambers. It is not clear just who this Eliashib was—the high priest
by that name (iii 1, 20, 21, xii 22, 23) or just one of the priests.
He was probably the latter—there were a number of persons with
that name in other groups at the time—since the high priest would
hardly have made himself responsible for the comparatively menial
task of overseeing the handling of temple supplies. This Eliashib
was close to Tobiah; he may have been a relative of his. In any
event, Nehemiah took quick action to rid the place of the unwel-
come intruder and had the chambers purified and then restored
to their original use. On the authority to intervene in cultic affairs
exercised by Nehemiah, see W. F. Albright, *The Archaeology of
Palestine and the Bible,* 3d ed., 1935, p. 175. For Cambyses' cleans-

ing and restoration of the cult of Neith at Sais in Egypt, see Kienitz, GÄJZ, pp. 56f., and the literature cited there.

[Levitical support renewed, 10–14]: Great pains had been taken earlier to bring new residents to Jerusalem (Neh xi), partly to fill the vacuum created by the repair of the walls and the consequent security of the city and partly to provide for the necessary temple services. Nehemiah's return to the Persian court signaled a relaxation in religious observances (vs. 10), which in turn brought about the withdrawal of the Levites to their old habitations. The Levites, possibly because of the menial character of their services, always had a hard time of it. There may be more than cultic concern behind the Chronicler's zeal for them. In any case, necessity forced them to seek a livelihood elsewhere. Nehemiah was perturbed by the course of events and immediately took steps to bring back the Levites from their farms and to reinstate them once more. He saw to it that their allotments were given to them through the exaction of the tithe from all Judah. He placed trusted officials (two priests and two Levites) in charge of the treasuries and held them responsible for the just and proper distribution of the proceeds.

[Sabbath observance, 15–22]: Nehemiah's observant eye is nowhere more vividly illustrated than here. He was particularly concerned with the religious welfare of the people because, as a student of history and as a realist, he knew that their existence depended on fidelity to Yahweh. One of the central features of the exilic and postexilic cult was the Sabbath, which had become utterly commercialized. Wine press operators, farmers, fruitgrowers, transportation workers—all disregarded the day, possibly because of the supposed economic needs of the community. The Phoenician traders peddled their wares on the Sabbath—with more than ordinary success, to judge from the vigorous protest of Nehemiah. It should be noted that the latter's caveat was due to profanation of the Sabbath and not to trade as such (cf. A. C. Welch, *Post-Exilic Judaism*, 1935, p. 76). He warned both vendors (vs. 15) and vendees (vs. 17). His reprimand to the chiefs of Judah is significant because they may have been implicated in a special way; possibly they were more than buyers. They should have known better, since they were aware of past experiences. Here Nehemiah reflects the dicta of the prophets (Jer xvii 19–27; Ezek xx 12–24), who attributed the misfortune of Judah to the violation of the Sabbath. Apparently

the warning went unheeded, since overt action followed. The gates
of the city were closed to mercantile traffic and guards posted to
prevent surreptitious operations. Since the Sabbath began at sunset,
violations could more easily have occurred during the hours of dark-
ness. Traders and dealers camped outside the walls for a while,
perhaps hoping to entice customers to come to them, until they were
threatened with arrest or bodily harm. To prevent any further desecration of the Sabbath in the future, Levitical guards were set at
the gates of the city, as they had been earlier at the gates of the
temple. Levitical guards were required because they could be consecrated for Sabbath duty, a requirement that could not be met by
laymen. Furthermore, the demands of the Sabbath observance, together with its sacred character, were sufficient to justify the assign-
ment of Levites as gatekeepers for that day.

[The problem of mixed marriages, 23–29]: Cultic purity was
not easy to achieve or to maintain when it was achieved. It was
persistently threatened by family relationships and economic interests. The most stubborn problem was that of intermarriage, which,
in the early days of the Exile, may have been necessary for survival.
Now, however, it was threatening the whole character of the community. Nehemiah observed it first in the speech of children—an
interesting point, since the mothers naturally taught their children
to speak the only language they knew.

Particularly reprehensible was the prevalence of the Ashdodite
tongue. The language of Moab and Ammon was very close to Hebrew, as we know from the Mesha inscription, and presumably
offered little or no great threat to the language aspect of the cult.
In any case, the phrase "Ammonite and Moabite" may be a secondary addition, as well as the phrase "or the language of one of
the other people" in vs. 24. What the Ashdodite language was is
not known—it could have been an Aramaic or Philistine dialect
(cf. A. Alt, PJB 25 [1929], 86, n. 1; Schneider, p. 261). Alt
thinks of Zech ix 6 in this connection. For references to other possibilities see Rudolph, pp. 208 f. On the Ashdodites in the time of
Nehemiah see Alt, KS, II, pp. 342 f., and Abel, AGP, II, pp. 121 f.
For interpretation see Cazelles (VT 4 [1954], 121 f.) who identifies the *mamzer* of Deut xxiii 3 with the Ashdodites. (See further
B. Otzen, *Studien über Deuterosacharaja,* 1964, pp. 109–13.)
The first concrete evidence for the Ashdodite language of the
fifth century B.C. has turned up recently. It is not conclusive but

suggests what might have been expected; namely, that there was very little difference between the language of Judah and that of Ashdod. Perhaps it was only a matter of dialectical variation, or merely of accent and pronunciation, which would be more than enough to arouse the ire of a man like Nehemiah. In view of Nehemiah's use of Hebrew, it is possible that he was trying to revive the ancient language. We do not know too much about the language of Judah and Jerusalem in the fifth century apart from seals and stamped jar handles and these seem to be divided between Aramaic and possibly some Hebrew. The fifth-fourth century ostraca from Arad are all in Aramaic. The Ashdod ostracon has the letters *krm* and the name *zbdyh,* i.e., "the vineyard of Zebadiah." The fact that it comes from a Jewish vineyard may mean that we have here a Judahite inscription rather than an Ashdodite one, though the difference cannot have been great. All the evidence at present points to a linguistic and commercial continuum in this area, with the lingua franca Aramaic though there may have been different dialects.

In any case, Nehemiah recognized how essential language was for the maintenance of national identity and, especially, religion. Hence he resorted to drastic measures to enforce his order. In contrast to Ezra, who chastised himself (Ezra ix 3), Nehemiah laid hands upon some of the guilty parties—the way of one who had more than moral authority. The text may indicate a progression in the harshness of the measures employed to break up the practice (vs. 25). Nehemiah did not go so far as Ezra (Ezra ix–x), who demanded divorce; he simply demanded an end to further intermarriage. The argument from the history of Solomon must be Nehemiah's, since the Chronicler omits any reference to Solomon's foreign wives, with the exception of Pharaoh's daughter, for whom a special dwelling was constructed (II Chron viii 11). Verse 26 recalls I Kings iii 12–13, xi 1–10. Verse 27, which draws a parallel between the culpability of Solomon (vs. 26) and the guilt of the Jews of Nehemiah's time, seems to be directed against the leaders of Judah. The son of Joiada, though he had not intermarried with any of the peoples mentioned above, had violated the general ban by marrying a daughter of Sanballat and so was driven out of the community. This statement has some bearing on the date of Nehemiah, as may be seen from the discussion of the problem in the Introduction. Josephus (*Antiquities* XI.vii.2) states that a brother of

Jaddua by the name of Manasseh married Nikaso, the daughter of Sanballat, but dates the affair in the time of Darius III (335–330 B.C.) and Alexander the Great. The new Samaria papyri would appear to go a long way in clearing up the confusion of Sanballats by Josephus. The Sanballat whose name occurs in these papyri is neither the one mentioned by Josephus nor the one named in the Bible and the Elephantine papyri. Since the governorship was presumably continued in the Sanballat family, in accordance with practices in the Persian empire, we may have, on the principle of papponymy, at least three Sanballats between the time of Nehemiah and Darius III. Josephus thus confused his Sanballats just as he did his Jadduas. For detailed suggestions on the problem in the light of the Samaria papyri, see the article by F. M. Cross, Jr., in BA 26 (1963), 120–21. For earlier discussion of the problem see Rudolph, pp. 210 f.

It is possible that the son of Joiada refused to divorce his wife— though that is not stated—and so was ostracized, or that he was chased out by virtue of Nehemiah's feeling toward Sanballat. Nehemiah then calls upon Yahweh to remember the defilement of the priesthood and the violation of the covenant by the priests and Levites. The high priest was enjoined from marrying a foreigner (Lev xxi 14), and although there is no specific prohibition against other priests and Levites marrying outsiders, they did have special obligations along this line. Expulsion of Joiada's son because he had married the daughter of Sanballat could be regarded as a natural extension of the prohibition about the high priest marrying a foreigner to male members of the family. Since the son of the high priest might conceivably become high priest, he might be enjoined from such a marriage on the basis of that possibility. As the commentators have pointed out, the violation of the covenant by priests and Levites is best illustrated by the complaint of Malachi (ii 1–8), who also inveighs bitterly against easy divorce (ii 13–16) because it violated the solemn agreement (covenant) involved in marriage.

[Summary statement of Nehemiah's cult reforms, 30–31]: The cult reforms of Nehemiah were undoubtedly thoroughgoing. The case of priestly aberration was an illustration of his determination to intervene effectively with the authority invested in him by the Persian king. He wielded a heavy hand to enforce the demands of the Torah as it applied to the clergy. His authority is clearly shown by the renewal of the priestly and Levitical orders of service which had been neglected (vs. 11). The renewal does not appear to have been a new arrangement; it was rather a reorganization of the temple services said by the Chronicler to have been instituted by David (I Chron xxiii–xxvi). It was recognized that the king was responsible for the maintenance of those orders (xi 23) and since Nehemiah had been appointed governor, the king's representative in the province of Judah, he was carrying out his obligation. In addition to filling the clerical orders and seeing after their proper functioning, he provided materials for the offerings and other cult operations. That too was a prerogative and, perhaps, responsibility of the king (II Chron viii 12–14, xxxi 2–3, xxxv 2–7). The book ends with Nehemiah's prayer that his work be remembered by Yahweh.

APPENDIXES

APPENDIX I. COMPARISON OF NEHEMIAH VII AND EZRA II (I ESDRAS V)

I. LIST IN MT (Neh vii 8–71; Ezra ii 3–69)

A. THE MEN OF ISRAEL

Neh vii	*Ezra ii*
Sons of Parosh, 2172	Sons of Parosh, 2172
Sons of Shephatiah, 372	Sons of Shephatiah, 372
Sons of Arah, 652	Sons of Arah, 775
Sons of Pahath-moab (Jeshua, Joab), 2818	Sons of Pahath-moab (Jeshua, Joab), 2812
Sons of Elam, 1254	Sons of Elam, 1254
Sons of Zattu, 845	Sons of Zattu, 945
Sons of Zaccai, 760	Sons of Zaccai, 760
Sons of Binnui, 648	Sons of Bani, 642
Sons of Bebai, 628	Sons of Bebai, 623
Sons of Azgad, 2322	Sons of Azgad, 1222
Sons of Adonikam, 667	Sons of Adonikam, 666
Sons of Bigvai, 2067	Sons of Bigvai, 2056
Sons of Adin, 655	Sons of Adin, 454
Sons of Ater (Hezekiah), 98	Sons of Ater (Hezekiah), 98
Sons of Hashum, 328	Sons of Bezai, 323
Sons of Bezai, 324	Sons of Jorah, 112
Sons of Hariph, 112	Sons of Hashum, 223
Sons of Gibeon, 95	Sons of Gibbar, 95
Men of Bethlehem and Netophah, 188	Sons of Bethlehem, 123
Men of Anathoth, 128	Men of Netophah, 56
Men of Beth-azmaveth, 42	Men of Anathoth, 128
Men of Kiriath-jearim (Chephirah, Beeroth), 743	Sons of Azmaveth, 42
Men of Ramah (Geba), 621	Sons of Kiriatharim (Chephirah, Beeroth), 743

Neh vii	*Ezra ii*
Men of Michmas, 122	Sons of Ramah (Geba), 621
	Men of Michmas, 122
Men of Bethel (Ai), 123	
Men of other Nebo, 52	Men of Bethel (Ai), 223
	Sons of Nebo, 52
Sons of other Elam, 1254	Sons of Magbish, 156
Sons of Harim, 320	Sons of other Elam, 1254
Sons of Jericho, 345	Sons of Harim, 320
Sons of Lod (Hadid, Ono), 721	
	Sons of Lod (Hadid, Ono), 725
Sons of Senaah, 3930	Sons of Jericho, 345
	Sons of Senaah, 3630

B. THE PRIESTS

Sons of Jedaiah of the house of Jeshua, 973	Sons of Jedaiah of the house of Jeshua, 973
Sons of Immer, 1052	Sons of Immer, 1052
Sons of Pashhur, 1247	Sons of Pashhur, 1247
Sons of Harim, 1017	Sons of Harim, 1017

C. THE LEVITES

Sons of Jeshua, to Kadmiel of the sons of Hodevah, 74	Sons of Jeshua and Kadmiel of the sons of Hodaviah, 74

D. THE SINGERS

Sons of Asaph, 148	Sons of Asaph, 128

E. THE GATEKEEPERS

Sons of Shallum	Sons of Shallum
Sons of Ater	Sons of Ater
Sons of Talmon	Sons of Talmon
Sons of Akkub }138	Sons of Akkub }139
Sons of Hatita	Sons of Hatita
Sons of Shobai	Sons of Shobai

Neh vii   *Ezra ii*

F. THE TEMPLE SLAVES

Sons of Ziha	Sons of Ziha
Sons of Hasupha	Sons of Hasupha
Sons of Tabbaoth	Sons of Tabbaoth
Sons of Keros	Sons of Keros
Sons of Sia	Sons of Siaha
Sons of Padon	Sons of Padon
Sons of Lebanah	Sons of Lebanah
Sons of Hagabah	Sons of Hagabah
Sons of Shalmai	Sons of Akkub
Sons of Hanan	Sons of Hagab
Sons of Giddel	Sons of Shamlai
Sons of Gahar	Sons of Hanan
Sons of Reaiah	Sons of Giddel
Sons of Rezin	Sons of Gahar
Sons of Nekoda	Sons of Reaiah
Sons of Gazzam	Sons of Rezin
Sons of Uzza	Sons of Nekoda
Sons of Paseah	Sons of Gazzam
Sons of Besai	Sons of Uzza
Sons of Meunim	Sons of Paseah
Sons of Nephushesim	Sons of Besai
Sons of Bakbuk	Sons of Asnah
Sons of Hakupha	Sons of Meunim
Sons of Harhur	Sons of Nephisim
Sons of Bazlith	Sons of Bakbuk
Sons of Mehida	Sons of Hakupha
Sons of Harsha	Sons of Harhur
Sons of Barkos	Sons of Bazluth
Sons of Sisera	Sons of Mehida
Sons of Temah	Sons of Harsha
Sons of Neziah	Sons of Barkos
Sons of Hatipha	Sons of Sisera
	Sons of Temah
	Sons of Neziah
	Sons of Hatipha

Neh vii	*Ezra ii*

G. SOLOMON'S SERVANTS

Sons of Sotai	Sons of Sotai
Sons of Sophereth	Sons of Hassophereth (the scribe)
Sons of Perida	Sons of Peruda
Sons of Jaala	Sons of Jaalah
Sons of Darkon	Sons of Darkon
Sons of Giddel	Sons of Giddel
Sons of Shephatiah	Sons of Shephatiah
Sons of Hattil	Sons of Hattil
Sons of Pochereth-hazzebaim	Sons of Pochereth-hazzebaim
Sons of Amon	Sons of Ami

H. TOTAL OF TEMPLE SLAVES AND SOLOMON'S SERVANTS
392

I. THOSE WHOSE ANCESTRY COULD NOT BE PROVEN

Laymen from:

Tel-melah	Tel-melah
Tel-harsha	Tel-harsha
Cherub	Cherub
Addon	Addan
Immer	Immer

Sons of Delaiah		
Sons of Tobiah	} 642	
Sons of Nekoda		

Sons of Delaiah		
Sons of Tobiah	} 652	
Sons of Nekoda		

Priests:

Sons of Hobaiah	Sons of Hobaiah
Sons of Hakkoz	Sons of Hakkoz
Sons of Barzillai	Sons of Barzillai

J. TOTALS GIVEN IN TEXT

Whole congregation, 42,360	Whole congregation, 42,360
Men and women servants, 7337	Men and women servants, 7337
Male and female singers, 245	Male and female singers, 200
Camels, 435	Horses, 736
Asses, 6720	Mules, 245
	Camels, 435
	Asses, 6720

Neh vii   *Ezra ii*

K. MONETARY AND OTHER CONTRIBUTIONS

Governor's gifts:
  1000 drachmas of gold
  50 bowls
  530 priestly garments
From heads of families:
  20,000 drachmas of gold   61,000 drachmas of gold
  2200 minas of silver   5000 minas of silver
                                   100 priestly garments

From the rest of the people:
  20,000 drachmas of gold
  2000 minas of silver
  67 priestly garments

II. ACCORDING TO LXX (Neh vii 8–72; Ezra ii 3–69; I Esdras v 10–44)

A. LAYMEN

Neh vii	*Ezra ii*	*Esdras v*
Phoros, 2172	Phores, 2172	Phoros, 2172 (LXX[B], 2070)
Saphatia, 372		
	Asaph (LXX[B], 472; LXX[A], 372)	Saphat, 472 (omitted by LXX[B])
Era, 652 (LXX[A], 672)	Era, 475	Ares, 756
Phaathmoab, 2818	Phalabmoab, 2812	Phthaleimoab, 2812 (LXX[B], 2802)
Iesou	Iesoue	Iesou
Iobab	Iobab	Roboab
Ailam, 1254	Mailam, 1254	Iolamou, 1254 (LXX[B], 2)
Zathouia, 840	Zathoua, 945	Zaton, 945 (LXX[B], 970)
Zathou, 860 (LXX[A], 870)	Zakchou, 760	Chorbe, 705
Banoui, 648	Banou, 642	Banei, 648
Bebi, 628	Babei, 623	Bebai, 623 (LXX[B], 633)
Asgad, 2328 (LXX[A], 2322)	Asgad, 3222 (LXX[A], 1322)	Argai, 1322

Neh vii	*Ezra ii*	*Esdras v*
Adeikam, 667	Adonikan, 666	Adoneikam, 667 (LXX^B, 37)
Batoei, 2067	Baogei, 2056	Bosai, 2066 (LXX^B, 2606)
Edein, 655 (LXX^A, 654)	Adin, 454	Adeiliou, 454
Ater of Ezekia, 98	Ater of Ezekia, 92 (LXX^A, 98)	Azer of Ezekiou, 92 (LXX^B, 607)
Esam, 328	Basou, 323	Keilan and Azetas, 67 (LXX^B, 607)
Besei, 324	Oura, 112	Azarou, 432
Areiph, 112	Asem, 223	Anneis, 101
Asen (Added by LXX^A), 223	Taber, 95	Arom, Bassai, 323
Gabaon, 95	Barthleem, 123	Arseiphoureith, 112 (XLX^B, 3005)
Bethleem, 123 ⎫	Netopha, 56	Baiterous, 3005 (LXX^B, 3005)
Netopha, 56 ⎬ om. by LXX^B	Anathoth, 128	Ragethlomon, 123
Anathoth, 128 ⎭	Asmoth, 42	Netebas, 55
Bethasmoth, 42	Kariothiarom ⎫ Kapheira ⎬ 743 Beroth ⎭	Enatou, 158
Karith-iareim ⎫ 721 Kapheira ⎬ (LXX^A, Beros ⎭ 743)	Aram ⎫ 621 Gabaa ⎭	Baitasmon-zammouth, 42 ⎫ LXX^B, ⎬ 25 Kartathei-areios, 25 ⎭
Arma ⎫ 621 Tamal ⎭	Machmas, 122	
Machemas, 122	Gaithel ⎫ 223; LXX^A, Aia ⎭ 423	Peiras 743, LXX^B, Berog 700
Bethel ⎫ 123 Aleia ⎭	Nabou, 52	Chadiasai ⎫ 422 Ammidioi ⎭
Nabia-aar, 52	Magebos, 156	Keiramas ⎫ 621 Kabbes ⎭
Magebos (Added by LXX^A), 156	Elamar, 2254; LXX^A, 1254	Makalon, 122
Elam-aar, 1250; (LXX^A, 1254)	Eram, 320	Betolio, 52

Neh vii	*Ezra ii*	*Esdras v*
Eram, 320	Lod ⎫ Aroth ⎬ 625; LXX^A, Onon ⎭ 725	Neipheis, 156
Iereicho, 345	Iereia, 345	Kalamokalou ⎫ 725 Onous ⎭
Lod ⎫ Adia ⎬ 721 Ono ⎭	Sana, 3630	Ierechou, 345; LXX^B, 245
Sananat, 930; LXX^A, 3930		Sama, 3330; LXX^B, 3301

B. Priests

Iodae (house of Iesou), 973	Ieouda (house of Iesoi), 973	Ieddou (of Iesou) ⎫ LXX^B, (of Sana- ⎬ 872 beis) ⎭ 972;
	Emmer, 1052	
Emmer (omitted by Lxx^B), 1052		Ermerou, 1052; LXX^B, 252
Phasedour, 1247	Phassour, 1247	Phassorou, 1247
Eram, 1017	Erem, 1007 (LXX^A)	Charme, 1017; LXX^B, 217

C. Levites

Iesou ⎫ Kabdiel ⎬74 Thoudia ⎭	Iesoue ⎫ ⎬ ⎬ 74 Sodouia ⎬ Kadmiel ⎭	Iesoueis ⎫ ⎬ Kadoelou ⎬ 74 ⎬ Bannou ⎬ Soudiou ⎭

D. Singers

Asaph, 148	Asaph, 148; LXX^A, 128	Asaph, 128

Neh vii	Ezra ii	Esdras v

E. DOORKEEPERS

Neh vii	Ezra ii	Esdras v
Saloum	Saloum	Saloum
Ater	Ater	Atar
Telamon	Telmon	Tolman
Akou } 138	Akoum } 139	Darkoubi } 139
Ateita	Ateta	Ateta
Satei	Abaou	Sabei

F. TEMPLE SLAVES

Neh vii	Ezra ii	Esdras v
Sea	Southia	Esau
Aspha	Asouphe	Taseipha
Gabaoth	Taboth	Tabaoth
Keira	Kades	Keras
Asouia	Soel	Soua
Phadon	Phadon	Phalaiou
Labana	Labano	Labana
Agaba	Agaba	Akkaba (omitted by LXX[B])
Salamei	Akaboth	Akoud
Anan	Agab	Outa
Gadel	Samalan	Ketab
Gaar	Anan	Akkaba
Raea	Kedad	Subaei
Rason	Gael	Anan
Nekoda	Reel	Koua
Gezam	Rason	Keddour
Ozei	Nechoda	Iaeirou
Phese	Gazem	Daisan
Besei	Ousa	Noeba
Meseinom	Phison	Chaseba
Nephosasei	Basei	Kazera
Bakbou	Asena	Ozeiou
Acheipha	Manoemein	Phinoe
Aroum	Napheison	Asara
Basaoth	Bakkouk	Basthai
Meeida	Apheika	Assana
Adasan	Arour	Manei
Barkou	Basadoe	Napheisei
Seseirath	Maouda	Akouph
Emath	Aresa	Acheiba

Neh vii	*Ezra ii*	*Esdras v*
Aseia	Barkous	Asour
Ateipha	Sisara (om. by LXX^B)	Pharakeim
	Thema	Basalem
	Nasous	Dedda
	Atoupha	Koutha
		Charea (omitted by LXX^B)
		Bachous
		Serar
		Thomthei
		Nasei
		Ateipha

G. SOLOMON'S SERVANTS	SONS OF ABDESELMA	
Soutei	Satei	Assapheioth
Sapharath	Asepherath	Phareida
Phereida	Phadoura	Ieielei
Ielel	Ieela	Lozon
Dorkon	Darkon	Isdael
Gadel	Gedea	Saphue
Saphatia	Saphateia	Agia
Egel	Ateia	Phakareth-sabein
Phacharath	Phasrath-aseboein	Sarothei
Sabaeim	Emei	Meisaias
Emeim		Gas
		Addous
		Soubas
		Apherra
		Barodeis
		Saphag
		Allon

H. NUMBERS OF TEMPLE SLAVES AND SOLOMON'S SERVANTS

392	392	372

Neh vii	*Ezra ii*	*Esdras v*

I. THOSE WHOSE ANCESTRY COULD NOT BE PROVED

Laymen: sons of

Dalea ⎫	Lachea ⎫	Asan ⎫
Tobia ⎬ 642	Boua ⎪	Baenan ⎬ 652
Nekoda ⎭	Tobeia ⎬ 652	Nekodan ⎭
	Nekoda ⎭	

Priests: sons of

Ebeia	Labeia	Obbeia
Akos	Akous	Akbos
Berzellei	Barbelthei	Iaddous

J. TOTALS GIVEN IN THE TEXT

Neh vii	*Ezra ii*	*Esdras v*
Whole congregation, 42,360; LXX[B], 42,308	Whole congregation, 42,360	Whole congregation, 42,360
Men and women servants, 7337; LXX[B], 337 (The *trischilioi* has fallen out.)	Men and women servants, 7337; LXX[B], 7334	Men and women servants, 7337
Male and female singers, 245	Male and female singers, 200	Male and female musicians, 245
Horses, 736 (omitted by LXX[B])	Horses, 736; LXX[B], 730	Horses, 7036
Mules, 245 (omitted by LXX[B])	Mules, 245	Mules, 245
Camels, 435 (omitted by LXX[B])	Camels, 435	Camels, 435
Asses, 6720; LXX[B], 2700	Asses, 6720; LXX[B], 720 (The *exakischilioi* has fallen out.)	Beasts of burden, 5525

Neh vii	*Ezra ii*	*Esdras v*

K. MONETARY AND OTHER CONTRIBUTIONS

Governor's gifts:
1000 (pieces) of
   gold
50 bowls
30 priestly gar-
   ments

From family heads:		
20,000 (pieces) of gold	61,000 minas (LXX^A, drachmas) of pure gold	1000 minas of gold
2200 minas of silver	5000 minas of silver	5000 minas of silver
	100 priestly garments	100 priestly garments

From the rest of
  the people:
20,000 (pieces)
  of gold
2200 minas of
  silver
67 priestly gar-
  ments

APPENDIX II. COMPARISON OF LISTS

A. PRIEST LISTS IN EZRA-NEHEMIAH

Ezra ii 36–39; Neh vii 39–42

The sons of Jedaiah, of the house of Jeshua
The sons of Immer
The sons of Pashhur
The sons of Harim

Ezra viii 2

Gershom, of the sons of Phinehas
Daniel, of the sons of Ithamar

Neh x 2–8	*Neh xii 1–7*	*Neh xii 12–21*	*I Chron xxiv 7–18*
(a) Seraiah	Seraiah (a)	Meraiah of Seraiah (a)	Jehoiarib
(b) Azariah	Jeremiah (c)	Hananiah of Jeremiah (c)	Jedaiah
(c) Jeremiah	Ezra (b?)	Meshullam of Ezra (b?)	Harim (i)
(d) Pashhur	Amariah (e)	Jehohanan of Amariah (e)	Seorim
(e) Amariah	Malluch (i)	Jonathan of Malluch (i)	Malchijah (f)
(f) Malchijah	Hattush (g)	Joseph of Shebaniah (h)	Mijamin (r)

(g) Hattush	Shecaniah (h?)	Adna of Harim (i)	Hakkoz
(h) Shebaniah	Rehum (i?)	Helkai of Meraioth (k?)	Abijah (q)
(i) Malluch	Meremoth (k)	Zechariah of Iddo (l?)	Jeshua
(j) Harim	Iddo (l?)	Meshullam of Ginnethon (n)	Shecaniah (h?)
(k) Meremoth	Ginnethoi (n)	Zichri of Abijah (q)	Eliashib
(l) Obadiah	Abijah (q)	—— of Miniamin (r?)	Jakim
(m) Daniel	Mijamin (r)	Piltai of Moadiah	Huppah
(n) Ginnethon	Maadiah	Shammua of Bilgah (t)	Jeshebab
(o) Baruch	Bilgah (t)	Jehonathan of Shemaiah (u)	Bilgah (t)
(p) Meshullam	Shemaiah (u)	Mattenai of Joiarib	Immer (e?)
(q) Abijah	Joiarib	Uzzi of Jedaiah	Hezir
(r) Mijamin	Jedaiah	Kallai of Sallai	Happizzez
(s) Maaziah	Sallu	Eber of Amok	Pethahiah
(t) Bilgai	Amok	Hashabiah of Hilkiah	Jehezqel
(u) Shemaiah	Hilkiah	Nethanel of Jedaiah	Jachin
	Jedaiah		Gamul
			Delaiah
			Maaziah (s)

Totals: 21   22   21   24

1 Chron ix 10–12	*Neh xi 10–13*	*Ezra x 18–22*
		Of the sons of Jeshua
Jedaiah	Jedaiah (son of)	son of Jozadak:
Jehoiarib	Joiarib	
Jachin	Jachin	Maaseiah
Azariah (son of)	Seraiah (son of)	Eliezer
↑	↑	Jarib
Hilkiah	Hilkiah	Gedaliah
↑	↑	
Meshullam	Meshullam	Of the sons of Immer:
↑	↑	
Zadok	Zadok	Hanani
↑	↑	Zebadiah
Meraioth	Meraioth	
↑	↑	
Ahitub	Ahitub	Of the sons of Harim:
Adaiah (son of)	Adaiah (son of)	Maaseiah
↑	↑	Elijah
Jeroham	Jeroham	Shemaiah
↑	↑	Jehiel
Pashhur	Pelaliah	Uzziah
↑	↑	
Malchijah	Amzi	
	↑	
Maasai (son of)	Zechariah	
↑	↑	
Adiel	Pashhur	Of the sons of Pashhur:
↑	↑	
Jahzerah	Malchijah	Elioenai
↑		Maaseiah
Meshullam	Amashsai (son of)	Ishmael
↑	↑	Nethanel
Meshillemoth	Azarel	Jozabad
↑	↑	Eleasah
Immer	Ahzai	
	↑	
	Meshillemoth	
	↑	
	Immer	

B. LISTS OF LEVITES

Ezra ii 40	*Ezra viii 18–19*	*Neh vii 43*
Sons of Jeshua	Sherebiah of the sons of Mahli	Sons of Jeshua
Kadmiel	Hashabiah ⎫	Kadmiel
Binnui (?)	Jeshaiah ⎬ of the sons of Merari	Binnui (?)
Hodaviah		Hodevah

Neh x 10–13	*Neh xii 8–9*	*Neh xii 24–25*
(a) Jeshua son of Azaniah	Jeshua (a)	Hashabiah (k) ⎫
(b) Binnui of sons of Henadad	Binnui (b)	Sherebiah (m) ⎬ chiefs Jeshua, son of Kadmiel (c?) ⎭
(c) Kadmiel	Kadmiel (c)	Mattaniah ⎫
(d) Shebaniah	Sherebiah (m)	Bakbukiah ⎬ singers
(e) Hodiah	Judah (e?)	Obadiah ⎭
(f) Kelita	Mattaniah	Meshullam ⎫
(g) Pelaiah	Bakbukiah	Talmon ⎬ gatekeepers
(h) Hanan	Unni	Akkub ⎭
(i) Mica		
(j) Rehob		
(k) Hashabiah		
(l) Zaccur		
(m) Sherebiah		
(n) Shebaniah		
(o) Hodiah		
(p) Bani		
(q) Beninu		

Neh ix 4–5		*Neh viii 7*
vs 4	*vs 5*	
Jeshua (a)	Jeshua (a)	Jeshua (a)
Bani (p)	Kadmiel (c)	Bani (p?)
Kadmiel (c)	Bani (p)	Sherebiah (m)
Shebaniah (d)	Hashabneiah (k?)	Jamin
Bunni (b?)	Sherebiah (m)	Akkub
Sherebiah (m)	Hodiah (e)	Shabbethai
Bani (p)	Shebaniah (n)	Hodiah (e), (o)
Chenani (h?)	Pethahiah	Maaseiah
		Kelita (f)
		Azariah
		Jozabad
		Hanan (h)
		Pelaiah (g)

Neh xi 15–17

Shemaiah←Hashshub←Azrikam←Hashabiah←Bunni (*b*?)
Shabbethai
Jozabad
Mattaniah←Micah←Zabdi←Asaph
Uzzi←Bani←Hashabiah←Mattaniah←Mica (*i*?) ←Asaph
Bakbukiah
Abda←Shammua←Galal←Jeduthun

I Chron ix 14–16

Shemaiah (son of)
    Hashshub
    Azrikam
    Hashabiah
    (Of sons of Merari)
Bakbakar
Heresh (?)
Galal
Mattaniah (son of)
    Micah
    Zichri
    Asaph
Obadiah (son of)
    Shemaiah
    Galal
    Jeduthun
Berekiah (son of)
    Asa
    Elkanah

C. LISTS OF LAYMEN

Neh x 15–28	*Neh vii 8 ff*	*Ezra ii 3 ff*
(*a*) Parosh	Parosh (*a*)	Parosh (*a*)
(*b*) Pahath-moab	Shephatiah	Shephatiah
(*c*) Elam	Arah	Arah
(*d*) Zattu	Pahath-moab (*b*)	Pahath-moab (*b*)
(*e*) Bani	Jeshua	Jeshua
(*f*) Bunni	Joab	Joab
(*g*) Azgad	Elam (*c*)	Elam (*c*)
(*h*) Bebai	Zattu (*d*)	Zattu (*d*)
(*i*) Adonijah	Zaccai	Zaccai
(*j*) Bigvai	Binnui (*f*?)	Bani (*e*)
(*k*) Adin	Bebai (*h*)	Bebai (*h*)
(*l*) Ater	Azgad (*g*)	Azgad (*g*)
(*m*) Hezekiah	Adonikam (*i*?)	Adonikam (*i*?)
(*n*) Azzur	Bigvai (*j*)	Bigvai (*j*)
(*o*) Hodiah	Adin (*k*)	Adin (*k*)
(*p*) Hashum	Ater (*l*)	Ater (*l*)
(*q*) Bezai	Hezekiah	Hezekiah
(*r*) Hariph	Hashum (*p*)	Bezai (*q*)
(*s*) Anathoth	Bezai (*q*)	Jorah
(*t*) Nobai	Hariph (*r*)	Hashum (*p*)
	[Towns]	
(*u*) Magpiash		Magbish (*u*)
(*v*) Meshullam		
	The other Elam	[Towns]
(*w*) Hezir		
		The other Elam
(*x*) Meshezabel	Harim (*qq*)	
		Harim (*qq*)
(*y*) Zadok	[Towns]	
		[Towns]
(*z*) Jaddua		
(*aa*) Pelatiah		
(*bb*) Hanan		
(*cc*) Anaiah		
(*dd*) Hoshea		
(*ee*) Hananiah		
(*ff*) Hasshub		
(*gg*) Hallohesh		
(*hh*) Pilha		

Neh x 15–28	Neh vii 8 ff	Ezra ii 3 ff
(ii) Shobek		
(jj) Rehum		
(kk) Hashabnah		
(ll) Maaseiah		
(mm) Ahijah		
(nn) Hanan		
(oo) Anan		
(pp) Malluch		
(qq) Harim		
(rr) Baanah		

Ezra viii 2c–14	Ezra x 25–43
Hattush (of sons of David)	Parosh (a)
———— (of sons of Shecaniah)	Elam (c)
Zechariah (of sons of Parosh) (a)	Zattu (d)
Eliehoenai son of Zerahiah (of the sons of Pahath-moab) (b)	Bebai (h)
Shecaniah son of Jahaziel (of the sons of Zattu) (d)	Bani (e)
Ebed son of Jonathan (of the sons of Adin) (k)	Pahath-moab (b)
Jeshaiah son of Athaliah (of the sons of Elam) (c)	Harim (qq)
Zebadiah son of Michael (of the sons of Shephatiah)	Hashum (p)
Obadiah son of Jehiel (of the sons of Joab)	Bani
Shelomith son of Josiphiah (of the sons of Bani) (e)	Binnui (f)
Zechariah son of Bebai (of the sons of Bebai) (h)	Nebo (t)
Johanan son of Hakkatan (of the sons of Azgad) (g)	

Eliphelet ⎫
Jeiel ⎬ ———————— (of the
Shemaiah ⎭   sons of Adonikam)

Uthai ⎫ ———————— (of the sons
Zabbud ⎭   of Bigvai) (j)

D. BUILDER'S LIST OF NEH III

Eliashib
Men of Jericho
Zaccur son of Imri

Sons of Hassenaah
Meremoth son of Uriah son of Hakkoz
Meshullam son of Berechiah son of Meshezabel
Zadok son of Baana

Tekoites
Joiada son of Paseah
Meshullam son of Besodeiah
Melatiah the Gibeonite
Jadon the Meronothite
Men of Gibeon and Mizpah
Uzziel son of Harhaiah
Hananiah
Rephaiah son of Hur
Jedaiah son of Harumaph
Hattush son of Hashabneiah
Malchijah son of Harim
Hasshub son of Pahath-moab
Shallum son of Hallohesh
Hanun
Malchijah son of Rechab
Shallun son of Colhozeh
Nehemiah son of Azbuk
Levites — Rehum son of Bani
        Hashabiah
        Bavvai son of Henadad

Ezer son of Jeshua
Baruch son of Zabbai
Meremoth son of Uriah son of Hakkoz
Priests
Benjamin

Hasshub

Azariah son of Maaseiah son of Ananiah
Binnui son of Henadad
Palal son of Uzai
Pedaiah son of Parosh
Tekoites
Priests
Zadok son of Immer
Shemaiah son of Shecaniah
Hananiah son of Shelemiah
Hanun son of Zalaph
Meshullam son of Berechiah
Malchijah
Goldsmiths' Guild
Merchants

E. TOWN LISTS OF BENJAMIN

Neh xi 31–35	1 Chron viii 1–40	1 Chron vii 20–29 (Ephraim)	Neh vii ‖ Ezra ii
Geba	Geba	Upper Beth-horon	Anathoth
Michmas	Ono	Lower Beth-horon	Ramah
Aijah	Lod	Uzzensheerah	Geba
Bethel	Aijalon	Bethel	Michmas
Anathoth	Jerusalem	Naaran	Bethel
Nob	Gibeon	Gezer	Ai
Ananiah		Shechem	Nebo
Hazor		Aijah	Lod
Ramah		Bethshan	Hadid
Gittaim		Taanach	Ono
Hadid		Megiddo	
Zeboim		Dor	
Neballat			
Lod			
Ono			

Josh xviii 21–27	Josh xix 41–46 (Dan)	(Towns mentioned in Neh iii)
Jericho	Zorah	Jericho
Beth-hoglah	Eshtaol	Tekoa
Emek-keziz	Irshemesh	Gibeon
Beth-haarabah	Shaalabbin	Mizpah (vss. 7, 15, 19)
Zemaraim	Aijalon	—Jerusalem
Beth-el	Ithlah	Zanoah
Haavvim	Elon	Beth-haccherem
Happarah	Timnah	Beth-zur
Ophrah	Ekron	Keilah
Chephar-haammonai	Eltekeh	
Haophni	Gibbethon	
Geba	Baalath	
Gibeon		
Haramah		
Beeroth		
Hamizpeh		
Hakkephirah		
Hammozah		
Rekem		
Irpeel		
Taralah		
Zela		
Haeleph		
Hajebusi (Jerusalem)		
Gibeath		
Kirjath-arim		

F. TOWN LISTS OF JUDAH

Neh xi 25–30	1 Chron iv 28 ff (Simeonite list)	Josh xv 21–62 (only those found in other lists here)
Kiriath-arba	Beer-sheba	
Dibon	Moladah	Kabzeel
Jekabzeel	Hazar-shual	[. . . .]
Jeshua	Bilhah	Dimonah
Moladah	Ezem	[. . . .]
Beth-pelet	Tolad	Shema (?)
Hazar-shual	Bethuel	Moladah
Beer-sheba	Hormah	[. . . .]
Ziklag	Ziklag	Beth-pelet
Meconah	Beth-marcaboth	Hazar-shual
En-rimmon	Hazar-susim	Beer-sheba
Zorah	Beth-biri	[. . . .]
Jarmuth	Shaaraim	Ziklag
Zanoah	(villages)	[. . . .]
Adullam	Etam	Ain
Lachish	Ain	Rimmon
Azekah	Rimmon	[. . . .]
	Tochen	Zorah
	Ashan	Ashnah
	(Baal)	Zanoah
		[. . . .]
		Jarmuth
		Adullam
		[. . . .]
		Azekah
		Shaaraim
		[. . . .]
		Lachish

Josh xix 2–8 (Simeon)	Josh xix 41–46 (Dan)	II Chron xi 6–10 (Rehoboam's fortified cities)
Beer-sheba	Zorah	Bethlehem
[. . . .]	[· · · ·]	Etam
Moladah		Tekoa
Hazar-shual		Beth-zur
[. . . .]		Soco
Ezem		Adullam
Eltolad		[. . . .]
Bethul		Lachish
Hormah		Azekah
Ziklag		Zorah
Beth-hammarkaboth		Aijalon
Hazar-susah		Hebron
Beth-lebaoth		
[. . . .]		
Ain		
Rimmon		
[. . . .]		
Ashan		

APPENDIX III: LEVITE FAMILIES

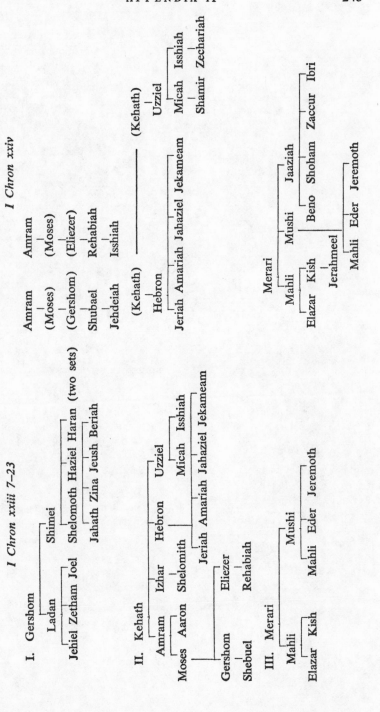

I Chron xxiii 7–23

I Chron xxiv

I. Gershom

Ladan — Shimei

Jehiel Zetham Joel — Shelomoth Haziel Haran (two sets)

Jahath Zina Jeush Beriah

II. Kehath

Amram Izhar Hebron Uzziel

Moses Aaron — Shelomith — Micah Isshiah

Gershom — Eliezer — Jeriah Amariah Jahaziel Jekameam

Shebuel — Rehabiah

III. Merari

Mahli — Mushi

Elazar Kish — Mahli Eder Jeremoth

Amram — Amram

(Moses) — (Moses)

(Gershom) — (Eliezer)

Shubael — Rehabiah

Jehdeiah — Isshiah

(Kehath) — (Kehath)

Hebron — Uzziel

Jeriah Amariah Jahaziel Jekameam — Micah Isshiah

Shamir Zechariah

Merari

Mahli — Mushi

Elazar Kish — Beno Shoham Zaccur Ibri

Jerahmeel — Jaaziah

Mahli Eder Jeremoth

INDEX OF PLACE AND PERSONAL NAMES

NOTES

1. The transcriptional spelling is generally that appearing in the first reference. Important variations are, however, noted where they do occur.

2. It is often difficult, perhaps impossible, to distinguish between personal and place names, especially those of the twelve tribes of Israel. The latter are all listed as personal names.

3. The general practice has been followed in transcriptions—

'=*aleph*	s=*samek*
'=*ayin*	ṣ=*tsade*
ḥ=*heth*	ś=*sin*
h=*he*	š=*shin*
ṭ=*teth*	y=*yod*
t=*taw*	

No attempt has been made to distinguish between consonants with or without *dagesh*.

PLACE NAMES

Across the River (*'br nhr (h)*) Ezra iv 10,11,16,17,20, v 3,6(*bis*), vi 6(*bis*), 8,13, vii 21,25, viii 36; Neh ii 7,9, iii 7.

Addan (*'dn*) Ezra ii 59.

Addon (*'dwn*) Neh vii 61.

Adullam (*'dlm*) I Chron xi 15; II Chron xi 7; Neh xi 30.

Ahava (*'hw'*) Ezra viii 15,21,31.

Ai (*h'y*) Ezra ii 28; Neh vii 32.

Aijah (*'yh*) I Chron vii 28; Neh xi 31.

Ananiah (*'nnyh*) Neh xi 32.

Anathoth (*'ntwt*) I Chron vi 60; Ezra ii 23; Neh vii 27, xi 32.

Egypt (*mṣrym*) I Chron xiii 5, xvii 21; II Chron i 17, v 10, vi 5, vii 8,22, ix 26,28, x 2(*bis*), xii 2,9, xx 10, xxvi 8, xxxv 20, xxxvi 3,4(*bis*); Neh ix 9,17(with Greek), 18.

En-rimmon (*'yn rmwn*) Neh xi 29.

Ephraim Gate (*š'r 'prym*) Neh viii 16, xii 39.

Fish Gate (*š'r hdgym*) Neh iii 3, xii 39.

Fountain Gate (*š'r h'yn*) Neh ii 14, iii 15, xii 37.

Geba (*gb'*) I Chron vi 60, viii 6; II Chron xvi 6; Ezra ii 26; Neh vii 30, xi 31, xii 29.

Gibeon (*gb'wn*) I Chron viii 29, ix 35, xiv 16, xvi 39, xxi 29; II Chron i 3,13; Neh iii 7, vii 25.

Gittaim (*gtym*) Neh xi 33.

Graves of David (*qbry dwyd*) Neh iii 16.

Hadid (*ḥdyd*) Ezra ii 33; Neh vii 37, xi 34.

Hakkephirim (*hkpyrym*) Neh vi 2.

Hazar-shual (*ḥṣr šw'l*) I Chron iv 28; Neh xi 27.

Hazor (*ḥṣwr*) Neh xi 33.

Heshbon (*ḥšbwn*) I Chron vi 81; Neh ix 22.

Hinnom (*hnm*) Neh xi 30.

Horse Gate (*š'r hswsym*) Neh iii 28.

House of David (*byt dwyd*) Neh xii 37.

House of the Mighty Men (*byt hgbrym*) Neh iii 16.

House of the Temple Slaves and of the Merchants (*byt hntynyn whrklym*) Neh iii 31.

Immer (*'mr*) Ezra ii 59.

Jarmuth (*yrmwt*) Neh xi 29.

Jekabzeel (*yqbṣ'l*) Neh xi 25.

Jericho (*yrḥw*) I Chron vi 78, xix 5; II Chron xxviii 15; Ezra ii 34; Neh iii 2, vii 36.

Jerusalem (*yrwšlm*) I Chron iii 4,5, vi 10,15,32, viii 28,32, ix 3, 34,38, xi 4, xiv 3,4, xv 3, xviii 7, xix 15, xx 1,3, xxi 4,15,16, xxiii 25, xxviii 1, xxix 27; II Chron i 4,13,14,15, ii 6,15, iii 1, v 2, vi 6, viii 6, ix 1,25,27,30, x 18, xi 1,5,14,16, xii 2,3,4,5,7,9, 13(*bis*), xiii 2, xiv 14, xv 10, xvii 13, xix 1,4,8(*bis*), xx 5,15,17, 18,20,27(*bis*), 28,31, xxi 5,11,13,20, xxii 1,2, xxiii 2, xxiv 1,6,9,

Persia (*prs*) II Chron xxxvi 20,22(*bis*); Ezra i 1(*bis*), 2,8, iii 7, iv 3,5(*bis*), 7,24, vi 14, vii 1, ix 9.
Pool of Shelah (*brkt hšlḥ*) Neh iii 15.
Pool of the King (*brkt hmlk*) Neh ii 14.
Prison Gate (*šʿr hmṭrh*) Neh xii 39.

Ramah (*hrmh*) II Chron xvi 1,5,6, xxii 6; Ezra ii 26; Neh vii 30, xi 33.
Reed Sea (*ym swp*) Neh ix 9.

Samaria (*šmrwn*) II Chron xviii 2,9, xxii 9, xxv 13,24, xxviii 8, 9,15, xxxiv 6; Ezra iv 10,17; Neh iii 34.
Senaah (*snʾh*) Ezra ii 35, Neh vii 38.
Sheep Gate (*šʿr hṣʾn*) Neh iii 1,32, xii 39.
Sinai (*sny*) Neh ix 13.
Susa (*šwšn*) Ezra iv 9; Neh i 1.

Tel-harsha (*tl ḥrš*) Ezra ii 59; Neh vii 61.
Tel-melah (*tl mlḥ*) Ezra ii 59; Neh vii 61.
Tower of Furnaces (*mgdl htnwrym*) Neh iii 11, xii 38.
Tower of Hananel (*mgdl ḥnnʾl*) Neh iii 1, xii 39.
Tower of the Hundred (*mgdl hmʾh*) Neh iii 1, xii 39.
Tower Projecting (*mgdl ywṣ*) Neh iii 25,26,27.

Upper Palace of the King (*byt hmlk hʿlywn*) Neh iii 25.
Upper Room at the Corner (*ʿlyt hpnh*) Neh iii 31,32.
Ur of the Chaldees (*ʾwr kśdym*) Neh ix 7.

Valley Gate (*šʿr hgyʾ*) Neh ii 13,15, iii 13.
Valley of Craftsmen (*gy hḥršym*) Neh xi 35.

Water Gate (*šʿr hmym*) Neh iii 26, viii 1,3,16, xii 37.

Zanoah (*znwḥ*) Neh iii 13, xi 30.
Zeboim (*zbʿym*) Neh xi 34.
Ziklag (*ṣyqlg*) I Chron iv 30, xii 1,21; Neh xi 28.
Zorah (*ṣrʿh*) II Chron xi 10; Neh xi 29.

PERSONAL AND OTHER NAMES

Amon (*'mwn*) I Chron iii 14; II Chron xviii 25, xxxiii 20,21,22, 23,25; Neh vii 59.

Amorite (*'mry*) I Chron i 14; II Chron viii 7; Ezra ix 1; Neh ix 8.

Amram (*'mrm*) I Chron vi 2,3,18, xxiii 12,13, xxiv 20, xxvi 23(Amramites); Ezra x 34.

Amzi (*'mṣy*) I Chron vi 46; Neh xi 12.

Anaiah (*'nyh*) Neh viii 4, x 23.

Anan (*'nn*) Neh x 27.

Ananiah (*'nnyh*) Neh iii 23.

Anathoth (*'ntwt*) I Chron vii 8; Neh x 20.

Arabian (*'rby*) Neh ii 19, vi 1.

Arabs (*'rby'ym, 'rbym, 'rbyym*) II Chron xvii 11, xxi 16, xxii 1, xxvi 7; Neh iv 1.

Arah (*'rḥ*) I Chron vii 39; Ezra ii 5; Neh vi 18, vii 10.

Ariel (*'ry'l*) Ezra viii 16.

Arkewite (*'rkwy*) Ezra iv 9.

Artaxerxes (*'rtḥššt', 'rtḥšst'*) Ezra iv 7(*bis*), 8,11,23, vi 14, vii 1,7,11,12,21, viii 1; Neh ii 1, v 14, xiii 6.

Asahel (*'śh'l*) I Chron ii 16, xi 26, xxvii 7; II Chron xvii 8, xxxi 13; Ezra x 15.

Asaph (*'sp*) I Chron vi 39(*bis*), ix 15, xv 17,19, xvi 5(*bis*), 7, 37, xxv 1,2(*tris*), 6,9, xxvi 1; II Chron v 12, xx 14, xxix 13, 30, xxxv 15(*bis*); Ezra ii 41, iii 10; Neh ii 8, vii 44, xi 17,22, xii 35,46.

Ashdodite (*'šdwdy, 'šdwdywt, 'šdwdyt*) Neh iv 1, xiii 23,24.

Asnah (*'snh*) Ezra ii 50.

Ater (*'ṭr*) Ezra ii 16,42; Neh vii 21,45, x 18.

Athaiah (*'tyh*) Neh xi 4.

Athaliah (*'tlyh*) I Chron viii 26; II Chron xxii 2,10,11,12, xxiii 12,13,21, xxiv 7; Ezra viii 7.

Athlai (*'tly*) Ezra x 28.

Azaniah (*'znyh*) Neh x 10.

Azarel (*'zr'l*) I Chron xii 7, xxv 18, xxvii 22; Ezra x 41; Neh xi 13, xii 36.

Azariah (*'zryh*) I Chron ii 8,38,39, iii 12, vi 9(*bis*), 10,11,13, 14,36, ix 11; II Chron xv 1, xxi 2(*bis*), xxiii 1(*bis*), xxvi 17,20, xxviii 12, xxix 12(*bis*), xxxi 10,13; Ezra vii 1,3; Neh iii 23,24, vii 7, viii 7, x 3, xii 33.

Azbuk (*'zbwq*) Neh iii 16.

Azgad (*'zgd*) Ezra ii 12, viii 12; Neh vii 17, x 16.

Aziza (*'zyz'*) Ezra x 27.

Azrikam (*'zryqm*) I Chron iii 23, viii 38, ix 14,44; II Chron xxviii 7; Neh xi 15.

Azzur (*'zwr*) Neh x 18.

Baana (*b'n'*) Neh iii 4.

Baanah (*b'nh*) I Chron xi 30; Ezra ii 2; Neh vii 7, x 28.

Babylonians (*bbly'*) Ezra iv 9.

Bakbuk (*bqbwq*) Ezra ii 51; Neh vii 53.

Bakbukiah (*bqbqyh*) Neh xi 17, xii 9,25.

Balaam (*bl'm*) Neh xiii 2.

Bani (*bny*) I Chron vi 46, ix 4; Ezra ii 10, viii 10(with Greek), x 29,34; Neh iii 17, viii 7, ix 4(*bis*), 5, x 14,15, xi 22.

Barkos (*brqws*) Ezra ii 53; Neh vii 55.

Baruch (*brwk*) Neh iii 20, x 7, xi 5.

Barzillai (*brzly*) Ezra ii 61(*bis*); Neh vii 63(*bis*).

Bavvai (*bwy*) Neh iii 18.

Bazlith (*bṣlyt*) Neh vii 54.

Bazluth (*bṣlwt*) Ezra ii 52.

Bebai (*bby*) Ezra ii 11, viii 11(*bis*), x 28; Neh vii 16, x 16.

Bedeiah (*bdyh*) Ezra x 35.

Benaiah (*bnyhw*) I Chron iv 36, xi 22,24,31, xv 18,20,24, xvi 5,6, xviii 17, xxvii 5,6,14,34; II Chron xx 14, xxxi 13; Ezra x 25,30,35,43.

Beninu (*bnynw*) Neh x 14.

Benjamin (*bnymn*) I Chron ii 2, vi 60,65, vii 6,10, viii 1,40, ix 3, 7, xi 31, xii 2,17,30, xxi 6, xxvii 21; II Chron xi 1,3,10,12,23, xiv 7, xv 2,8,9, xvii 17, xxv 5, xxxi 1, xxxiv 9,32; Ezra i 5, iv 1, x 9,32; Neh iii 23, xi 4,7,31,36, xii 34.

Berechiah (*brkyh*) I Chron iii 20, vi 39, ix 16, xv 17,23; II Chron xxviii 12; Neh iii 4,30, vi 18.

Besai (*bsy*) Ezra ii 49; Neh vii 52.

Besodeiah (*bswdyh*) Neh iii 6.

Bezai (*bṣy*) Ezra ii 17; Neh vii 23, x 19.

Bezalel (*bṣl'l*) I Chron ii 20; II Chron i 5; Ezra x 30.

Bigvai (*bgwy*) Ezra ii 2,14, viii 14; Neh vii 7,19, x 17.

Bilgah (*blgh*) I Chron xxiv 14; Neh xii 5,18.

Bilgai (*blgy*) Neh x 9.

Bilshan (*blšn*) Ezra ii 2; Neh vii 7.

Binnui (*bnwy*) Ezra viii 33, x 30,38; Neh iii 24, vii 15, x 10, xii 8.

Bukki (*bqy*) I Chron vi 5(*bis*), 51; Ezra vii 4.

Bunni (*bny, bwny*) Neh ix 4, x 16, xi 15.

Canaanites (*kn'ny*) Ezra ix 1; Neh ix 8,24.

Chaldeans (*kśdyym, ksdy'*) II Chron xxxvi 17; Ezra v 12.

Chelal (*kll*) Ezra x 30.

Cheluhi (*klhy*) Ezra x 35.

Chenani (*knny*) Neh ix 4.

Colhozeh (*kl ḥzh*) Neh iii 15, xi 5.

Cyrus (*kwrš*) II Chron xxxvi 22(*bis*), 23; Ezra i 1(*bis*), 2,7,8, iii 7, iv 3,5, v 13(*bis*), 14,17, vi 3(*bis*), 14.

Daniel (*dny'l*) I Chron iii 1; Ezra viii 2; Neh x 7.

Darius (*drywš*) Ezra iv 5,24, v 5,6,7, vi 1,12,13,14,15; Neh xii 22.

Darkon (*drqwn*) Ezra ii 56; Neh vii 58.

David (*dwyd*) I Chron ii 15, iii 1,9, iv 31, vi 31, vii 2, ix 22, x 14, xi 1,3(*bis*), 4,5(*tris*), 6,7(*bis*), 9,10,11,13,15,16,17,18(*bis*), 25, xii 1,9,17,18,19(*bis*), 20,22,23,24,32,34,39(*tris*), 40, xiii 2, 5,6,8,11,12,13(*bis*), xiv 1,2,3,8(*tris*), 10,11(*bis*), 12,14,16,17, xv 1,2,3,4,11,16,25,27(*bis*), 29(*bis*), xvi 2,7,43, xvii 1(*bis*), 2, 4,7,15,16,18,24, xviii 1,2,4(*bis*), 5,6(*tris*), 7,8,9,10,11,13(*bis*), 14,17, xix 2(*tris*), 3,4,5,6,8,17(*bis*), 18,19, xx 1,2(*bis*), 3,7,8, xxi 1,2,5,8,9,10,11,13,16(*bis*), 17,18(*bis*), 19,21(*tris*), 22,23, 24,25,26,28,30, xxii 1,2,3,4,5(*bis*), 6,7,17, xxiii 1,4,6,25,27, xxiv 3,31, xxv 1, xxvi 26,31,32, xxvii 18,23,24,31,32, xxviii 1,2, 11,20, xxix 1,9,10(*bis*), 20,22,23,24,26,29; II Chron i 1,4(*bis*), 8,9, ii 2,6,11,13,16, iii 1(*bis*), v 1,2, vi 4,6,7,8,10,15,16,17,42, vii 6(*bis*), 10,17,18, viii 11(*bis*), 14(*bis*), ix 31, x 16(*bis*), 19, xi 17,18, xii 16, xiii 5,6,8,23, xvi 14, xxi 1,7(*bis*), 12,20, xxiii 3,9,18(*bis*), xxiv 16,25, xxvii 9, xxviii 1, xxix 2,25,26,27,30, xxx 26, xxxii 5,30,33, xxxiii 7,14, xxxiv 2,3, xxxv 3,4,15; Ezra iii 10, viii 2,20; Neh iii 15,16, xii 24,36,37(*bis*), 45,46.

Delaiah (*dlyh*) I Chron iii 24, xxiv 18; Ezra ii 60; Neh vi 10, vii 62.

Ebed (*'bd*) Ezra viii 6.

Eber (*'br*) I Chron i 18,19,25, v 13, viii 12,22; Neh xii 20.

256

Egyptian (*mṣry*) I Chron ii 34, xi 23(*tris*); Ezra ix 1.

Elam (*'ylm*) I Chron i 17, viii 24, xxvi 3; Ezra ii 7,31, viii 7, x 2 [Q(ere)], 26; Neh vii 12,34, x 15, xii 42.

Elamite (*'lmy'*) Ezra iv 9.

Eleasah (*'l'śh*) I Chron ii 39,40, viii 37, ix 43; Ezra x 22.

Eleazar (*'l'zr*) I Chron vi 3,4,50, ix 20, xi 12, xxiii 21,22, xxiv 1,2,3,4(*bis*), 5,6,28; Ezra vii 5, viii 33, x 25; Neh xii 42.

Eliakim (*'lyqym*) II Chron xxxvi 4; Neh xii 41.

Eliashib (*'lyšyb*) I Chron iii 24, xxiv 12; Ezra x 6,24,27,36; Neh iii 1,20,21(*bis*), xii 10(*bis*), 22,23, xiii 4,7,28.

Eliehoenai (*'lyhw'yny*) I Chron xxvi 3; Ezra viii 4.

Eliezer (*'ly'zr*) I Chron vii 8, xv 24, xxiii 15,17(*bis*), xxvi 25, xxvii 16; II Chron xx 37; Ezra viii 16, x 18,23,31.

Elijah (*'lyhw*) II Chron xxi 12; Ezra x 21,26.

Elioenai (*'lyw'yny, 'lyw'ny*) I Chron iii 23,24, iv 36, vii 8; Ezra x 22,27; Neh xii 41.

Eliphelet (*'lyplṭ*) I Chron iii 6,8, viii 39, xiv 7; Ezra viii 13, x 33.

Elnathan (*'lntn*) Ezra viii 16(*tris*).

Esarhaddon (*'srḥdn*) Ezra iv 2.

Ezer (*'zr*) I Chron iv 4, vii 21, xii 10; Neh iii 19, xii 42.

Ezra (*'zr'*) Ezra vii 1,6,10,11,12,21,25, x 1,2,5,6,10,16; Neh viii 1,2,4,5,6,9,13, xii 1,13,26,33,36.

Gabbai (*gby*) Neh xi 8.

Gahar (*gḥr*) Ezra ii 47; Neh vii 49.

Galal (*gll*) I Chron ix 15,16; Neh xi 17.

Gashmu (*gšmw*) Neh vi 6.

Gazzam (*gzm*) Ezra ii 48; Neh vii 51.

Gedaliah (*gdlyhw*) I Chron xxv 3,9; Ezra x 18.

Gershom (*gršm, gršwm*) I Chron vi 16,17,20,43,62,71, xv 7, xxiii 15,16, xxvi 24; Ezra viii 2.

Geshem (*gšm*) Neh ii 19, vi 1,2.

Gibbar (*gbr*) Ezra ii 20.

Gibeonite (*gb'wny*) I Chron xii 4; Neh iii 7.

Giddel (*gdl*) Ezra ii 47,56; Neh vii 49,58.

Gilalai (*glly*) Neh xii 36.

Gileadite (*gl'dy*) Ezra ii 61; Neh vii 63.

Ginnethoi (*gntwy*) Neh xii 4.

Ginnethon (*gntwn*) Neh x 7, xii 16.

Girgashite (*grgšy*) I Chron i 14; Neh ix 8.

Gishpa (*gšp'*)   Neh xi 21.
Goldsmiths' guild (*ṣrpy, ṣrpym*)   Neh iii 8,31,32.

Hacaliah (*ḥklyh*)   Neh i 1, x 2.
Hagab (*ḥgb*)   Ezra ii 46.
Hagabah (*ḥgbh*)   Ezra ii 45; Neh vii 48.
Haggai (*ḥgy*)   Ezra v 1, vi 14.
Haggedolim (*hgdwlym*)   Neh xi 14.
Hakkatan (*ḥqṭn*)   Ezra viii 12.
Hakkoz (*ḥqwz*)   I Chron xxiv 10; Ezra ii 61; Neh iii 4,21, vii 63.
Hakupha (*ḥqwp'*)   Ezra ii 51; Neh vii 53.
Hallohesh (*hlwḥš*)   Neh iii 12, x 25.
Hanan (*ḥnn*)   I Chron viii 23,38, ix 44, xi 43; Ezra ii 46; Neh vii
    49, viii 7, x 11,23,27, xiii 13.
Hananel (*ḥnn'l*)   Neh iii 1, xii 39.
Hanani (*ḥnny*)   I Chron xxv 4,25; II Chron xvi 7, xix 2, xx 34;
    Ezra x 20; Neh i 2, vii 2, xii 36.
Hananiah (*ḥnnyh*)   I Chron iii 19,21, viii 24, xxv 4,23; II Chron
    xxvi 11; Ezra x 28; Neh iii 8,30, vii 2, x 24, xii 12,41.
Hanun (*ḥnwn*)   I Chron xix 2(*bis*), 3,4,6; Neh iii 13,30.
Harhaiah (*ḥrhyh*)   Neh iii 8.
Harhur (*ḥrḥwr*)   Ezra ii 51; Neh vii 53.
Harim (*ḥrm*)   I Chron xxiv 8; Ezra ii 32,39, x 21,31; Neh iii 11,
    vii 35,42, x 6,28, xii 15.
Hariph (*ḥryp*)   Neh vii 24, x 20.
Harsha (*ḥrš'*)   Ezra ii 52; Neh vii 54.
Harumaph (*ḥrwmp*)   Neh iii 10.
Hashabiah (*ḥšbyh*)   I Chron vi 45, ix 14, xxv 3,19, xxvi 30, xxvii
    17; II Chron xxxv 9; Ezra viii 19,24; Neh iii 17, x 12, xi 15,22, xii
    21,24.
Hashabnah (*ḥšbnh*)   Neh x 26.
Hashabneiah (*ḥšbnyh*)   Neh iii 10, ix 5.
Hashbaddanah (*ḥšbdnh*)   Neh viii 4.
Hashum (*ḥšm*)   Ezra ii 19, x 33; Neh vii 22, viii 4, x 19.
Hassenaah (*hsn'h*)   Neh iii 3.
Hassenuah (*hsn'h, hsnw'h*)   I Chron ix 7; Neh xi 9.
Hasshub (*ḥšwb*)   I Chron ix 14; Neh iii 11,23, x 24, xi 15.
Hassophereth (*hsprt*)   Ezra ii 55.
Hasupha (*ḥśwp'*)   Ezra ii 43; Neh vii 46.
Hatipha (*ḥṭyp'*)   Ezra ii 54; Neh vii 56.

23,25(*bis*), 26,27,30; II Chron i 2(*bis*), 13, ii 3,11,16, v 2(*bis*),
3,4,6,10, vi 3(*bis*), 4,5(*bis*), 6,7,10(*bis*), 11,12,13,14,16(*bis*),
17,21,24,25,27,29,32,33, vii 3,6,8,10,18, viii 2,7,8,9,11, xix 8,30,
x 1,3,16(*tris*), 17,18,19, xi 1,3,13,16(*bis*), xii 1,6,13, xiii 4,
5(*bis*), 12,15,16,17,18, xv 3,4,9,13,17, xvi 1,3,4,7,11, xvii 1,4,
xviii 3,4,5,7,8,9,16,17,19,25,28,29(*bis*), 30,31,32,33,34, xix 8, xx
7,10,19,29,34,35, xxi 2,4,6,13(*bis*), xxii 5, xxiii 2, xxiv 5,6,9,
16, xxv 6,7(*bis*), 9,17,18,21,22,23,25,26, xxvii 7, xxviii 2,3,5,
8,13,19,23,26,27, xxix 7,10,24(*bis*), 27, xxx 1(*bis*), 5(*bis*),
6(*tris*), 21,25(*bis*), 26, xxxi 1(*bis*), 5,6,8, xxxii 17,32, xxxiii 2,7,
8,9,16,18(*bis*), xxxiv 7,9,21,23,26,33(*bis*); xxxv 3(*tris*), 4,17,
18(*bis*), 25,27, xxxvi 8,13; Ezra i 3, ii 2,59,70, iii 1,2,10,11, iv
1,3(*bis*), v 1,11, vi 14,16,17(*bis*), 21(*bis*), 22, vii 6,7,11,13,15,
28, viii 18,25,29,35(*bis*), ix 1,4,15, x 1,2,5,10,25; Neh i 6(*bis*),
ii 10, vii 7,61,72(*bis*), viii 1,14,17, ix 1,2, x 40, xi 3,20, xii 47,
xiii 2,3,18,26(*bis*).

Isshiah (*yšyh*) I Chron vii 3, xii 7, xxiii 20, xxiv 21,25(*bis*);
Ezra x 31.

Ithamar (*'ytmr*) I Chron vi 3, xxiv 1,2,3,4(*bis*), 5,6; Ezra viii 2.

Ithiel (*'yty'l*) Neh xi 7.

Izziah (*yzyh*) Ezra x 25.

Jaala (*y'l'*) Neh vii 58.

Jaalah (*y'lh*) Ezra ii 56.

Jaasu (*y'św*) Ezra x 37.

Jachin (*ykyn*) I Chron ix 10, xxiv 17; II Chron iii 17; Neh xi 10.

Jaddai (*ydw,* Kethib) Ezra x 43.

Jaddua (*ydw'*) Neh x 22, xii 11,22.

Jadon (*ydwn*) Neh iii 7.

Jahaziel (*yhzy'l*) I Chron xii 5, xvi 6, xxiii 19, xxiv 23; II Chron
xx 14; Ezra viii 5.

Jahzeiah (*yhzyh*) Ezra x 15.

Jamin (*ymyn*) I Chron ii 27, iv 24; Neh viii 7.

Jarib (*yryb*) I Chron iv 24; Ezra viii 16, x 18.

Jashub (*yšwb*) I Chron vii 1(Kethib, *yšyb*); Ezra x 29.

Jebusite (*ybwsy*) I Chron i 14, xi 4,6, xxi 15,18,28; II Chron
iii 1, viii 7; Ezra ix 1; Neh ix 8.

Jedaiah (*yd'yh*) I Chron ix 10, xxiv 7; Ezra ii 36; Neh vii 39,
xi 10, xii 6,7,19,21.

Jedaiah (*ydyh*) I Chron iv 37; Neh iii 10.

Jonathan (*ywntn*) I Chron ii 32,33, x 2, xi 34; Ezra viii 6, x 15; Neh xii 11(*bis*), 14, xii 35.

Jorah (*ywrh*) Ezra ii 18.

Joseph (*ywsp*) I Chron ii 2, v 1,2, vii 29, xxv 2,9; Ezra x 42; Neh xii 14.

Josiphiah (*ywspyh*) Ezra viii 10.

Jozabad (*ywzbd*) I Chron xii 5,21(*bis*); II Chron xxxi 13, xxxv 9; Ezra viii 33, x 22,23; Neh viii 7, xi 16.

Jozadak (*ywṣdq*) Ezra iii 2,8, v 2, x 18; Neh xii 26.

Judah (*yhwdh*) I Chron ii 1,3(*bis*), 10, iv 1,21,27,41, v 2,17, vi 15,55,65, ix 1,3,4, xii 17,25, xiii 6, xxi 5, xxvii 18, xxviii 4(*bis*); II Chron ii 6, ix 11, x 17, xi 1,3(*bis*), 5,10,12,14,17,23, xii 4,5, 12, xiii 1,13,14,15(*tris*), 16,18, xiv 3,4,5,6,7,11, xv 2,8,9,15, xvi 1(*bis*), 6,7,11, xvii 2(*bis*), 5,6,7,9(*bis*), 10,12,13,14,19, xviii 3,9,28, xix 1,5,11, xx 3,4(*bis*), 5,13,15,17,18,20,22,24,27,31,35, xxi 3(*bis*), 8,10,11(*bis*), 12,13,17, xxii 1,6,8,10, xxiii 2(*bis*), 8, xxiv 5,6,9,17,18,23, xxv 5(*bis*), 10,12,13,17,18,19,21(*bis*), 22, 23,25,26,28, xxvi 1,2, xxvii 4,7, xxviii 6,9,10,17,18,19(*bis*), 25, 26, xxix 8,21, xxx 1,6,12,24,25(*bis*), xxxi 1(*bis*), 6(*bis*), 20, xxxii 1,8,9,12,23,25,32,33, xxxiii 9,14,16, xxxiv 3,5,9,11,21,24, 26,29,30, xxxv 18,21,24,27, xxxvi 4,8,10,14,23; Ezra i 2,3,5,8, ii 1(*bis*), iii 9, iv 1,4,6, v 1,8, vii 14, ix 9, x 7,9,23; Neh ii 5,7, iv 4,10, v 14, vi 7,17,18, vii 6, xi 3,4(*bis*), 9,20,24,25,36, xii 8, 31,32,34,36,44, xiii 12,15,16,24.

Judeans (*yhwdym*) Neh i 2.

Kadmiel (*qdmy'l*) Ezra ii 40, iii 9; Neh vii 43, ix 4,5, x 10, xii 8,24.

Kallai (*qly*) Neh xii 20.

Kelaiah (*qlyh*) Ezra x 23.

Kelita (*qlyṭ'*) Ezra x 23; Neh viii 7, x 11.

Keros (*qrs, qrys*) Ezra ii 44; Neh vii 47.

Kolaiah (*qwlyh*) Neh xi 7.

Lebanah (*lbnh*) Ezra ii 45; Neh vii 48.

Levi (*lwy*) I Chron ii 1, vi 1,16,38,43,47, ix 18, xxi 6, xxiii 6, 14,24; Ezra viii 18.

Levite(s) (*lwy, lwym*) I Chron vi 19,48,64, ix 2,14,26,31,33,34, xii 27, xiii 2, xv 2,4,11,12,14,15,16,17,22,26,27, xvi 4, xxiii 2,3, 26,27, xxiv 6(*bis*), 20,30,31, xxvi 20, xxvii 17, xxviii 13,21; II

Chron v 4,5,12, vii 6, viii 14,15, xi 13,14, xiii 9,10, xvii 8(*bis*),
xix 8,11, xx 14,19, xxiii 2,4,6,7,8,18, xxiv 5(*bis*), 6,11, xxix 4,5,
12,16,25,26,30,34(*bis*), xxx 15,16,17,21,22,25,27, xxxi 2(*bis*),
4,8,12,14,17,19, xxxiv 9,12(*bis*), 13,30, xxxv 3,5,8,9(*bis*), 10,
11,14,15,18; Ezra i 5,40, ii 70, iii 8(*bis*), 9,10,12, vi 16,18,20,
vii 7,13,24, viii 15,20,29,30,33, ix 1, x 5,15,23; Neh iii 17, vii 1,
43,72, viii 7,9,11,13, ix 4,5, x 1,10,29,35,38(*bis*), 39(*bis*),
40, xi 3,15,16,18,20,22,36, xii 1,8,22,23,24,27,28,30,44(*bis*),
47(*bis*), xiii 5,10(*bis*), 13,22,29,30.

Maadai (*m'dy*) Ezra x 34.
Maadiah (*m'dyh*) Neh xii 5.
Maai (*m'y*) Neh xii 36.
Maaseiah (*m'śyhw*) I Chron xv 18,20; II Chron xxiii 1, xxvi 11,
    xxviii 7, xxxiv 8; Ezra x 18,21,22,30; Neh iii 23, viii 4,7,
    x 26, xi 5,7, xii 41,42.
Maaziah (*m'zyhw*) I Chron xxiv 18; Neh x 9.
Machnadbai (*mkndby*) Ezra x 40.
Magbish (*mgbyš*) Ezra ii 30.
Magpiash (*mgpy'š*) Neh x 21.
Mahalalel (*mhll'l*) I Chron i 2; Neh xi 4.
Mahli (*mḥly*) I Chron vi 19,29,47, xxiii 21(*bis*), 23, xxiv 26,28,
    30; Ezra viii 18.
Malchijah (*mlkyh*) I Chron vi 40, ix 12, xxiv 9; Ezra x 25(*bis*),
    31; Neh iii 11,14,31, viii 4, x 4, xi 12, xii 42.
Malluch (*mlwk*) I Chron vi 44; Ezra x 29,32; Neh x 5,28, xii
    2,14(Kethib, *mlwky*).
Manasseh (*mnšh, mnšy*) I Chron iii 13, v 18,26, vi 61,62,70,71,
    vii 14,17,29, ix 3, xii 20,21(*bis*), 32,38, xxvi 32, xxvii 20,21; II
    Chron xv 9, xxx 1,10,11,18, xxxi 1, xxxii 33, xxxiii 1,9,10,11,13,
    14,18,20,22(*bis*), 23, xxxiv 6,9; Ezra x 30,33.
Mattaniah (*mtnyh*) I Chron ix 15, xxv 4,16; II Chron xx 14,
    xxix 13; Ezra x 26,27,30,37; Neh xi 17,22, xii 8,25,35, xiii 13.
Mattattah (*mtth*) Ezra x 33.
Mattenai (*mtny*) Ezra x 33,37; Neh xii 19.
Mattithiah (*mttyh*) I Chron ix 31, xv 18,21, xvi 5, xxv 3,21;
    Ezra x 43; Neh viii 4.
Mehetabel (*mḥyṭb'l*) I Chron i 50; Neh vi 10.
Mehida (*mḥyd'*) Ezra ii 52; Neh vii 54.

Melatiah (*mlṭyh*) Neh iii 7.

Meraiah (*mryh*) Neh xii 12.

Meraioth (*mrywt*) I Chron vi 6,7,52, ix 11; Ezra vii 3; Neh xi 11, xii 15.

Merari (*mrry*) I Chron vi 1,16,19,29,44,47,63,77, ix 14, xv 6,17, xxiii 6,21, xxiv 26,27, xxvi 10,19; II Chron xxix 12, xxxiv 12; Ezra viii 19.

Merchants (*rklym*) Neh iii 32.

Meremoth (*mrmwt*) Ezra viii 33, x 36; Neh iii 4,21, x 6, xii 3.

Meronothite (*mrnty*) I Chron xxvii 30; Neh iii 7.

Meshezabel (*mšyzb'l*) Neh iii 4, x 22, xi 24.

Meshillemoth (*mšlmwt*) II Chron xxviii 12; Neh xi 13.

Meshullam (*mšlm*) I Chron iii 19, v 13, viii 17, ix 7,8,11,12; II Chron xxxiv 12; Ezra viii 16, x 15,29; Neh iii 4,6,30, vi 18, viii 4, x 8,21, xi 7,11, xii 13,16,25,33.

Meunim (*m'ynym, m'wnym*) II Chron xx 1, xxvi 7,8; Ezra ii 50; Neh vii 52.

Mica (*myk'*) I Chron ix 15; Neh x 12, xi 22.

Micah (*mykh*) I Chron v 5, viii 34,35, ix 40,41, xxiii 20, xxiv 24(*bis*), 25; II Chron xviii 14, xxxiv 20; Neh xi 17.

Micaiah (*mykyh, mykhw*) II Chron xiii 2, xvii 7, xviii 7,8,12,13, 23,24,25,27; Neh xii 35,41.

Michael (*myk'l*) I Chron v 13,14, vi 40, vii 3, viii 16, xii 21, xxvii 18; II Chron xxi 2; Ezra viii 8.

Mijamin (*mymn*) I Chron xxiv 9; Ezra x 25; Neh x 8, xii 5.

Milalai (*mlly*) Neh xii 36.

Miniamin (*mnymn*) II Chron xxxi 15; Neh xii 17,41.

Mishael (*myš'l*) Neh viii 4.

Mispar (*mspr*) Ezra ii 2.

Mispereth (*msprt*) Neh vii 7.

Mithredath (*mtrdt*) Ezra i 8, iv 7.

Moab, Moabite (*mw'b, mw'by*) I Chron iv 22, xi 22,46, xviii 2; II Chron xx 1,10,22,23, xxiv 26; Ezra ix 1; Neh xiii 1,23.

Moadiah (*mw'dyh*) Neh xii 17.

Mordecai (*mrdky*) Ezra ii 2; Neh vii 7.

Moses (*mšh*) I Chron vi 3,49, xv 15, xxi 29, xxii 13, xxiii 13,14, 15, xxvi 24; II Chron i 3, v 10, viii 13, xxiii 18, xxiv 6,9, xxv 4, xxx 16, xxxiii 8, xxxiv 14, xxxv 6,12; Ezra iii 2, vi 18, vii 6; Neh i 7,8, viii 1,14, ix 14, x 30, xiii 1.

Perida (*pryd'*) Neh vii 57.
Perizzite (*przy*) II Chron viii 7; Ezra ix 1; Neh ix 8.
Persian (*prsy*) Neh xii 22.
Peruda (*prwd'*) Ezra ii 55.
Pethahiah (*pthyh*) I Chron xxiv 16; Ezra x 23; Neh ix 5, xi 24.
Pharaoh (*pr'h*) I Chron iv 18; II Chron viii 11; Neh ix 10.
Phinehas (*pynḥs*) I Chron vi 4(*bis*), 50, ix 20; Ezra vii 5, viii 2,33.
Pilha (*plḥ'*) Neh x 25.
Piltai (*plṭy*) Neh xii 17.
Pochereth-hazzebaim (*pkrt-hṣbyym*) Ezra ii 57; Neh vii 59.

Raamiah (*r'myh*) Neh vii 7.
Ramiah (*rmyh*) Ezra x 25.
Reaiah (*r'yh*) I Chron iv 2, v 5; Ezra ii 47; Neh vii 50.
Rechab (*rkb*) Neh iii 14.
Reelaiah (*r'lyh*) Ezra ii 2.
Rehob (*rḥwb*) Neh x 12.
Rehum (*rḥwm*) Ezra ii 2, iv 8,9,17,23; Neh iii 17, x 26, xii 3.
Rephaiah (*rpyh*) I Chron iii 21, iv 42, vii 2, ix 43; Neh iii 9.
Rezin (*rṣyn*) Ezra ii 48; Neh vii 50.

Sallai (*sly*) Neh xi 8, xii 20.
Sallu (*slw', sl', slw*) I Chron ix 7; Neh xi 7, xii 7.
Sanballat (*snblṭ*) Neh ii 10,19, iii 33, iv 1, vi 1,2,5,12,14, xiii 28.
Seraiah (*śryh*) I Chron iv 13,14,35, vi 14(*bis*); Ezra ii 2, vii 1; Neh x 3, xi 11, xii 1,12.
Shabbethai (*šbty*) Ezra x 15; Neh viii 7, xi 16.
Shallum (*šlwm*) I Chron ii 40,41, iii 15, iv 25, vi 12,13, vii 13, ix 17(*bis*), 19,31; II Chron xxviii 12, xxxiv 22; Ezra ii 42, vii 2, x 24,42; Neh iii 12, vii 45.
Shallun (*šlwn*) Neh iii 15.
Shalmai (*šlmy*) Neh vii 48.
Shamlai (*šmlai*) Ezra ii 46.
Shammua (*šmw'*) I Chron xiv 4; Neh xi 17, xii 18.
Shashai (*ššy*) Ezra x 40.
Sheal (*š'l*) Ezra x 29.
Shealtiel (*š'lty'l*) I Chron iii 17; Ezra iii 2,8, v 2; Neh xii 1.
Shebaniah (*šbnyhw*) I Chron xv 24; Neh ix 4,5, x5,11,13, xii 14.

Tabbaoth (*ṭbʿwt*) Ezra ii 43; Neh vii 46.

Tabeel (*ṭbʾl*) Ezra iv 7.

Talmon (*ṭlmn, ṭlmwn*) I Chron ix 17; Ezra ii 42; Neh vii 45, xi 19, xii 25.

Tattenai (*ttny*) Ezra v 3,6, vi 6,13.

Telem (*ṭlm*) Ezra x 24.

Temah (*tmḥ*) Ezra ii 53; Neh vii 55.

Tekoite (*tqwʿy*) I Chron xi 28, xxvii 9; Neh iii 5,27.

Thummin (*tmym, twmym*) Ezra ii 63; Neh vii 65.

Tikvah (*tqwh*) Ezra x 15.

Tirshata (*tršʾ*) Ezra ii 63; Neh vii 65.

Tobiah (*ṭwbyhw, ṭbyh*) II Chron xvii 8; Ezra ii 60; Neh ii 10, 19, iii 35, iv 1, vi 1,12,14,17(*bis*), 19, vii 62, xiii 4,7,8.

Tyrian (*ṣry*) I Chron xxii 4; II Chron ii 13; Ezra iii 7; Neh xiii 16.

Uel (*ʾwʾl*) Ezra x 34.

Unni (*ʿny, ʿnw*) I Chron xv 18,20; Neh xii 9(Q[ere]).

Uri (*ʾwry*) I Chron ii 20(*bis*); II Chron i 5; Ezra x 24.

Uriah (*ʾwryh*) I Chron xi 41; Ezra viii 33; Neh iii 4,21, viii 4.

Urim (*ʾwrym*) Ezra ii 63; Neh vii 65.

Uthai (*ʾwty*) I Chron ix 4; Ezra viii 14.

Uzai (*ʾwzy*) Neh iii 25.

Uzza (*ʿz*) I Chron viii 7, xiii 7,9,10,11; Ezra ii 49; Neh vii 51.

Uzzi (*ʿzy*) I Chron vi 5,6,51, vii 2,3,7, ix 8; Ezra vii 4; Neh xi 22, xii 19,42.

Uzzia (*ʿzy*) I Chron xi 44.

Uzziah (*ʿzyh*) I Chron vi 24, xxvii 25; II Chron xxvi 1,3,8,9,11, 14,18(*bis*), 19,21,22,23, xxvii 2; Ezra x 21; Neh xi 4.

Uzziel (*ʿzyʾl*) I Chron iv 42, vi 2,18, vii 7, xv 10, xxiii 12,20, xxiv 24, xxv 4, xxvi 23; II Chron xxix 14; Neh iii 8.

Vaniah (*wnyh*) Ezra x 36.

Zabad (*zbd*) I Chron ii 36,37, vii 21, xi 41; II Chron xxiv 26; Ezra x 27,33,43.

Zabbai (*zby*) Ezra x 28; Neh iii 20.

Zabbud (*zbwd*) Ezra viii 14.

Zabdi (*zbdy*) I Chron viii 19, xxvii 27; Neh xi 17.

Zabdiel (*zbdyʾl*) I Chron xxvii 2; Neh xi 14.

Zaccai (*zky*) Ezra ii 9; Neh vii 14.

KEY TO THE TEXT

EZRA

Chapter	Verse	§	Chapter	Verse	§
i	1–11	1	vi	1–22	6
ii	1–70	2	vii	1–28	7
iii	1–13	3	viii	1–36	8
iv	1–24	4	ix	1–15	9
v	1–17	5	x	1–44	10

NEHEMIAH

Chapter	Verse	§	Chapter	Verse	§
i	1–11	1		4–72a	10
ii	1–10	2		72b	11
	11–20	3	viii	1–12	11
iii	1–32	4		13–18	12
	33–38	5	ix	1–37	13
iv	1–17	5	x	1–40	14
v	1–13	6	xi	1–36	15
	14–19	7	xii	1–26	16
vi	1–14	8		27–43	17
	15–16	9		44–47	18
	17–19	8	xiii	1–3	18
vii	1–3	9		4–31	19